Nijay Gupta's volume on 1 and 2 Thessalonians in the new and much-anticipated Zondervan Critical Introductions to the New Testament series is certain to become the standard critical introduction to Paul's Thessalonian correspondence. Here we have critical yet faithful scholarship at its finest! Gupta includes a discussion of the Greek text and all the significant text-critical issues. To that he adds an in-depth treatment of the background and historical situation of both letters. He continues with a prodigious and insightful investigation of the letter's theological themes, major interpretive issues, and history of interpretation. To top it off, Gupta provides an even-handed interaction with the best and most recent New Testament scholarship on the letters. No serious scholarship related to Paul's Thessalonian correspondence can afford to neglect Gupta's marvelous contribution. Indeed, this should be the first resource consulted.

J. SCOTT DUVALL, Fuller Professor of New Testament and chair, department of biblical studies, Ouachita Baptist University

Nijay Gupta has given students of the New Testament an invaluable resource. His volume on the Thessalonian correspondence in the Zondervan Critical Introductions to the New Testament series is more robust than a typical commentary. Gupta interacts with influential scholars whose works span many years, including those in German and French. He also covers the history of interpretation of 1 and 2 Thessalonians. In addition to giving detailed discussion of key themes, Gupta treats important exegetical issues as well. I will frequently grab this book off the shelf to assist me in my studies. The Zondervan Critical Introductions to the New Testament series will become the consistent, dependable reference for every New Testament student.

DENNIS R. EDWARDS, associate professor of New Testament, Northern Seminary

Having written a fine commentary on the Thessalonian correspondence, Nijay Gupta now deftly reviews the main critical and theological issues in the analysis of those letters, including the major interpreters for the principal issues. Gupta's engaging prose makes the details of scholarly debate and the history of interpretation anything but dull. Moreover, we are also treated to the author's wise take on these various matters. All scholars and serious students of 1 and 2 Thessalonians are greatly in Gupta's debt.

MICHAEL J. GORMAN, Raymond E. Brown Professor of Biblical Studies and Theology, St. Mary's Seminary & University

In this balanced introduction, Nijay Gupta presents an up-to-date survey of all the major issues pertaining to the Pauline letters to Thessalonian Jesus-followers. Gupta is well versed in scholarly conversations and explores issues expertly and clearly. This is a welcome addition to the best of scholarship on these important texts.

BRUCE LONGENECKER, professor of Christian origins and W. W. Melton Chair of Religion, Baylor University

The new and promising series, the Zondervan Critical Introductions to the New Testament, boldly addresses the frequently ignored yet paramount introductory issues (authorship, date, text, etc.) and redirects the readers, whether scholars, students, or pastors, to a fresh and improved understanding of the New Testament. The maiden voyage for the series comes from Nijay Gupta, who provides succinct analysis in articulate prose of each issue in 1 and 2 Thessalonians. The readers will only benefit from the vast research and careful deliberation Gupta provides throughout the volume.

M. SYDNEY PARK, associate professor of divinity, Beeson Divinity School

Nijay Gupta's introduction to the Thessalonian letters is critical in the best sense of that word: he skillfully asks and answers penetrating questions without falling prey to the critical scholar's ever-tempting intellectual vice of skepticism. Instead, with balanced, level-headed argumentation and prose Gupta explores both standard and fresh questions, thus wisely guiding students of 1 and 2 Thessalonians to be better readers. His labors have bequeathed a great gift to future commentators on Paul's early epistles. This volume shows great promise for the Zondervan Critical Introductions to the New Testament series.

JONATHAN T. PENNINGTON, associate professor of New Testament interpretation, Southern Seminary

Matthew 13:52 likens a Jesus-following scribe to a house owner who brings out of his storeroom treasures new and old. In his critical introduction to 1 and 2 Thessalonians, Nijay K. Gupta collects and considers afresh a significant swath of scholarship, both ancient and modern, on these Pauline letters. More than a collation of, an introduction to, or even an examination of academic work on 1 and 2 Thessalonians from multiple angles regarding sundry matters over the sweep of interpretative history, this volume adds appreciably to the serious scholarly study of these early pastoral letters through independent investigation and cogent argumentation. As I continue to explore 1 and 2 Thessalonians in conversation with other interpreters, I will have Gupta's critical introduction nearby as a rich bibliographic resource and as an insightful guide through the nettle of the fertile field that is Thessalonian scholarship.

TODD D. STILL, Hinson Professor of
Christian Scriptures, Truett Seminary

Here in one volume is everything we need to know to help us to read these two lively letters of Paul with greater depth and understanding. Written with great clarity and an impressively thorough grasp of scholarship on these letters, Gupta provides us with in-depth discussions of matters such as the background, theology, major exegetical and interpretive issues, and the history of interpretation for 1 and 2 Thessalonians. The new series of Zondervan Critical Introductions, launched by this excellent volume by Gupta, is to be warmly welcomed as broad-ranging volumes that will greatly help us to read Scripture carefully, and with richer insight.

PAUL TREBILCO, theology programme,
University of Otago

This welcome study breaks new ground in coverage of scholarly study of Paul's Thessalonian letters. Going beyond what either New Testament introductions or Thessalonian commentaries typically provide, Gupta surveys the discussion on text, authorship, background, and situation of both epistles. He also devotes whole chapters to the themes of each letter and how key passages are understood. On top of that, there are chapters on the history of interpretation of each letter going all the way back to patristic writers, including nonacademic appropriation, as in hymns. The result is a must-read for scholars and advanced students seeking a thorough description and assessment of Thessalonian studies. Gupta's own conclusions are well-informed, judicious, and clear. This is a truly fresh take on a wide expanse of top scholarship.

ROBERT W. YARBROUGH, professor of New
Testament, Covenant Theological Seminary

ZONDERVAN
CRITICAL INTRODUCTIONS
TO THE NEW TESTAMENT

1 & 2 THESSALONIANS

NIJAY K. GUPTA

Michael F. Bird,
series editor

ZONDERVAN
ACADEMIC

ZONDERVAN ACADEMIC

1 & 2 Thessalonians
Copyright © 2019 by Nijay K. Gupta

ISBN 978-0-310-51871-6 (hardcover)

ISBN 978-0-310-51872-3 (ebook)

Requests for information should be addressed to:
Zondervan, *3900 Sparks Dr. SE, Grand Rapids, Michigan 49546*

Cover design: Tammy Johnson
Cover photo: Morphart Creation/Shutterstock.com
Interior design: Kait Lamphere

Printed in the United States of America

19 20 21 22 23 24 25 26 27 28 29 /LSC/ 15 14 13 12 11 10 9 8 7 6 5 4 3 2 1

To Roy Ciampa

CONTENTS

ACKNOWLEDGMENTS

I want to thank Michael Bird for inviting me to write this critical introduction to the Thessalonian correspondence. This is the longest and most challenging research project I have ever attempted. It has required me to strengthen my German, French, and Latin reading skills, and I spent many afternoons chasing down difficult-to-find articles and books. In many ways, this experience was like working on a second dissertation! As one can imagine, it required painstaking research and analysis, but there was also the excitement of new ideas and the tracing of trends and crosscurrents. Many friends and colleagues have helped me along the way, and I wish to thank a few in particular: Gene Boring, John Byron, Karl Donfried, Andy Johnson, Michael Gorman, and Todd Still. Kent Yinger graciously helped me with some German translation (but I take responsibility for any mistaken or infelicitous English translations in the book). I wish to note the generosity of Wipf & Stock, who let me adapt some material from my commentary for this reference work.

I am also grateful to George Fox University and Portland Seminary for supporting my research, and to my family as well. Finally, I want to thank Katya Covrett for her excellent work as an editor at both the conceptual and page levels. Her expertise helps potentially esoteric and convoluted books become more readable and more interesting! This book is dedicated to Roy Ciampa, my mentor and friend, and the one who first taught me how to sit at the apostle's feet.

ABBREVIATIONS

ACCS	Ancient Christian Commentary on Scripture
ACT	Ancient Christian Texts
ANF	*Ante-Nicene Fathers*
ANTC	Abingdon New Testament Commentaries
ABD	*Anchor Bible Dictionary.* Edited by David Noel Freedman. 6 vols. New York: Doubleday, 1992
ANRW	*Aufstieg und Niedergang der römischen Welt: Geschichte und Kultur Roms im Spiegel der neueren Forschung.* Part 2, *Principat.* Edited by Hildegard Temporini and Wolfgang Haase. Berlin: de Gruyter, 1972–
APOT	*The Apocrypha and Pseudepigrapha of the Old Testament.* Edited by Robert H. Charles. 2 vols. Oxford: Clarendon, 1913
AThR	*Anglican Theological Review*
AYB	Anchor Yale Bible
BBR	*Bulletin for Biblical Research*
BETL	Bibliotheca Ephemeridum Theologicarum Lovaniensium
BECNT	Baker Exegetical Commentary on the New Testament
BibInt	*Biblical Interpretation*
BFCT	Beiträge zur Förderung christlicher Theologie
BSac	*Bibliotheca Sacra*
BJRL	*Bulletin of the John Rylands University Library of Manchester*
BNTC	Black's New Testament Commentaries
BTB	*Biblical Theology Bulletin*
BZNW	*Beihefte zur Zeitschrift für die neutestamentliche Wissenschaft*
CBQ	*Catholic Biblical Quarterly*
CurBR	*Currents in Biblical Research*
ConBNT	Coniectanea Neotestamentica or Coniectanea Biblica: New Testament Series

CTJ	*Calvin Theological Journal*
DBI	*Dictionary of Biblical Imagery.* Edited by Leland Ryken, James C. Wilhoit, and Tremper Longman III. Downers Grove, IL: InterVarsity Press, 1998
DNTD	Das Neue Testament Deutsch
DSD	*Dead Sea Discoveries*
ECC	Eerdmans Critical Commentary
EKKNT	Evangelisch-katholischer Kommentar zum Neuen Testament
ETL	*Ephemerides Theologicae Lovanienses*
EvQ	*Evangelical Quarterly*
ExpTim	*Expository Times*
GRBS	*Greek, Roman, and Byzantine Studies*
HBT	*Horizons in Biblical Theology*
HTR	*Harvard Theological Review*
HvTSt	*Hervormde teologiese studies*
IBC	Interpretation: A Bible Commentary for Teaching and Preaching
ICC	International Critical Commentary
IVPNTC	InterVarsity Press New Testament Commentary
JBL	*Journal of Biblical Literature*
JECS	*Journal of Early Christian Studies*
JSJSup	Journal for the Study of Judaism Supplement Series
JSNT	*Journal for the Study of the New Testament*
JSNTSup	Journal for the Study of the New Testament Supplement Series
JSPL	*Journal for the Study of Paul and His Letters*
JTI	*Journal of Theological Interpretation*
JTS	*Journal of Theological Studies*
KEK	Kritisch-exegetischer Kommentar über das Neue Testament (Meyer-Kommentar)
L&N	Louw, Johannes P., and Eugene A. Nida, eds. *Greek–English Lexicon of the New Testament: Based on Semantic Domains.* 2nd ed. New York: United Bible Societies, 1989
LCL	Loeb Classical Library
LNTS	Library of New Testament Studies
MM	Moulton, James H., and George Milligan. *The Vocabulary of the Greek New Testament.* London, 1930. Repr. Peabody, MA: Hendrickson, 1997
NA[28]	*Novum Testamentum Graece*, Nestle-Aland, 28th ed.

NCBC	The New Century Bible Commentary
NCCS	New Covenant Commentary Series
NIBC	New International Biblical Commentary
NICNT	New International Commentary on the New Testament
NIDB	*New Interpreter's Dictionary of the Bible.* Edited by Katharine Doob Sakenfeld. 5 vols. Nashville: Abingdon, 2006–2009
NIGTC	New International Greek Testament Commentary
NIVAC	The NIV Application Commentary
NovT	*Novum Testamentum*
NovTSup	Novum Testamentum Supplements
NPNF[1]	*Nicene and Post-Nicene Fathers*, Series 1
NTAbh	Neutestamentliche Abhandlungen
NTOA	Novum Testamentum et Orbis Antiquus
NTL	New Testament Library
NTR	New Testament Readings
NTS	*New Testament Studies*
NTT	New Testament Theology (Cambridge)
NTTS	New Testament Tools and Studies
NTTSD	New Testament Tools, Studies, and Documents
OGIS	*Orientis Graeci Inscriptiones Selectae.* Edited by Wilhelm Dittenberger. 2 vols. Leipzig: Hirzel, 1903–1905
PAST	Pauline Studies
PNTC	Pillar New Testament Commentary
PRSt	*Perspectives in Religious Studies*
RevExp	*Review and Expositor*
RHPR	*Revue d'histoire et de philosophie religieuses*
SBLDS	Society of Biblical Literature Dissertation Series
SBLGNT	Society of Biblical Literature Greek New Testament
SemeiaSt	Semeia Studies
SHBC	Smyth & Helwys Bible Commentary
SIG3	*Sylloge Inscriptionum Graecarum.* Edited by Wilhelm Dittenberger. 4 vols. 3rd ed. Leipzig: Hirzel, 1915–1924
SNT	Studien zum Neuen Testament
SNTSMS	Society for New Testment Studies Monograph Series
SP	Sacra Pagina
TDNT	*Theological Dictionary of the New Testament.* Edited by Gerhard Kittel and Gerhard Friedrich. Translated by Geoffrey W. Bromiley. 10 vols. Grand Rapids: Eerdmans, 1964–1976

THGNT   Tyndale House Greek New Testament
THKNT   Theologischer Handkommentar zum Neuen Testament
THNT   Two Horizons New Testament
TLNT   *Theological Lexicon of the New Testament.* Ceslas Spicq.
         Translated and edited by James D. Ernest. 3 vols. Peabody,
         MA: Hendrickson, 1994
TLZ   *Theologische Literaturzeitung*
TU   Texte und Untersuchungen
TynBul   *Tyndale Bulletin*
UBS⁵   *The Greek New Testament,* United Bible Societies, 5th ed.
WBC   Word Biblical Commentary
WUNT   Wissenschaftliche Untersuchungen zum Neuen Testament
ZAW   *Zeitschrift für die alttestamentliche Wissenschaft*
ZECNT   Zondervan Exegetical Commentary on the New Testament
ZIBBC   Zondervan Illustrated Bible Background Commentary
ZNW   *Zeitschrift für die neutestamentliche Wissenschaft und die Kunde*
         der älteren Kirche
ZPE   *Zeitschrift für Papyrologie und Epigraphik*
ZTK   *Zeitschrift für Theologie und Kirche*

1 THESSALONIANS

CHAPTER 1

TEXT OF 1 THESSALONIANS

The first port of call in this study is to identify the origins of 1 Thessalonians with a focus on the integrity of the text, authorship, and date, followed by an extended discussion of genre, style, and structure. Thereafter, I will discuss some of the possible sources behind 1 Thessalonians.

TEXTUAL WITNESSES AND SIGNIFICANT TEXT-CRITICAL CONCERNS

Textual Witnesses to 1 Thessalonians

For 1 Thessalonians, the consistently cited witnesses of the NA[28] text are as follows:[1]

PAPYRI

$\mathfrak{P}^{30}$: 4:12–13, 16–17; 5:3, 8–10, 12–18, 25–28
$\mathfrak{P}^{46}$: 1:1; 1:9–2:3; 5:5–9, 23–28
$\mathfrak{P}^{61}$: 1:2–3
$\mathfrak{P}^{65}$: 1:3–2:1, 6–13

MAJUSCULES

א (01): Pauline corpus
A (02): Pauline corpus
B (03): Pauline corpus
C (04): lacking 1:1, 2:9–5:28 (end)

---

1. See Barbara and Kurt Aland et al., eds., *Novum Testamentum Graece*, 28th ed. (Stuttgart: Deutsche Bibelgesellschaft, 2012); hereafter NA[28]. In the NA[28], the consistently cited witnesses for 1 Thessalonians are found on page 64*. Roy Ciampa deserves credit for compiling relevant information in a database pertaining to the specific contents of these witnesses; see http://www.viceregency.com/Manual_08_Contents.pdf.

D (06): Pauline corpus
F (010): Pauline corpus
G (012): Pauline corpus
H (015): contains only 2:9–13; 4:5–11
I (016): contains only 1:1–2, 9–10; 2:7–9, 14–16; 3:2–5, 11–13; 4:7–10; 4:16–5:1, 9–12, 23–27
K (018): Pauline corpus
L (020): Pauline corpus
P (025): lacking 3:5–4:17
Ψ (044): Pauline corpus
048: contains only 1:1, 5–6
0183: contains only 3:6–9; 4:1–5
0208: 2:4–7, 12–17
0226: 4:16–5:5
0278: all of 1 Thess

MINUSCULES

33: Pauline corpus
81: Pauline corpus
104: Pauline corpus
365: Pauline corpus
630: Pauline corpus
1175: lacking 1:10–3:2
1241: Pauline corpus
1505: Pauline corpus
1739: Pauline corpus
1881: Pauline corpus
2464: Pauline corpus

LECTIONARIES

l 249: Pauline corpus
l 846: Pauline corpus

Major Textual Variants in 1 Thessalonians

There are fourteen verses in 1 Thessalonians with textual variant discussions worth consideration.[2]

---

2. For the latest discussion of the practice of textual criticism, see B. D. Ehrman and M. W.

1:1 χάρις ὑμῖν καὶ εἰρήνη

The NA²⁸/UBS⁵ text of 1 Thessalonians 1:1 ends with χάρις ὑμῖν καὶ εἰρήνη. Some manuscripts contain a longer salutation such as ἀπὸ θεοῦ πατρὸς καὶ κυρίου Ἰησοῦ Χριστοῦ (e.g., D 0150 256 263 1319 1573 2127 *l* 593).³ Similarly, we also find ἀπὸ θεοῦ πατρὸς ἡμῶν καὶ κυρίου Ἰησοῦ Χριστοῦ (e.g., ℵ A I 6 33 81 104). The best and earliest manuscripts support the short reading. Furthermore, the longer readings can be explained as assimilation to Pauline style (see 1 Cor 1:3).

1:5 εὐαγγέλιον ἡμῶν

While the reading "our gospel" is widely attested, apparently some copyists found the language of "our" inappropriate, thus omitting it. The witnesses ℵᶜ and C read εὐαγγέλιον τοῦ θεοῦ (no ἡμῶν); similarly ℵ* has εὐαγγέλιον τοῦ θεοῦ ἡμῶν.

2:7 νήπιοι

This is one of the most controversial text-critical issues in the whole Pauline corpus. We will devote more attention to historical and theological issues related to this text on pages 106–14. Here we will reserve ourselves primarily to comment only on the manuscript witnesses and potential unintentional scribal behavior. The two main options for textual readings are νήπιοι, which means "infants," and ἤπιοι, "gentle."

νήπιοι: 𝔓⁶⁵ ℵ* B C* D* F G I Ψ* 0150 104* 263 459 1962 *l* 147 *l* 592 *l* 593 *l* 603ᶜ itᵃʳ, ᵇ, ᵈ, ᶠ, ᵍ, ᵐᵒⁿ, ᵒ vgᶜˡ, ʷʷ copˢᵃᵐˢ, ᵇᵒ eth Origen⁽ᵍʳ¹/³⁾, ˡᵃᵗ; Ambrosiaster Jerome Pelagius Augustine

ἤπιοι: ℵᶜ A C² D² Ψᶜ 075 6 33 81 104ᶜ 256 365 424 436 1241 1319 1573 1739 1852 1881 1912 2127 2200 2464 *Byz* [K L P] *Lect* vgˢᵗ (syrᵖ, ʰ) copˢᵃᵐˢˢ, ᶠᵃʸ arm (geo) slav Clement Origen²/³ Basil Chrysostom Theodoreˡᵃᵗ

Metzger notes that νήπιοι could have occured by dittography (accidental repeating of a letter), or ἤπιοι by haplography (accidental omission of a

Holmes, eds., *The Text of the New Testament in Contemporary Research: Essays on the Status Quaestionis*, 2nd ed., NTTS 42 (Leiden: Brill, 2013); cf. K. Wachtel and M. W. Holmes, *The Textual History of the Greek New Testament: Changing Views in Contemporary Research* (Atlanta: SBL Press, 2011).
    3. For a detailed critical apparatus, see UBS⁵.

letter).[4] Nevertheless, Metzger's committee preferred νήπιοι on account of "what is admittedly the stronger external attestation."[5]

2:12 καλοῦντος

The weight of extant manuscript evidence favors καλοῦντος (present tense), but there are some manuscripts that have the aorist καλέσαντος (e.g., ℵ A 104 459 1912 2464). The aorist variant could be explained as assimilation to Paul's use of the aorist form in 1 Corinthians 1:9, Galatians 1:6, and 1 Thessalonians 4:7.[6]

2:15 προφήτας

Again, external evidence overwhelmingly supports the short reading, but some witnesses (including most minuscules, as well as the Textus Receptus) have the reading ἰδίους προφήτας, understood as "their own prophets" (i.e., *Jewish* prophets versus *Christian* prophets). Metzger wonders whether those witnesses that include the longer reading may have been influenced by Marcion's text.[7]

2:16 ὀργή

Some later Western-type manuscripts add τοῦ θεοῦ to ὀργή to clarify the reference to God's wrath. In the context, though, this addition is unnecessary and thus superfluous.

3:2 καὶ συνεργὸν τοῦ θεοῦ ἐν τῷ εὐαγγελίῳ τοῦ Χριστοῦ

Some manuscripts have διάκονον instead of συνεργόν. Another matter is τοῦ θεοῦ—it is occasionally omitted. Metzger argues that on external evidence alone, the reading καὶ διάκονον τοῦ θεοῦ is very strong, but the UBS choice {B} seems best able to explain how the other readings came into existence. He reasons that some copyists may have been uncomfortable with the idea of being "coworkers of God," thus removing τοῦ θεοῦ to avoid

---

4. B. M. Metzger, *A Textual Commentary on the Greek New Testament*, 2nd ed. (Stuttgart: German Bible Society, 1994), 561.

5. *Textual Commentary*, 562. Both the SBLGNT and the THGNT prefer ἤπιοι. Philip Comfort strongly prefers νήπιοι as the original reading. Comfort explains that the change to ἤπιοι may have occurred because of the uncomfortable dual metaphor presented by νήπιοι, but the external support for νήπιοι is decisive. See P. W. Comfort, *A Commentary on the Manuscripts and Text of the New Testament* (Grand Rapids: Kregel, 2015), 355–56.

6. See R. L. Omanson, *A Textual Guide to the Greek New Testament* (Stuttgart: Deutsche Bibelgesellschaft, 2006), 425.

7. Metzger, *Textual Commentary*, 562.

confusion (is God a "coworker"?). Others preferred διάκονον to soften the language. Some manuscripts have both διάκονον and συνεργόν (F G it^(f, g)).[8]

3:13 αὐτοῦ, [ἀμήν].

One cannot decide on the originality of ἀμήν based on external evidence alone, since both readings are strongly attested. Not much hangs on its *inclusion*, though one wonders why a copyist would exclude it.

4:1 καθὼς καὶ περιπατεῖτε

Though the *inclusion* of this clause is strongly attested, it is lacking in many minuscules. The most likely reason why it was dropped is because it could appear redundant.

4:11 [ἰδίαις]

There is fairly even manuscript support for the *inclusion* of ἰδίαις: ἐργάζεσθαι ταῖς [ἰδίαις] χερσὶν ὑμῶν. The UBS committee was undecided {C}. It may have been dropped because it could appear unnecessary.

> Includes: ℵ* A D¹ 33 81 424* 436 1241 1852 1962 2200 *Byz* [K L]
> Omits: ℵ² B D* F G Ψ 075 0150 6 104 256 263 365 424^c

4:13 κοιμωμένων

The Western and Byzantine witnesses tend to read here κεκοιμημένων, while the Alexandrian witnesses favor κοιμωμένων. The latter is preferred, supported by more ancient texts; moreover, κοιμωμένων (present tense) is the more difficult reading.

5:25 [καί]

Does the text read "pray for us" or "pray *also* for us"? Encouragement for apostolic prayer is found in Colossians 4:3: προσευχόμενοι ἅμα καὶ περὶ ἡμῶν. External evidence does not support one reading as stronger. Most translations do not add "also."

5:27 ἀδελφοῖς

A number of minuscules (and evidence from non-Greek ancient translations) include ἅγιος (τοῖς ἁγίοις ἀδελφοῖς). The external evidence

---

8. See Metzger, *Textual Commentary*, 563.

supports the shorter reading, and perhaps the addition of ἅγιος can be explained by its use in 5:26.

5:28 ὑμῶν

In the Alexandrian-type texts, 1 Thessalonians ends with ὑμῶν ("The grace of our Lord Jesus Christ be with you"). A large number of manuscripts (including ℵ A Dᶜ K L P Ψ 614 1739ᶜ), though, include a final ἀμήν, though this might be explained based on liturgical use.

TEXTUAL INTEGRITY

In the last few decades, Thessalonian scholarship has lost much interest in theories that question the integrity of the text of 1 Thessalonians as we have it in the manuscript traditions (besides the possible interpolation of 1 Thessalonians 2:13/14–16, discussed below). In a previous generation, it was more common to see division theories;[9] among contemporary academic commentaries, only that of Earl Richard entertains (and in his case adopts) a division theory. Richard notes that the two thanksgiving sections of the letter have raised concern for some (2:1–10; 2:13). However, Richard finds more problematic the way 2:13–4:2 sits within the text. He postulates that 2:13–4:2 could be read as a "short earlier missive" with a later text being comprised of 1:1–2:12 + 4:3–5:28.[10]

It must be underscored again, though, that Richard is unique among recent commentators; nearly all other commentaries defend integrity, and some ignore the topic altogether.[11] Part of this involves the *theory* of integrity. Richard is quite transparent on this: "It should be stressed that the

---

9. For a survey of the discussion up to the 1970s, see R. F. Collins, "Apropos the Integrity of 1 Thess," *ETL* 65 (1979): 67–106, republished in R. F. Collins, *Studies on the First Letter to the Thessalonians*, BETL 66 (Leuven: Leuven University Press, 1984), 96–135. An important theory was put forth by W. Schmithals (*Paul and the Gnostics* [Nashville: Abingdon, 1972], 123–218), which divided up both 1 and 2 Thessalonians into a total of four letters: {A} 2 Thess 1:1–12 + 3:6–16; {B} 1 Thess 1:1–2:12 + 4:2–5:28; {C} 2 Thess 2:13f., 2:1–12 + 2:15–3:3 (5) + 17f.; {D} 1 Thess 2:13–4:1. For a refutation of Schmithals's reconstruction, see R. Jewett, *The Thessalonian Correspondence: Pauline Rhetoric and Millenarian Piety* (Philadelphia: Fortress, 1986), 33–36. Brief mention can also be made here of G. Friedrich's proposal that 5:1–11 is an interpolation; see G. Friedrich, "I. Thessalonicher 5, 1–11, der apologetische Einschub eines Späteren," *ZTK* 70.3 (1973): 288–315. See refutation of the latter in I. H. Marshall, *1 and 2 Thessalonians*, NCBC (Grand Rapids: Eerdmans, 1983), 12–13.

10. See E. J. Richard, *First and Second Thessalonians*, SP (Collegeville, MN: Liturgical Press, 1995), 11–12.

11. Note, for example, the absence of the matter in G. D. Fee, *The First and Second Letters to the Thessalonians*, NICNT (Grand Rapids: Eerdmans, 2009).

presumption of integrity is an assumption unless it explains satisfactorily serious structural and temporal anomalies."[12] In my estimation, many scholars begin from the opposite assumption: a theory seeking to question literary integrity must make an especially convincing case.[13]

The only serious matter related to integrity still debated currently is the text of 1 Thessalonians 2:13–16. From a text-critical standpoint, there are no extant Greek manuscripts that omit 2:13, 14, 15, or 16.[14] However, because so many scholars find material in these verses *either* unpauline in thought *or* historically implausible (or both), it is up for discussion.

As Jewett notes, the matter first emerged in the academic sphere in 1905 via Rudolf Knopf, who proposed that 2:16c was a marginal note that later merged into the text in the late first century.[15] The most influential proponent of an interpolation theory in the late twentieth century is Birger Pearson.[16] We will reserve the matter of the so-called "anti-Judaism" of 1 Thessalonians 2:13–16 for a later discussion (see pp. 114–23). Here, as we consider textual-integrity matters, we will deal only with the issue of historical plausibility—*is there sufficient evidence that this is a text "out of its time," that is, anachronistic? In other words, is this a text that could not be written by the historical Paul?*

A major concern for those that propose an interpolation for 2:13–16 is the aorist ἔφθασεν (2:16). How has the wrath (of God) come upon them *already*?[17] Pearson urges that it *must* refer retrospectively to the destruction

---

12. Richard, *First and Second Thessalonians*, 12.

13. Thus note Wanamaker's mindset on this matter: "Unless and until further evidence is forthcoming in support of the interpolation hypothesis, it should be assumed that 2:13–16 formed part of the original text of the letter" (C. A. Wanamaker, *The Epistles to the Thessalonians: A Commentary on the Greek Text*, NIGTC [Grand Rapids: Eerdmans, 1990], 33).

14. See W. O. Walker Jr., *Interpolations in the Pauline Letters*, JSNTSup 213 (Sheffield: Sheffield Academic Press, 2001), 210, though Walker considers 1 Thessalonians 2:13–16 a "likely interpolation"; see pp. 210–23. There is, it should be noted, a Latin manuscript that lacks 2:16d (Vatic. Lat. 5729; eleventh century). As Luckensmeyer explains, the omission may nevertheless be due to a mistake. Thus, "since the witness is exceptionally isolated it is unlikely that the trajectory of this decision goes back to a Greek manuscript" (162). Nevertheless, Luckensmeyer is right to lament that this witness to the 2:16d omission is too often neglected in the discussion (D. Luckensmeyer, *The Eschatology of First Thessalonians*, NTOA 71 [Göttingen: Vandenhoeck & Ruprecht, 2009], 115–72).

15. See R. Knopf, *Das nachapostolische Zeitalter* (Tübingen: Mohr, 1905), 139; see Jewett, *Thessalonian Correspondence*, 36–37.

16. See B. A. Pearson, "1 Thessalonians 2:13–16: A Deutero-Pauline Interpolation," *HTR* 64 (1971): 79–94; see also D. Schmidt, "1 Thess 2:13–16: Linguistic Evidence for an Interpolation," *JBL* 102 (1983): 269–79; cf. H. Koester, Introduction to the New Testament: History and Literature of Early Christianity II (Philadelphia: Fortress, 1982), 113.

17. Most scholars do indeed try to read this in terms of a *past* event (see below), but Luckensmeyer makes the reasonable point that the subject is the *wrath of God*, which tends to have a future orientation in Pauline thought; see *Eschatology*, 163.

of the temple (70 CE). Yet Robert Jewett supplies an important coun-
terargument. While hindsight tells us of the pervasive impact of the
Jewish-Roman war, we must remember that "to someone who lived before
that catastrophe, several [other] events could easily have appeared to be
a final form of divine wrath."[18] Jewett includes reference to the death of
Agrippa (44 CE), the insurrection of Theudas (44–46 CE), the Judean
famine (46–47 CE), the Jerusalem riot (48–51 CE), the expulsion of Jews
from Rome by Claudius (49 CE), or (pointing to the research of Sherman
Johnson) the bloody riot in Jerusalem (after 49 CE).[19]

Another historical matter is the reference to Jewish persecution of
Judean churches. Is it possible that at such an early period Jews were
actively persecuting followers of Jesus? Is this not a phenomenon of a later
period where "the ways had parted" enough to underscore distinction, so to
speak? Perhaps; however, Jeffrey Weima points to Paul's own persecution
of believers in Jerusalem and the wider area (see 1 Cor 15:9; Gal 1:13,
22–23; Phil 3:6). Weima also mentions, as the most likely reference, a
Judean Zealot movement (ca. 46–51 CE; see Josephus, *Ant.* 20.102–15)
that sought to rid Palestine of gentile influence; this may have included
harassment of Judean churches.[20]

Perhaps I should register my personal concern with theories of interpolation in Pauline letters (lacking manuscript evidence for omission/dis-
placement); it is not that interpolations are impossible, but rather I wonder
if so much energy on deconstruction and reconstruction leads, in the end,
to any sort of clarity and settledness about the matter. At best, I believe
we can only label the authenticity of a text like 1 Thessalonians 2:13–16
"dubious" when we lack clear(er) extant evidence of textual disunity.[21]

---

18. Jewett, *Thessalonian Correspondence*, 37. See his argumentation more generally on pp. 31–46.

19. *Thessalonian Correspondence*, 37; cf. S. Johnson, "Notes and Comments," *ATR* 23 (1941):
173; see further the discussion in J. A. D. Weima, *1–2 Thessalonians*, BECNT (Grand Rapids: Baker
Academic, 2014); Weima notes that most scholars who take ἔφθασεν as past sense (imagining the
time period before 50 CE) prefer Claudius's expulsion (p. 177).

20. See Weima, *1–2 Thessalonians*, 30–40.

21. I resonate with the concerns of Fee, a respected textual critic, when he asks (the interpo-
lation-theorist), "Why has it [1 Thess 2:14–16] been inserted *here* and not in a more 'logical' place
in other letters?" (*Thessalonians*, 91); note too the important work of I. Broer in reference to how
2:14–16 fits into 1 Thessalonians in "'Der ganze Zorn ist schon über sie gekommen': Bemerkungen
zur Interpolationshypothese und zur Interpretation von 1 Thes 2,14–16," in *The Thessalonian Correspondence*, ed. R. F. Collins, BETL 87 (Leuven: Leuven University Press, 1990), 137–59; cf. idem,
"'Antisemitismus' und Judenpolemik im Neuen Testament: Ein Beitrag zum besseren Verständnis
von 1 Thess 2:14–16," *Biblische Notizen* 20 (1983): 59–91; similarly, see E. W. Stegemann, "Zur
antijudischen Polemik in 1 Thess 2,14–16," in *Paulus und die Welt: Aufsätze*, ed. C. Tuor and P. Wick
(Zürich: Theologischer Verlag, 2005), 62–63. Stegemann writes: "Even though Paul would clearly
be relieved of one controversy of this hypothesis, this would only shift the problem to a younger

AUTHORSHIP AND DATE

The authenticity of 1 Thessalonians has not been seriously questioned in recent history. It was, of course, included in the Muratorian Canon as well as Marcion's list (see Tertullian, *Marc.* 5.15). The most well-known advocate of the *exclusion* of 1 Thessalonians from a genuine Pauline corpus is F. C. Baur. He argued that the similarities between 1 Thessalonians and 1 Corinthians are too great not to assume dependence. Baur pointed out, as another concern, discrepancies between 1 Thessalonians and Acts. There have also been concerns raised on occasion with the vocabulary of 1 Thessalonians, though it is commonly recognized today that playing the *hapax legomena* game leads to all manner of fallacies.[22]

A much more controversial and serious matter today involves the proper dating of 1 Thessalonians and whether or not it should be considered the first extant letter of Paul (or whether perhaps it should come after Galatians).[23] A conventional assessment of Paul's apostolic *curriculum vitae* requires an integration of the bits of timeline information from 1 Thessalonians combined with the general movements (including geography and duration) from Acts and critical nonbiblical resources such as the Gallio inscription (*SIG3* 2:492–94, §801). Acts narrates a journey of Paul to Macedonia (particularly Philippi and Thessalonica), and then on to the southern part of Achaia (Athens and Corinth). According to Acts 18:1–5, Paul moved from Athens to Corinth by himself, and Timothy joined him later (18:5; cf. 1 Thess 3:1–13). This makes Corinth the most likely place

---

anonymous figure. To assume a later interpolation is always precarious and should be at best an exegetical last resort. Material and formal considerations necessitate no literary critical solutions. Ingo Broer has recently made a careful examination of the chief arguments for the interpolation theory and concludes that retaining the text as an integral part of 1 Thessalonians is more plausible than seeing it as an interpolation in whole or in part. I find his arguments convincing even if one cannot attain absolute certainty" (trans. mine).

22. See H. W. Hoehner, "Did Paul Write Galatians?" in *History and Exegesis: New Testament Essays in Honor of Dr. E. Earle Ellis for His 80th Birthday*, ed. S.-W. (Aaron) Son (New York: T&T Clark, 2006), 150–69. See too the discussion by F. W. Hughes, "Thessalonians, First and Second Letters to the," in *New Testament: History of Interpretation*, ed. J. H. Hayes (Nashville: Abingdon, 2004), 111–16.

23. On the general discussion of chronology of Paul and his letters, see N. Hyldahl, *Die paulinische Chronologie*, Acta Theologica Danica 19 (Leiden: Brill, 1986); J. D. G. Dunn, *Beginning from Jerusalem*, Christianity in the Making 2 (Grand Rapids: Eerdmans, 2009), 497–518; R. Riesner, *Paul's Early Period: Chronology, Mission Strategy, Theology*, trans. D. Stott (Grand Rapids: Eerdmans, 1998); idem, "Pauline Chronology," in *Blackwell Companion to Paul*, ed. S. Westerholm (Oxford: Wiley-Blackwell, 2011), 9–29. Hyldahl and Dunn both propose a possibly earlier dating of Paul's time in Corinth (respectively, 49–51 CE, and 49/50–51/52 CE) than most scholars, including Riesner (50–51 CE).

from which Paul sent 1 Thessalonians. We can place his extended stay in Corinth in history relatively well thanks to the Gallio inscription, as it indicates that Gallio was named proconsul in 51 CE.[24] Working backwards a bit, scholars offer the general period of Paul's writing of 1 Thessalonians as 49–51 CE.[25]

It is difficult to determine how long Paul was in Thessalonica, and after how long following his departure from the city he wrote 1 Thessalonians. Acts 17:2 mentions Paul's ministry in the synagogue that lasted "three Sabbath days," which sets a minimum time of about three to four weeks. However, the impression from 1 Thessalonians itself is that Paul would have spent enough time in Thessalonica with the new believers to have given them instruction in the faith (4:2) as well as time to share his *life* with them (2:8). Regarding how soon *after* his departure he wrote 1 Thessalonians, Malherbe gives a hypothesis of four months, enough time to travel through Beroea (Berea), Athens, and then to settle in Corinth.[26]

It behooves us to mention here a more recent approach developed by Douglas A. Campbell regarding not just the dating of 1 Thessalonians but all of Paul's missionary work and letters. This is outlined in his book *Framing Paul: An Epistolary Biography* (2014). While most NT scholars have used the book of Acts in companion with the Pauline letters to sketch a life of Paul, Campbell works only with the epistles. This approach yields results starkly different than the consensus view of Paul's ministry. Campbell argues for a very early "mission to Macedonia" (ca. 40–42 CE) where Paul went to Philippi, Thessalonica, Achaia, and then Corinth. During this period, he would have written 1–2 Thessalonians. Thus Campbell's chronology pushes 1 Thessalonians up several years. Time will tell whether other scholars find Campbell's approach appealing and compelling.

---

24. Gallio's time in office lasted at least from July of 51 CE through June of 52 CE.

25. For a discussion from a nonbiblical ancient historian, see D. J. Kyrtatas, "Early Christianity in Macedonia," in *Brill's Companion to Ancient Macedon*, ed. R. J. L. Fox (Leiden: Brill, 2011), 585–99.

26. See A. J. Malherbe, *The Letters to the Thessalonians*, AB (New Haven: Yale University Press, 2004), 72–73. He offers this sketch: one week of travel from Thessalonica to Beroea, three weeks from Beroea to Athens, another three weeks before Paul's companions return to Beroea from Athens (see Acts 17:15), six weeks to account for Timothy's journey to Athens and return to Thessalonica (1 Thess 3:1–3), four weeks for Timothy's journey from Thessalonica to Corinth.

LETTER FEATURES

We now turn our attention to various textual features of 1 Thessalonians, including scholarly discussion of genre, Paul's Greek writing style, proposals regarding the structure of the letter, and possible sources and influences for the letter.

Genre

Obviously 1 Thessalonians is a *letter*, and thus it has been studied *as a letter*. But there has been much debate for generations about *how* it should be studied as a letter. Thus, George Milligan's comments are apt: "It must be clear that they are in no sense literary documents, still less theological treatises, but genuine letters intended to meet passing needs, and with no thought of any wider audience than those to whom they were originally addressed."[27] Yet Milligan goes on to note that just because Paul's words are directed at particular problems does not preclude the possibility of understanding his theological thinking in a broader sense (perhaps here anticipating Beker's famous contingency/coherence discussion).[28]

As Stanley Porter reminds us, the interest in reading Paul's writings *as letters* boomed with the discovery of the Greek documentary papyri from Oxyrhynchus (Egypt).[29] Especially in the later twentieth century, epistolary analysis pushed toward differentiating various *types* of letters in the Greco-Roman world and then considering where Paul's letters fit on a letter-by-letter examination. Objectively distinguishing letter types is a tricky matter; Stanley Stowers has advocated drawing from the work of Pseudo-Libanius and Pseudo-Demetrius.[30] Pseudo-Demetrius

---

27. G. Milligan, *St. Paul's Epistles to the Thessalonians* (London: Macmillan 1908), xli.

28. *Thessalonians*, xli; see J. C. Beker, *Paul the Apostle: The Triumph of God in Life and Thought* (Philadelphia: Fortress, 1984).

29. See S. E. Porter and S. A. Adams, "Pauline Epistolography: An Introduction," in *Paul and the Ancient Letter Form*, ed. S. E. Porter and S. A. Adams, PAST 6 (Leiden: Brill, 2010), 1; Porter rightly notes the influence of A. Deissmann, *Light from the Ancient East: The New Testament Illustrated by Recently Discovered Texts of the Graeco-Roman World*, 4th ed., trans. L. R. M. Strachan (London: Hodder and Stoughton, 1927); cf. also L. H. Blumell, *Lettered Christians: Christians, Letters, and Late Antique Oxyrhynchus*, NTTSD 39 (Leiden: Brill, 2012); L. Doering, *Ancient Jewish Letters and the Beginnings of Christian Epistolography*, WUNT 298 (Tübingen: Mohr Siebeck, 2012).

30. See S. K. Stowers, *Letter Writing in Greco-Roman Antiquity* (Philadelphia: Westminster, 1986), 51–57; cf. H.-J. Klauck, *Ancient Letters and the New Testament* (Louisville: Westminster John Knox, 1986), 202–3; C. Poster, "A Conversation Halved: Epistolary Theory in Greco-Roman Antiquity," in *Letter-Writing Manuals and Instructions from Antiquity to the Present: Historical and Bibliographic Studies*, ed. C. Poster and L. C. Mitchell, Studies in Rhetoric/Communication (Columbia, SC: University of South Carolina Press, 2007), 21–51.

distinguishes twenty-one types: friendly, commendatory, reproachful, censorious, threatening, praising, supplicatory, responding, accounting, apologetic, ironic, blaming, consoling, admonishing, vituperative, advisory, inquiring, allegorical, accusing, congratulatory, and thankful.[31] Pseudo-Libanius's list is much longer, and he includes a category of "mixed" (μικτή), identifying that there are cases where forms and styles of letters are combined.

When it comes to the study of 1 Thessalonians, broadly speaking there are two directions in which scholars go vis-à-vis an epistolary label. Some prefer to identify 1 Thessalonians as a consoling letter (i.e., paracletic), including Karl Donfried,[32] Abraham Smith,[33] and Donald Hagner.[34] Other scholars urge that it is better to identify 1 Thessalonians as paraenetic, emphasizing moral exhortation. Such proponents of this view include Abraham Malherbe,[35] Stanley Stowers,[36] David Aune,[37] and Luke Timothy Johnson.[38] For my part, I am skeptical about the usefulness of assigning 1 Thessalonians to a specific epistolary letter-type. If I had to choose, I might prefer the "mixed" type because I think the reader ought not to be forced to decide between "consoling" and "paraenetic."

---

31. See J. Murphy-O'Connor, *Paul the Letter-Writer* (Collegeville, MN: Liturgical, 1995), 97. Note that different Anglophone scholars may translate the Greek words a bit differently, so there is no standard English terminology for these types.

32. K. P. Donfried, "The Theology of 1 Thessalonians as a Reflection of Its Purpose," in *To Touch the Text*, ed. M. P. Horgan and P. J. Kobelski (New York: Crossroad, 1989), 243–60. Note the pushback against Donfried's interpretation by J. Chapa, "Is First Thessalonians a Letter of Consolation?" *NTS* 40 (1994): 150–60; cf. also idem, "Consolatory Patterns? 1 Thes 4,13–18; 5,11," in Collins, *Thessalonian Correspondence*, 220–28.

33. A. Smith, *The Social and Ethical Implications of the Pauline Rhetoric in 1 Thessalonians* (PhD diss., Vanderbilt University, 1989).

34. See D. A. Hagner, *The New Testament: A Historical and Theological Introduction* (Grand Rapids: Baker, 2012), 457–75. Probably B. R. Gaventa falls into this category as well: "In common with the crafters of love letters, Paul does not write to convey data, but to express his affection and communicate his concern" (*First and Second Thessalonians*, IBC [Louisville: Westminster John Knox, 1998], 40).

35. A. Malherbe, "Exhortation in First Thessalonians," in *Light from the Gentiles: Hellenistic Philosophy and Early Christianity: Collected Essays, 1959–2012, by Abraham J. Malherbe*, ed. C. R. Holladay et al., 2 vols. (Boston: Brill, 2013), 1:167–86; cf. idem, *Letters to the Thessalonians*, 81–86. Malherbe takes his reading of 1 Thessalonians a step further than most scholars by bringing the Paul of 1 Thessalonians into conversation with the moral philosophers of his age; Malherbe reads 1 Thessalonians from this viewpoint not only as a hortatory letter but as a *pastoral* one, as the apostle sought to give assurance to the unsure and encouragement to those walking in truth and love; see idem, *Paul and the Thessalonians: The Philosophic Tradition of Pastoral Care* (Philadelphia: Fortress, 1987).

36. Stowers, *Letter Writing*, 96.

37. See D. Aune, *The New Testament in Its Literary Environment* (Louisville: Westminster John Knox, 1987), 206; Aune points especially to the lengthy hortatory section (1 Thess 4:1–5:22) as a clear indicator of the centrality of this paraenesis for the letter's purpose as a whole.

38. L. T. Johnson, *Writings of the New Testament: An Interpretation*, rev. ed. (Minneapolis: Fortress, 1999), 282.

In the last thirty years, we have seen a swell of interest in turning the discussion of genre away from letter analysis toward the study of ancient rhetoric.[39] Steve Walton has provided a succinct "state of the discussion" regarding rhetorical criticism and 1 Thessalonians.[40] It is widely understood that there were three species of rhetoric—deliberative, judicial, and epideictic. Kennedy reasons that 1 Thessalonians is *deliberative* because it has the aim of convincing the audience to follow a particular path (1 Thess 3:8; chs. 4–5). Walton places Bruce Johanson in this category as well, particularly as Johanson puts emphasis on the consolatory purpose of the letter.[41] The *deliberative* view has not gained wide approval.

Much more attractive is the position that 1 Thessalonians fits an epideictic rhetorical category.[42] Here the idea is that Paul was not concerned with getting the Thessalonians to evaluate something in the past particularly (i.e., judicial/forensic), nor to make a specific decision in the future (i.e., deliberative), but rather to reinforce certain values and to offer affirmation and encouragement. Duane Watson represents this majority opinion and defends the epideictic interpretation on these grounds:

> Paul is trying to persuade the Thessalonians to reaffirm or adhere more closely to received values and theology. With the choice of epideictic rhetoric Paul functions as a consoling pastor addressing congregational concerns, with no adversaries in mind.[43]

According to Watson (and I deeply resonate with his analysis), the disturbance created by the death of Thessalonian believers—along with the ongoing persecution—rattled the community significantly.

---

39. For an accessible overview, see B. Witherington III, *New Testament Rhetoric: An Introductory Guide to the Art of Persuasion in and of the New Testament* (Eugene, OR: Wipf & Stock, 2009); note the importance of the work of G. A. Kennedy, *New Testament Interpretation through Rhetorical Criticism* (Chapel Hill: University of North Carolina Press, 1984); idem, *Classical Rhetoric and Its Christian and Secular Tradition from Ancient to Modern Times*, 2nd ed. (Chapel Hill: University of North Carolina Press, 1999); cf. C. C. Black and D. F. Watson, eds., *Words Well Spoken: George Kennedy's Rhetoric of the New Testament*, Studies in Rhetoric and Religion 8 (Waco, TX: Baylor University Press, 2008).

40. S. Walton, "What Has Aristotle to Do with Paul? Rhetorical Criticism and 1 Thessalonians," *TynBul* 46.2 (1995): 229–50. On the history of the study of 1 Thessalonians, Walton underscores the ground-breaking work of Malherbe and Jewett.

41. B. Johanson, *To All the Brethren: A Text-Linguistic and Rhetorical Approach to 1 Thessalonians*, ConBNT 16 (Stockholm: Almqvist & Wiksell, 1987), 165–66.

42. See Jewett, *Thessalonian Correspondence*, 71–72; cf. G. Lyons, *Pauline Autobiography: Toward A New Understanding*, SBLDS 73 (Atlanta: Scholars, 1985), 219–21.

43. D. F. Watson, "The Three Species of Rhetoric and the Study of the Pauline Epistles," in *Paul and Rhetoric*, ed. J. P. Sampley and P. Lampe (London: Bloomsbury, 2013), 30; cf. the similar conclusion by Wanamaker, *Thessalonians*, 47.

Paul's "apostolic perspective" offered guidance through a refashioned "symbolic world" that would enable the Thessalonians to imagine their situation as part of "Satan's forces arrayed against God and God's righteous followers in an end-time battle."[44] Paul's goal was not (merely?) to move the Thessalonians to take a particular course of action but rather to "adhere to values they have already come to hold."[45]

Ben Witherington bolsters his own case for reading 1 Thessalonians as epideictic by noting that the text does not offer intense logical arguments (e.g., as in Galatians and Romans), but more so we see *pastoral* language in the letter, words of encouragement from "one who loves his new converts and is anxious about them since they are under fire."[46]

Giving some pushback against interpreting 1 Thessalonians as epideictic (especially Jewett's reading), Margaret Mitchell notes that "praise and blame" (and the desire to comfort and reinforce values) appear in all the rhetorical categories (not just epideictic). Furthermore, epideictic itself tends to be more *present*-oriented, while 1 Thessalonians is clearly *future*-oriented.[47]

Ultimately, the discussion about genre raises the question regarding whether Paul's texts are meant to be analyzed as *letters* (fitting into ancient letter-writing conventions) or as textualized *speeches* (that would draw from rhetorical conventions).[48] One can easily see the folly of making this an *either-or* matter. Judith Lieu reminds us that Paul's letters are peculiar because while, on the one hand, they are personal letters such as we find in the Oxyrhynchus collection, on the other hand his letters are unusually long.[49] Lieu also encourages caution when focusing solely on rhetorical categorization because Paul does not come to us through recorded speeches, but letters.[50] She rightly asks, "Is it possible to retain

---

44. Watson, "Three Species," 31.

45. Watson, "Three Species," 31.

46. B. Witherington III, *1 and 2 Thessalonians: A Socio-Rhetorical Commentary* (Grand Rapids: Eerdmans, 2006), 29. Witherington adds here a comment that 1 Thessalonians may relate to the subcategory of epideictic rhetoric that he calls the "consolatory speech" (for funerals). He notes that Menander urges that such speeches ought to direct attention to the hope of the next life.

47. See M. M. Mitchell, *Paul and the Rhetoric of Reconciliation: An Exegetical Investigation* (Louisville: Westminster John Knox, 1991), 12n41.

48. See M. F. Bird, "Reassessing a Rhetorical Approach to Paul's Letters," *ExpTim* 119.8 (2008): 374–79.

49. See J. Lieu, "Letters," in *The Oxford Handbook of Biblical Studies*, ed. Judith M. Lieu and J. W. Rogerson (Oxford: Oxford University Press, 2006), 449; cf. E. R. Richards, *Paul and First-Century Letter Writing: Secretaries, Composition and Collection* (Downers Grove, IL: InterVarsity Press, 2004).

50. See Lieu, "Letters," 449.

an awareness of Paul's letters as letters while also analyzing them as rhetorical artefacts?"[51]

Not too far from this is the perspective of Wanamaker: "The two systems [epistolary and rhetoric] have in common that they both help us to assess the literary intention of the author. This in turn sheds light on the socio-historical situation that the author addressed."[52] Wanamaker is saying that both approaches end up offering approximately the same level of satisfaction in terms of using genre to properly read and interpret 1 Thessalonians.

Style

At a different time in history (about a century ago), probably because NT scholars were more classically trained, it was more common to see discussions of Paul's Greek writing style. It has become extremely rare to see such comments today. George Milligan was one of these early twentieth-century commentators who noted the style of 1 Thessalonians. He remarks that Paul had a comfortable, though not sophisticated, handle on the Greek language. His Greek is smooth enough to imply that he constructed his thoughts in Greek, and probably did not actively "translate" into Greek (from Aramaic).[53] First Thessalonians has a tendency toward drawn-out sentences (e.g., 1:2ff.; 2:14ff.) and ellipses (e.g., 1:8; 2:2; 4:4, 14). This communicated to Milligan that Paul wrote the letter out of the gushing fountain of his love and regard for the Thessalonians that sometimes came across as spontaneous and terse.[54]

In Malherbe's commentary, he also gives attention to the style of 1 Thessalonians. He observes that the "constituent" parts of a traditional Greco-Roman letter are present, but Paul shapes the letter toward his audience and his communicative purposes. Thus, we see a "creative adaptability of epistolary conventions."[55] In terms of the Greek style of 1 Thessalonians, Malherbe offers these observations:

---

51. Lieu, "Letters," 449; cf. D. Kremendahl, *Die Botschaft der Form: Zum Verhältnis von antiker Epistolographie und Rhetorik im Galaterbrief* (Göttingen: Vandenhoeck & Ruprecht, 2000). The debate on this matter is ongoing; see F. W. Hughes, "The Rhetoric of Letters," in *The Thessalonians Debate: Methodological Discord or Methodological Synthesis?*, ed. K. P. Donfried and J. Beutler (Grand Rapids: Eerdmans, 2000), 194–240; cf. idem, *Early Christian Rhetoric and 2 Thessalonians*, JSNTSup 30 (Sheffield: JSOT, 1989), 19–50.

52. Wanamaker, *Thessalonians*, 47.

53. Milligan, *Thessalonians*, lv.

54. Milligan, *Thessalonians*, lvi.

55. Malherbe, *Thessalonians*, 90–91.

- Paul liked to play with prepositions as in 1:5;
- there are several occurrences of asyndeta (2:11; 5:14–22);
- Paul tends to front-load imperatives;
- there is a heavy use of personal pronouns[56];
- there is a repeated use of disjunctive/adversative conjunctions[57];
- there are regular uses of rhetorical questions (e.g., 2:19; 3:9);
- there are emphatic uses of καί (e.g., 2:19; 4:14);
- there is the presence of interjections (e.g., 4:10).[58]

Structure

Weima helpfully identifies three approaches to outlining the structure of 1 Thessalonians: thematic, rhetorical, and epistolary.[59] That is, some choose to follow, for example, a classical rhetorical arrangement (e.g., Jewett, Wanamaker, Witherington) where various categories are identified such as *exordium, narratio, probatio,* and *peroratio.*[60] There is also the natural consideration of epistolary conventions in terms of structure. Thus, it is common to see the partitioning of a prescript and greeting, introductory thanksgiving, body (middle), and closing statement.[61] Scholars tend to gravitate toward either analyzing structure/arrangement according to an epistolary framework or a rhetorical one, though some opt for a combination.

Moreover, there are those who use neither (at least in a thoroughgoing fashion), but opt for a "thematic" approach, looking for logical-discourse breaks. Those who prefer a thematic approach are reluctant to assign to Paul (for 1 Thessalonians) the limitation of "following" a particular genre convention for structure and arrangement.

Weima himself prefers the epistolary structural analysis. He expresses his conviction that the fact that Paul wrote *letters* should guide the process of examining structure.[62] Wanamaker and Jewett follow a rhetorical

---

56. He notes, "The personal pronouns have the effect of making the letter more personal" (*Thessalonians*, 91).

57. See also N. K. Gupta, "The 'Not . . . But' (*ou . . . alla*) New Testament Rhetorical Pattern," *Ashland Theological Journal* 42 (2010): 13–24.

58. See, for all these, Malherbe, *Thessalonians*, 90–91.

59. See Weima, *1–2 Thessalonians*, 55; cf. Jewett, *Thessalonian Correspondence*, 71–85.

60. See Kennedy, *Classical Rhetoric*, 4–5.

61. See Porter and Adams, *Paul and the Ancient Letter Form*, passim; L. A. Jervis, *The Purpose of Romans: A Comparative Letter Structure Investigation*, JSNTSup 55 (Sheffield: JSOT, 1991), 29–68; cf. J. A. D. Weima, *Paul the Ancient Letter Writer: An Introduction to Epistolary Analysis* (Grand Rapids: Baker Academic, 2016).

62. Weima, *1–2 Thessalonians*, 55–56. For Weima, though, this does not preclude the possibility of Paul using rhetorical devices.

arrangement.[63] Fee appears to follow a more thematic approach.[64] Jewett is rather critical of the thematic approach, urging that outlining in this way tends to be rather arbitrary: "In the case of the Thessalonian letters, there is very little discussion in the commentaries as to why one outline is preferred over another, which indicates the unmethodical quality of the research up to this point [1986]."[65]

For my own part, I am not convinced that a rhetorical-arrangement approach is beneficial. Perhaps it depends on *why* one is outlining the structure. If it is simply to make sense of the arguments of the letter and how they fit together as a whole, I think that a "thematic" approach (with attention to conventional epistolary-framing features) is sufficient; thus, I am more drawn to Fee's approach. If one wants to consider how ancient genre elements may have shaped, inspired, and limited Paul's discourse, then giving more attention to macro-rhetorical arrangement might prove useful.

When it comes to the "seams" of the structure of 1 Thessalonians, there is widespread agreement among Thessalonian scholars on most of the major divisions. First Thessalonians 1:1 tends to be treated on its own as the address/opening/prescript. The rest of chapter one is treated as some form of thanksgiving (vv. 2–10). Next, 2:1–12 is generally recognized as a discrete section of personal narrative or autobiography for Paul. Verses 13–16 tend to be partitioned off, seeming to be a kind of digression (depending on how it is interpreted). Next, 2:17–3:10 is treated as another narrative section emphasizing the ongoing relationship between Paul (and his team) and the Thessalonians. There is then another break, where 3:11–13 is treated as a liturgical pause or transition to the next section. Without exception, scholars agree that chapter four begins a whole new section (largely partitioned as 4:1–5:22). Most scholars label this section as "exhortation" broadly speaking, but those who are inclined toward rhetorical structures label this as *probatio* (proof). The last section (5:23–28) is considered some form of "concluding matters" or *peroratio*.[66]

---

63. Jewett argues against an epistolary analysis of structure, positing that such an approach tells us very little about how the letter parts actually relate to one another. Moreover, Jewett reasons that if one were to assume epistolary structure, the majority of the first few chapters would relate to a "thanksgiving section," and the so-called letter "body" would not appear until chapter four, "which leads to a misconstrual of the main argument of the letter" (*Thessalonian Correspondence*, 68).

64. Fee, *Thessalonians*, 111.

65. Jewett, *Thessalonian Correspondence*, 68.

66. See the appendix at the end of this chapter for a visual presentation of the outlines of several scholars.

Sources and Influences

The matter of considering the possible sources behind 1 Thessalonians is complicated. Traditionally nineteenth- and twentieth-century scholarship considered the Old Testament (and other Jewish texts) and the Jesus tradition as potential sources (and we will consider the relationship between 1 Thessalonians and these below), but it is far less common in the twenty-first century to see discussion of sources. The concept of sources tends to presume Paul was sitting at his writing desk with his "Bible" (i.e., the Greek-language Jewish Scriptures) open on his left and some kind of "Jesus document" open on his right, and as he wrote his letter to the Thessalonians, he purposefully included excerpts from such "sources." Because there are no explicit quotations from Scripture in 1 Thessalonians, nor from Jesus tradition, it would be difficult to accept such a scenario.[67] Instead of thinking in terms of sources, it is preferable in the case of 1 Thessalonians to employ the language of "influences."

Milligan's commentary makes the classic case for the dual influences of "the Greek O.T. and certain Sayings of Jesus."[68] Milligan makes special note that, despite Paul's text being written in Greek to gentiles, he does *not* cite pagan texts at all.[69] Milligan urges that the influence of the LXX is pervasive, as demonstrated in Paul's vocabulary (ἀγάπη, ἁγιασμός, ἐκκλησία, δόξα, etc.).[70] He explains, "So minute was his acquaintance with its phraseology, so completely had it passed *in sucum et sanguinem*, that, though in these alone of all his Epistles there is no direct quotation from the O.T., there are whole passages which are little more than a mosaic of O.T. words and expressions."[71]

I begin with Milligan (from well over a century ago!) because most commentaries today and much Pauline scholarship in general have dis-

---

67. S. E. Porter offers an insightful essay on Paul's life and his access and use of Scripture entitled "Paul and His Bible: His Education and Access to the Scriptures of Israel," in *As It Is Written: Studying Paul's Use of the Old Testament*, ed. S. E. Porter and C. D. Stanley (Atlanta: SBL Press, 2008), 97–124. Leonard Greenspoon offers a thoughtful discussion of how Paul went about citing Scripture, and particularly what role his own memorization of Scripture played in how he used Scripture in his writings ("By the Letter? Word for Word? Scriptural Citation in Paul," in *Paul and Scripture: Extending the Conversation*, ed. C. D. Stanley [Atlanta: SBL Press, 2012], 9–24); see also C. D. Stanley, *Arguing with Scripture: The Rhetoric of Quotations in the Letters of Paul* (London: T&T Clark, 2004), 41–43; J. D. H. Norton, *Contours in the Text: Textual Variation in the Writings of Paul, Josephus, and the Yahad*, LNTS 430 (London: T&T Clark, 2011), 1–38 (see esp. 31–34).

68. Milligan, *Thessalonians*, xviii.

69. Milligan, *Thessalonians*, xlv.

70. Milligan, *Thessalonians*, lii.

71. Milligan, *Thessalonians*, lviii.

counted OT influence on 1 Thessalonians because it ostensibly does not quote Scripture verbatim. Milligan underscores, rightly I believe, that it is suffused with scriptural language and imagery. So why did Paul *not* quote Scripture in 1 Thessalonians the way he does in, say, 1 Corinthians and Romans? The answer to this question is complex and contested—and falls beyond the purview of our discussion here—but suffice it to say that it is unquestionable that Jewish Scripture strongly influenced how and what Paul communicated to the Thessalonians. In the late twentieth century, Richard Hays made a strong case for the presence and importance of "echoes of Scripture" in Paul, and in more recent years there has been more attention paid to scriptural echoes and allusions in 1 Thessalonians.[72] It is difficult to make a case that a *particular* Old Testament text or texts served as specific influences for 1 Thessalonians, so we will not speculate here.[73]

There have been much more concrete and fruitful discussions about the possibility of the use of Jesus material or tradition in 1 Thessalonians.[74] As for Milligan, he mentioned a number of possible influences (see table below).

Milligan's List of Possible Influences of Jesus Material in 1 Thessalonians

2:14–16	(influenced by) Matthew 23:31–34
4:8	Luke 10:16
5:2	Matthew 24:43; Luke 12:39 (he found the Lukan connection more convincing)
5:3	Luke 21:34
5:5	Luke 16:8
5:6	Matthew 24:42
5:7	Matthew 24:48–49

72. See R. B. Hays, *Echoes of Scripture in the Letters of Paul* (New Haven: Yale University Press, 1989); on 1 Thessalonians in particular see S. C. Keesmaat, "In the Face of the Empire: Paul's Use of Scripture in the Shorter Epistles," in *Hearing the Old Testament in the New Testament*, ed. S. E. Porter (Grand Rapids: Eerdmans, 2006), 182–213 (esp. 204–8); J. Weima, "1–2 Thessalonians," in *Commentary on the New Testament Use of the Old Testament*, ed. G. K. Beale and D. A. Carson (Grand Rapids: Baker Academic, 2007), 871–90; E. E. Johnson, "Paul's Reliance on Scripture in 1 Thessalonians," in Stanley, *Paul and Scripture*, 143–62.

73. One can see suggestions for OT allusions in the NA[28] Greek text margins.

74. For a general discussion, see J. D. G. Dunn, "Jesus Tradition in Paul," in *Studying the Historical Jesus*, ed. B. Chilton and C. A. Evans, NTTS 19 (Leiden: Brill, 1998), 155–78.

We will reserve the examination of 1 Thessalonians 2:(13+)14–16 for another occasion, and the possible influence on 4:8 is unconvincing to most scholars. That leaves us with 1 Thessalonians 5:1–7, and one might also include 4:15–17 (Matt 24:3–42).

There is almost no doubt that Paul would have received the "thief in the night" language from early Christian tradition.[75] It is difficult to know *how* Paul received such a tradition. It is facile to imagine that Paul carried around a copy of Q or copies of notes from (pre-)Matthew or (pre-) Luke. I think it best to recognize the point that Victor Furnish makes regarding the connection (especially from a literary perspective) between Jesus and Paul. Furnish notes the problem of trying to directly link "the individual, Jesus of Nazareth, to the individual, Paul of Tarsus." Following Schweitzer, Furnish directs attention to that great mediating factor, "primitive Christianity."[76] It was about a couple of decades between the death of Jesus and the writing of 1 Thessalonians; Paul would have undoubtedly absorbed some of the language, imagery, traditions, and liturgy that were developing out of Jesus's following. We will return to the influence of "primitive Christianity" in a moment.

What about 1 Thessalonians 4:15 where Paul refers to a teaching that came to him "by the word of the Lord" (related to the raising of dead believers before those still alive)? This is a major debate in the study of 1 Thessalonians, and at least one monograph is entirely dedicated to this subject.[77] There is a segment of scholarship that is very much open to the possibility that "the word of the Lord" means a saying of Jesus.[78] Obviously what Paul refers to as this "word" does not clearly match any known saying of Jesus in the Gospels. Thus, either it is an *agraphon*[79] or a loose reference to something from the Gospels. David Wenham tries to make such a case

---

75. See T. Holtz, "Paul and the Oral Gospel Tradition," in *Jesus and the Oral Gospel Tradition*, ed. Henry Wansbrough (London: Bloomsbury, 2004), 380–93; cf. C.-P. März, "Das Gleichnis vom Dieb: Überlegungen zur Verbindung von Lk 12,39 par Mt 24,43 und 1 Thess 5,2.4," in *The Four Gospels: Festschrift for Franz Neirynck*, ed. F. van Segbroeck, 3 vols., BETL 100 (Leuven: Leuven University Press, 1992), 1:633–49. For a more skeptical perspective see C. Tuckett, "Synoptic Tradition in 1 Thessalonians," in *From the Sayings to the Gospels* (Tübingen: Mohr Siebeck, 2014), 316–39.

76. See V. P. Furnish, "The Jesus-Paul Debate: From Baur to Bultmann," in *Paul and Jesus: Collected Essays*, ed. A. J. M. Wedderburn (Sheffield: Sheffield Academic Press, 1989), 45.

77. M. W. Pahl, *Discerning the "Word of the Lord": The "Word of the Lord" in 1 Thessalonians 4:15*, LNTS 389 (London: T&T Clark, 2009).

78. See, e.g., J. Jeremias, *Unknown Sayings of Jesus*, 2nd ed. (London: SPCK, 1964), 81–83.

79. See C. R. Nicholl, *From Hope to Despair in Thessalonica: Situating 1 and 2 Thessalonians*, SNTSMS 126 (Cambridge: Cambridge University Press, 2004), 38–41, for an argument in favor of this view.

for the latter by observing that Paul refers to his previous eschatological teaching based on "traditions" he passed on to them (e.g., 1 Thess 5:1–2). Wenham believes that it makes perfect sense that some of this Christian tradition related to teachings of the earthly Jesus.[80] He goes on then to underscore the similarities and resonances between Paul's eschatological teaching and the "synoptic eschatological traditions" (e.g., Matt 24:40, 41/ Luke 17:34, 35). Specifically on the matter of the return of Jesus, Wenham points to the saying, "Truly I tell you, some who are standing here will not taste death before they see the Son of Man coming in his kingdom" (Matt 16:28/Mark 9:1/Luke 9:27). Perhaps it was about the Son of Man gathering the elect (Mark 13:27), Wenham wonders. He is open to a link to Johannine tradition as well: "I am the resurrection and the life. The one who believes in me will live, even though they die; and whoever lives by believing in me will never die" (John 11:25–26).[81] Nevertheless, I find links to sayings from the Jesus tradition tenuous; the *agraphon* theory is more attractive, though in the end I believe the saying is best understood as "new" prophetic insight.

We have considered the matter enough to say that Paul probably did not work with concrete Jesus tradition *sources*, but certainly we can detect influence from the stream of Jesus's teachings passed down. And that brings us to a third area of "influences"—primitive or earliest Christianity.

Because 1 Thessalonians is probably the very earliest extant piece of literature from early Christianity, it is difficult to know what is *Pauline* (marks of Paul's unique vocabulary and imagination) and what is *pre-Pauline* (what language and concepts he received from those before him).[82] Nevertheless, *because* Paul makes reference to traditions, we know he was influenced by and passed on such. Probably the safest bet is to recognize that certain terminology and titles he used came from that tradition, such as "brothers and sisters" (ἀδελφοί), "believers" (πιστεύω), "church(es)" (ἐκκλησία), and also perhaps παρουσία.[83]

---

80. See D. Wenham, *Paul: Follower of Jesus or Founder of Christianity?* (Grand Rapids: Eerdmans, 1995), 305–6.

81. Wenham, *Paul*, 332–33.

82. Interestingly, in Rom 16:7 Paul commends Andronicus and Junia whom he specifically mentions as those who "were in Christ before I was"—*those with a longer history of following Jesus than he.*

83. On the first three items, see P. R. Trebilco, *Self-Designations and Group Identity in the New Testament* (Cambridge: Cambridge University Press, 2014), 16–120, 164–205.

RECOMMENDED READING

Textual Criticism and 1 Thessalonians

Comfort, P. W. *A Commentary on Textual Additions to the New Testament*. Grand
Rapids: Kregel, 2017.

———. *A Commentary on the Manuscripts and Text of the New Testament*. Grand
Rapids: Kregel, 2015.

Ehrman, B. D., and M. W. Holmes, eds. *The Text of the New Testament in Contemporary Research: Essays on the Status Quaestionis*. 2nd ed. NTTSD 42. Leiden:
Brill, 2013.

Metzger, B. M. *A Textual Commentary on the Greek New Testament*. 2nd ed.
Stuttgart: German Bible Society, 1994.

Royse, J. R. "The Early Text of Paul (and Hebrews)." Pages 175–203 in *The Early
Text of the New Testament*. Edited by C. E. Hill and M. J. Kruger. Oxford:
Oxford University Press, 2012.

Textual Integrity of 1 Thessalonians

Collins, R. F. "Apropos the Integrity of 1 Thess." *ETL* 65 (1979): 67–106. Republished on pages 96–135 of *Studies on the First Letter to the Thessalonians*. BETL
66. Leuven: Leuven University Press, 1984.

Pearson, B. A. "1 Thessalonians 2:13–16: A Deutero-Pauline Interpolation." *HTR*
64 (1971): 79–94.

Schmidt, D. "1 Thess 2:13–16: Linguistic Evidence for an Interpolation." *JBL* 102
(1983): 269–79.

Authorship and Date

Campbell, D. A. Pages 190–253 in *Framing Paul: An Epistolary Biography*. Grand
Rapids: Eerdmans, 2014.

Dunn, J. D. G. *Beginning from Jerusalem*. Christianity in the Making 2. Grand
Rapids: Eerdmans, 2009.

Riesner, R. *Paul's Early Period: Chronology, Mission Strategy, Theology*. Grand Rapids:
Eerdmans, 1998.

APPENDIX A

	JEWETT	WANAMAKER	MALHERBE	FEE	WEIMA	GUPTA*
1:1	Exordium (1:1–5) [includes Epistolary prescript + Thanksgiving]	Epistolary Prescript (1:1)	Address (1:1)	**Thanksgiving, Narrative, and Prayer (1:1–3:13):** Salutation (1:1)	Letter opening (1:1)	Prescript (1:1)
1:2–3		Exordium (1:2–10)	**Autobiography (1:2–3:13):** Thanksgiving (1:2–3:10): The Conversion of the Thessalonians (1:2–10)	**Thanksgiving, Narrative, and Prayer (1:1–3:13):** Thanksgiving (1:2–3)	Thanksgiving (1:2–10)	Thanksgiving for the Thessalonians' praiseworthy trust (1:2–10)
1:4–7	**Narratio of Grounds for Thanksgiving (1:6–3:13):** Congregational imitation (1:6–10)			**Thanksgiving, Narrative, and Prayer (1:1–3:13):** Narrative Part I: The Thessalonians' Conversion and Following (1:4–10): Paul Reminds the Thessalonians of Their Experience of Conversion (1:4–7)		
1:8–10				**Thanksgiving, Narrative, and Prayer (1:1–3:13):** Narrative Part I: The Thessalonians' Conversion and Following (1:4–10): The Thessalonians' Following Christ Had Become Well Known to Others (1:8–10)		

* See Nijay K. Gupta, *1–2 Thessalonians*, NCCS (Eugene, OR: Wipf & Stock, 2016).

	JEWETT	WANAMAKER	MALHERBE	FEE	WEIMA	GUPTA
2:1–7b	**Narratio of Grounds for Thanksgiving (1:6–3:13):** Clarification of apostolic example (2:1–12)	**Narratio (2:1–3:10):** Paul's Missionary Style among the Thessalonians (2:1–12)	**Autobiography (1:2–3:13):** Thanksgiving (1:2–3:10): Paul's Ministry in Thessalonica (2:1–12)	**Thanksgiving, Narrative, and Prayer (1:1–3:13): Narrative Part 2: Paul's Conduct in Thessalonica** (2:1–12): What Paul was NOT like among the Thessalonians (2:1–7b)	**Defense of Apostolic Actions and Absence (2:1–3:13):** Defense of Paul's actions in Thessalonica (2:1–16)	Paul's blameless ministry (2:1–12)
2:7b–12				**Thanksgiving, Narrative, and Prayer (1:1–3:13): Narrative Part 2: Paul's Conduct in Thessalonica** (2:1–12): What Paul WAS like among the Thessalonians (2:7b–12)		
2:13	**Narratio of Grounds for Thanksgiving (1:6–3:13):** Clarification of Judean example (2:13–16)	**Narratio (2:1–3:10):** Digression within the Narratio (2:13–16)	**Autobiography (1:2–3:13):** Thanksgiving (1:2–3:10): The Word under Persecution (2:13–16)	**Thanksgiving, Narrative, and Prayer (1:1–3:13):** The Thanksgiving Renewed (2:13)		Praiseworthy endurance amid persecution (2:13–16)
2:14–16				**Thanksgiving, Narrative, and Prayer (1:1–3:13):** Narrative Part 3: The Thessalonians' (and Paul's) Ill Treatment (2:14–16)		

	JEWETT	WANAMAKER	MALHERBE	FEE	WEIMA	GUPTA
2:17–20	**Narratio of Grounds for Thanksgiving (1:6–3:13):** Paul's desire for apostolic visit (2:17–3:10)	*Narratio* **(2:1–3:10):** Paul's Continuing Relationship with His Persecuted Converts at Thessalonica (2:17–3:10): His Desire to See the Thessalonians and Attempts to Revisit Them (2:17–20)	**Autobiography (1:2–3:13):** Thanksgiving (1:2–3:10): Reestablishing Contact (2:17–3:10)	**Thanksgiving, Narrative, and Prayer (1:1–3:13):** Narrative Part 4: In the Meantime (2:17–3:10): Paul Had Been Thwarted from Returning (2:17–20)	**Defense of Apostolic Actions and Absence (2:1–3:13):** Defense of present absence from Thessalonica (2:17–3:10)	Paul's love, pride, and concern (2:17–3:13)
3:1–5		*Narratio* **(2:1–3:10):** Paul's Continuing Relation with His Persecuted Converts at Thessalonica (2:17–3:10): The Sending of Timothy (3:1–5)		**Thanksgiving, Narrative, and Prayer (1:1–3:13):** Narrative Part 4: In the Meantime (2:17–3:10): The Sending of Timothy (3:1–5)		
3:6–10		*Narratio* **(2:1–3:10):** Paul's Continuing Relationship with His Persecuted Converts at Thessalonica (2:17–3:10): Timothy's Return (3:6–10)		**Thanksgiving, Narrative, and Prayer (1:1–3:13):** Narrative Part 4: In the Meantime (2:17–3:10): The Return of Timothy (3:6–10)		

(cont.)

	JEWETT	WANAMAKER	MALHERBE	FEE	WEIMA	GUPTA
3:11–13	**Narratio of Grounds for Thanksgiving (1:6–3:13):** Transitus in benedictory style (3:11–13)	*Transitus from Narratio to Probatio* (3:11–13)	**Autobiography (1:2–3:13):** Concluding Prayer (3:11–13)	**Thanksgiving, Narrative, and Prayer (1:1–3:13):** The Prayer Report (3:11–13)	**Defense of Apostolic Actions and Absence (2:1–3:13):** Transitional Prayer (3:11–13)	Paul's love, pride, and concern (2:17–3:13)
4:1–2	**Probatio (4:1–5:22):** The proof concerning the marriage ethic (4:1–8)	**Probatio (4:1–5:22):** Ethical Exhortation (4:1–12): Exhortation to Continue in Current Behavior (4:1–2)	**Exhortation (4:1–5:22):** Introduction (4:1–2)	**Supplying What is Lacking (4:1–5:11):** Introduction (4:1–2)	**Exhortations to the Thessalonians (4:1–5:22):** Increasing in conduct that pleases God (4:1–12)	Exhortation to persevere and grow in holiness, love, and integrity (4:1–12)
4:3–8		**Probatio (4:1–5:22):** Ethical Exhortation (4:1–12): Reinforcement of Sexual Norms (4:3–8)	**Exhortation (4:1–5:22):** On Marriage (4:3–8)	**Supplying What is Lacking (4:1–5:11):** Avoiding Sexual Immorality (4:3–8)		
4:9–12	**Probatio (4:1–5:22):** The second proof concerning the communal ethic (4:9–12)	**Probatio (4:1–5:22):** Ethical Exhortation (4:1–12): Familial Love and the Quiet Life (4:9–12)	**Exhortation (4:1–5:22):** On Brotherly Love and Self-Sufficiency (4:9–12)	**Supplying What is Lacking (4:1–5:11):** Loving Others by Working with One's Own Hands (4:9–12)		

	JEWETT	WANAMAKER	MALHERBE	FEE	WEIMA	GUPTA
4:13–18	**Probatio (4:1–5:22):** The third proof concerning the dead in Christ (4:13–18)	**Probatio (4:1–5:22):** Instruction concerning the Parousia and Assumption (4:13–18)	**Exhortation (4:1–5:22):** Eschatological Exhortation (4:13–5:11)	**Supplying What is Lacking (4:1–5:11):** About the Believers Who Have Died (4:13–18)	**Exhortations to the Thessalonians (4:1–5:22):** Comfort concerning deceased Christians at Christ's return (4:13–18)	The hopeful fate of the Christian dead (4:13–18)
5:1–3	**Probatio (4:1–5:22):** The fourth proof concerning the eschaton (5:1–11)	**Probatio (4:1–5:22):** Eschatological Expectation and Parenesis (5:1–11)		**Supplying What is Lacking (4:1–5:11):** About the Day of the Lord (5:1–11): The Day of the Lord and Unbelievers (5:1–3)	**Exhortations to the Thessalonians (4:1–5:22):** Comfort concerning living Christians at Christ's return (5:1–11)	The day of the Lord: preparedness and perseverance, not prediction (5:1–11)
5:4–11				**Supplying What is Lacking (4:1–5:11):** About the Day of the Lord (5:1–11): The Day of the Lord and the Thessalonian Believers (5:4–11)		

	JEWETT	WANAMAKER	MALHERBE	FEE	WEIMA	GUPTA
5:12–13	**Probatio (4:1–5:22):** The fifth proof concerning congregational life (5:12–22)	General Exhortations (5:12–22) [W. separates 5:19–22 as a unique section he calls "The Unity and Purpose of 5:19–22]	**Exhortation (4:1–5:22):** Intracommunal Relations (5:12–22)	**Concluding Matters (5:12–28):** Summary Exhortations (5:12–22): Attitude toward Their Leaders (5:12–13)	**Exhortations to the Thessalonians (4:1–5:22):** Exhortations on congregational life and worship (5:12–22)	Final instructions (5:12–28)
5:14–15				**Concluding Matters (5:12–28):** Summary Exhortations (5:12–22): Imperatival Summation of the Letter (5:14–15)		
5:16–18				**Concluding Matters (5:12–28):** Summary Exhortations (5:12–22): Exhortation to Continue Basic Christian Piety (5:16–18)		
5:19–22				**Concluding Matters (5:12–28):** Summary Exhortations (5:12–22): About Christian Prophecy (5:19–22)		
5:23–24	**Peroratio** (5:23–28)	**Peroratio and Epistolary Closing** (5:23–28)	**Conclusion** (5:23–28)	**Concluding Matters (5:12–28):** Benediction (5:23–24)	**Letter Closing (5:23–28)**	
5:25–28				**Concluding Matters (5:12–28):** Closing Greetings and Final Grace (5:25–28)		

CHAPTER 2

BACKGROUND AND SITUATION OF 1 THESSALONIANS

In this chapter we address the history of Thessalonica as well as the background and situation that gave rise to 1 Thessalonians. The chapter concludes with a brief discussion of the academic debate over the ordering of the Thessalonian letters.

THESSALONICA

City

In 316 BCE, Thessalonica was built on the site of Therme below the Hortiates Mountains.[1] Macedonian military leader (and later king) Cassander named the city he founded after his wife, the daughter of Philip II and half-sister of Alexander.[2] Thanks in no small part to Thessalonica's port, it became a prominent city.[3] In 187 BCE, king Philip V permitted Thessalonica to issue its own coinage, further boosting its economy.[4]

When Rome took control of Macedonia (168 BCE), it was divided into

---

1. An excellent summary chapter can be found in P. Adam-Veleni, "Thessalonike," in Fox, *Brill's Companion to Ancient Macedon*, 545–62. For an important methodological discussion regarding how to use and interpret archaeological findings to make sense of social history, see H. Koester, "Archäologie und Paulus in Thessalonike," in *Frühchristliches Thessaloniki*, ed. C. Breytenbach, Studien und Texte zu Antike und Christentum 44 (Tübingen: Mohr Siebeck, 2007), 1–9.

2. See the eminent historical work of C. vom Brocke, *Thessaloniki—Stadt der Kassander und Gemeinde des Paulus: eine frühe christliche Gemeinde in ihrer heidnischen Umwelt*, WUNT 2/125 (Tübingen: Mohr Siebeck, 2001).

3. P. Nigdelis, "Thessaloniki: The Age of the Macedonian Kingdom and the Period of Roman Rule," http://site.lpth.gr/en/texts/Nigdelis_en.pdf (online only).

4. See K. Dahmen, "The Numismatic Evidence," in *A Companion to Ancient Macedonia*, ed. J. Roisman and I. Worthington (West Sussex: Wiley-Blackwell, 2010), 54.

four districts, and Thessalonica became capital of the second district.[5] In the following years Thessalonica made several important political moves. First, it refused to support a revolt against Rome among Macedonian cities led by Andriscus (149 BCE). Instead, it hailed Roman praetor Quintus Caecilius Metellus (Macedonicus), suppressor of the revolt, as "savior."[6] A few years later, Thessalonica was named the capital of the province of Macedonia. The Romans took special interest in this city largely for its size and location.[7] They built the Via Egnatia, a roadway that ran east-west from Dyrrhachium on the Adriatic Sea to Thessalonica. It was intended, in the first place, for military use, but it became a major thoroughfare for trade and travel more broadly.[8]

About a century later, after Julius Caesar was murdered, Thessalonica again shrewdly supported Octavian and Mark Antony over against Brutus and Cassius.[9] In return for this loyalty, Antony bestowed upon Thessalonica the status of *civitas libera* (free city).[10] This special privilege meant that Thessalonians could operate with considerable autonomy while also receiving support from Rome.[11] Additionally it received tax concessions. It is no exaggeration to say, then, that this status "ushered in a prosperous

---

5. As V. Allamani-Souri notes, this fragmentation was strategic "to prevent once and for all the revival of a strong unified state that would constitute a threat to Rome" ("The Province of Macedonia in the Roman Imperium," in *Roman Thessaloniki*, ed. D. Grammenos [Thessaloniki: Archaeological Museum of Thessaloniki, 2003], 68).

6. See A. Smith, "'Unmasking the Powers': Toward a Postcolonial Analysis of 1 Thessalonians," in *Paul and the Roman Imperial Order*, ed. R. A. Horsley (London: Bloomsbury, 2004), 57; cf. R. Bernhardt, *Polis und römische Herrschaft in der späten Republik* (Berlin: de Gruyter, 1985).

7. Nigdelis, "Thessaloniki."

8. See C. G. Thomas, "The Physical Kingdom," in Roisman and Worthington, *Companion to Ancient Macedonia*, 76–77; see also J. Vanderspoel, "Provincia Macedonia," in Roisman and Worthington, *Companion to Ancient Macedonia*, 272. Allamani-Souri's commentary on this city's relationship with Rome is insightful: "Although it became a distinctly cosmopolitan city with a multinational population, it was also concerned to preserve its Greek core, though always in a dialectical relationship with the new cultural situation" ("Province of Macedonia," 75).

9. A coin has been unearthed from Thessalonica jointly issued in the names of Antony and Octavian; see Dahmen, "Numismatic Evidence," 57.

10. See Adam-Veleni, "Thessalonike," 554; cf. Brocke, *Thessaloniki*, 83–85; cf. Allamani-Souri, "Province of Macedonia," 69. Amphipolis and Skotousa were the only other Macedonian cities under this classification. But Philippi, Pella, Dion, Cassandreia, and Stobi were "purely Roman cities founded for soldiers and veterans, and for a significant number of Augustus' political enemies" (Allamani-Souri, "Province of Macedonia," 70).

11. See Adam-Veleni, "Thessalonike," 554; M. J. Smith, "The Thessalonian Correspondence," in *All Things to All Cultures: Paul among Jews, Greeks, and Romans*, ed. M. Harding and A. Nobbs (Grand Rapids: Eerdmans, 2013), 270; for a general discussion of "free cities" under Rome, see A. Lintott, *Imperium Romanum: Politics and Administration* (London: Routledge, 1993), 36–41. M. Tellbe adds that free cities did not have oversight from a Roman proconsul, and they were governed by their own counsel (βουλή), politarchs, and local assembly (*Paul between Synagogue and State: Christians, Jews, and Civic Authorities in 1 Thessalonians, Romans, and Philippians*, ConBNT 34 [Stockholm: Almqvist & Wiksell, 2001], 82).

new era for Thessalonica."[12] By the time of Paul, Thessalonica was a large, cosmopolitan city; Antipater of Thessalonica referred to it as the "mother of all Macedonia."[13] The largest ethnic population in Thessalonica at that time was Greek, but there is evidence for the presence of other groups, including Italians, Thracians, and Jews.[14]

Religion in Thessalonica

The religious atmosphere in Roman Thessalonica was remarkably diverse.[15] The traditional Greek deities were widely honored, including Athena, Artemis, Aphrodite, Demeter, Hermes, Poseidon, Dionysus, and Zeus.[16] Thessalonians also had an interest in the cult of Cabirus (or Kaberios).[17] We learn from Clement of Alexandria the legend of two brothers who killed a third sibling and buried him near Mount Olympus. Cabirus is depicted in worship as a young man with no beard. Devotees worshiped the murdered Cabirus as a savior who would return and bless the people, especially the poor.[18]

---

12. K. P. Donfried, *Paul, Thessalonica, and Early Christianity* (London: T&T Clark, 2002), 35.

13. *Palatine Anthology* 4.228.

14. Cf. V. Allamani-Souri, "The Social Composition of the City," in Grammenos, *Roman Thessaloniki*, 92; cf. Brocke, *Thessaloniki*, 94–96. Adam-Veleni nevertheless observes that despite the presence of "powerful Roman families" in Thessalonica in the mid-imperial period, "the inhabitants of the city were not Latinized, a fact that is proven by the quantity of inscriptions in Greek" ("Thessalonike," 555).

15. See Brocke, *Thessaloniki*, 114–42. E. Carney, "Macedonian Women," in Roisman and Worthington, *Companion to Ancient Macedonia*, comments that "new cults entered Macedonia, probably primarily through the great port of Thessaloniki. The cult of the Egyptian gods became important, especially for women" (425).

16. See K. Tzanavari, "The Worship of Gods and Heroes in Thessaloniki," in Grammenos, *Roman Thessaloniki*, 177–262. Tzanavari looks at evidence for worship of these gods: Aphrodite, Artemis, Asklepios, Athena, Demeter, Dionysus, Herakles, Hermes, Kaberios (Cabirus), Korybantes, Nemesis, Poseidon, Tyche, Zeus Hypsistos; heroes: Rider God, Heros Aulonites, Aineias; Egyptian deities; Oriental deities: Kybele, Mithras, Sol Invictus; and also Dea Roma and Epona. Christopher Steimle's important monograph focuses on the devotion to Egyptian gods, the emperor, and cult associations (*Vereinigungen*) in Roman Thessaloniki; see Steimle, *Religion im römischen Thessaloniki: Sakraltopographie, Kult und Gesellschaft* (Tübingen: Mohr Siebeck, 2008); cf. Adam-Veleni, "Thessalonike," 559.

On Egyptian deities, see H. Koester, "Egyptian Religion in Thessalonike: Regulation for the Cult," in *From Roman to Early Christian Thessalonikē*, ed. L. Nasrallah, C. Bakirtzis, and S. J. Friesen (Cambridge: Harvard University Press, 2010), 133–50. A total of sixty-nine inscriptions from Thessalonica refer to the worship of Egyptian deities. We can infer too that Egyptian cults had a presence in Thessalonica as far back as at least 200 BCE. Koester explains that in the Roman imperial period, the Egyptian religion became popular especially due to the expansive powers and often intimate attentiveness attributed to the Egyptian gods. Devotees sometimes attributed to Sarapis power equal to Zeus.

17. See Brocke, *Thessaloniki*, 117–21.

18. See Donfried, *Paul, Thessalonica, and Early Christianity*, 25–26. While it was once common for scholars to assume the prominence of this cult in Paul's time, this is now questioned; see E. Pillar, *Resurrection as Anti-Imperial Gospel: 1 Thessalonians 1:9b–10 in Context* (Minneapolis: Fortress, 2013), 103–5.

In Thessalonica, there is well-attested evidence of the worship of Egyptian deities.[19] In 1917 an ancient temple was discovered in Thessalonica that is now called the Sarapeion (or Sarapeum; dedicated to the deity Sarapis).[20] This temple probably dates to the third century BCE. This building was located in the southwestern part of ancient Thessalonica. A miniature replica can be found in Thessaloniki's Archaeological Museum.

As the excavation of the remains reveals, the Sarapeion had an anteroom that led to a great hall. Several small items have been found at the site, including several dozen inscriptions. One such inscription recounts a communication from Philip V (187 BCE) "in which he prohibited the use of the Sarapeion's funds for extra-cultic purposes and declared specific penalties for contraventions of the regulations." Thus, it is believed this inscription proves that Egyptian gods were worshiped in Thessalonica before the first-century BCE.[21] Many of the other inscriptions have proven useful for understanding life in ancient Macedonia, even beyond "cult."[22]

Even though it is called the Sarapeion, it may simply be a matter of convenience to call it thus, as other deities may have been worshiped there. It is true that a statue head of Sarapis was found in the vicinity, and the name Sarapis appears in inscriptions from Thessalonica. Yet Koester finds it unlikely that this Sarapeion was *the* temple of Sarapis in Thessalonica. Rather, he wonders whether it could have served as a "healing shrine" (in agreement with C. Bakirtzis).[23]

Roman Thessalonica

In recent years, New Testament studies have become more interested in the social and sociopolitical dimensions of life in the Roman world.[24] In terms of the study of the context and background of 1–2 Thessalonians in particular, credit must go to Holland Hendrix for his massively influential,

---

19. Brocke, *Thessaloniki*, 132–38.

20. For a full account of the history of the excavations of the Sarapeion, see Koester, "Egyptian Religion in Thessalonike," 133–50; also Brocke, *Thessaloniki*, 37–41, 138.

21. See H. Koester, *Cities of Paul* (Minneapolis: Fortress, 2005), Logos Bible Software.

22. See Koester, *Cities of Paul*; see J. S. Kloppenborg and R. S. Ascough, *Greco-Roman Associations: Texts, Translations, and Commentary: I. Attica, Central Greece, Macedonia, Thrace* (Berlin: de Gruyter, 2011), 361–62; on collected inscriptions see C. F. Edson, *Inscriptiones Thessalonicae et Viciniae* (Berlin: de Gruyter, 1972).

23. See Koester, "Egyptian Religion in Thessalonike," 139.

24. See W. Carter, *The Roman Empire and the New Testament* (Nashville: Abingdon, 2006); P. S. Oakes, ed., *Rome in the Bible and the Early Church* (Grand Rapids: Baker, 2002); note also the important reference work *Aufstieg und Niedergang der römischen Welt [ANRW]* (Berlin: de Gruyter, 1972–); regarding Paul in particular see J. P. Sampley, ed., *Paul in the Greco-Roman World*, 2nd ed. (London: Bloomsbury, 2016), and S. E. Porter, ed., *Paul: Jew, Greek, and Roman*, PAST (Boston: Brill, 2008).

though unpublished, Harvard dissertation entitled "Thessalonicans Honor Romans" (written under Dr. Helmut Koester).[25] Hendrix did not set out to investigate something directly related to the apostle Paul or 1–2 Thessalonians; rather, his interest was squarely on Thessalonica in the Roman period. He set his sights on the history of honors given to Romans by this Macedonian city between approximately 200 BCE and 100 CE.

Hendrix makes the claim, meticulously defended, that Thessalonica sought to ally themselves with those powers that could preserve and prosper their city. As Rome became a significant political factor, the Romans "became the objects of a distinct system of honors which rewarded positive administrative policies and other philanthropic activity beneficial to the city."[26]

Such honors included the production and hosting of contests and games honoring Rome (with the establishment of the priest and agonothete), and the *inclusion* of the Roma cult.[27] Hendrix also points to extant evidence of the honoring of Romans.[28] As a notable case study, Hendrix mentions the relationship between Antipater of Thessalonica and Lucias Calpunius Piso, the former a client of the latter Roman benefactor and fellow poet. Hendrix explains, "Antipater's stewardship of Piso's patronage represents a microcosm of the city's honorific institutions: the demonstration of gratitude for patronage was an explicit strategy in soliciting further benefaction."[29]

The Cult of Roma and Divine Honors for Caesar in Thessalonica

As noted above, Thessalonica established a cult in honor of the goddess Roma[30] and also erected a temple for Caesar during the reign of Augustus.[31]

---

25. Hendrix's work is rather exhaustive (444 pages!) and has stood the test of time; see H. Hendrix, "Thessalonicans Honor Romans" (ThD diss., Harvard Divinity School, 1984); cf. Brocke, *Thessaloniki*, 45–74.

26. Hendrix, "Thessalonicans," 336; see key summary on p. 253 as well (also cf. 153–54). See similarly Allamani-Souri, "Province of Macedonia," 76: "During the Roman civil wars under the Republic, the city seems to have sided invariably with the victor, even if this entailed changing ideological camps" (76).

27. Hendrix, "Thessalonicans," 337.

28. See Hendrix, "Thessalonicans," 143, 188. According to Hendrix, a significant piece of early extant evidence comes from an inscription of Thessalonica officially honoring Metellus Macedonicus for his "salvation" of the city in the uprising of Andriscus (post 147 BCE); see Hendrix, "Thessalonicans," 21; cf. 146–48, 192. Perhaps the earliest evidence comes from the Paramonos inscription (ca. 95 BCE; see Hendrix, "Thessalonicans," 195; Tellbe, *Paul between Synagogue and State*, 83). Hendrix estimates that it was about a half century later that Roma began to receive honors (193).

29. Hendrix, "Thessalonicans," 281.

30. See A. Powell, *The Greek World* (London: Routledge, 2002), 376; Adam-Veleni, "Thessalonike," 558–60.

31. See Brocke, *Thessaloniki*, 138–41, 142; cf. Tellbe, *Paul between Synagogue and State*, 80–86. In general, on the topic of the imperial cult, see S. R. F. Price, *Rituals and Power: The Roman Imperial Cult in Asia Minor* (Cambridge: Cambridge University Press, 1984); H. Hendrix, "Beyond

Again, this was associated with the Thessalonian desire to show loyalty and respect to Rome.[32] Indeed, so enamored was Thessalonica with Rome that it was granted the title *tetrakis neokoros* (allowing it to dedicate *four* temples to the emperor).[33] Numismatic evidence informs us that Thessalonica extended to the emperor the title *divus*.[34] Does that mean that the emperor was considered divine and worshiped as a deity?[35] This is a debated matter. Allamani-Souri urges that while Romans themselves would not have felt comfortable using the religious language of worship to show devotion to the supreme human leader, matters were rather different among Greeks who did not hold such a religio-political distinction.[36]

Nevertheless, scholars like Hendrix encourage caution when referring to the so-called imperial cult and assuming it entailed worship. Hendrix argues that "sacrifices *to* Romans and emperors were not the norm."[37] He prefers to see emperors as *indirect* objects of sacrifice. Thus, Hendrix

---

'Imperial Cult' and 'Cults of Magistrates,'" *SBL Seminar Papers* 25 (1986): 301–8; S. J. Friesen, *Twice Neokoros: Ephesus, Asia and the Cult of the Flavian Imperial Family* (Leiden: Brill, 1993); I. Gradel, *Emperor Worship and Roman Religion* (Oxford: Clarendon, 2002); D. Horrell, "The Imperial Cult and the New Testament," *JSNT* 27.3 (2005): 251–373; D. Fishwick, "A Critical Assessment: On the Imperial Cult in Religions of Rome," *Religious Studies and Theology* 28.2 (2009): 129–74; C. Miller, "The Imperial Cult in the Pauline Cities of Asia Minor and Greece," *CBQ* 72.2 (2010): 314–32; Allamani-Souri remarks that no emperor ever visited Thessalonica. We do have record of letters and edicts from emperors, such as a note from second century (CE) Antoninus Pius to the leaders of Thessalonica; see "Province of Macedonia," 72–73. As for the location of the temple of Caesar, J. Harrison speculates that the cult may have been located in the western sector of the city. While there are no material remains that identify such a temple in that location, portions of a statue of the emperor were found in the western region (J. R. Harrison, *Paul and the Imperial Authorities at Thessalonica and Rome: A Study in the Conflict of Ideology*, WUNT 273 [Tübingen: Mohr Siebeck, 2011], 55).

32. V. Allamani-Souri comments that the Greek East accepted the imperial cult (for the purposes of supporting Rome), but they did not worship Roman deities because they found their own cultural deities to be superior; see V. Allamani-Souri, "The Imperial Cult," in Grammenos, *Roman Thessaloniki*, 98. Allamani-Souri points out that the early devotion to Roma would have been an exception, but certainly spread throughout the Greek East for political capital (99); see also K. P. Donfried, "The Imperial Cults of Thessalonica and Political Conflict in 1 Thessalonians," in *Paul and Empire*, ed. R. A. Horsley (Harrisburg, PA: Trinity Press International, 1997), 217–18.

33. Allamani-Souri, "Imperial Cult," 100.

34. See Dahmen, "Numismatic Evidence," 57; cf. C. Breytenbach, "Der Danksagungsbericht des Paulus," in *Grace, Reconciliation, Concord* (Boston: Brill, 2010), 163; cf. B. W. Winter, *Divine Honours for the Caesars: The First Christians' Responses* (Grand Rapids: Eerdmans, 2015), 67.

35. On the use of *divus* versus *deus* as titles for emperors, see Winter, *Divine Honours*, 63–67.

36. See Allamani-Souri, "Imperial Cult," 98; cf. Donfried, "Imperial Cults," 218. Donfried and others draw attention to the fact that some coins (dating to late first-century BCE) have the head of Augustus in just the place where formerly the head of Zeus would have appeared. Such a phenomenon is certainly remarkable (see Donfried, "Imperial Cults," 218), but I would think hardly irrefutable evidence that Augustus was considered a god on par with Zeus (contra M. J. Harris, "The Thessalonian Correspondence," Pages 269–301 in *All Things to All Cultures*, ed. M. Harding and A. Nobbs [Grand Rapids: Eerdmans, 2013], 274).

37. Hendrix, "Thessalonicans," 333–34.

proposes a clearer academic label, something like "cult for emperors" (or Roman benefactors).[38]

Jews in Thessalonica

When and why Jews first migrated to Thessalonica is unknown, but their presence in the city can be confidently traced back as early as the second-century BCE.[39] There is a broad consensus that Jews tended to form a cohesive subcommunity even in the diaspora.[40] According to Nigdelis, the Romans would not have classified the Jews as an ethnic group, but rather a social one. The Jewish community in Thessaloniki was particular in the sense that it was the only one in the region that came to have more than one synagogue.[41] If (later) evidence from Beroea is instructive more broadly, the Jewish community would have been led by elected elders, not unlike pagan associations.[42] In terms of their values and level of Hellenistic assimilation, the extant funerary inscriptions are in Greek, but attest to their strong religious identification.[43] As for their civic life, Bradley Ritter makes this important note in view of the portrayal in Acts:

---

38. Hendrix, "Thessalonicans," 334.

39. See A. Ovadiah, "Ancient Jewish Communities in Macedonia and Thrace," in *Hellenic and Jewish Arts: Interaction, Tradition and Renewal*, ed. A. Ovadiah (Tel Aviv: Ramot, 1998), 185–98; Adam-Veleni, "Thessalonike," 553. Adam-Veleni associates the attraction to Thessalonica (by Italians as well as Jews) with the prosperity stimulated by Roman conquest of the region; see also T. Stefanidou-Tiveriou, "Thessaloniki from Cassander to Galerius," http://site.lpth.gr/en/texts/Tiveriou_en.pdf (online only). According to Nigdelis, Jews settled in all four of Macedonia's prominent cities: Philippi, Thessaloniki, Beroea, and Stobi; see P. Nigdelis, "Roman Thessalonica," in *The History of Macedonia*, ed. I. Koliopoulos (Thessaloniki: Museum of the Macedonian Struggle Foundation, 2007), 62. Tellbe notes Philo's information about Jews in the Roman Empire, including Macedonia. Tellbe remarks that "given the wide dispersion of Jews in the eastern half of the Roman Empire, and that there is evidence of other Jewish communities close to Thessalonica, it would indeed have been remarkable if there would have been at this time no Jewish community in the Macedonian metropolis [of Thessalonica] with an estimated population of more than 50,000" (*Paul between Synagogue and State*, 88).

40. See Nigdelis, "Roman Thessalonica," 51–87; Allamani-Souri, "Social Composition," 93–95. D. J. Kyrtatas's treatment of early Christianity in Thessaloniki examines interaction between Paul and local Jews, drawing significantly from the account in Acts 17 ("Early Christianity in Macedonia," 585–99); see below for more discussion of the use of Acts as a historical source.

41. Nigdelis, "Roman Thessalonica," 62. A sarcophagus inscription apparently bears witness to a synagogue in Thessalonica (third century CE), and here it even mentions "synagogues" (plural). For an important discussion, see P. Nigdelis, "Synagoge(n) und Gemeinde der Juden in Thessaloniki: Fragen Aufgrund einer neuen jüdischen Grabinschrift der Kaiserzeit," *ZPE* 120 (1994): 298–306. The inscription reads: "Marcus Aurelius Iakob also (called) Eutychios while he was alive (made this) for his wife Anna also (called) Asyncrition and for himself. In memory. If anyone places another (body in the sarcophagus) he shall give to the synagogues 75,000 shiny *denarii*." This translation is found in Kloppenborg and Ascough, *Greco-Roman Assocations*, 375–76; cf. Brocke, *Thessaloniki*, 217–233; Tellbe, *Paul between Synagogue and State*, 86.

42. Nigdelis, "Roman Thessalonica," 62.

43. Nigdelis, "Roman Thessalonica," 63.

While there is no evidence for or against distinctions in legal status between the Judean residents of Thessalonica and the rest, Luke hardly presents the Judeans in his account as in any way politically disenfranchised or as political outsiders. Certainly they might have been resident foreigners. Status is unimportant to Luke's account. But in the assembly, their presentation convinced the gathered citizens and the politarchs to take a pledge from Jason and the rest. . . . The Judeans understood the political climate of Thessalonica and were able to use it for their own ends by bringing legal action in the assembly against fellow residents.[44]

THE SITUATION BEHIND 1 THESSALONIANS

When we attempt to reconstruct the situation behind 1 Thessalonians, we are dealing primarily with three key sources: (a) 1 Thessalonians, (b) 2 Thessalonians, and (c) Luke's Acts of the Apostles. It has been customary to bring all three together with the caveat that Paul's own firsthand information (1 Thessalonians) is the most important.[45] Regarding Acts, questions about how to categorize it in terms of *genre* are complex, but it is fair to say that most scholars comfortably place it under a "genre of history."[46] The key

---

44. B. Ritter, *Judeans in the Greek Cities of the Roman Empire* (Boston: Brill, 2015), 237.

45. Because of both the traditional ordering (1 Thess, then 2 Thess) and also the concern of pseudepigraphy for the second canonical letter, 1 Thessalonians is usually given priority in scholarly historical reconstruction.

46. See the summary of the history of scholarship on this matter by S. A. Adams, *The Genre of Acts and Collected Biography*, SNTSMS 156 (Cambridge: Cambridge University Press, 2013), 13; cf. Dunn, *Beginning from Jerusalem*, 68; J. Schröter, "Lukas als Historiograph. Das lukanische Doppelwerk und die Entdeckung der christlichen Heilsgeschichte," in *Die antike Historiographie und die Anfänge der christlichen Geschichtsschreibung*, ed. E.-M. Decker (Berlin: de Gruyter, 2005), 246–47. Craig Keener concludes that "Acts is history, probably apologetic history in the form of a historical monograph with a narrow focus on the expansion of the gospel message from Jerusalem to Rome. Luke's approach focuses on primary characters and their deeds and speeches, as was common in the history of his day. Stating that Acts is history rather than a novel affects how we should read it" (C. S. Keener, *Acts: An Exegetical Commentary, Volume 1: Introduction and 1:1–2:47* [Grand Rapids: Baker, 2012], 115). J. Fitzmyer offers a kind of both-and perspective by urging that Luke indeed was *doing history writing*, but (a) within the boundaries of his own literary culture and (b) with obvious concerns for style and coherence. Fitzmyer writes, "In judging the historical character of the many narratives in Acts, one has to reckon with the author's possible abridgement of details and even tendentious presentation of some of the events recounted. The lucan story line at times bears an apologetic thrust; yet to admit that is not to write off the whole episode as unhistorical" (J. Fitzmyer, *The Acts of the Apostles*, AB [New Haven: Yale University Press, 1998], 125). What this means is that Luke's account can be taken at face value in the broader depiction of historical occurrences. Even still, as Fitzmyer observes, we find that Luke happens to get certain details right that we have been able to corroborate elsewhere; in the case of Thessalonica, for example, the reference to "politarchs" (τοὺς

question seems to be how *accurately* Luke intended to recount the events he describes. A central criticism of those who treat Acts as trustworthy historical reporting is that Luke clearly stylizes his story and portrays certain literary-narrative patterns. Because of this, when the material we can glean from 1 Thessalonians cannot be harmonized with the account in Acts, the latter is brought into question. Let us look briefly at Acts 17:1–10a and then discuss the interpretive challenges and debates after that.

According to Luke, many people responded to Paul's messages in the synagogue; some were Jews, but many were Godfearers and "prominent women" (Acts 17:4). Comparing this to 1 Thessalonians, some scholars, such as Richard Ascough, put Acts into doubt, arguing that Luke has embellished this account and that one cannot rely on this narrative to establish that Thessalonica even had a synagogue at this time.[47] Much is made by Ascough (and also G. Lüdemann on whom he relies methodologically) of Luke's redactional tendencies, such as the recounting of conversions from upper classes, the positive reaction of gentile Godfearers, and the resistance of the Jews.[48]

Mark Allan Powell gives insight into the standard interpreting procedure of many interpreters of Acts, whereby any feature that seems to serve Luke's theological agenda is placed into the category of "dubious" in terms of historicity.[49] Chris Mount's approach represents perhaps the most extreme perspective on the historical limits of Acts in view of its literary design:

πολιτάρχας) in local leadership (17:6; see Fitzmyer, *Acts*, 126). Dunn reminds us that Luke could not have learned the term for "politarch" from "literary sources" since the word does not appear in any Greek literature that we have, though it does appear in Macedonian inscriptions (Dunn, *Beginning from Jerusalem*, 80). Concerning Acts and historiography, see too L. T. Johnson, *Acts of the Apostles*, SP (Collegeville, MN: Liturgical Press, 2006), 7.

47. See R. S. Ascough, *Paul's Macedonian Associations: The Social Context of Philippians and 1 Thessalonians*, WUNT 2/161 (Tübingen: Mohr Siebeck, 2003), 205–6; see also the critical concerns of E. J. Richard, "Early Pauline Thought: An Analysis of 1 Thessalonians," in *Pauline Theology*, ed. J. M. Bassler (Minneapolis: Fortress, 1991), 71–85. Though note the comment by historian Bradley Rittler regarding the historical usefulness of Acts and its portrayal of Jewish social relationships: "Because Acts only provides a snapshot of Judean life, it is frustratingly limited, although its vivid, anecdotal account of Judean interaction in the life of Greek cities in Ephesus, Thessalonica and Corinth can at times offer a more revealing picture of the relations between Judeans and the cities in which they lived" (B. Rittler, *Judeans in the Greek Cities of the Roman Empire* [Leiden: Brill, 2015], 229).

48. Ascough, *Paul's Macedonian Associations*, 206–12. H. Koester makes similar remarks, adding furthermore that a Pauline mission within the synagogue is not a clear feature within Paul's own letters; see Koester, *Introduction to the New Testament*, 115.

49. See M. A. Powell, *What Are They Saying about Acts?* (Mahwah, NJ: Paulist, 1991), 90; again, see, e.g., Richard, *First and Second Thessalonians*: "One must conclude that the Acts account of the mission owes more to Luke's project and remote acquaintance with the Apostle's role than to first-hand data. Scholars are thus correct in favoring the Pauline account both in terms of chronology and treatment of the mission and correspondence" (6).

The narrative of 17:1–15 is of the type of narrative found in the apoc-
ryphal acts—the preaching of the gospel by an apostle, the conversion
of women, often prominent in the community, and the anger of the
men of the community against the apostle. Any apostle and any city
could be placed into this pattern. The author has superimposed the
theme of opposition between Paul (and Pauline Christians) and Jews
on a story pattern that presupposes no particular relation to Paul.
What information the author had in his sources for Christianity at
Thessalonica associated with Jason cannot be determined.[50]

Again, this sort of perspective tends to treat Luke as unhelpful from
a historical standpoint. But let us take one example—the hostility of Jews.
As Fearghus Ó Fearghail reminds us, when we look at the overall portrayal
of Jews in Acts, we see remarkable variety, even despite Luke's episodic
patterns. The Jews in Beroea are described as εὐγενέστεροι (Acts 17:11)
compared to the Jews in Thessalonica; εὐγενέστεροι meaning here "noble-
minded, generous, liberal, free from prejudice."[51] In Rome, Fearghail
explains, the response by Jews is even more unusual (i.e., breaking from
any supposed Lukan pattern). Paul calls the Jewish leadership to the site
of his house arrest (28:17); they respond positively (28:21–23). While not
everyone approved of Paul's teaching (28:24b), still "Luke's account does
not give any hint of active opposition toward him. Instead, the narrative
ends on a positive note (28.30–31) with Paul preaching boldly and without
hindrance to all-comers, Jews and Greek alike."[52] Fearghail's concluding
words underscore this point:

> While Luke paints a picture that is probably much more consistent
> than it actually was, his representation of the Jews in the diaspora as
> on the whole more tolerant toward "messianic" Jews than their coun-
> terparts in Jerusalem may well reflect the original situation in which
> the word was preached. Some are described as more tolerant than
> others, and in various cities of the diaspora (e.g., Thessalonica, Beroea,
> Ephesus) probably reflect the varied nature of Judaism in that period.[53]

---

50. C. Mount, *Pauline Christianity: Luke-Acts and the Legacy of Paul*, NovTSup 104 (Boston:
Brill, 2002), 141; see also C. Coulet, "Paul à Thessalonique (1Th 2.1–12)," *NTS* 52.3 (2006): 377–93.
    51. See F. Ó Fearghail, "The Jews in the Hellenistic Cities of Acts," in *Jews in the Hellenistic
and Roman Cities*, ed. J. R. Bartlett (London: Routledge, 2002), 45.
    52. Fearghail, "Jews in the Hellenistic Cities," 47.
    53. Fearghail, "Jews in the Hellenistic Cities," 49–50. On the matter of Paul's regular visitation

Again, contrary to the conclusions of Ascough and Mount, Luke Timothy Johnson in his commentary on Acts defends the view that the information in Acts 17:1–10a fits rather nicely with the information derived from 1 Thessalonians itself.[54] For example, Luke and Paul agree on the apostle's prior suffering in Philippi, opposition in Thessalonica, a subsequent visit to Athens, and cooperation with Timothy.[55] At the end of the day, any attempt to understand Paul's life and even his letters apart from Luke's accounts is irresponsible and perhaps even impossible, as Martin Hengel urges.[56] Furthermore, Hengel adds the point that just because we may label a passage as a legend or type scene does not obviate its historical value, "because they tend to indicate the essential characteristics of a person or event and the general impression that they made, and because they express the earliest influence exerted by such a person or event."[57]

Hengel also adds the important point that Acts should be regarded by historians of no less value than Josephus's works.[58] One way to underscore this is to note how nonreligion historians approach Acts. Well-informed ancient historians are, of course, cautious and aware of the possibility of embellishments in ancient sources, including Acts, but most nonreligion

---

to synagogues, Fearghail notes that some scholars are skeptical. Fearghail responds that Luke would not need to fabricate these visits with such frequency later in Acts, because the point is made clearly and early on in Acts about this practice of Christians preaching in Jewish religious settings (2:14–36, 39; 3:12–26). Furthermore, according to 2 Cor 11:24, it is in keeping with Paul's own testimony that "he did retain his contact with the synagogue despite its occasionally painful repercussions" (Fearghail, "Jews in the Hellenistic Cities," 52). Similarly, note the comment by Krodel (also with 2 Cor 11:24 in mind): "He would hardly have been subjected to flogging five times by synagogue officials (forty lashes less one) had he persistently avoided any contact with them. In short Paul did preach in diaspora synagogues and encountered opposition, but Luke generalized this into a schematic pattern for the sake of his theological program" (G. Krodel, *Acts* [Minneapolis: Augsburg, 1986], 92).

54. Johnson, *Acts*, 308–9: "More than at any other place in Paul's career, we are able with confidence and some precision to trace his movements. In 1 Thessalonians, Paul recounts for his readers his earliest experiences with them, as well as his present circumstances. These agree in outline with the presentation in Luke's narrative."

55. Johnson, *Acts*, 309. Similarly, Bornkamm, while he discounts the possibility that Luke was an eyewitness and confesses that the "details" in Acts cannot be trusted as historical, still "for the most important features the account furnishes a perfectly credible picture," including Paul's visitations at the synagogue with Jews and Godfearers (G. Bornkamm, *Paul*, trans. D. M. G. Stalker [New York: Harper & Row, 1971], 62).

56. M. Hengel, *Acts and the History of Earliest Christianity* (London: SCM, 1979), 36–38; see also 59–68.

57. Hengel, *Acts*, 41; see similarly D. Binder, *Into the Temple Courts: The Place of the Synagogues in the Second Temple Period*, SBLDS 169 (Atlanta: SBL Press, 1999), 78–81: "We should consider the possibility that Luke's pattern may well be a generalization based on one or more actual incidents—a possibility that takes on greater weight when we factor in the supporting evidence we have seen from Paul's own writings" (81; see more generally 78–81).

58. Hengel, *Acts*, 39.

historians take Luke's account more or less at face value.[59] Dimitris Kyrtatas, for example, a professor of archaeology and social anthropology at the University of Thessaly, considers Luke a "well-informed author" despite the obvious presence of theological interests in the text. Kyrtatas writes:

> I find no reason to disregard [Acts 17:1–10a's] historical reliability, despite the obvious fact that its author had his own theological agenda. The epistles of Paul, on which almost all scholars depend for a historical reconstruction of events, had clearly his own theological priorities.[60]

The same perspective seems to be true for Victoria Allamani-Souri, retired deputy director of the 16th Ephorate of Prehistoric and Classical Antiquities in Thessaloniki,[61] and Pantelis Nigdelis, professor of history in the department of ancient Greek, Roman, Byzantine, and Medieval History, School of History and Archaeology, Aristotle University of Thessaloniki.[62]

---

59. A good example of this is L. I. Levine, professor of Jewish history and archaeology at Hebrew University of Jerusalem. He is a leading expert on the subject of ancient Jewish synagogues, and here is his statement about the use of Acts as a historical source: "Much has been written about the historical reliability of Acts—from the more skeptical to the largely accepting. Theological agenda aside, one may assume that the specific events reported, especially those relating to the synagogue, are largely credible. The author was certainly familiar with the Jewish Diaspora and wrote for Christian Diaspora communities. It is hard to imagine that he would invent accounts for a population that knew a great deal about the synagogue, its workings, and Paul's activities. At the very least, even were one to doubt the specific details included in Acts, one would have to admit that such events could well have taken place, even if not precisely in the manner recorded" (*The Ancient Synagogue: The First Thousand Years* [New Haven: Yale University Press, 2005], 116).

60. Kyrtatas, "Early Christianity in Macedonia," 586n4. I hasten to add here that Kyrtatas claims that "the first Macedonian Christians appear to have been, for the most part, either Hellenised Jews or Hellenised Jewish sympathisers" (598); he writes furthermore: "The earliest opposition to Christian missionary activity came from Jews. Some Greeks may have accused the Christians for religious purposes as well, but the authorities reacted with moderation. . . . They only started persecuting energetically from the mid-third century onwards" (598).

61. See Allamani-Souri, "Brief History of Imperial Thessaloniki as Derived from Epigraphic and Archaeological Evidence," in Grammenos, *Roman Thessaloniki*, 93–94. Again, it is interesting to observe how Luke differentiates the Jews in Thessalonica from Beroea and that Allamani-Souri underscores the competitive/rivalry spirit between these cities. Allamani-Souri writes: "Note should be taken of the constant competition between Thessaloniki and the equally important city of Beroea and the strong rivalry that developed between them for first position in the province" ("Province of Macedonia," 75–76). In a different essay, Allamani-Souri points out that Thessaloniki petitioned Rome for the title of *neokoros* (city with imperial cult), yet Thessaloniki "made efforts through diplomatic channels to have the privilege removed from Beroea" ("Imperial Cult," 100).

62. Nigdelis, "Roman Thessalonica," 62, 67–68; cf. Nigdelis, "Thessaloniki," 7, http://site.lpth .gr/en/texts/Nigdelis_en.pdf.

We may proceed, then, by taking Luke's account of Paul's experiences in Thessalonica seriously, with full awareness that Luke was writing a *story* and not simply recounting history *wie es eigentlich gewesen* ("how it really was").[63] If a *bona fide* contradiction appears between Acts 17 and 1 Thessalonians, it makes sense to put doubt on Luke's account, but every effort should be made to integrate all the available information first before taking such a step.

Paul and the Thessalonians according to Luke's Acts

While in Troas (Asia Minor), Paul received a vision of a "man of Macedonia" begging him to cross over into Macedonia to help his people (Acts 16:9). Paul and Silas wasted no time setting sail into Samothrace and Neapolis to bring the gospel to the Macedonians (vv. 10–11). They eventually went to Philippi where his ministry caused a stir and locals accused them before the authorities (vv. 12–21). They were beaten and imprisoned, but the Lord miraculously delivered them (vv. 22–34). Before departing from Philippi, Paul and Silas encouraged the new believers there including Lydia, the first convert of Europe (v. 40).

Paul and Silas traveled through Amphipolis and Apollonia to Thessalonica (17:1). They went to the Thessalonian Jewish synagogue, and Paul preached about Messiah Jesus on three Sabbath days (vv. 2–3). Luke recounts that "some of the Jews were persuaded and joined Paul and Silas, as did a large number of God-fearing Greeks and quite a few prominent women" (v. 4).

Some jealous Jews incited ruffians (F. F. Bruce refers to them as a "rentamob"!)[64] to turn the city against Paul and Silas (v. 5). Unable to locate the two strangers, the mob attacked Paul's host Jason and other new believers in Jesus. They were brought before the city authorities under this accusation: "These men who have caused trouble all over the world have now come here, and Jason has welcomed them into his house. They are all defying Caesar's decrees, saying that there is another king, one called Jesus" (vv. 6–7).

While Jason and the others were released when they posted bail, still

---

63. See L. von Ranke, "Preface to the First Edition of the Histories of the Latin and Germanic Nations," in *The Theory and Practice of History*, ed. G. G. Iggers (London, Routlege, 2011), 86. For an example of this kind of careful but "open" use of Acts regarding Paul and the Thessalonians, see O. Wischmeyer, *Paul: Life, Setting, Work, Letters* (London: Bloomsbury, 2012), 142–44.

64. F. F. Bruce, *1 and 2 Thessalonians*, WBC (Waco, TX: Word, 1982), xxii.

the city was perturbed by this matter (vv. 8–9). Paul and Silas took their leave under the cover of darkness, making their way to Beroea (v. 10). Luke makes it a point to say that the Jews there were more receptive to the gospel than in Thessalonica (vv. 11–12). Still, Paul's Thessalonian troubles were far from over. Some Jews from Thessalonica heard about Paul's successful ministry in Beroea and traveled there to turn those people against him as well (v. 13). Thus, Paul was forced on to Athens (vv. 14–15). After Acts 17, Luke offers no more clues regarding the situation in Thessalonica.[65] What we surmise about the situation that led to Paul's writing of the Thessalonian letters must come primarily from historical reconstruction and guesswork based on information from the letters themselves.

The Situation in Thessalonica: Evidence from the Text of 1 Thessalonians

Again, the challenge in addressing this matter is that the only real evidence we have (aside from some of the information listed above related to Acts 16–17) must come from guesswork based on the letter of 1 Thessalonians itself. Howard Marshall underscores the difficulty with this illustration: "It is rather like the problem of trying to form a picture of a modern church simply on the basis of the official minutes of its business meeting; we should know very little about what actually happened in its services and other activities or about the kind of people who made up the congregation."[66] Nevertheless, we ought to learn what we can and be able to distinguish what is certain from what is probable, and then also consider what is plausible.[67]

PERSECUTION AND LOYALTY

It is immediately clear when reading Paul's first letter that the Thessalonians experienced persecution from the beginning (1 Thess 1:6; 2:14). This would not have been a state-enforced persecution but rather harassment from neighbors and community members who were troubled by their newfound religion and practices. The Thessalonian believers would have been taught by Paul to devote themselves exclusively to the one God; thus,

---

65. Note that Luke does mention certain Thessalonian believers who cross paths with Paul, i.e., Aristarchus and Secundus (20:4; cf. 27:2).

66. Marshall, *1 and 2 Thessalonians*, 4; in relation especially to gleaning from Acts 17:1–10a.

67. For methodology on historical reconstruction, see J. M. G. Barclay, "Mirror-Reading a Polemical Letter: Galatians as a Test Case," *JSNT* 31 (1987): 73–97; N. K. Gupta, "Mirror-Reading Moral Issues in Paul's Letters," *JSNT* 34 (2012): 361–81.

they would have withdrawn from local pagan rites, festivities that typically had important political dimensions. In all probability, they would have been charged with "atheism." As Philip Esler explains, "To be respectable and decent meant taking part in the [local, religious] cult; old was good and new was bad; thus, religion served to strengthen the existing social order. To deny the reality of the gods was absolutely unacceptable—one would be ostracized for that, even stoned in the streets."[68]

Knowing of the Thessalonians' persecution (3:1–6; see further below), Paul and his apostolic associates were concerned about the Thessalonians' πίστις. Typically this word is translated "faith" (1:3, 8; 3:2, 5–7, 10; 5:8). However, πίστις is a polyvalent Greek noun and can cover a range of meanings from belief to trust to faithfulness and loyalty. Due to the way that Paul talks about the strength of the Thessalonians' πίστις, he is almost certainly *not* referring to their "beliefs" if by this we mean "religious views." Rather, πίστις was a term used in the Greco-Roman world especially in relation to *loyalty*.[69] Around the time of Paul, Jews too became comfortable using the Greek word πίστις to refer to pledges of loyalty within a covenantal relationship.[70] Particularly in chapter three of 1 Thessalonians, Paul refers to his concern for their πίστις in the context of affliction. Timothy was dispatched to see about their πίστις lest the tempter overwhelm them (3:5). Again, Paul was not worried about their *beliefs per se* but the "whole package" of their commitment to Jesus Christ and their complete trust in him. Therefore, the best terms to translate πίστις here are probably "trust," "loyalty," or "faithfulness."[71]

ANXIETY OVER ESCHATOLOGY

Another problem among the Thessalonian believers apparently pertained to the death of some members of the church (4:13–18). Paul felt the need to comfort them by urging that the recently deceased believers would

---

68. P. E. Esler, "1 Thessalonians," in *The Oxford Bible Commentary*, ed. J. Barton and J. Muddiman (Oxford: Oxford University Press, 2001), 1200; see also J. M. G. Barclay, "Conflict in Thessalonica," *CBQ* 55 (1993): 512–30.

69. See Z. Crook, *Reconceptualising Conversion: Patronage, Loyalty, and Conversion in the Religions of the Ancient Mediterranean*, BZNW 130 (Berlin: de Gruyter, 2004).

70. See esp. LXX Neh 10:1; also Josephus *Ant.* passim.

71. I believe the translation "faith" is best justified when Paul clearly appears to be using πίστις in reference to trust that goes against natural senses, "believing the unbelievable," so to speak; see 2 Cor 5:7. For similar argumentation regarding the best translation of πίστις in 1–2 Thessalonians, see Andy Johnson, *1 & 2 Thessalonians*, THNT (Grand Rapids: Eerdmans, 2016), 39–40, on πίστις in 1:3.

be especially honored at the return of the Lord. Many scholars believe that the Thessalonians naively thought that everyone would remain alive until the return of Christ, so the death of church members was perplexing and even traumatizing. This is possible, but it does not account for the unusual emphasis Paul places on the dead in Christ being raised *first* before the living at the return of Jesus (4:15). Why would they receive this honor of priority? A minority of scholars (including myself) hypothesize that those who died had been *martyred*, killed by persecutors.[72] This view accords well with how it could be possible that several people died in the same small, believing community around the same time a short while after Paul left. Furthermore, it explains why Paul focuses on their position of honor—those who died for their allegiance to Christ deserve such a special role. (See ch. 3 of this book.)

THE RETURN OF THE LORD

A third notable concern that Paul raises relates to the timing of the coming of the Lord (5:1–11). Paul is unwilling to say more than that it will be unexpected (5:2–3). He turns their attention away from timetable theories toward faithfulness and upright behavior *today*. The *timing* doesn't matter if, in waiting for the master, you are *always* at work in your duties (cf. Luke 12:41–48). Somewhere along the way, a fear struck them that they might not be ready. Paul comforts them by reminding them of their firmly anchored identity in Christ (5:9) but challenges them to live faithfully in light of that identity.

POSSIBLE OTHER REASONS FOR 1 THESSALONIANS

The above exigencies seem to be most explicit and pressing (persecution, dead in Christ, return of the Lord), but there could be other "problems" as well, perhaps minor ones that still needed addressing.

Sexual purity. Paul calls for control over the body, lest the Thessalonians succumb to heathen lust (4:3–4). The Greco-Roman lifestyle was highly permissive when it came to male sexuality. Men often had sex with multiple people, though it was considered especially inappropriate to

---

72. See J. S. Pobee, *Persecution and Martyrdom in the Theology of Paul*, JSNTSup 6 (Sheffield: JSOT Press, 1985); K. P. Donfried, "Imperial Cults," 221–23; Witherington, *Thessalonians*, 139; L. T. Johnson, *The Writings of the New Testament*, rev. ed. (Minneapolis: Fortress, 1999), 285; Gorman is open to this possibility as well; see M. J. Gorman, *Apostle of the Crucified Lord*, 2nd ed. (Grand Rapids: Eerdmans, 2017), 188–210; also idem, *Becoming the Gospel* (Grand Rapids: Eerdmans, 2015), 63–105.

commit adultery by sleeping with another man's wife. Paul called for a strict kind of holiness and purity that sought to honor one another and God (4:6).

Doubting Paul. Some scholars wonder whether Paul felt the need to defend himself in 1 Thessalonians (especially to maintain the integrity of the gospel he preached). Many scholars, myself included, detect a defensive tone in Paul's self-description in 2:1–12 (see detailed discussion on pp. 75–76). Paul felt the need to say that he was not deceitful and did not resort to trickery. He was neither a flatterer nor motivated by greed or popularity. He did not want their money and tried to remain blameless before them. In chapter three, he communicates his relief when he heard the report from Timothy that the Thessalonians remembered him fondly and wanted to see him (3:6).

Other minor concerns? There is some evidence that the church may have had internal divisions and communal problems; Paul seems briefly to address these (see 4:9–11; 5:12–15). Also, Paul may have had a small concern for those he calls ἄτακτοι (the idle troublemakers), but his mention of them is brief enough that apparently it is not significant at this point for him (5:14). Moreover, it is possible that the Thessalonian believers had been thrown into confusion by (false?) prophecies (5:20–21). Again, a variety of such minor concerns may have stood behind 1 Thessalonians.

Leading Scholarship on the Situation behind 1 Thessalonians

Scholarly interest in the Thessalonian correspondence lags behind texts like Romans, 1 Corinthians, and Galatians in terms of wider scholarly attention.[73] Nevertheless, several significant studies have been written in the last few decades.

THE THESSALONIAN CORRESPONDENCE, BY R. JEWETT (1986)

In 1986, Robert Jewett published his important study called *The Thessalonian Correspondence: Pauline Rhetoric and Millenarian Piety*.[74] Jewett offers his thesis statement in the preface:

---

73. J. M. G. Barclay called the Thessalonian letters the "neglected children in the Pauline family" ("Conflict in Thessalonica," *CBQ* 55 [1993]: 512); similarly, Donfried commented that until the twentieth century, "1 Thessalonians has been the stepchild of modern Pauline studies" (*Paul, Thessalonica, and Early Christianity*, 69). Just as a personal anecdote, at a recent SBL annual meeting, I was on the lookout for papers on 1–2 Thessalonians, and, based on paper titles and abstracts in the program I could not find more than three or four papers (out of *hundreds*) that gave central interest to the Thessalonian correspondence.

74. This book grew out of a paper Jewett published in 1972. The influence of the study can be noted in all kinds of ways, but it is noteworthy that ATLA database indexes more than ten critical

Paul was faced with a situation of millenarian radicalism in Thessalonica, presenting a unique profile not matched elsewhere in early Christianity. While other Pauline churches were millenarian in the general sense, believing that they were part of a dawning new age and that the end of history would occur in the near future, only in Thessalonica do we encounter a group that proclaimed the actual arrival of the millennium and then proceeded to act on that assumption. The distinctive political and religious background of Thessalonica and the unusually narrow profile of the congregation led to this millenarian construal of Paul's apocalyptic gospel, evoking the emergence of radicals who behaved as if the new age were already in effect for them.[75]

Jewett defines millenarianism in Thessalonia in terms of "religious movements that expect the total transformation of this world to occur in connection with a cataclysm in the near future."[76] Such groups tend to focus on an impending crisis; they maintain a "this-worldly orientation."[77] One can detect ecstatic behavior and also antinomian behavior. And this mindset can lead to competition between inspired prophets and local organizers.

The exigency or crisis that led to Paul's first letter to the Thessalonians involves a "sudden deflation of the millenarian faith."[78] Jewett offers a rather sophisticated methodology for classifying and interpreting 1 Thessalonians (combining traditional historical-critical, rhetorical, and social-scientific analyses), but suffice it to say here that he categorizes the letter as "demonstrative rhetoric." Yet he hastens to underscore that despite the positive tone of comfort and encouragement in the letter, one should not conclude that he was not concerned with local problems.[79] Jewett addresses the problem of deaths in the community and how some "were assuming the separation of death would be permanent."[80]

---

reviews of his book, many from leading NT scholars such as S. Barton (*ExpTim*), D. Garland (*RevExp*), J. Gillman (*CBQ*), S. Kraftchick (*Interpretation*), H. Hendrix (*JBL*), M. Bockmuehl (*Themelios*), T. Holtz (*TLZ*), E. Ellis (*Southwestern Journal of Theology*), and C. Black (*Dialog*).

75. Jewett, *Thessalonian Correspondence*, xiii.

76. Jewett, *Thessalonian Correspondence*, 161. Jewett links the unique situation in Thessalonica to influences from the Cabirus cult that led to certain utopic yearnings for a golden age that could ostensibly be fulfilled by the gospel of Jesus. As Hendrix and others have pointed out, however, "there is no unequivocal evidence for a cult of the single Cabirus at the city before the late second or early third century CE" (review of *The Thessalonian Correspondence*, by R. Jewett, *JBL* 107.4 [1988]: 766; see also Pillar, *Resurrection as Anti-Imperial Gospel*, 103–5).

77. Jewett, *Thessalonian Correspondence*, 161.

78. Jewett, *Thessalonian Correspondence*, xiii.

79. Jewett, *Thessalonian Correspondence*, 91.

80. Jewett, *Thessalonian Correspondence*, 94.

Jewett spends a significant amount of time (re)evaluating the social, economic, political, and religious setting of the Thessalonians. In particular, he argues that the community of Thessalonian believers would have come from a "non-slave lower-class population in poverty."[81] In terms of religious culture, Jewett again underscores the popularity of the Cabirus cult at the time. According to Jewett, clear parallels can be drawn between the identity and beliefs of this cult and that of the early Christians, especially in terms of apocalyptic expectation.[82] Here was a martyred hero who was expected to return to rescue the poor. Jewett explains that during the Augustan age, the worship of Cabirus was merged with the civic cult of Thessalonica. A consequence of this absorption was the honoring of Cabirus by elites as well as non-elites, and thus Cabirus was no longer the patron of the poor *per se*; thus "the craftmen and laborers of Thessalonica [were left] without a viable benefactor"—that is, until Paul came into town.[83]

As for the ἀτάκτοι, he rejects the reading that views them as mere "loafers"; rather, they were rebellious (here following C. Spicq's interpretation).[84] In an attempt to put all the problematic pieces together, Jewett wonders whether the problem of sexual ethics pertained to the ἀτάκτοι's resistance to apostolic instruction.[85] Jewett also has a theory regarding their refusal to work: they pushed back against the "structures of everyday life," which included labor.[86]

We will revisit Jewett's book when we eventually turn to 2 Thessalonians, but we can simply note here Jewett's argument that 1 Thessalonians failed in its rhetorical objectives. Instead of pacifying the Thessalonians, the letter inadvertently provoked them to "intensify their activities in directions that countered the thrust of Paul's intended argument."[87] The second letter was written as another attempt to correct the problem and to "set the record straight."[88]

Jewett is generally commended for his incisive critique of (then) common approaches to 1–2 Thessalonians. He is also lauded for his circumspection regarding methodology, and he raised the bar in terms of

---

81. Jewett, *Thessalonian Correspondence*, 121–22.
82. See *Thessalonian Correspondence*, 127–29.
83. See *Thessalonian Correspondence*, 131.
84. Jewett, *Thessalonian Correspondence*, 104. Jewett is comfortable connecting 1 Thess 5 to 2 Thess 2, something many other scholars are reluctant to do.
85. Jewett, *Thessalonian Correspondence*, 106.
86. Jewett, *Thessalonian Correspondence*, 176.
87. Jewett, *Thessalonian Correspondence*, 177.
88. See Jewett, *Thessalonian Correspondence*, xiv.

interpreters seeking to become more familiar with discoveries and insights from the world of archaeology.[89] He is also applauded for his desire to paint a comprehensive picture of the Thessalonian situation—so many commentaries have their heads buried in the minutiae of the trees that they never bother to step back and try to outline the forest. Of course, reviews and interactions with Jewett's work are not without serious criticism. For example, John Gillman remarks that Jewett has made too much of a central role for the ἀτάκτοι, who probably had "[n]either the identity [n]or the influence ascribed to them" by Jewett.[90]

"CONFLICT IN THESSALONICA," BY JOHN M. G. BARCLAY (1993)

In 1993 John Barclay published an important article on the Thessalonian situation with particular interest in the reasons for the persecution of the Thessalonian believers.[91] To start with, Barclay urges that the defensive tone Paul takes in 1 Thessalonians 2:3–12 demonstrates that his character was under attack, and Barclay surmises that the criticisms probably came from unbelievers in Thessalonica. Furthermore, the Thessalonians were suffering persecution (1:6), which Barclay interprets as "social harassment."[92] He explains that the persecution came from gentiles (not Jews) and probably related to the problem of the converts' "offensive abandonment of common Greco-Roman religion."[93]

Later in the essay, Barclay sketches out Paul's preaching to the Thessalonians based on clues in 1 Thessalonians. Paul apparently placed an emphasis on the imminent coming of Jesus. The Thessalonians probably anticipated escape from pain and suffering. The death of members of their community consequently disturbed their faith. While they did not give up hope in general, they did lose hope for the recently deceased.[94]

Nevertheless, Paul had equipped them with an "apocalyptic perspec-

---

89. See D. Garland, review of *The Thessalonian Correspondence*, by R. Jewett, *RevExp* 85 (1988): 132–33. On the other hand, S. Kraftchick finds Jewett's methodological discussion inspiring in *theory* but disappointing in *practice*: "Only four pages are used for the rhetorical analysis itself, causing it to be minimal and in the end superficial as a method of control [for exegesis]. The result casts doubt upon rhetoric's role in the book and Jewett's ability to substantiate his initial claims" (review of *The Thessalonian Correspondence*, by R. Jewett, *Interpretation* 42.4 [1988]: 411).

90. J. L. Gillman, review of *The Thessalonian Correspondence*, by R. Jewett *CBQ* 50 (1988): 326.

91. Barclay, "Conflict in Thessalonica," 512–30.

92. Barclay, "Conflict in Thessalonica," 514. Though Barclay sees this as largely verbal, he entertains the possibility that it could have included physical harm (515).

93. Barclay, "Conflict in Thessalonica," 514.

94. Barclay, "Conflict in Thessalonica," 517.

tive" that could deal with persecution if properly understood.[95] Barclay detects signs in 1 Thessalonians that Paul was aware that at least some of the Thessalonian believers were retaliating against opposition (1 Thess 5:15). When it comes to Paul's teaching that they should live "quiet" lives (4:11–12), Barclay pursues the unique thesis that some believers in Thessalonica urgently began to preach the gospel but in a heavy-handed and obnoxious manner.[96]

> It is sufficient to posit that some of Paul's enthusiastic converts, taking very seriously the threat of the imminent outpouring of God's wrath, committed themselves and all their time to aggressive evangelistic activity. Their insistent attacks on the morals and beliefs of the "children of darkness," however, could endanger the safety of the church, which is already in quite enough trouble; Paul, therefore, urges any with such tendencies to live quietly, to mind their own affairs, and to get (back) to work. His concern is, as he puts it in 4:12, that his converts should not behave indecently toward outsiders.[97]

Barclay tries to buttress his hypothesis by pointing to Paul's several appeals to his own manner of ministry, where he mentions his gentleness and graciousness (2:7–9). Later in the article Barclay notes Paul's appeal to his previous teaching (e.g., 4:11), arguing that "such tendencies were present in the Thessalonian church from the beginning."[98]

Barclay's brief work here has been well received, mostly for his perceptive sociopolitical-religious analysis of why the Thessalonians were being persecuted.[99] Much less convincing has proven his argument that the Thessalonians were overzealous in their evangelistic work. One would suppose that if this were really the situation, Paul would have gone out of

---

95. In this section Barclay focuses the discussion on the social-constructive dimensions of apocalyptic discourses/teachings that create a particular "symbolic world" structured by oppositions, contrasts, and conflicts ("Conflict in Thessalonica," 518–19).

96. Barclay, "Conflict in Thessalonica," 522; Barclay later calls this "provocative evangelism" (525). Barclay does find some support for this in the work of Dobschütz, but parts ways from him in terms of the argument that there was some sort of political dimension to this tension; see E. von Dobschütz, *Die Thessalonicher-Briefe* (Göttingen: Vandenhoeck & Ruprecht, 1909), 180.

97. Barclay, "Conflict in Thessalonica," 522. Barclay goes further in wondering whether the reference to the outward echoing of the faith of the Thessalonians (1:8) implies that their evangelism went beyond the borders of their own city (see 522–23).

98. Barclay, "Conflict in Thessalonica," 525.

99. See Fee, *Thessalonians*, 94n29; A. Paddison, *Theological Hermeneutics and 1 Thessalonians*, SNTSMS (Cambridge: Cambridge University Press, 2005), 3–4.

his way, even if he wanted to soften their tone, to continue to encourage their sharing of the gospel—but we do not see such.

CONFLICT AT THESSALONICA, BY TODD D. STILL (1999)

Todd D. Still wrote his doctoral thesis under Barclay at Glasgow University, and his research was published as *Conflict at Thessalonica*.[100] Still takes a similar interest as Barclay in the persecution and suffering (θλῖψις) of the Thessalonian believers and analyzes this matter with special interest in social-scientific perspectives on deviance and conflict.[101] Much in line with Barclay, Still argues that the persecution had strong sociopolitical dimensions, involving "intergroup conflict between Christians and non-Christians in Thessalonica."[102] Paul's role was to help the Thessalonians to make sense of this tension.

Still defends 1 Thessalonians 2:13–16 as part of Paul's first letter to the Thessalonians, countering form-critical, grammatical/syntactical, historical, and theological concerns.[103] He concludes that "even though Paul was convinced that those Jews who refused to accept the gospel and opposed his efforts to share his message with the Gentiles were subject to God's wrath, he does not categorically condemn the Jewish people here or elsewhere."[104] He also affirms the careful use of Acts to help make sense of the Thessalonian situation.[105] While he is more open than most scholars to the involvement of Jewish opposition to Paul in Thessalonica, he also urges that Luke did not seem to be properly informed about the gentile conflict.[106]

Regarding the earlier part of the letter, he again agrees with Barclay that 2:1–12 reflects Paul's response to concerns and criticism. Regarding the nature of the suffering of the Thessalonians, Still argues that this involved "verbal harassment, social ostracism, political sanctions and perhaps even some sort of physical abuse, which on the rarest occasions may have resulted in martyrdom."[107]

In chapter nine, Still examines the word θλῖψις and Paul's perspective on persecution from outsiders. Pushing against Malherbe's theory that

---

100. T. D. Still, *Conflict at Thessalonica: A Pauline Church and Its Neighbors*, JSNTSup 183 (Sheffield: Sheffield Academic, 1999).
101. See chapters four and five respectively (*Conflict*, 84–106, 107–25).
102. Still, *Conflict*, 17.
103. Still, *Conflict*, 25–45.
104. Still, *Conflict*, 44.
105. Still, *Conflict*, 61–83.
106. Still, *Conflict*, 73–74.
107. Still, *Conflict*, 217.

Paul had in mind primarily *mental* stress, Still points to texts like 2:14 to demonstrate that the Thessalonians "were subject to suffering as a result of their having received the gospel."[108] As parallels, he notes Philippians 1:27–30 and 2 Corinthians 8:2.[109] Obviously the Thessalonians were not threatened by a systematic, state-enforced persecution. Following Barclay's lead, Still imagines the affliction to include social pressures and verbal harassment: "One can imagine that Paul's converts were criticized, marginalized and perhaps ostracized by non-Christian family, friends and associates for joining an upstart religious movement whose leader encouraged a fair degree of social dislocation from the 'rest.'"[110] Later in this chapter Still takes up the complex matter of the meaning of συμφυλέτης (1 Thess 2:14). We have reserved a more extensive discussion of this matter for later (see p. 177), but suffice to say here that Still defends a view that interprets these as fellow *gentile* countrymen.[111]

In chapter ten, Still explores the reasons for the persecution from other Thessalonians. While acknowledging that the evidence we have offers little more than an opportunity for educated speculation, Still dwells on sociopolitical and religious factors. There were many social entailments for someone abandoning his or her own cultic customs and traditions.[112] Because Jews and Christians did not worship "other gods," they were treated as "strange and snobbish," perhaps too "disruptive or even subversive."[113] The welfare of a village or city was often assumed to lie in the hands of patron deities whose favor could thwart outside evil and whose wrath could raze the town.

Regarding political factors, Still argues that Paul's message would have been interpreted as dangerous and did in fact lead to his flight from the city; thus "political issues played an important role in the conflict with their compatriots which Paul's Thessalonian converts experienced."[114]

Still's last formative chapter handles the matter of believers' conflict with each other. Looking at a text like 5:12–13, he does conceive of there being internal problems in the Thessalonian church. Nevertheless, he is

---

108. Still, *Conflict*, 212.
109. Still, *Conflict*, 212–13.
110. Still, *Conflict*, 214.
111. Still, *Conflict*, 218–27.
112. See Still, *Conflict*, 228–32. Still also considers Barclay's theory that the Thessalonians were not making friends with their evangelistic activity.
113. Still, *Conflict*, 255.
114. Still, *Conflict*, 266.

far more hesitant to place the blame and focus on the so-called ἀτάκτοι (cf. Jewett). Even with the many commands in 5:12–22, "Paul does not explicitly mention actual congregational divisions at any point in 1 (and 2) Thessalonians."[115] Overall, Still surmises, Paul must have been content with their unity. Toward the close of this chapter, Still also considers how eschatological concerns led to turmoil in the community. His second letter to this church appears to be Paul's "attempt to support his converts in the throes of intensified inter-group conflict and to correct what he considered to be potentially disastrous eschatological excesses which were linked to, if not spawned by, the church's experience of external hostility."[116]

Still accomplishes, in a more detailed way, part of what Barclay was also working to achieve—a comprehensive portrait of the situation in Thessalonica that tries to integrate all aspects of life as well as all pieces of evidence—literary, archaeological, historical. Works like Still's offer poignant reminders of the "contingency" of Paul's letters, driven as they were by exigencies and conflict in Christian communities trying to live out their new and peculiar faith in a world that often found Paul's gospel intolerable.

Less likely to be accepted are his arguments about the identity of the persecutors, especially pointing to Jewish persecution. There is simply too little acceptance of the portrait from Acts 17 among Thessalonian scholars on this. As for myself, I resonate strongly with Still, but it should be admitted that his view is accepted by few.[117]

PAUL'S MACEDONIAN ASSOCIATIONS, BY RICHARD ASCOUGH (2003)

R. S. Ascough has been one of the most important contributors to the modern discussion of the Thessalonian situation. His influential monograph *Paul's Macedonian Associations* was published in 2003,[118] though he had already made some important shorter contributions about early Christianity and Greco-Roman associations as early as 1997.[119] Ascough is

---

115. Still, *Conflict*, 278.

116. Still, *Conflict*, 284.

117. It is a bit of an unusual criticism for L. M. Bridges to fault Still for not engaging with her and Goulder's theory that the opposition was a Jewish Christian group from Jerusalem, people "who represent the religious status quo of the Petrine, Jerusalem, Christian church"; see L. M. Bridges, review of *Conflict at Thessalonica*, by T. D. Still, *RevExp* 97 (2000): 110–11.

118. Ascough, *Paul's Macedonian Associations*.

119. See his "Translocal Relationships among Voluntary Associations and Early Christianity," *JECS* 5.2 (1997): 223–41; also *What Are They Saying about the Formation of Pauline Churches?* (New York: Paulist, 1999); "The Thessalonian Christian Community as a Professional Voluntary Association," *JBL* 119.2 (2000): 311–28.

recognized not only as an expert on the Thessalonian correspondence (and Paul's ministry in Macedonia) but also on Greco-Roman associations.[120]

Ascough's dissertation (under John Kloppenborg), later published as *Paul's Macedonian Associations*, makes the case that the earliest Christian communities would have had much in common with Greco-Roman associations or guilds. While scholars often try to find parallels, influences, and antecedents to the early Christian churches in the synagogue, Ascough found the Greco-Roman associations too often neglected. Thus, his monograph endeavored to give a full treatment of the background and nature of the voluntary associations and compare them to the Pauline communities (in Thessalonica and Philippi in particular).

Much of the evidence for associations in Macedonia comes from inscriptions.[121] This evidence shows that "in large cities of the Greco-Roman world voluntary associations can be found in abundance."[122] Ascough distinguishes three kinds of associations: burial/funerary (for proper burial of the deceased members), religious, and professional. The associations had a strong social component—meeting for meals, various traditional ceremonies, etc.

Ascough notes tension between civic leaders and associations. Sometimes Roman leadership intervened and even suppressed associations.[123] Groups ranged in size from ten to a hundred on average, though large ones are rarely attested. Members of associations came from the lower end of society, mostly slaves, freedmen, and the poor.[124] Women were rarely members of professional associations; they were much more commonly found in religious ones, even as leaders.[125]

We turn our attention now to Ascough's argument regarding Paul and the Thessalonians. On preliminary matters, Ascough treats the subject of the authenticity of 1 Thessalonians 2:13–16. He finds the arguments from both sides inconclusive, but in the end omits it as evidence for his historical reconstruction.[126] Ascough commences his socio-historical reconstruction

---

120. See R. S. Ascough and P. A. Harland, *Associations in the Greco-Roman World: A Sourcebook* (Minneapolis: Fortress, 2012).

121. E.g., honorific inscriptions, cultic dedications, membership lists, clerical documentation (*Paul's Macedonian Associations*, 20).

122. *Paul's Macedonian Associations*, 19.

123. *Paul's Macedonian Associations*, 42–46.

124. *Paul's Macedonian Associations*, 51.

125. Apparently, some were exclusively comprised of women (*Paul's Macedonian Associations*, 57).

126. *Paul's Macedonian Associations*, 164. With a similar mindset, he also excludes 2 Thessalonians as historical evidence for the situation (164–65).

with a study of the Thessalonian believers' social location. Ascough argues that they appear to be "among the poor."[127] He explains, "The financial contributions of the Philippians [see Phil 4:15–16] along with the necessity for Paul to work at his trade suggest that there was not even a patron of the Thessalonian Christians who would support Paul during his time among them."[128]

In terms of work, Ascough takes ἐργάζομαι as pointing to manual labor, as well as the command to work with their hands (4:11).[129] Ascough surmises that this group of Thessalonians had a similar trade to Paul, which explains how they came to be acquainted. It may have been while at work that Paul preached the gospel to them.[130] Perhaps he found a leatherworkers' guild in Thessalonica.[131]

Ascough argues that if the Thessalonian church is viewed as a converted artisan association, some of the perplexities of 1 Thessalonians can be resolved. For example, regarding the ἀτάκτοι, Ascough explains that "disorderly behavior" was not uncommon in associations.[132] And regarding 4:11 and Paul's command for them to "live quietly," it may have pertained to the problem of honor-competitiveness within associations.[133]

Toward the end of this chapter, Ascough takes a closer look at 1 Thessalonians 1:9b. He argues that this does not relate the experience of an *individual* conversion to Paul's gospel but a collective "turning." Thus, "we could imagine that over time Paul managed to persuade the members of the existing professional association to switch their allegiance from their patron deity or deities 'to serve a living and true God.'"[134]

A further element of his reconstruction—admittedly speculative—is the idea that it was a male-only group, "since women would not be members of an association of artisans in a trade dominated by males even if they worked in the same occupation."[135] His particular reconstruction of the Thessalonian situation is only adumbrated in this monograph, but it is

---

127. *Paul's Macedonian Associations*, 167.
128. *Paul's Macedonian Associations*, 167.
129. *Paul's Macedonian Associations*, 169–72.
130. *Paul's Macedonian Associations*, 174–75.
131. *Paul's Macedonian Associations*, 175–76.
132. *Paul's Macedonian Associations*, 181.
133. *Paul's Macedonian Associations*, 183.
134. *Paul's Macedonian Associations*, 185.
135. *Paul's Macedonian Associations*, 186. As supporting evidence for this within 1 Thessalonians, Ascough points to 1 Thess 4:4–6 (see 186–90).

worked out more fully in his 2014 book *1 and 2 Thessalonians: Encountering the Christ Group at Thessalonike*.[136]

The reception of Ascough's work is mixed. Some have found his argument regarding the Thessalonian situation comprehensively persuasive—for example, Linda McKinnish Bridges, who develops her 1–2 Thessalonians commentary based on Ascough's work.[137] Others find it limited or unpersuasive. Eckhard Schnabel regards Ascough too bent on drawing parallels between associations and Paul's churches such that he overplays similarities and underplays differences.[138] Christoph Stenschke considers Ascough's assumption that the Thessalonian church was an artisan group to be based on insufficient evidence.[139] Both Schnabel and Stenschke push back on Ascough's skepticism toward using Acts 17 as a source for historical reconstruction of the Thessalonian situation. Stenschke writes, "This evaluation of Acts does not follow the general tendency in the research of the past decade concerning the historical reliability of Acts, neither for the reliability of all of Acts nor specifically for chapters 16 and 17."[140]

THE WORK OF ABRAHAM MALHERBE

It should probably go without saying that Abraham Malherbe was perhaps the premier expert on the Thessalonian correspondence during the late twentieth and early twenty-first centuries until his death in 2012. His now classic essay on "The Cynic Background to 1 Thess 2" appeared in 1970.[141] In 1987 he published *Paul and the Thessalonians: The Philosophic Tradition of Pastoral Care*.[142] And, of course, his acclaimed Anchor Bible commentary appeared in 2000. A three-volume collection of his essays

---

136. R. S. Ascough, *1 and 2 Thessalonians: Encountering the Christ Group at Thessalonike* (Sheffield: Sheffield Phoenix Press, 2014).

137. See L. M. Bridges, *1 & 2 Thessalonians*, SHBC (Macon, GA: Smyth & Helwys, 2008); see also W. E. Arnal, "Bridging Paul and the Corinthians Together? A Rejoinder and Some Proposals on Redescription and Theory," in *Redescribing Paul and the Corinthians*, ed. R. Cameron and M. P. Miller (Atlanta: SBL Press, 2011), 85–86.

138. E. Schnabel, review of *Paul's Macedonian Associations*, by R. S. Ascough, *Trinity Journal* 26.2 (2005): 335–36. Among the differences, Schnabel mentions frequency of meetings, the "translocal" nature of the early churches, and the use of Scripture.

139. See C. W. Stenschke, review of *Paul's Macedonian Associations*, by R. S. Ascough, *Religion & Theology* 12.1 (2005): 77; cf. L. M. Trozzo, "Thessalonian Women: The Key to the 4:4 Conundrum," *PRSt* 39.1 (2012): 39–52; also G. S. Shogren, *1 and 2 Thessalonians*, ZECNT (Grand Rapids: Zondervan, 2012), 24n17.

140. Stenschke, review of *Paul's Macedonian Associations*, 77; cf. C. W. Stenschke, "Hinweise zu einem wiederentdeckten Gebiet der Actaforschung . . . ," *Communio Viatorum* 41 (1999): 65–91.

141. A. Malherbe, "Gentle as a Nurse: The Cynic Background to 1 Thess 2," *NovT* 12.2 (1970): 203–17.

142. Published by Fortress Press.

was published in 2013 under the title *Light from the Gentiles*.[143] The first volume contains several essays that relate thematically to the Thessalonian correspondence, and seven are explicitly focused on them.[144]

The thread that runs through much of Malherbe's scholarship on 1–2 Thessalonians relates Paul to the Greco-Roman moral philosophers.[145] In his work *Paul and the Thessalonians*, Malherbe argues that 1 Thessalonians bears witness to an apostle who approached the Thessalonian church with a ministry of pastoral care and whose perspective on and approach to pastoral care bears remarkable similarity to those of the moral philosophers of his age.[146] Malherbe does not make a case for this comparison directly but rather presumes this connection and underscores the thematic and sometimes terminological connectivity. For example, Paul shared with popular philosophers the desire to "convert people to a new way of life."[147] Malherbe is convinced that Paul drew from Greco-Roman *topoi* in his letters; for example, the father-son imagery Paul uses in 1 Thessalonians 2:11–12 resembles what we find in philosophical texts about teacher-student relationships.[148] That does not mean that *everything* Paul said and did could be traced to philosophy; rather, his letters bear *some* clear marks of that influence and relationship.[149] Malherbe summarizes what 1 Thessalonians tells us about Paul and philosophy this way:

> The intention of this book [*Paul and the Thessalonians*] has not been to make Paul a moral philosopher, but to illuminate his practice by comparing it to that of his contemporaries who were engaged in a similar, if not identical, enterprise. We have seen that in many respects Paul's methods had their counterparts in those of the philosophers. . . . Paul consciously used the conventions of his day in attempting to shape a community with its own identity, and he did so with considerable originality. . . . A complete portrayal of Paul as pastor will do justice

---

143. Holladay et al., *Light from the Gentiles*.

144. "Gentle as a Nurse" (ch. 4); "Exhortation in First Thessalonians" (ch. 10); "'Pastoral Care' in the Thessalonian Church" (ch. 14); "Did the Thessalonians Write to Paul?" (ch. 15); "God's New Family at Thessalonica" (ch. 19); "Anti-Epicurean Rhetoric in 1 Thessalonians" (ch. 23); "Ethics in Context: The Thessalonians and their Neighbors" (ch. 32).

145. See especially his *Paul and the Thessalonians*; cf. *Paul and the Popular Philosophers* (Minneapolis: Fortress, 1989).

146. *Paul and the Thessalonians*, 1–4.

147. *Paul and the Thessalonians*, 10, 21, 58.

148. *Paul and the Thessalonians*, 56.

149. *Paul and the Thessalonians*, 69.

to the theological dimension of Paul's understanding of his own task and of the nature of the little communities.[150]

Perhaps the most well-known and most influential argument that Malherbe has made about the influence of philosophy on Paul's ministry relates to 1 Thessalonians 2:1–12, where Paul writes at length about the blameless nature of his work among them. A previous generation of scholarship (and some today as well) understood Paul's tone as *defensive*; that is, Paul was reacting to potential or real accusations that he was not trustworthy.[151] In contrast to this tendency, Malherbe argued that Paul was taking up the mode of a Cynic philosopher who would regularly appeal to his own character in an exemplary fashion. In particular, Malherbe pointed to the case of Dio Chrysostom ("orator-turned-Cynic philosopher") as one who identified himself as an ideal moral philosopher—bold, noble, and even gentle.[152] Malherbe also highlights how Dio Chrysostom describes the model Cynic in antithetical terms to distinguish counterfeit philosophers from himself.[153] Thus, Malherbe believes Paul's statements in 1 Thessalonians 2:1–12 are strikingly parallel and resonant. And this seems to solve an important puzzle regarding the interpretation of 1 Thessalonians 2:1–12: in the same way Dio Chrysostom sought to distinguish himself from hack philosophers without reacting to direct accusations, so Malherbe concludes that Paul was not necessarily reacting to direct accusations from the Thessalonians.[154]

While a number of scholars are attracted to Malherbe's proposal,[155] there are some important concerns with the parallels Malherbe has posited between Paul and Dio Chrysostom. Taking on the parallels themselves, I. Howard Marshall argues that Dio Chrysostom made specific appeal that his audience imitate him, but Paul did not do this in 2:1–12.[156] Robin Griffith-Jones adds his own critique. First, Malherbe takes too little account of Dio Chrysostom's own context—namely, his address to the Alexandrians and the fact that the published form of his speech would

150. *Paul and the Thessalonians*, 109.
151. See Donfried and Beutler, *Thessalonians Debate*.
152. See Malherbe, "Gentle as a Nurse," 208–11.
153. See Malherbe, "Gentle as a Nurse," 214–15; Dio Chrysostom, *Ad Alexandrinos* (*Or.* 32) 11ff.
154. See Malherbe, "Gentle as a Nurse," 217.
155. See Gaventa, *First and Second Thessalonians*, 5, 25; A. Smith, "The First Letter to the Thessalonians: Introduction, Commentary, and Reflections," in vol. 9 of *The New Interpreter's Bible Commentary*, ed. L. E. Keck, 10 vols. (Nashville: Abingdon, 2015), 698.
156. Marshall, *1 and 2 Thessalonians*, 61.

make it to Vespasian, who banned all Cynics from Rome and held all philosophers in contempt except Musonius. Griffith-Jones wonders whether Alexandria itself was home to one of the emperor's named detractors; thus, Dio Chrysostom had to consider his "delicate position in Alexandria."[157] Second, in another review Griffith-Jones explains further regarding the local context in Alexandria that Dio Chrysostom had to endure "cat-calls" (*Ad Alexandrinos* [*Or.* 32] 1–2) and needed to stop his speech midway (*Ad Alexandrinos* [*Or.* 32] 99–101). "Dio had expected his audience to be difficult, but not this difficult; the trouble he encountered in delivering his speech became in good measure the point of it. If Paul was thinking as Dio thought before the speech (let alone, during it), Paul was working hard."[158]

Other scholars disagree with Malherbe regarding some of the inferences he makes about the Thessalonian context based on these ostensible similarities between Paul's discourse in 2:1–12 and Dio's speech. Robert Jewett criticizes Malherbe's argument by noting that simply because shared themes and even shared language and ideas exist between Paul and Dio, that does not prove that Paul was *not* addressing local problems in Thessalonica.[159] Karl Donfried adds that the way Dio criticizes and repudiates huckster philosophers would indeed fit in well with an "apologetic" strategy if Paul were on the defense.[160]

We can now move on to discussing some of the distinctive features of Malherbe's Anchor Bible commentary on 1–2 Thessalonians.

Reliability and usefulness of Acts. Malherbe finds the heavy skepticism of the historicity of Acts "extreme."[161] While, with others, he acknowledges that Luke's accounts have their shortcomings, still one can continue with a "discriminating use of its evidence to supplement Paul's letters."[162] He argues that historians simply cannot paint a full picture of Paul's ministry

---

157. R. Griffith-Jones, review of *The Thessalonians Debate*, by K. P. Donfried and J. Beutler, *JTS* 52.2 (2001): 817–18.

158. R. Griffith-Jones, review of *The First and Second Letters to the Thessalonians*, by G. D. Fee, *JTS* 62.1 (2011): 324.

159. See Jewett, *Thessalonian Correspondence*, 192.

160. Donfried, *Paul, Thessalonica, and Early Christianity*, 44; cf. 164–65. It should be noted, however, that Donfried still resists the apologetic reading of 1 Thessalonians 2:1–12 (see 194). For my part, while the similarities between Paul and Dio are intriguing, I do not find the parallels compelling enough to expect some kind of conscious Pauline "use" of Dio's methods, specific wording, or particular moral-philosophical perspective. See further N. K. Gupta, "Paul and the *Militia Spiritualis* Topos in 1 Thessalonians," in *Paul and the Greco-Roman Philosophical Tradition*, ed. J. R. Dodson and A. W. Pitts, LNTS (London: Bloomsbury, 2017), 13–32.

161. Malherbe, *Letters to the Thessalonians*, 55.

162. Malherbe, *Letters to the Thessalonians*, 55.

without Acts.[163] In a section of his commentary called "Evidence of Acts," Malherbe suggests that the basic people, places, and events offer a credible portrayal of Paul's activity in Thessalonica. Indeed, there are many parallels between Acts and 1 Thessalonians, such as Paul's companions (Timothy and Silvanus/Silas), the movement from Philippi to Thessalonica, and the problem of his departure from Thessalonica.[164]

What kind of affliction? Three times in 1 Thessalonians we find the word θλῖψις (1:6; 3:3, 7). Most scholars define this in terms of social harassment with the possibility of some physical abuse (see Barclay and Still above). Malherbe makes the unique case that this word relates to *mental* stress, "the distress of the anguished heart."[165] Paul is concerned that the Thessalonians have been "shaken" in their thinking.[166] Malherbe turns to 2 Corinthians 4:8–10 for parallels, where Paul lists his own hardships. Malherbe counts "internal distress" as among these, relating to "the personal distress he suffered in his ministry."[167] The vast majority of scholars disagree with Malherbe on this, taking the θλῖψις of 1 Thessalonians to be a more demonstrably external, social form of harassment. As Dunn notes, "The tie-in with the events recalled in Acts 17.5–9 and their sequel is still the most persuasive."[168]

THE WORK OF KARL P. DONFRIED

As with Malherbe, Karl Donfried has left a lasting mark on Thessalonian scholarship. In 1984 he published his important essay, "Paul and Judaism: 1 Thessalonians 2:13–16 as a Test Case."[169] He was a contributor to the seminal 1990 Leuven volume *The Thessalonian Correspondence*. He also

---

163. Though, again, see D. A. Campbell, Framing Paul: An Epistolary Biography (Grand Rapids: Eerdmans, 2014).

164. Malherbe, *Letters to the Thessalonians*, 57–61.

165. Malherbe, *Letters to the Thessalonians*, 77. See also idem, "Conversion to Paul's Gospel," in Holladay et al., *Light from the Gentiles*, 1:358–59.

166. See Malherbe, *Letters to the Thessalonians*, 193; see also 202.

167. Malherbe, "Conversion to Paul's Gospel," 359.

168. Dunn, *Beginning from Jerusalem*, 704; cf. G. Haufe, *Der erste Brief des Paulus an die Thessalonicher*, THKNT 12.1 (Leipzig: Evangelische Verlagsanstalt, 1999), 27. Witherington also argues against Malherbe, noting 1 Thess 2:14–15 where the suffering of the Thessalonians is compared to that of Jesus: "We have no evidence that Jesus suffered such internal distress on receiving the word" (Witherington, *Thessalonians*, 72). Still disagrees with Malherbe's larger argument about the "internal distress" reading of θλῖψις but acknowledges that in Malherbe's "Conversion" essay there is a good amount of nuance where Malherbe refers to their "social dislocation" and "public criticism." Still writes, "This type of conflict certainly extends beyond the private, psychological sphere!" (Still, *Conflict*, 210).

169. "Paul and Judaism: 1 Thessalonians 2:13–16 as a Test Case," *Interpretation* 38.3 (1984): 242–53.

wrote for the collection *Paul and Empire* edited by Horsley with the essay "The Imperial Cults of Thessalonica and Political Conflict in 1 Thessalonians."[170] In 2000 his work on 1 Thessalonians 2:1–12 was published in the volume *The Thessalonians Debate*.[171] A couple of years later, a collection of his work on Paul was published under the title *Paul, Thessalonica, and Early Christianity*.[172] Since that time he has written important scholarship on 1 Timothy, but he is also presently writing the 1–2 Thessalonians volume for the International Critical Commentary. Because our focus here is on the Thessalonian situation, we will examine two important essays from *Paul, Thessalonica, and Early Christianity*: "1 Thessalonians, Acts and the Early Paul" and "The Cults of Thessalonica and the Thessalonian Correspondence."

In the former essay ("1 Thessalonians, Acts and the Early Paul"), Donfried begins, as many are inclined to do, with a discussion of sources with respect to examining the Thessalonian situation. When it comes to Acts, Donfried expresses skepticism of its historical reliability due to Luke's tendency to reshape traditions to fit his theological concerns.[173] Still, some value comes from Acts when taking these tendencies into account. When it contradicts the Pauline letters, Acts should not be given priority. This admittedly leads to gaps in the reconstruction of Paul's ministry, thus *"there can be no absolutely definitive chronology of this period*; all attempts must be tentative and subject to correction and revision."[174] Be that as it may, Donfried does not pit Luke's portrait of Paul against what we see in the Pauline letters. On the contrary, Donfried argues (1) that 1 Thessalonians is very early (i.e., before any conflict with Jewish Christian opponents), and (2) the Paul of 1 Thessalonians coheres remarkably with the depiction of Paul found in Acts.[175]

Donfried expresses the wider thought of 1 Thessalonians as this: "God has chosen, elected, the believers in Thessalonica and . . . they, because the

---

170. "The Imperial Cults of Thessalonica and Political Conflict in 1 Thessalonians," in *Paul and Empire*, ed. R. A. Horsley (Harrisburg, PA: Trinity Press International, 1997), 215–23.

171. "The Epistolary and Rhetorical Context of 1 Thess. 2.1–12," 163–94.

172. *Paul, Thessalonica, and Early Christianity* (London: T&T Clark, 2002).

173. Donfried, *Paul, Thessalonica, and Early Christianity*, 72. According to Donfried's chronological study, Paul was "commissioned" in 33 CE; c. 36 he visited Jerusalem. He made a first visit to Corinth somewhere in the period of 41–44. The Jerusalem conference took place in 50 and in the period of 50–52 he made an intermediate visit to Corinth. Donfried dates 1 Thessalonians to ca. 43 CE (see pp. 75–76).

174. Donfried, *Paul, Thessalonica, and Early Christianity*, 72 (emphasis original).

175. See basic explanation on p. 70 of *Paul, Thessalonica, and Early Christianity*, and then *passim*.

gospel had been proclaimed to them in all power, have responded positively and joyfully, despite persecution, to this word of God."[176] Donfried argues that 1 Thessalonians contains a significant amount of pre-Pauline material: "Over and over again Paul simply takes over traditions circulating in the Hellenistic church and appropriated by that church from a variety of sources including Hellenistic Judaism and, through it, popular Hellenistic philosophy."[177] Of course, Paul did write this letter with his own advice and thoughts, such as the comforting words in light of recent deaths in the community. Moreover, Donfried sees Paul at work applying his eschatology of the "triumph of God" in Christ to the Thessalonian crises. In particular, Donfried takes interest in 1 Thessalonians 1:9–10 and 4:13–18. He points out that many of the terms we have come to associate with Paul (body, flesh, death, life, sin, freedom, law, righteousness/justification, cross) are remarkably absent from such key texts. The emphasis lies on the parousia in Paul's early thought.[178] Only *after* the Antioch incident do we see the development of Paul's interest in justification and the problem of the law.

Coming back to Acts, Donfried affirms again at the end of his essay that the Paul of Acts closely aligns with 1 Thessalonians (e.g., compare 1 Thess 2:13–16 and Acts 28:17–31).[179] For those that try to pit "the Lukan Paul" vs. the Paul of his letters, Donfried asks, *Which should we consider the "real Paul"? The "early Paul" or "later Paul"?*[180]

The second essay by Donfried regarding the Thessalonian situation is "The Cults of Thessalonica and the Thessalonian Correspondence."[181] Here Donfried urges that one must read 1–2 Thessalonians in light of "the religious and political history of Thessalonica."[182] He is interested in the social world of Thessalonica and what kind of context created the exigencies for Paul's correspondence. He separates the so-called "religious" cults from civic and political features of life in Thessalonica, though he notes that in reality these overlapped and interpenetrated in the first-century Roman world.[183]

In terms of religious cults, Donfried surveys extant knowledge of the

---

176. Donfried, *Paul, Thessalonica, and Early Christianity*, 77.
177. Donfried, *Paul, Thessalonica, and Early Christianity*, 78.
178. Donfried, *Paul, Thessalonica, and Early Christianity*, 83–84.
179. He offers a more comprehensive study of similarities on pp. 92–97.
180. See Donfried, *Paul, Thessalonica, and Early Christianity*, 91.
181. Donfried, *Paul, Thessalonica, and Early Christianity*, 21–48.
182. Donfried, *Paul, Thessalonica, and Early Christianity*, 22.
183. Donfried, *Paul, Thessalonica, and Early Christianity*, 22.

worship of Dionysus and the classic Greek deities, but he gives particular attention to the cult of Cabirus.[184] Donfried relates this knowledge of religious life to the Thessalonian believers' turn *from idolatry* (1 Thess 1:9) and their problems with sexual immorality, perhaps linked to the permissiveness of pagan religion (4:5).[185]

Next Donfried discusses "civic cults" and Thessalonica. Combining information from Acts 17:1–9 as well as clues from 1 Thessalonians (e.g., 5:3), Donfried concludes that elements of Paul's original preaching "could be understood or misunderstood in a distinctly political sense."[186] For instance, Donfried takes 5:3 as "a frontal attack on the *Pax et Securitas* program of the early Principate."[187] Donfried also points to some of Paul's Greek words, particularly παρουσία, ἀπάντησις, and κύριος as politically charged terms. Thus, Donfried posits, one can see how Thessalonian residents could find Paul's message disturbing to the peace of the city.[188] Paul's eschatologically oriented proclamation carried a heavy royal ideology that would have clashed with the Thessalonian political atmosphere. The following quotation summarizes his overall approach to the Thessalonian situation:

> The Greeks who were attracted to the Pauline mission grew up in a city filled with mystery cults and royal theology. Surely they would compare the gospel proclaimed by Paul with their pagan past; for this reason Paul skillfully selects his terminology for protreptic purposes. The language Paul uses, on the one hand, reveals sharp discontinuities with their pagan past and intends to show them how the totality of their existence has been transformed through the death of Christ into a new living relationship with him—whether awake or asleep. . . . It is our hope to have shown, even though in a cursory manner, that a knowledge of the interrelated cultic and historical background of Thessalonica, particularly the strong Roman presence and domination at the time of Paul, is an indispensable first step in the interpretation of the Thessalonian correspondence.[189]

---

184. On Cabirus, see Donfried, *Paul, Thessalonica, and Early Christianity*, 25–29.

185. See Donfried, *Paul, Thessalonica, and Early Christianity*, 30. He also briefly tries to link Paul's teachings in 1 Thess 5:5–7 to vices related to mystery cults; and perhaps also 5:19–22 (see pp. 30–31).

186. Donfried, *Paul, Thessalonica, and Early Christianity*, 34.

187. Donfried, *Paul, Thessalonica, and Early Christianity*, 34.

188. In his discussion of Thessalonica's relationship with Rome, Donfried draws significantly from and affirms the work of H. Hendrix; see Donfried, *Paul, Thessalonica, and Early Christianity*, 35–38.

189. Donfried, *Paul, Thessalonica, and Early Christianity*, 48.

Before moving on, we might add that Donfried's approach to the interpretation of 1 Thessalonians and the Thessalonian situation offers these two distinctive features. First, Donfried is rather rare among 1 Thessalonians interpreters in affirming the argument that those who died in the Thessalonian community were probably martyred.[190] Secondly, Donfried takes 1 Thessalonians 2:13–16 as genuine and original to the letter.[191]

FROM HOPE TO DESPAIR IN THESSALONICA,
BY COLIN R. NICHOLL (2004)

The Society of New Testament Studies monograph *From Hope to Despair in Thessalonica* is the product of Colin Nicholl's doctoral thesis written under the supervision of Morna Hooker.[192] Nicholl sets out to explain the situation behind the Thessalonian letters, attempting to make sense of the continuity between the two letters as well as the differences. Is there a scenario one can imagine that could fit both texts together?[193] Naturally, emphasis is placed on eschatological problems in Thessalonica.

In the introduction, Nicholl engages in the debate over the authenticity of 2 Thessalonians (we will return to this on pp. 197–220). He discusses literary parallels, the possible hints of pseudepigraphy detected in 2 Thessalonians 2:2 and 3:17, and the tone of the second letter. The most important factor in the discussion, and the only one Nicholl deals with in depth, is the matter of historical and theological compatibility: "The perceived contradiction between the eschatology of the second letter and the first, specifically between premonitory signs in 2 Thessalonians and imminence/suddenness in 1 Thessalonians."[194]

Nicholl's second chapter investigates 1 Thessalonians 4:13–18, concentrating on the problem of the recent death of community members. According to Nicholl, "the deaths have brought to the surface a serious lack in the Thessalonians' eschatology."[195] Nicholl follows a traditional interpretation that imagines the remaining Thessalonian believers confused at these deaths, presuming that all would remain alive in view of

---

190. See Donfried, *Paul, Thessalonica, and Early Christianity*, 120–34.
191. See Donfried, *Paul, Thessalonica, and Early Christianity*, 195–208; cf. 1–20.
192. This book, while technically a revised version of a doctoral thesis, contains so much attention to detail and commentary-like exegesis that it functions similar to a commentary, yet it has become influential in the study of 1–2 Thessalonians and easily belongs in this situational discussion.
193. See *From Hope to Despair*, 3; cf. 49.
194. See *From Hope to Despair*, 3–4.
195. *From Hope to Despair*, 48.

Jesus's impending return. After some perished, the community lost hope. As Nicholl explains, "Certainly the deaths seemed to declare that among the number of the converted were at least some whom God had not elected to salvation at the Parousia, which meant that the elect status and eschatological destiny of the whole community was subject to suspicion."[196]

First Thessalonians 5:1–11 is the focus of the next chapter. Nicholl argues that Paul here is trying "to reassure the community that they are not destined to wrath, but rather to salvation on the Day of the Lord."[197] Apparently, Nicholl surmises, the Thessalonians worried that "in dying, the dead had been placed beyond the pale of Parousia salvation."[198] Non-Christian family and friends (as well as enemies) may have stoked the flames of their imagination by convincing them that these deaths were an omen of divine wrath. Nicholl writes, "It is not inconceivable that those loyal to the Greco-Roman deities would have been looking for *prodigia* (τέρατα), expecting that their gods would soon express unhappiness concerning the apostasy of those who had converted to the new religious movement in Thessalonica."[199]

They had expectant hope in the parousia and quickly went from hope to dejection and "nervous dread."[200] Thus, Nicholl concludes "that the unexpected passing away of community members is the primary exigency of 1 Thessalonians, filling the survivors with despair both for their dead and for themselves."[201]

In terms of how to reconstruct the situation in Thessalonica, Nicholl spends a short bit of space discussing Acts 17:1–10a. He takes the common approach of detecting clues from 1 Thessalonians 1:9, concluding that the majority of Thessalonian believers were former pagans, but (with a side glance to Luke's account) he leaves it open as to whether the church included a minority of Jews.[202] He also wonders whether the believing community contained smaller groups of house churches, split by culture and ethnicity. Specifically, "the Jewish believers may have been largely

---

196. *From Hope to Despair*, 48. Nicholl posits that the Thessalonians were apparently not properly instructed about the resurrection of the Christian dead (74). I personally find it unlikely that the problem was too little instruction, given the centrality of the resurrection in Paul's theology. What may have been more likely is that they *misunderstood* the concept of the resurrection.

197. *From Hope to Despair*, 73.

198. *From Hope to Despair*, 74.

199. *From Hope to Despair*, 75.

200. *From Hope to Despair*, 111.

201. *From Hope to Despair*, 112.

202. *From Hope to Despair*, 112; see note 92.

confined to the band of leaders mentioned in 5:12–13, who it seems had not yet managed to command the community's full respect."[203]

Much of the remainder of Nicholl's book is dedicated to 2 Thessalonians and the interrelationship between the two letters and what can be understood about the underlying situation. We will return to Nicholl's arguments in chapter six (pp. 212–14). Ultimately he proposes a solution that can explain a situation that could give rise to both letters (as authentically from Paul).[204]

Nicholl's work has received a lot of positive discussion, owing especially to his detailed study and analysis of the Thessalonian correspondence.[205] Again, because his monograph does the kind of work one sees in a commentary, many of the contributions he makes are in those finer points. This leads perhaps to the greatest weakness of the book, one pointed out by reviewer Alan Mitchell, that his overall interpretation of the Thessalonian situation is rather traditional—he does not offer a "brand new theory."[206] Still, this ranks as one of the most important academic works on 1–2 Thessalonians written in the last fifteen years and should be consulted by all who are interested in the Thessalonian situation and the interrelation of the letters from Paul.

CONCLUSION ON THE THESSALONIAN SITUATION

When we look over this selective survey of influential works on the Thessalonian situation, a few patterns and themes are apparent and warrant brief comment.

Ancient contextualization. Paul's letters have long been recognized as occasional documents and not independent theological treatises. Still, it was not really until the last few decades that we have seen this kind of surge in thorough contextualization. I do not know all the reasons why this is happening *now*, but I can venture a few guesses. First, new findings in archaeology have led to fresh insights into the Jewish and Greco-Roman world (e.g., the Dead Sea scrolls, unearthed synagogues, inscriptions, Oxyrhynchus papyri transcribed). Second, scholars are benefitting from digitization and online dissemination of archaeological information.

---

203. *From Hope to Despair,* 112n92.
204. See the concluding comments on p. 208.
205. See, e.g., P. Oakes, review of *From Hope to Despair,* by C. Nicholl, *JSNT* 27.5 (2005): 113–14.
206. See A. C. Mitchell, review of *From Hope to Despair,* by C. Nicholl, *Journal of Religion* 85.4 (2005): 654–56.

Common to almost all the studies mentioned above is a deep desire to "get into" the world of first-century Thessalonica and discover the pressures, motivations, and circumstances that led to 1–2 Thessalonians.

One dimension that has come to the forefront is *sociopolitical* factors regarding the harassment of Paul and the Thessalonians. This raises the question about whether the θλῖψις should be understood to convey persecution; one often thinks today of persecution as intolerance of "religion." What many of the above studies have shown is that the θλῖψις no doubt related to what we think of as "religion," yet also was bound up with Christian disturbance of social cohesion, failure to honor Rome, and perhaps infringement or at least criticism of civic laws, traditions, and expectations.

Acts 17:1–9? A point of tension and disagreement between several of the above scholars regards the use of Acts to reconstruct the Thessalonian situation. Almost none of the scholars mentioned above discount Acts entirely, but several hesitate to rely too heavily on the Lukan details. As I noted above, however, historians that are not biblical scholars tend to be less finicky, recognizing that (a) most sources, including Acts, do indeed have biases and embellishments, but also believing that (b) historians tend to have no other choice than to press forward carefully and use as much of the information as possible.

Jewish or gentile converts? Jewish or gentile opposition? Again, not unrelated to the above two issues is determining the culture and ethnicity of the converts to Paul's gospel as well as the identity of the opposition. If Acts is discounted, then a combination of common readings of 1 Thessalonians 1:9 and 2:14 leads to the assumptions that the church was almost exclusively (if not exclusively) gentile and that the persecutors were gentile as well.[207] If the information from Acts is given more weight, there is more openness to imagining that the church in Thessalonica was comprised of *some* Jews and a good portion of God-fearing gentiles. Then there would also be more willingness to take seriously the notion that *Jewish* opposition and persecution were happening in Thessalonica (alongside of or perhaps inciting gentile opposition).

Eschatology and anxiety. Scholars like Jewett and Nicholl have invested much time and energy in determining what, and to what extent,

---

207. One would also probably need to add the common remark that a gentile readership of 1 Thess is in view because Paul does not quote from the Jewish Scriptures; see below.

eschatological teaching, questions, and misunderstanding led to anxiety and social problems within the Thessalonian church.

Order of the Thessalonian Letters

Most scholars simply take it for granted that 1 Thessalonians was written before 2 Thessalonians.[208] The most significant modern voice that favors an alternative (i.e., that 2 Thessalonians precedes 1 Thessalonians) is C. Wanamaker.[209] First, Wanamaker notes that the placement of the letters in the canon do not assume chronological ordering—they were set into that sequence according to length.[210] For support in his case for the priority of 2 Thessalonians, Wanamaker turns to T. W. Manson's important essay "St. Paul in Greece: The Letters to the Thessalonians."[211] Manson argues that 2 Thessalonians was penned by Paul in Athens and sent to the Thessalonians via Timothy (1 Thess 3:1–6). The second letter (1 Thessalonians) was later written from Corinth. To establish this scenario, Manson notes the following:

- The persecution seems to have been intense in 2 Thessalonians 1:4–7 but seen only in retrospect in 1 Thessalonians 2:14.[212]
- The problem of idleness is "introduced" in 2 Thessalonians 3:11–15 but assumed in 1 Thessalonians 4:10–12.[213]
- In 2 Thessalonians 3:17, the mention of his signature used in all his letters makes more sense if 2 Thessalonians precedes 1 Thessalonians.[214]
- Concerning eschatological matters, in 1 Thessalonians 5:1 Paul tells the Thessalonians they need no further instruction, hinting that he had already informed them (as in 2 Thess 2:1–12).[215]
- First Thessalonians 4:9, 13, and 5:1 ("now about . . .") is a formula referring back to earlier instruction.[216]

---

208. Fee does not entertain another possibility at all (*Thessalonians*, 1–8); Weima places a brief dismissal in a footnote (*1–2 Thessalonians*, 39n32), simply referring the reader to antecedent scholarly conversations.
209. Wanamaker, *Thessalonians*.
210. Wanamaker, *Thessalonians*, 38.
211. "St. Paul in Greece: The Letters to the Thessalonians," *BJRL* 35 (1953): 428–47. This essay comes from a lecture delivered in the John Ryland Library on November 12, 1952.
212. See Manson, "St. Paul in Greece," 441.
213. "St. Paul in Greece," 441–42.
214. "St. Paul in Greece," 442–43.
215. "St. Paul in Greece," 443.
216. "St. Paul in Greece," 443–45.

Important to Manson's overall argument is the drawing of a trajectory of Pauline teaching from 2 Thessalonians to 1 Thessalonians; Manson argues that several passages in 2 Thessalonians appear to be connected to teaching in 1 Thessalonians (1 Thess 4:9–13 → 2 Thess 3:6–15; 1 Thess 4:13; 5:1 → 2 Thess 2:1–12).

Wanamaker seems favorable toward several of these arguments, but he focuses his argument on picking apart assumptions about the priority of 1 Thessalonians. Jewett, writing prior to Wanamaker, put forward several arguments in support of the traditional ordering:[217]

1. Second Thessalonians refers to a previous letter (2:2, 15; 3:17), whereas 1 Thessalonians does not.
2. Regarding 2 Thessalonians 2:15, Jewett argues that ἐδιδάχθητε is a clear reference to teaching from 1 Thessalonians.
3. Second Thessalonians 3:17 implies that the Thessalonians *know from experience* that Paul gives a personal authentication in his letters.

Regarding the first matter, Wanamaker responds that 2 Thessalonians 2:2 refers not to 1 Thessalonians but to a presumed forgery, or perhaps "he may have included the reference for rhetorical affect."[218] Moreover, Wanamaker repeats Best's suggestion that if the Thessalonians had misunderstood 1 Thessalonians 4:13–5:11, Paul would have offered a clarification that was more direct.[219] As for the second point regarding ἐδιδάχθητε, Wanamaker notes that it could easily refer to the teaching of traditions (in person) rather than via letter according to 2 Thessalonians 2:15.[220] And what about the evidence from 2 Thessalonians 3:17? Wanamaker does not find this to be proof of their possession of 1 Thessalonians. First, Wanamaker argues that Paul may have merely tried to give them a way to test a genuine letter from a forgery (if in fact they had received a Pauline forgery).[221] Second, if the Thessalonians already had 1 Thessalonians in

---

217. Jewett, *Thessalonian Correspondence*, 27ff.
218. Wanamaker, *Thessalonians*, 40.
219. *Thessalonians*, 40; see E. Best, *First and Second Epistles to the Thessalonians*, BNTC (Peabody, MA: Hendrickson, 1972), 279.
220. See Wanamaker, *Thessalonians*, 40–41. I think Wanamaker is right on this pushback against Jewett. Much less convincing is his argument that if the Thessalonians had 1 Thessalonians in hand, Paul would have said *letters* (plural) in 2 Thess 2:15 rather than *letter* (singular); see p. 41. Because he is referring here to *previous* teaching, I doubt that the singular/plural distinction is absolutely necessary.
221. Wanamaker, *Thessalonians*, 41.

hand, why was Paul not more specific about it in 2 Thessalonians 3:17? Why such a general remark?[222] I do agree with Wanamaker that it *would* have made more sense for Paul to have encouraged the Thessalonians to check 2 Thessalonians against 1 Thessalonians if indeed the latter was written first; nevertheless, this argument is not strong proof in favor of 2 Thessalonians's temporal priority. Second Thessalonians 3:17 can be understood with either ordering.

Another level on which the debate takes place concerns the way Paul's teaching develops with the situation in Thessalonica. Jewett argues that Paul presumes they have accepted his imminent apocalyptic teaching, and in 2 Thessalonians Paul must put the brakes on to cool their overrealized hysteria.[223] Wanamaker reads the situation differently, especially pertaining to the persecution. It is obvious that the persecution is a clear and present danger in 2 Thessalonians, but Wanamaker argues that according to 1 Thessalonians 2:14 it is "a thing of the past."[224] Wanamaker bases this on Paul's use of the aorist tense, but that seems like too much certainty placed on the tense of the verb. Furthermore, while Paul does look *back* on their affliction in 1 Thessalonians 1–2, he is certainly concerned with *present* vigilance in 5:1–11.

Abraham Malherbe takes a fresh look at the whole issue—with both Jewett and Wanamaker in view—and concludes that Jewett's arguments for the traditional sequencing of letters are not as cogent as they could be, but neither is he convinced by Wanamaker's rebuttals and justifications of a reversed sequencing.[225] In fact, though Malherbe himself ultimately supports a traditional ordering, he imagines that the following interpretation of 2 Thessalonians *could* offer a historical reconstruction that favors it as the earlier letter:

> Paul had converted the Thessalonians (2:14)[226] and taught them eschatological doctrine (2:5) as well as social responsibility (3:10) and perhaps other matters (2:15). He remained with them long enough to expect that his personal example would carry weight (3:7–9). After leaving them, he received alarming news that there was a threat of

---

222. Wanamaker, *Thessalonians*, 41.
223. See Jewett, *Thessalonian Correspondence*, 28ff.
224. Wanamaker, *Thessalonians*, 42.
225. See Malherbe, *Thessalonians*, 361–64.
226. All his references here are to 2 Thess.

doctrinal error (2:2), that some of his converts were disobeying his command that they should work (3:11), and that the Thessalonian believers were being persecuted (1:4). He then writes 2 Thessalonians, long enough after he had left Thessalonica for him to suspect that a letter had been written in his name (2:2). On such a reading, 1 Thessalonians does not appear anywhere in the letter.[227]

This intriguing scenario notwithstanding, as mentioned above Malherbe still finds the traditional ordering of the letters to be the most sensible. Though his comments about this are brief,[228] he points to the material in 1 Thessalonians 2:17–3:10 that sets up the background relationship between Paul and the Thessalonians, the kind of information that makes much more sense in the earliest contact.[229] Malherbe's preferred situational reconstruction—which is rather traditional—follows this basic outline: Paul wrote 2 Thessalonians after the first letter upon hearing of problems in Thessalonica. The believers there were struggling with persecution and false teaching regarding the parousia. Furthermore, some had abandoned work. Thus, Paul wrote another letter aiming at both encouragement but also admonishment.[230]

RECOMMENDED READING

City and Background

Adam-Veleni, P. "Thessalonike." Pages 545–62 in *Brill's Companion to Ancient Macedon: Studies in the Archaeology and History of Macedon, 650 BC–300 AD*. Edited by R. J. L. Fox. Leiden: Brill, 2011.

Brocke, C. vom. *Thessaloniki-Stadt des Kassander und Gemeinde des Paulus: eine frühe christliche Gemeinde in ihrer heidnischen Umwelt*. WUNT 2/125. Tübingen: Mohr Siebeck, 2001.

Fearghail, F. Ó. "The Jews in the Hellenistic Cities of Acts." Pages 39–54 in *Jews in the Hellenistic and Roman Cities*. Edited by J. R. Bartlett. London: Routledge, 2002.

Grammenos, D. V., ed. *Roman Thessaloniki*. Translated by D. Hardy. Thessaloniki: Archaeological Museum of Thessaloniki, 2003.

---

227. Malherbe, *Thessalonians*, 363.
228. Malherbe, *Thessalonians*, 364.
229. See too M. E. Boring, *1 and 2 Thessalonians*, NTL (Louisville: Westminster John Knox, 2015), 8–9.
230. See Malherbe, *Thessalonians*, 364.

Hendrix, H. L. "Thessalonians Honor Romans." ThD diss., Harvard Divinity School, 1984.

Kyrtatas, D. J. "Early Christianity in Macedonia." Pages 585–99 in *Brill's Companion to Ancient Macedon: Studies in the Archaeology and History of Macedon, 650 BC–300 AD*. Edited by R. J. L. Fox. Leiden: Brill, 2011.

Nasrallah, L., C. Bakirtzis, and S. J. Friesen, eds. *From Roman to Early Christian Thessalonikē: Studies in Religion and Archaeology*. Cambridge: Harvard University Press, 2010.

Nigdelis, P. "Roman Thessalonica." Pages 51–87 in *The History of Macedonia*. Edited by I. Koliopoulos. Thessaloniki: Museum of the Macedonian Struggle Foundation, 2007.

——. "Thessaloniki: The Age of the Macedonian Kingdom and the Period of Roman Rule." http://site.lpth.gr/en/texts/Nigdelis_en.pdf. Online only.

Stefanidou-Tiveriou, T. "Thessaloniki from Cassander to Galerius," http://site.lpth .gr/en/texts/Tiveriou_en.pdf. Online only.

For further on the background of Thessalonica, see P. Nigdelis, Επιγραφικά Θεσσαλονίκεια. Συμβολή στην πολιτική και κοινωνική ιστορία της Αρχαίας Θεσσαλονίκης. (*Epigraphica Thessalonicensia: A Contribution to the Political and Social History of Ancient Thessaloniki*). Thessaloniki: University Studio Press, 2006.

Situation

Ascough, R. S. *Paul's Macedonian Associations: The Social Context of 1 Thessalonians and Philippians*. WUNT 2/161. Tübingen: Mohr Siebeck, 2003.

Barclay, J. M. G. "Conflict in Thessalonica." *CBQ* 55 (1993): 512–30.

Donfried, K. P. *Paul, Thessalonica and Early Christianity*. London: T&T Clark, 2002.

Jewett, R. *The Thessalonian Correspondence: Pauline Rhetoric and Millenarian Piety*. Philadelphia: Fortress, 1986.

Nicholl, C. R. *From Hope to Despair in Thessalonica: Situating 1 and 2 Thessalonians*. SNTSMS 126. Cambridge: Cambridge University Press, 2004.

Still, T. D. *Conflict at Thessalonica: A Pauline Church and Its Neighbours*. JSNTSup 183. Sheffield: Sheffield Academic, 1999.

CHAPTER 3

THEMES AND INTERPRETATION OF 1 THESSALONIANS

I n this chapter we will examine the theological themes of 1 Thessalonians as well as the major exegetical and interpretive cruxes and debates.

THEMES

Eschatology and Hope

By the account of most scholars, the most prominent theological category in the Thessalonian correspondence is final eschatology; that is, as far as 1 Thessalonians is concerned, the emphasis is on life shaped in light of the hope of the parousia.[1]

From as early as on in the letter as 1 Thessalonians 1:3, Paul refers to the Thessalonians' praiseworthy commitment to the gospel, particularly their "faith," "love," and their "endurance inspired by hope in our Lord Jesus Christ." As he reminds them of their conversion (a few verses later), he notes their reliance on the expectant hope of God's "Son from heaven,

---

1. Note that L. Morris's Word Biblical Themes volume on 1–2 Thessalonians gives major attention to "The Last Things" (*1, 2 Thessalonians*, Word Biblical Themes [Dallas: Word, 1989]). In M. J. Gorman's respected Pauline textbook, *Apostle of the Crucified Lord*, the title of the 1 Thess chapter is "Holiness and Hope in Faithful Witness to a Pagan World," 188–210. K. P. Donfried's NTT volume contribution to the theology of 1–2 Thess strongly emphasizes the parousia (K. P. Donfried, *Theology of the Shorter Pauline Letters*, with I. H. Marshall, NTT [Cambridge: Cambridge University Press, 1993], 45). Dunn states matter-of-factly that "the parousia theme dominates these letters [1–2 Thess], as it does none of Paul's other letters" (J. D. G. Dunn, *The Theology of Paul the Apostle* [Grand Rapids: Eerdmans, 1998], 298). See too I. H. Marshall's *New Testament Theology* where he underscores "the strong future orientation" of the Thessalonian correspondence, particularly the parousia (Downers Grove, IL: InterVarsity Press, 2010), 249–50; cf. also Johnson, *1 and 2 Thessalonians*, 256–70. D. Luckensmeyer makes the claim that "eschatology is the best hermeneutical key to interpret Paul's pattern of exhortation in First Thessalonians" (*Eschatology*, 2).

whom he raised from the dead—Jesus, who rescues us from the coming wrath" (1:10). Paul recognizes the persecution, suffering, and shame endured by the Thessalonian believers and states that Jewish persecutors of Jesus-followers cannot avoid the final wrath of God (2:16). As Paul reflects on his own affection for the Thessalonians, he reminds them that they are his hope and joy, a "crown in which we will glory" when the Lord Jesus returns (2:19–20). Twice in the letter Paul offers a wish-prayer for their maturity and holiness in view of the parousia (3:12–13; 5:23).

A set of key topics related to eschatological matters are introduced in chapter four of the letter. In 1 Thessalonians 4:13–18, Paul addresses the problem of those believers in Thessalonica who have recently died, in particular their fate and dignity when the living and dead are summoned at the parousia. In 5:1–11 Paul transitions to the topic of "times and dates." Rather than prognosticate about the eschatological timeline, Paul shifts the concern to right living as people of day and light (5:6–8).

Three key themes seem to emerge in relation to the eschatology of 1 Thessalonians: hope, vigilance and holiness, and divine justice.

HOPE

Again, it is easy to recognize that "hope" (1:3; 2:19; 4:13; 5:8) is a *leitmotif* of 1 Thessalonians.[2] Hope for Paul is not wishful thinking; nor is it stargazing, imagining future worlds and ages. Michael J. Gorman rightly explains that Pauline hope is "anticipatory *participation* in the future, specifically God's eschatological promise of glory."[3] This parousia becomes, then, an occasion when hope is fulfilled; in expectation it increases in urgency when one experiences persecution.

Alexandra Brown nevertheless aptly points out that Paul does not represent the parousia as *the* salvific event.[4] Early on in 1 Thessalonians Paul recounts the work of the Holy Spirit at the Thessalonians' conversion (1:5–6) and the unmistakeable transformation that they underwent as a result of receiving the truth of the gospel (2:13). Paul implies that, whether dead or alive, the Thessalonian believers are identified as "in Christ" (4:16), representing a sense of security.

---

2. See J. Plevnik, *Paul and the Parousia: An Exegetical and Theological Investigation* (Peabody, MA: Hendrickson, 1997), 197–220.

3. Gorman, *Becoming the Gospel*, 100 (emphasis original).

4. A. Brown, "Paul and the Parousia," in *The Return of Jesus in Early Christianity*, ed. J. T. Carroll (Peabody, MA: Hendrickson, 2000), 48.

While Paul inspires their confidence in a guarantee of salvation, salvation is not described in 1 Thessalonians as something completed and in the past but rather as something secured yet awaiting completion (the "hope of salvation," 5:8). Brown sums up well the perspective on salvation offered in 1 Thessalonians: "Having already won cosmic victory through the death and resurrection of Jesus Christ, God will, at Christ's return, make the victory manifest to the whole creation, defeating the enemies of God and bringing their tyranny to an end."[5]

VIGILANCE AND HOLINESS

No doubt the Thessalonians conveyed to Paul questions regarding what things would happen at the end and when they would happen. Paul does offer them some clues, but he places the emphasis on the proper mindset and attitude to have because Jesus will return suddenly, like a thief in the night (5:2).[6] Much like the use of the night-thief image in Matthew 24:43 (cf. Luke 12:39), Paul's concern is with readiness regarding character and obedience (and not necessarily being "in the know").[7]

There is some sense in which Paul sees his role as apostle and "father" to his converts as one of preparing these gentiles for judgment at the parousia. They are called to be "blameless and holy" (3:13), like a perfect offering.[8] James Thompson is right to represent this objective as part of Paul's pastoral mission and ministry. With 1 Thessalonians and Philippians specifically in view, Thompson notes how Paul "articulates a vision of the ultimate outcome of God's work and the community's progress toward that goal."[9] The church is "unfinished business," and Paul sought to shape these believers in preparation for and anticipation of the return of Christ.[10]

DIVINE JUSTICE

Because of the obvious care and concern that Paul expresses in 1 Thessalonians vis-à-vis the persecution and suffering of the believers

---

5. Brown, "Paul and the Parousia," 48; cf. A. Thiselton, *The Living Paul* (Downers Grove, IL: InterVarsity Press, 2009), 135–47, esp. 146–47.

6. See C. D. Stanley, "Who's Afraid of a Thief in the Night?" *NTS* 48.4 (2002): 468–86.

7. On the complicated matter of how Matthew and 1 Thess (and Luke) share this same motif, see März, "Das Gleichnis vom Dieb."

8. See N. K. Gupta, *Worship that Makes Sense to Paul*, BZNW 175 (Berlin: de Gruyter, 2010), 55–60.

9. J. W. Thompson, *Pastoral Ministry according to Paul* (Grand Rapids: Baker, 2006), 59.

10. See too the general discussion on pp. 20–22. For another helpful discussion of how interpreting Paul's eschatology relates to his pastoral ministry, see P. Foster, "The Eschatology of the Thessalonian Correspondence: An Exercise in Pastoral Pedagogy and Constructive Theology," *JSPL* 1.1 (2011): 57–82; cf. Plevnik, *Paul and the Parousia*, 239–43.

in Thessalonica, his appeal to the parousia relates to the ultimate divine recompense.[11] While sometimes it is easy for us today to balk at the notion of final judgment (especially those like me who live relatively comfortable lives with few concerns for wrongs done to them), it can be a real relief to those who long for a world where things are fair. Let us take the word ὀργή, often translated as "wrath." This term occurs three times in 1 Thessalonians (1:10; 2:16; 5:9), all pertaining to divine judgment. We tend to have a knee-jerk negative reaction to this word, perhaps finding it embarrassing that God should seem so volatile. However, Scripture represents divine wrath *not* as unbridled and limitless rage but as a holy *response* to injustice in God's world. Thus, in my own commentary on 1–2 Thessalonians, I chose to translate ὀργή as "anger for justice."[12] According to Paul, believers can look forward to the parousia because on that day of reckoning the world will be restored to a place of peace and prosperity. Brown writes, "Paul points to the parousia of Christ as the culmination of the cosmic struggle when 'every rule, authority, and power' is put under subjection to Christ and, ultimately, under subjection to God who will at last be 'all in all' (1 Cor 15:28)."[13]

Faith(fulness) and Loyalty

Though Pauline scholars debate the ordering of the first two extant letters of Paul, almost all agree that the earliest two letters are 1 Thessalonians and Galatians. And both letters make frequent use of the word πίστις.[14] However, this word is used a bit differently in 1 Thessalonians and pertains to perseverance in light of the persecution and suffering that the Thessalonians were facing.

Paul commends the Thessalonians' πίστις, which inspires their tireless work (1:3). He reminds them of how they embraced the message of the gospel despite opposition, such that their πίστις became well known throughout the region and beyond (1:8). In chapters two and three, Paul expresses his concern that they had become estranged from him; Timothy was sent to check on the Thessalonians and reported back to Paul about

---

11. See Plevnik, *Paul and the Parousia*, 221–27. This relates to Paul's appeal that one must not take justice into his or her own hands because the Lord will pay back wrongdoing (4:6).

12. Gupta, *Thessalonians*.

13. Brown, "Paul and the Parousia," 75; cf. N. T. Wright, *Surprised by Hope: Rethinking Heaven, the Resurrection, and the Mission of the Church* (New York: HarperOne, 2008), 98–108.

14. In 1 Thess, πίστις appears eight times (1 Thess 1:3, 8; 3:2, 5, 6, 7, 10; 5:8); in Galatians, about twenty times (*passim*); compare that to the five occurrences of πίστις in Philippians.

their robust πίστις (3:2), especially how they had resisted the tempter (3:5). They reciprocated Paul's love, and their πίστις brought great comfort to Paul and his apostolic companions (3:6–7). He expressed his ongoing hope for the security of their πίστις (3:10).

Typically πίστις is translated into English as "faith" (so NIV, NRSV, NET, RSV, ASV, KJV). However, it should be recognized that πίστις is a polyvalent word and "faith" is one of several possible nuances. The noun πίστις can cover a range of semantic values from belief to trust to faithfulness and loyalty.[15] How one translates πίστις really depends on the context in which it is used.[16] Beverly Gaventa is undoubtedly correct that what we see in 1 Thessalonians in general is Paul's encouragement to those believers to persevere in the midst of perplexities and afflictions, thus leading the interpreter to the preferred translation of "faithfulness" or "loyalty."[17] The Common English Bible has generally preferred this translation of πίστις, but perhaps to a fault (not discerning carefully when indeed it should be rendered "faith").[18]

This distinction is critically important for the study of a text like 1 Thessalonians because Paul's counsel to a suffering and grieving church was not simply that they ought to have a renewed (doctrinal? cerebral?) "faith" but that they should be commended for fidelity in their ongoing walk with God in hope and love.[19] This comes into more clarity if we compare Paul's language in 1 Thessalonians with the similar encouragement offered to the church of Thyatira in Revelation 2:19: "I know your deeds, your τὴν ἀγάπην καὶ τὴν πίστιν καὶ τὴν διακονίαν καὶ τὴν ὑπομονήν σου" (cf. Rev 13:10). This is obviously a list of virtues that resembles the

---

15. See Crook, *Reconceptualising Conversion*, 199–259; Teresa Morgan, *Roman Faith and Christian Faith: Pistis and Fides in the Early Roman Empire and Early Churches* (Oxford: Oxford University Press, 2015); P. Fredriksen, "Paul's Letter to the Romans, the Ten Commandments, and Pagan 'Justification by Faith,'" *JBL* 133.4 (2014): 801–8; idem, "Judaizing the Nations: The Ritual Demands of Paul's Gospel," *NTS* 56 (2010): 232–52; S. Young, "Paul's Ethnic Discourse on 'Faith': Christ's Faith and Gentile Access to the Judean God in Rom 3:21–5:1," *HTR* 108 (2015): 30–51; K. W. McFadden, "Does Πίστις Mean Faith(fulness) in Paul?" *TynBul* 66.2 (2015): 251–70. For a more popular-level study that addresses these issues, see M. W. Bates, *Salvation by Allegiance Alone: Rethinking Faith, Works, and the Gospel of Jesus the King* (Grand Rapids: Baker, 2017).

16. See A. Thiselton, *The First Epistle to the Corinthians*, NIGTC (Grand Rapids: Eerdmans, 2000), 223.

17. See the helpful discussion of πίστις by M. Barth, *The Letter to Philemon*, ECC (Grand Rapids: Eerdmans, 2000), 273.

18. See the methodological comments by R. B. Hays, "Lost in Translation: A Reflection on Romans in the Common English Bible," in *The Unrelenting God: Essays on God's Action in Scripture in Honor of Beverly Roberts Gaventa*, ed. D. J. Downs and M. L. Skinner (Grand Rapids: Eerdmans, 2013), 83–101; esp. pp. 90–95 where Hays discusses the translation of πίστις in the CEB.

19. See Johnson, *1 and 2 Thessalonians*, 39–40.

commendations given to the Thessalonians, and a translation of πίστις as "faithfulness" in Rev 2:19 would be quite natural (so CEB).

Taking this perspective helps the reader of 1 Thessalonians to see how 1 Thessalonians 5:5–12 offers a kind of *inclusio* with the beginning of the letter. Just as Paul commends the Thessalonians for their steadfastness, loyalty, and love in 1:3, he returns toward the close of the letter to the exhortation that they live as good soldiers who don the breastplate πίστεως καὶ ἀγάπης—again, best rendered "faithfulness and love."

This emphasis in Paul fits into a wider concern in early Christianity for perseverance in persecution and adversity.[20] According to Luke, Jesus taught that followers of Jesus ought to consider themselves blessed "when people hate you, when they exclude you and insult you and reject your name as evil, because of the Son of Man. Rejoice in that day and leap for joy, because great is your reward in heaven. For that is how their ancestors treated the prophets" (Luke 6:22–23). In Acts we learn that a band of persecuted apostles, after being beaten and threatened, left the Sanhedrin with joy because "they had been counted worthy of suffering disgrace for the Name" of Jesus (Acts 5:41). Paul and Barnabas similarly warned some disciples, "We must go through many hardships to enter the kingdom of God" (Acts 14:22). As for Paul, he explains to the Romans that being true children of God is confirmed by sharing in the sufferings of Jesus "in order that we may also share in his glory" (Rom 8:17).

The idea is neither that suffering *earns* salvation nor that God desires to see people suffer as retribution for sin. Rather, the early Christians would have shared the view of many ancient peoples that adversity tests the soul, that suffering leads to maturity. As Charles Talbert's illuminating study *Learning through Suffering* sums up, many ancient Jews and gentiles believed that suffering should be seen as training that leads one to strength and virtue.[21]

Thanksgiving and Joy

Typically Philippians is granted the status of being Paul's most "joyful" letter, especially within the context of his imprisonment and uncertain fate. Nevertheless, 1 Thessalonians also demonstrates a Paul who—despite

---

20. See Pobee, *Persecution and Martyrdom in the Theology of Paul*; L. A. Jervis, *At the Heart of the Gospel* (Grand Rapids: Eerdmans, 2007).

21. See C. Talbert, *Learning through Suffering: The Educational Value of Suffering in the New Testament and Its Milieu* (Collegeville, MN: Liturgical Press, 1991), see a helpful summary on p. 20.

harrowing recent events (see 1 Thess 2:2)—is filled with thanksgiving and joy. Students of 1 Thessalonians often point out the letter's intimate tone and warmth.[22] Paul is thankful for his Thessalonian brothers and sisters who accepted the gospel with joy and faith (1:6; 2:13) and who showed great resilience in affliction (1:2–3). Paul himself rejoiced in their life (2:19–20); they became a source of deep happiness for him (3:9). He passed on a ministry of thanksgiving to them as well (5:18).

On the subject of the "thanksgiving" sections of Paul's letters, P. T. O'Brien's classic study *Introductory Thanksgivings in the Letters of Paul* is still an illuminating work, with some updated discussions since then from others.[23] On the theological theme of thanksgiving in Paul, David Pao offers a comprehensive study.[24]

When it comes to studying the subject of joy in Paul, there are of course some useful thematic studies.[25] In more recent years, scholars have begun to examine emotions in the Bible with attention to emotion studies in psychology, sociology, literary theory, and contemporary philosophy.[26] An important essay, particularly on joy and the New Testament, comes from Stephen Barton, "Spirituality and the Emotions in Early Christianity: The Case of Joy."[27] Barton first offers some insights on the emotion of joy from philosophy, literary theory, and the social sciences. Then he turns to Luke-Acts and Paul. Barton concludes that joy and rejoicing are "among the *pre-eminent* emotions in early Christianity."[28] With the new resurrection life of Jesus, the early Christians discovered a fresh sense of fullness and vitality deep within themselves, something that they communicated with the word "joy."

---

22. See, e.g., Witherington, *Thessalonians*, 28; E. Krentz, "2 Thessalonians," in *The Blackwell Companion to the New Testament*, ed. D. E. Aune (Oxford: Wiley-Blackwell, 2010), 518–19.

23. See especially P. Arzt-Grabner, "Paul's Letter Thanksgiving," in *Paul and the Ancient Letter Form*, ed. S. E. Porter and S. A. Adams, PAST 6 (Leiden: Brill, 2010), 129–58. In the same volume see too Raymond F. Collins, "A Significant Decade: The Trajectory of the Hellenistic Epistolary Thanksgiving," 159–84.

24. D. Pao, *Thanksgiving: An Investigation of a Pauline Theme* (Downers Grove, IL: InterVarsity Press, 2002); see too idem, "Gospel within the Constraints of an Epistolary Form: Pauline Introductory Thanksgivings and Paul's Theology of Thanksgiving," in Porter and Adams, *Paul and the Ancient Letter Form*, 101–28.

25. E.g., R. Kampling, "Freude bei Paulus," *Trierer theologische Zeitschrift* 101 (1992): 69–79.

26. E.g., the Society of Biblical Literature annual meeting and its recent "Bible and Emotions" section.

27. "Spirituality and the Emotions," in *The Bible and Spirituality*, ed. A. T. Lincoln et al. (Eugene, OR: Wipf & Stock, 2013), 171–93.

28. Barton, "Spirituality and the Emotions," 178.

Metamorphosis

It is not typical for scholars to identify a theme of "transformation"[29] or "metamorphosis" in 1 Thessalonians (or any of Paul's letters for that matter), but perhaps such a consideration can be entertained based on the use of the word γίνομαι in 1 Thessalonians. Paul employs this verb twelve times in this letter (four times in 1:5–7). The Thessalonians *became* imitators of the apostles and the Lord Jesus (1:6; 2:14). They *became* an example for the Macedonians and Achaians (1:7). The apostles *became* holy and blameless among them (2:10). One way in which Paul uses the word γίνομαι in 1 Thessalonians is to demonstrate Christian integrity and maturity, the transformation into something better, just as we expect in light of a text like 2 Corinthians 3:18: "And we all, who with unveiled faces contemplate the Lord's glory, are being transformed into his image with ever-increasing glory, which comes from the Lord, who is the Spirit." Paul here is expressing that as believers are gravitationally pulled into the orbit of God's grace and sanctifying power, they are reshaped into "the image of [God's] Son" (Rom 8:29).

This can make it seem like Paul's vision of the Christian life is simply one of glorious transformation, like an unassuming caterpillar becoming a beautiful butterfly. However, a glorious transformation is not the *only* kind of change that Paul expects believers to undergo. In several of his letters, including 1 Thessalonians, Paul notes that in a sinful, hostile world, another kind of "becoming" emerges where believers must *become* something less glorious in the eyes of the world. When writing to the Corinthians, he told them that he had to suffer, becoming (γίνομαι) like garbage in the world's eyes in order to bring them the gospel (1 Cor 4:13). There is, then, an ignoble transformation that must happen when one identifies with the gospel of the humble Christ, the Christ of the cross. Thus Paul tells the proud Corinthians who mock Paul's grotesque and morbid ministry: "Death is at work in us, but life is at work in you" (2 Cor 4:12). We can see this modeled by Jesus in Philippians 2:5–11 where the text states that he took upon himself the humble station of a human who had to face the degradation of death on a cross (Phil 2:8).

This may be what Paul means when he tells the Thessalonians that he *became* an infant (see below on pp. 106–14) when he was with them (2:7b).

---

29. Although see the excellent study by D. deSilva, *Transformation: The Heart of Paul's Gospel* (Bellingham, WA: Lexham, 2014).

In this context, the implication is that becoming a νήπιος would not come naturally to Paul. For the sake of the Thessalonians, Paul had to undergo a change, a *metamorphosis*, but not always into something more attractive from a worldly perspective. Yet this *becoming* is inspired by Christ and empowered by the Spirit.[30]

Work and Labor

Above we treated the subject of faith(fulness) and loyalty (πίστις) and touched on the relationship in 1 Thessalonians between faith and work. Here we give some space to the latter subject as a theme. In popular reflections on Paul's theology, the apostle is sometimes represented as being "anti-works," often with appeal to a text like Galatians 2:16 ("a person is not justified by the works of the law but by faith in Jesus Christ"; cf. Rom 3:27–28; 4:5). In 1 Thessalonians we see no such faith/works dichotomy. In fact, Paul treats πίστις and ἔργον as if they exist in a healthy relationship, πίστις demonstrating itself in ἔργον (1 Thess 1:3).[31]

In addition to some more abstract ways that Paul talks about work (e.g., 2:13, the work of the word of God in believers), 1 Thessalonians places special emphasis on laborious human work. Beginning in 1 Thessalonians 2:9, Paul mentions the way that he toiled (in manual labor) night and day "in order not to be a burden to anyone while we preached the gospel of God to you."[32] The language Paul uses here of "labor" (κόπος) connotes difficult or tedious work, work that saps energy and strength (especially when it is combined with μόχθος as it is here).

Some of this emphasis in 1 Thessalonians seems to be apologetic, a defense of the integrity of the apostolic ministry among the Thessalonians. Paul and his fellow apostles were not hucksters looking to take advantage of them. Furthermore, they did not want to pose a financial burden on them, even though taking support from them was considered to be an acceptable practice for the apostles (cf. 1 Cor 9:11–15). Nevertheless, Paul also seemed to be raising the matter of his own self-sustaining labor

---

30. There are some important connections here to Morna Hooker's work on interchange; see *From Adam to Christ* (Eugene, OR: Wipf & Stock, 1990), in particular the chapters "Interchange and Suffering" (42–55) and "Interchange in Christ and Ethics" (55–72). See too the relevant work by M. J. Gorman on transformation in Paul from the perspective of theosis entitled *Inhabiting the Cruciform God: Kenosis, Justification, and Theosis in Paul's Narrative* (Grand Rapids: Eerdmans, 2009).

31. Truth be told, though, those who see Galatians as setting up a works/faith dichotomy trip over Paul's statement in Gal 5:6 (where "faith" "works").

32. The matter comes up again in 2 Thess (3:8); we will treat this theme again on p. 236.

as a model for these Thessalonian believers. In 4:11 he exhorts them to "lead a quiet life . . . mind your own business and work with your hands," something he apparently taught them previously.[33] There have been robust discussions about how Paul's work practices give clues toward his social status and attitudes toward social status, but our concern here is simply the theme of work and labor in 1 Thessalonians.[34]

The study of a Christian theology of work has grown in the last few decades, with many offerings from theologians,[35] and a few from biblical scholars.[36] Those biblical scholars who have tried to discover a theology of work in Scripture have often come to the honest conclusion that there is no overt discussion of this in the Bible, except that labor is a reality of life. As Shillington admits, "Work is necessary for physical human life in the present scheme of things. . . . To be sure we should thank God for the ability to work; for skills to build structures and talents to create art; thank him also for the soil, the rain, the sun, and the generative process; but the labor is ours. Without it we perish."[37]

Despite the lackluster reality of this statement, Shillington touches on that notion of perseverance and integrity that is indicative of Paul's attitude

---

33. We will address the various arguments for the proper context and meaning of 4:11 below (see pp. 130–39).

34. On the sociohistorical discussion, see especially R. Hock, *The Social Context of Paul's Ministry: Tentmaking and Apostleship* (Philadelphia: Fortress, 1980), as well as his most recent offering on the subject, "The Problem of Paul's Social Class: Further Reflections," in *Paul's World*, ed. S. E. Porter, PAST 4 (Leiden: Brill, 2008), 7–18; see T. Still's engagement with Hock and this topic in "Did Paul Loathe Manual Labor? Revisiting the Work of Ronald F. Hock on the Apostle's Tentmaking and Social Class," *JBL* 125.4 (2006): 781–95.

35. See M. Volf, *Work in the Spirit: Toward a Theology of Work* (Oxford: Oxford University Press, 1991); R. P. Stevens, *The Other Six Days: Vocation, Work, and Ministry in Biblical Perspective* (Grand Rapids: Eerdmans, 2000); D. Cosden, *The Heavenly Good of Earthly Work* (Peabody, MA: Hendrickson, 2006); cf. R. O. Bystrom, "God as Worker: How It Affects Life and Ministry," *Direction* 32.2 (2003): 166–72; for an insightful "reception" perspective see J. Ellul, "From the Bible to a History of Non-Work," *Cross Currents* (1985): 43–48 (trans. D. Lovekin).

36. E.g., B. Witherington, *Work* (Grand Rapids: Eerdmans, 2011); also C. vom Brocke, "Work in the New Testament and in Greco-Roman Antiquity," in *Dignity of Work*, ed. K. Mtata (Minneapolis: Lutheran University Press, 2011), 23–34. This short chapter covers broadly the NT and the first-century context, where Brocke argues that Greeks and Romans carried an "ideal image" of the free citizen who "did not depend on income produced by the work of his own hands, but rather, was able to use others (mainly slaves) to work for him, while he in his leisure time took an active part in the political activities of his city" (25). Of course, as Brocke notes, common people had to depend on manual labor for work. Still, this Greco-Roman image became a kind of cultural dream, one even shared by some Jewish writers (27). Whether with Paul or other NT figures, Brocke concludes that there does not appear to be a unique "theology of work" articulated. Nevertheless, work is apparently conceived of as "a necessary activity whose objective it is to ensure one's own livelihood and to succor—when necessary—neighbors in need. It is precisely this aspect that differentiated early Christianity from its Greco-Roman context" (34).

37. V. G. Shillington, "A New Testament Perspective on Work," *Conrad Grabel Review* 10 (1992): 139–55.

in 1 Thessalonians regarding work: "Work is a necessary and proper part of the social conventions while God works out his purpose for history. Until the plan of God is complete, history continues, and the necessary convention of the human experience of work continues as well."[38]

Another kind of "work" that is discussed in 1 Thessalonians is the work of ministry. In passing, Paul mentions that he sent Timothy to check on the Thessalonians, especially their ongoing commitment to the gospel and their love and concern for Paul, because Paul was afraid they might be weakening in faith, which would mean that "our labors [κόπος] might have been in vain" (3:5). Furthermore, toward the end of the letter, in Paul's final instructions, he requests of the Thessalonian believers that they "acknowledge those who work hard among you [τοὺς κοπιῶντας ἐν ὑμῖν], who care for you in the Lord and who admonish you" (5:12; cf. 5:13). There are many insightful books on Paul's theology of the work of ministry,[39] but it is worth noting here in 1 Thessalonians that Paul does not use a separate, spiritual, or professional vocabulary for the work of ministry. Rather, the word κόπος (and its cognates) can refer to any kind of labor for Paul, whether ministry or otherwise.[40]

Holiness, Purity, and Integrity

Despite the fact that Paul does *not* refer to the believers in Thessalonica as ἅγιοι, still there is a prominent emphasis in 1 Thessalonians on holiness and purity (and the related notion of integrity). Holiness is a concept central to Israel's religious imagination and is imprinted deeply within the Old Testament. One of the key moments in the story of Israel comes when they are freed from slavery in Egypt so that they might worship YHWH. The Lord pronounces over Israel the vocation of being a "kingdom of priests and a holy nation" (Exod 19:6). The notion of Israel being a holy nation involves being set apart from the other nations for a special relationship with God and to be transformed by this unique association. This idea of

---

38. Shillington, "New Testament Perspective on Work," 152.

39. See, e.g., Thompson, *Pastoral Ministry according to Paul*; cf. idem., "Paul as Missionary Pastor," in *Paul as Missionary*, ed. T. Burke and B. Rosner (London: T&T Clark, 2011), 25–36; also D. L. Bartlett, *Ministry in the New Testament* (Philadelphia: Fortress, 1993); E. Peterson, "Pastor Paul," in *Romans and the People of God*, ed. S. Soderlund and N. T. Wright (Grand Rapids: Eerdmans, 1999), 283–94; J. Weima, "Infants, Nursing Mother, and Father: Paul's Portrayal of a Pastor," *CTJ* 37.2 (2002): 209–29; A. D. Clarke, *A Pauline Theology of Church Leadership* (London: T&T Clark, 2008); J. Lo, "Pastoral Theology in the Letters of Paul: The Basis for Paul's Pastoral Responsibility," *Hill Road* 17.2 (2014): 25–50.

40. Cf. Rom 16:6, 9, 12; 1 Cor 3:8–9; 16:16; 1 Tim 5:17.

holiness also includes being so identified with God's own identity and purpose that Israel is absorbed into the work of God to bless the world (hence the idea of being a "priestly" kingdom, i.e., performing a vicarious ministry).[41]

In 1 Thessalonians, Paul presents the Thessalonians in a way remarkably like how Israel is portrayed in the Old Testament. Paul reminds them how they are "beloved by God" and how "he has chosen you" (1 Thess 1:4 NRSV). Not only does this seem to echo Exodus 19:5–6 ("out of all nations you will be my treasured possession"), but perhaps more closely it compares to Isaiah 44:1–2:

> But now listen, Jacob, my servant, Israel, whom I have chosen. This is what the LORD says—he who made you, who formed you in the womb, and who will help you: Do not be afraid, Jacob, my servant, Jeshurun, whom I have chosen.[42]

No doubt Paul's concern is similar to that of Isaiah 44, reminding God's people regarding their "holy" status and that they are precious and uniquely close to God and cared for by him. Therefore, Paul does indeed portray the Thessalonians as those who have a holy status without actually calling them ἅγιοι.[43]

Paul also calls the Thessalonians to live out holy lives, and this is an expectation, even a *demand* for God's people, particularly in light of the parousia. In a rather pointed manner, Paul tells the Thessalonians that God's will for them is their sanctification or consecration (ὁ ἁγιασμὸς ὑμῶν; 4:3b). He immediately goes on to define this ἁγιασμός in terms of sexual integrity, "that you keep away from sexual immorality" (NET 4:3c). In Roman and Greek religion in general, one's "religious views" hardly affected one's sexual practices.[44] Paul's response and challenge to the Thessalonians is that the living God that rescued them in Jesus Christ expects consecration and exclusive devotion to him. Paul reminds them that their lives must be directed toward pleasing God (4:1). Knowing God—and

---

41. For theoretical discussions about Paul's use of holiness imagery and metaphors, see my *Worship That Makes Sense to Paul*, 40–42.

42. For further exposition of 1 Thess 1:4, see Gupta, *Thessalonians*, 43–44.

43. Notice, though, how Paul treats these *gentile* Thessalonian believers as those who "know better" about how to live to please God, unlike "the pagans, who do not know God" (4:5).

44. See L. Hurtado, *Destroyer of the Gods: Early Christian Distinctiveness in the Roman World* (Waco, TX: Baylor University Press, 2016), 143–81.

being known by God in Christ—has freed them from slavery to their own lustful passions (4:5).

In 4:7 Paul offers an important clue to his understanding of his own ministry as well as to his soteriology: "For God did not call us to be impure, but to live a holy life." Given the context, this seems to mean that the Thessalonian believers are called to purity in their relationships (4:6). Again, this would be something particularly difficult for those from a pagan background to understand.

In Paul's final exhortations, he adds this prayer: "May God himself, the God of peace, sanctify you through and through. May your whole spirit, soul and body be kept blameless at the coming of our Lord Jesus Christ" (5:23; cf. 1 Thess 3:13). The language Paul uses here makes it sound as if these Thessalonian believers will be presented to God as a sacrifice, and thus they must be without blemish ("blameless") and set apart ("sancti-f[ied]").[45] The holiness and purity imagery of 1 Thessalonians is ultimately about the expectation God has that his people will be like him, set apart and displaying his own character as a testimony to his glory in the world.[46]

Love

It might be easy to overlook "love" (especially ἀγάπη and its cognates) as an important theological theme, either because of Christian familiarity with this word or because it appears in all of Paul's letters. But when we read 1 Thessalonians by itself, the emphasis Paul places on love should be obvious. The language of love appears eight times in this letter overall, and it appears in every single chapter.

In chapter one, Paul commends the Thessalonians for their "labor of love" (NRSV), that is, labor driven by their deep love for God. For Paul, love is not a fleeting or shallow emotion but rather (to borrow the words of V. P. Furnish) "a total disposition of one's life that involves deliberate choice and determined effort."[47] No doubt for Paul Christian love is responsive. Christians can love because God has taught them to love. Hence, in 1:4 Paul calls the Thessalonian believers "brothers and sisters beloved by God [NRSV; ἀδελφοὶ ἠγαπημένοι ὑπὸ θεοῦ]." Also in 1:4 Paul reminds the Thessalonians that their response to the gospel shows their connection to

---

45. See Gupta, *Worship That Makes Sense to Paul*, 55–59.

46. See A. Johnson, *Holiness and the Missio Dei* (Eugene, OR: Wipf & Stock, 2016).

47. V. P. Furnish, *1 and 2 Thessalonians*, ANTC (Nashville: Abingdon, 2007), 42; as cited in A. Johnson, *1 and 2 Thessalonians*, 40.

God through Jesus and God's election of them (τὴν ἐκλογὴν ὑμῶν). This language is not about predestination but more about the active participation of God in reaching out to them, a demonstration and reaffirmation of his careful "choice" and love for them.

The love God showed to the Thessalonians is modeled in the apostles in their ministry to them. In chapter two Paul divulges that he and his companions went above and beyond merely sharing a message; they shared their *lives* (τὰς ἑαυτῶν ψυχάς), because, literally, "you became beloved to us" (ἀγαπητοὶ ἡμῖν ἐγενήθητε, 2:8). In light of the way 2:8 parallels 1:4 in wording, I do not believe it is going too far to say that Paul was communicating that he fell in love with them the way *God* did.

In chapter three, Paul recounts how he feared for the Thessalonians' well-being after his sudden departure. He sent Timothy for a report, and Paul was overwhelmed by the "good news about your faith and love" (εὐαγγελισαμένου ἡμῖν τὴν πίστιν καὶ τὴν ἀγάπην, 3:6). Here we see a complement to 1:3. In chapter one Paul refers to the Thessalonians' love *for God*, and in 3:6 Paul addresses their love *for Paul*, remembering and longing to see him. Yet then later in chapter three, Paul offers a prayer for their ongoing and increasing love for one another, imitating the way Paul has loved them (v. 12).

In chapter four, Paul goes out of his way to make a special topic of φιλαδελφία ("sibling-love"). Paul affirms that they need not be instructed in detail on this, because they have been "taught by God" (θεοδίδακτοι, 4:9). Still, he offers a word of encouragement that they have come to show their love toward all the brothers and sisters in Macedonia, and they should press forward to do so even more (v. 10).

The language of φιλαδελφία here at 4:9 is remarkable, since this term was not often used for people that were not biologically siblings.[48] The sibling-bond associated with early Christian fellowship became a mainstay in Christian ecclesiology, so much so that Marcus Cornelius Fronto (in the second century) criticized Christians in this way: "They recognize each other by secret marks and signs; hardly have they met when they love each other, throughout the world uniting in the practice of a veritable religion of lusts. Indiscriminately they call each other brother and sister, thus turning even ordinary fornication into incest by the intervention of these hallowed

---

48. R. Aasgaard notes the relative rarity of this word in Greek literature, extant use numbering less than a dozen times; see R. Aasgard, *My Beloved Brothers and Sisters: Christian Siblingship in Paul*, JSNTSup 265 (London: T&T Clark, 2004), 151.

names."[49] Minucius Felix offered this response to Fronto: "It is true that we do love one another—a fact that you deplore—since we do not know how to hate. Hence it is true that we call one another brother—a fact which rouses your spleen—because we are men of the one and same God the Father, copartners in faith, coheirs in hope."[50]

What does the use of the word φιλαδελφία mean for Christian theology? It is certainly an indication of the power of the kinship metaphor and imagery in relation to the people that make up the church. Paul makes it clear that believers have been adopted into God's family through God's (only) Son, Jesus Christ (Rom 8:29). Looking at an important essay by Plutarch called *De fraterno amore* ("On sibling-love"), we come to learn how in the Greco-Roman world claiming a family bond implied a special obligation to care for and protect the other.[51]

Joseph Hellerman adds to our understanding of Greco-Roman sibling relations from the perspective of honor and shame. In Paul's world, there was a general expectation that people would compete for honor to bring glory to their own family and clan. However, within a family there existed a different mentality. According to Hellerman, "The honor game was off-limits."[52] Rather, family members sought to *honor* members of their own family and defer to them.[53] David deSilva furthermore explains that even within a family the sibling relationship "is the closest, strongest and most intimate of relationships in the ancient world."[54] Thus, this background would all the more short-circuit any competitiveness between believers and suspicion against believers who differed in terms of ethnicity or status.

All this helps to put Paul's theology of love into perspective. At the end of the letter, the apostle calls on the Thessalonians to don the armor of vigilant loyalty, including the breastplate of "faith and love" (5:8). This clearly serves as an *inclusio* that is meant to reinforce the affirmation of their "work of faith" and "labor of love" mentioned in 1:3 (cf. NRSV).

---

49. See Minucius Felix, *Oct.* 8–9 (from *Tertullian: Apologetical Works and Minucius Felix: Octavius*, trans. E. J. Daly, R. Arbesmann, and E. A. Quain [New York: Fathers of the Church, 1950]).

50. See *Oct.* 31.18 (*The Octavius of Marcus Minucius Felix*, trans. Graeme Clarke, Ancient Christian Writers 39 [New York: Newman, 1974]).

51. Aasgaard further explains that in Plutarch's view sibling-love was characterized by "tolerance, loyalty, and forgiveness" (*My Beloved Brothers and Sisters*, 106).

52. J. Hellerman, *Embracing Shared Ministry: Power and Status in the Early Church and Why It Matters Today* (Grand Rapids: Kregel, 2013), 186.

53. See J. Hellerman, "Brothers and Friends in Philippi: Family Honor in the Roman World and in Paul's Letter to the Philippians," *BTB* 39.1 (2009): 16.

54. D. deSilva, *Honor, Patronage, Kinship, and Purity* (Downers Grove, IL: InterVarsity Press, 2000), 166.

Lastly, Paul encourages the Thessalonians to treat those who have charge of and lead them with the utmost respect and love, though not because of their status but because of their commitment to the work of the church (5:12–13a). Ultimately this kinship love expected of believers is meant to lead to a peaceful community (5:13b).

Study of the topic of love in Paul is sparse in scholarship except when it appears in wider discussions of his ethics.[55] Some key studies on Paul's theology of love include Thomas Söding, *Das Liebesgebot bei Paulus*,[56] and the relevant sections on love in Michael Gorman's works *Cruciformity* and *Becoming the Gospel*.[57]

Christian Tradition and Teachings

When one thinks of the concept of traditions and the passing down of inherited, authoritative teachings, very few think of Paul, at least not the "early Paul." Paul is generally conceived of as a free thinker, a ground-breaking theologian, and a maverick apostle. For example, in the beginning of Galatians Paul underscores the notion that he was not educated as a believer in a particular apostolic school, but rather his authority came directly from Christ (Gal 1:1, 10–12). Nevertheless, it should be rather obvious that Paul *must* have received teachings and traditions that laid out the foundation of his understanding of the gospel (see Gal 1:18–19).

One might presume then that an early letter like 1 Thessalonians would possibly ignore or even eschew such traditions, but the opposite seems to be true. On several occasions Paul refers to inherited traditions and general Christian teaching in a positive manner. This comes out most clearly in chapter four.

As for other matters, brothers and sisters, we instructed you how to live in order to please God, as in fact you are living. Now we ask you and urge you in the Lord Jesus to do this more and more. For you know what instructions we gave you by the authority of the Lord Jesus. (1 Thess 4:1–2)

---

55. E.g., see D. Horrell, *Solidarity and Difference: A Contemporary Reading of Paul's Ethics*, 2nd ed. (London: T&T Clark, 2015); J. P. Sampley, *Walking in Love: Moral Progress and Spiritual Growth with the Apostle Paul* (Minneapolis: Fortress, 2016).

56. T. Söding, *Das Liebesgebot bei Paulus: Die Mahnung zur Agape im Rahmen der paulinischen Ethik*, NTAbh 26 (Münster: Aschendorff, 1995).

57. *Cruciformity: Paul's Narrative Spirituality of the Cross* (Grand Rapids: Eerdmans, 2001), 63–74, and *Becoming the Gospel*, 63–105, respectively.

Not long after writing these words, Paul mentions that calling for mutual love is not explicitly necessary because they are "taught by God" (4:9). Almost certainly this should not be taken at face value to mean that there was no need for teachings and traditions. Rather, Paul seems to be saying that they already have taken this expectation to heart (presumably having *already* been instructed in love previously). Another place where previous instruction is brought up is 4:6, where the Thessalonians are reminded how they have been taught not to take revenge, knowing that the Lord is attentive to injustice. On the topic of tradition in the New Testament, the recent book by Edith Humphrey, *Scripture and Tradition*, is highly recommended. Humphrey notes how Protestant English translations tend to refuse to refer to good Christian teaching as "traditions," choosing instead to represent any *negative* references to traditions using such terminology. Yet she observes that on several occasions Paul does indeed appeal positively to traditions that should be passed down.[58]

INTERPRETIVE ISSUES IN 1 THESSALONIANS

In the study of 1 Thessalonians, there are five major interpretive challenges related to the following texts: 2:7b, 2:13–16, 4:4, 4:11, and 5:3. We will discuss these below.

Infants or Gentle? (2:7b)

This verse from 1 Thessalonians includes one of the most discussed and debated text-critical issues in the whole of the New Testament. The verse is as follows:

δυνάμενοι ἐν βάρει εἶναι ὡς Χριστοῦ ἀπόστολοι. ἀλλ᾿ ἐγενήθημεν [νήπιοι/ἤπιοι] ἐν μέσῳ ὑμῶν, ὡς ἐὰν τροφὸς θάλπῃ τὰ ἑαυτῆς τέκνα

The word in question here is either νήπιοι ("infants") or ἤπιοι ("gentle").[59] As is well recognized in scholarship, there is significant extant Greek

---

58. E. Humphrey, *Scripture and Tradition: What the Bible Really Says* (Grand Rapids: Baker, 2013).

59. As S. Fowl points out, a similar textual problem appears in 2 Tim 2:24 where, in that case, ἤπιον is the preferred reading, though some manuscripts have νήπιον; see S. Fowl, "A Metaphor in Distress: A Reading of νήπιοι in 1 Thessalonians 2.7," *NTS* 36.3 (1990): 469–73.

manuscript support for both readings.[60] The latter boasts the support of numerous manuscripts, mostly medieval minuscules, though a few early manuscripts as well (ℵ^c A Ψ^c). The former enjoys the support of 𝔓^{65}, ℵ*, B, C, and D* (and also several minuscules). Few scholars doubt that νήπιοι carries stronger external support (see pp. 21–22). Nevertheless, a case could be made that early νήπιοι support is simply a mistake or deviation from a (hypothetically) *earlier* reading of ἤπιοι. The role of the text critic is to consider the ways in which a variant reading came to be.

One route has been to consider the variant to be a scribal error, a serious possibility since the difference is a mere letter (ν). Given the phrase ἐγενήθημεν (ν)ηπιοι ἐν μέσῳ ὑμῶν, it is imaginable that a scribe was guilty of haplography, with an original text reading ἐγενήθημεν νήπιοι ἐν μέσῳ ὑμῶν and the scribe writing ἤπιοι instead (the scribe assuming that he had *already* written the ν of νήπιοι). Alternatively, it could be a case of dittography, the scribe seeing ΕΓΕΝΗΘΗΜΕΝΗΠΙΟΙ and associating the "N" with ΗΠΙΟΙ instead of ΕΓΕΝΗΘΗΜΕΝ. There is no compelling reason to imagine that either haplography or dittography was more likely to occur, all things being equal.

Text critics, translators, and commentators have spent more of their energy considering how one reading or the other might make better sense of Paul's argumentation here. First, we will consider the basic arguments of those who decide in favor of the ἤπιοι reading. Then we will do the same for the νήπιοι reading. Finally, we will consider insights and discussion from recent research.

Most late twentieth-century treatments of 1 Thessalonians 2:7b have preferred the ἤπιοι variant as original.[61] In 1983, for example, I. H. Marshall offered the explanation that Paul employed the adjective ἤπιοι, but given that it is an uncommon word (see 2 Tim 2:24, the only other NT occurrence), a scribe confused it with the more popular word νήπιοι (used often by Paul; e.g., Rom 2:20; 1 Cor 3:1; 13:11; Gal 4:1, 3).[62]

---

60. Codex Augiensis (ninth century) attests to a spelling variation, νεπιοι.

61. See Malherbe, *Thessalonians*, 145, and the comment by Fowl in 1990 ("Distress," 469): "Almost all of the major commentators on this text read ἤπιοι, 'gentle'"; cf. B. Rigaux, *Les Épitres aux Thessaloniciens* (Paris: Gabalda, 1956); W. Marxsen, *Der erste Brief an die Thessalonicher* (Zürich: Theologischer, 1979); Richard, *First and Second Thessalonians*. Furthermore, as Controzzi explains (in 1999) in his examination of twenty-seven European-language translations of the Bible, only *two* represent (and thus prefer) the νήπιοι reading (S. Controzzi, "1 Thes 2:7—A Review," *Filologia Neotestamentaria* 12.23–24 (1999): 155.

62. Marshall, *1 and 2 Thessalonians*, 70. Coulet is a rare twenty-first century advocate of the ἤπιοι reading (2006), though he gives no direct defense and merely appeals to the arguments of S. Légasse,

Some have rejected the νήπιοι reading, giving the explanation that Paul tends to use νήπιος only with a negative connotation (as in 1 Cor 3:1). That is, Paul did not use νήπιος in his other letters to refer to infants in a neutral manner, but rather to refer to those who were immature. For example, George Milligan, finding the νήπιοι reading interpretively weak compared to ἤπιοι, mentions that if νήπιοι did somehow prove to be original it could only (uncomfortably) be understood as Paul implying that he had to resort to "baby-language to those who were still babes in the faith."[63] Similarly, Stefan Controzzi reasons, "So, by putting himself on a level with his Thessalonian converts, Paul would implicitly call himself and his readers immature and inexperienced, and that does not seem likely in the present context."[64] Important pushback has come from those who urge that in several instances Paul's use of νήπιος is neutral, referring to a younger stage of life, not to immaturity specifically, as in Galatians 4:1–3 and Romans 2:20.[65]

By far the most common concern *against* the νήπιοι reading (and in favor of ἤπιοι) is the problem of how Paul appears to be mixing metaphors and thus the confusion caused by his flow of thought. As Ernest Best explains, "'Infant' requires a sudden inversion of metaphor in the next clause and though Paul can change his metaphors rapidly (2 Cor 3:13–16; Rom 7:1ff) this is no argument that he would have done so here; gentle fits appropriately with the defence Paul puts up in vv. 5, 6, contrasting vividly with 'exploit.'"[66] Charles Wanamaker adds to this line of thought the way "gentle" fits as a contrast with ἐν βάρει εἶναι that comes before and is in alignment with the image of the "caring nurse" that follows.[67]

Les épitres de Paul aux Thessaloniciens (Paris: Cerf, 1999), 124; see Coulet, "Paul à Thessalonique (1Th 2.1–12)," 377–93.

63. G. Milligan, *Thessalonians*, 21, following Augustine.

64. Controzzi, "1 Thes 2:7," 157. Nevertheless, Controzzi himself is convinced based on external manuscript support that νήπιοι is the right reading; he urges that νήπιοι cannot mean "innocent" (babies) here (based on Pauline usage of the word elsewhere), but can mean "humble" (babies); see pp. 159–60.

65. See J. H. McNeel, *Paul as Infant and Nursing Mother: Metaphor, Rhetoric, and Identity in 1 Thessalonians 2:5–8* (Atlanta: SBL Press, 2014), 39.

66. Best, *Thessalonians*, 101; cf. Bruce, *Thessalonians*, 31.

67. Wanamaker, *Thessalonians*, 100. M. Holmes is one of the only experts in textual criticism that I could find that supports the ἤπιοι reading. Holmes acknowledges that νήπιοι has strong manuscript support, but because of the possibility of a "scribal slip," the external evidence "is of little help." Instead Holmes urges that the "most decisive consideration" is the structure of 1 Thess 2:5–8, where a set of three contrasts expect that the first item in 2:7–8 will pertain to "means or motive." And in the case of the variant readings, this favors ἤπιοι; see M. W. Holmes, *1 & 2 Thessalonians*, NIVAC (Grand Rapids: Zondervan, 1998), 64.

While it will become clear that I myself favor the νήπιοι reading, the fact should be noted that the preponderence of interest and argumentation in the last couple of decades has shifted in support of νήπιοι. We will consider these arguments with three key points in view. First, the external evidence (i.e., the superiority of the manuscript witnesses in favor of νήπιοι) should outweigh concerns regarding internal "coherence." Second, studies of metaphors in the New Testament have been written in recent years, many specifically on Paul, and these open up fresh ways of thinking about Paul's style of communication. Third, a reconsideration of punctuation and proper clausal division could weaken the ostensible awkwardness of the mixed metaphors.

It is helpful to begin with Timothy B. Sailor's important 2000 article, "Wedding Textual and Rhetorical Criticism to Understand the Text of 1 Thessalonians 2.7."[68] Sailors begins by rehearsing the text-critical discussion, concluding as most scholars do regardless of which reading they prefer, that νήπιοι is transparently favored as "older, at least as widely attested geographically, and much more widely attested among the textual families than ἤπιοι."[69]

With respect to *transcriptional* tendencies, Sailors briefly addresses the notion that scribes tended to replace unfamiliar words with more common ones. He dismisses this concern, since both words in question were well known at the time (or perhaps more accurately, neither was notably *uncommon*).[70] Second, Sailors rules the principle of *lectio brevior* to be irrelevant. Third, Sailors addresses the more pressing matter of *lectio difficilior* (all things being equal, a scribe is more likely to alter an unclear or "difficult" text; thus the more "difficult" reading is probably earlier).[71] Sailors argues that ἤπιοι has been preferred by translators and commentators *because* it is

---

68. T. B. Sailors, "Wedding Textual and Rhetorical Criticism to Understand the Text of 1 Thessalonians 2.7," *JSNT* 80 (2000): 91–98.

69. Sailors, "Wedding Textual Criticism," 85.

70. Sailors, "Wedding Textual Criticism," 86.

71. The longer explanation of this principle articulated by S. E. Porter and A. W. Pitts is helpful for the sake of clarity: "The reading that appears initially to be difficult to grasp, but when studied in greater detail makes good sense, is probably closer to the original. The logic behind this principle is that scribes tended to correct/change what was difficult for them." Porter and Pitts add the important qualification that this principle does *not* apply when a variant is so difficult as to be completely nonsensical (which then implies that the introduction of an error has occurred): "So if a reading is most difficult because it makes no sense, that reading is not likely original even though it may be the most difficult reading." See *Fundamentals of New Testament Textual Criticism* (Grand Rapids: Eerdmans, 2015), 116–17. The earliest expression of this principle I could find comes from J. S. Porter, *Principles of Textual Criticism* (London: Simms and M'Intyre, 1848), 34.

such a smooth reading of 1 Thessalonians 2:1–12, but that makes νήπιοι the more difficult reading.

Sailors adds a second piece to his argumentation in favor of the νήπιοι reading: insight from rhetorical criticism in terms of both lexis (word choice) and synthesis. As for the former, Sailors notes that νήπιος could be used to emphasize, not the immaturity of babies, but their innocence. According to Sailors, Paul could leverage this metaphor because babies do not seek to flatter or deceive; thus they are not seekers of status.[72] Thus, Sailors pushes against the perspective of those who insist that Paul would not apply to *himself* a term (νήπιος) that he tends to use pejoratively.[73] Sailors explains, "An examination of the term in literature from the first centuries BCE and CE shows that the vast majority of the time (75%) it is used as a neutral, purely descriptive term meaning 'infant.'"[74]

Regarding the other element of Sailor's appeal to rhetorical criticism, synthesis (arrangement of clauses/sentences; e.g., syntax, literary structure), Sailors supports the notion that Paul's flow of thought and argumentation would make good sense with the νήπιοι reading if there was a "high-point" (a full stop or period) between 7b and 7c. (Fee strongly supports this clausal break, and we will offer Fee's explanation in more detail below.) Furthermore, Sailors, tracing Paul's line of reasoning, posits that the metaphor of infants/babies in 2:7b "argues for the moral impunity of Paul and his coworkers," and the second image of τροφός (a nurse or mother) focuses more on how they openly shared their lives with the Thessalonian believers.[75] This rhetorical analysis is intended to diffuse the argument that using νήπιοι would make Paul guilty of offering "mixed metaphors"; rather, Sailors urges, it should perhaps be seen as "peculiar adjacent metaphors."[76]

The same year that Sailors published his article on 1 Thessalonians 2:7b, Jeffrey Weima presented his perspective on the matter in "'But We Became Infants Among You': The Case for ΝΗΠΙΟΙ in 1 Thess 2.7."[77] In terms of external evidence, Weima covers essentially the same ground that

---

72. "Wedding Textual Criticism," 90. See Plutarch, *Mor.* 1045A; Diodorus Siculus, *Hist.* 20.72.2; Philo, *Joseph* 225.6; Josephus, *Ant.* 6.138; *J.W.* 3.304; 3.337.

73. See Wanamaker, *Thessalonians*, 100.

74. Sailors, "Wedding Textual Criticism," 91.

75. "Wedding Textual Criticism," 97.

76. "Wedding Textual Criticism," 97.

77. J. Weima, "'But We Became Infants Among You': The Case for ΝΗΠΙΟΙ in 1 Thess 2.7," *NTS* 46.4 (2000): 547–64.

Sailors does. Weima notes that the 𝔓⁶⁵ attestation to νήπιοι comes about two entire centuries earlier than the earliest witness to ἤπιοι (i.e., Alexandrinus).[78] Weima underscores too that it should be taken for granted (but currently is not fully appreciated) that the external evidence ought to outweigh internal considerations from a methodological standpoint.[79]

In terms of internal considerations, Weima begins by refuting four common arguments in favor of ἤπιοι. First, could the νήπιοι reading be accounted for by dittography? Weima counterbalances that with the equal possibility of haplography. Second, did a scribe seek to replace the less common word ἤπιοι with the more common νήπιοι? Following a similar line of thought as Sailors, Weima reasons that neither word, generally speaking, has the advantage of being more familiar according to the evidence. A more formidable argument in Weima's estimation relates to the concern that Paul uses νήπιοι pejoratively. Weima concedes that Paul *does* use it negatively in some cases (1 Cor 3:1), but in 1 Corinthians 13:11 the employment of νήπιος is neutral.[80] Furthermore, Weima offers numerous examples where νήπιος is used positively by Greek writers outside the New Testament. Finally, Weima addresses the so-called "mixed metaphor" problem. Weima first appeals to this as actually *favoring* this reading since it presents the *lectio difficilior.* He then reinforces the idea of a sentence break at the end of 7b (7c starting a new idea). Again, similar to Sailors' reading, Weima notes how the "infants" image underscores Paul's innocence, whereas the "nursing mother" metaphor focuses on Paul's *love.*[81]

An original piece that Weima adds to the puzzle is his articulation of the way Paul shifts metaphors later in chapter two, first presenting himself as a "father" (2:11) and then as if a child being "orphaned" (ἀπορφανισθέντες ἀφ᾽ ὑμῶν; 2:17). This is not as sudden a shift as in 2:7, but it shows that the employment of a cluster of metaphors is clearly demonstrated in the letter. Weima draws even further from the orphan metaphor in 2:17 to show that already Paul demonstrates in 1 Thessalonians the notion that he is like a child.[82]

---

78. Weima, "But We Became Infants," 548.
79. Weima, "But We Became Infants," 549; so he argues that "the burden of proof, therefore, rests on those who reject the compelling testimony of the external evidence."
80. Weima, "But We Became Infants," 552. Weima adds that the use of the cognate verb νηπιάζω in 1 Cor 14:20 is "positive" (552).
81. Weima, "But We Became Infants," 556.
82. Weima, "But We Became Infants," 557–58.

In the remainder of his article, Weima offers his own reading of 1 Thessalonians 2:5–7b, presuming νήπιοι to be the original reading. He argues that Paul's reference to himself as an "infant" was intended to capitalize on the idea that he and his companions were guileless, thus reinforcing apostolic integrity.

In the twenty-first century, probably with a swing of interpretation propelled in no small part by Sailors and Weima, the νήπιοι reading is now favored by the majority of translations and commentaries. So, for example, the NET, NIV 2011, and NLT all place an English translation of νήπιοι in the text.[83] Perhaps one can attribute *some* of this change to the increased interest in metaphors and conceptual metaphor theory among biblical scholars. But before we address that, we will briefly note the defense of the νήπιοι reading by Gordon Fee in his commentary, largely because Fee is one of the only New Testament scholars trained in textual criticism who has given lengthy attention to this matter.[84]

From the standpoint of text-critical theory, Fee makes the following four points in his commentary. First, Fee points out, similar to Weima, that neither dittography or haplography is more likely, given that the difference in this case is one letter.[85] Second, the external evidence is decisively in support of νήπιοι. Fee adds an important concern above and beyond Sailors and Weima here. Because νήπιοι is attested earlier in the extant manuscripts, an explanation must be given as to how an accidental corruption occurred so early and often that it became pervasive in those early centuries only for the so-called original reading of ἤπιοι to emerge again and proliferate. Put another way, how could it be (if ἤπιοι is correct) that "the 'accident' is universally known in the first four centuries."[86]

In terms of what we know of actual manuscript recensions, Fee notes that in all cases but one (manuscript 326), the correction is a change from νήπιοι to ἤπιοι.[87] This is telling (a) as proof that the difference between these readings is not one of unintentional error, and (b) that almost certainly these changes occured because νήπιοι was found to be too difficult or confusing.

We turn now to advanced discussions of the study of metaphors in

---

83. A notable exception is the CEB: "We were gentle with you."
84. Of course, M. Holmes is another such scholar, see above.
85. Fee, *Thessalonians*, 69.
86. Fee, *Thessalonians*, 70.
87. Fee, *Thessalonians*, 70.

the Bible and how that has shaped treatments of 1 Thessalonians 2:7 and Paul's letters in general. In the latter part of the twentieth century, biblical scholars began to catch on to work being done in linguistics, literary studies, and psychology about the nature of communication and the use of metaphors in relation to cognitive operations. A pivotal work in this area is G. Lakoff and M. Johnson's *Metaphors We Live By.*[88] Lakoff and Johnson cogently made the case that metaphors are not simply word tricks but rather shape the platform of thought; that is, metaphors are fundamental to the way we think and the way we process information. By attending more carefully to the theological *weight* of Paul's metaphors, thanks to insights from conceptual metaphor theory, there have been numerous studies of the way the apostle uses imagery to reflect his thought and his concerns.[89] Beverly Gaventa is an example of someone who has invested deeply in Paul's kinship metaphors and in particular his maternal imagery.[90] When it comes to 1 Thessalonians, Gaventa insists that Paul was careful in his choice of metaphors because they are central to his communication, including the representation of his apostolic ministry as father, infant, and nursing mother. Regarding 1 Thessalonians 2:5–7, Gaventa does not see a shift in imagery (from infant to nurse) as a problem; rather, it is rhetorically *intentional*—it creates a purposeful, destabilizing effect.[91] To understand the role and work of Paul requires of the Thessalonians "categories [that] seem outrageous outside the context of Pauline paradox."[92]

More careful study of metaphors in communication and thought has led to more sophisticated methods for the study of metaphors. One development in our understanding of metaphor has been that an image (a source concept) does not import *all* that it could possibly mean into the target concept. Rather, usually one or two themes or values are carried forward. When it comes to Paul's use of νήπιος, just because he may draw a negative value from the image in one text (e.g., 1 Cor 3:1), does not mean it is restricted to doing so always. Jennifer H. McNeel has published an extensive study of Paul's metaphorical imagery called *Paul as Infant and*

---

88. G. Lakoff and M. Johnson, *Metaphors We Live By* (Chicago: University of Chicago Press, 1980).

89. See, e.g., R. F. Collins, *The Power of Images in Paul* (Collegeville, MN: Liturgical Press, 2008).

90. B. R. Gaventa, *Our Mother Saint Paul* (Louisville: Westminster John Knox, 2007).

91. See also M. Aymer, "'Mother Knows Best': The Story of Mother Paul Revisited," in *Mother Goose, Mother Jones, Mommie Dearest: Biblical Mothers and Their Children*, ed. C. A. Kirk-Duggan and T. Pippin, SemeiaSt 61 (Atlanta: SBL Press, 2009), 187–98.

92. Gaventa, *Our Mother Saint Paul*, 27; similarly, see U. Schmidt, "1 Thess 2.7b, c: 'Kleinkinder, die wie eine Amme Kinder versorgen,'" *NTS* 55.1 (2009): 116–20.

Nursing Mother. McNeel demonstrates that while the concepts of infant and nurse seem contradictory or dissonant in terms of authority, they are similar in terms of intimacy and tenderness.[93]

Again, scholarship has been moving steadily toward favoring νήπιοι, and for good reason. First, I too believe that the external evidence should stand as decisive (as one of the least subjective considerations in the mix). Second, I find no personal concern with a mixed metaphor. Two notes should be registered here: (a) we ought not to impose our own expectations for consistency on Paul, and (b) is it such a problem if Paul did end up using a less-than-perfect set of analogies in his argument? Almost no one I know consciously attributes to Paul, either by dint of his education or "inspiration," perfection in literary artistry.[94]

Moreover, I simply do not find νήπιοι problematic as a reading, even though it is clearly the more "difficult" reading. Paul's point appears to me to be that he wishes to portray himself as innocent. Comparing himself to the status and innocence of an infant certainly could convey that sentiment.[95]

Is Paul Anti-Semitic? (2:13–16)

Just as 1 Thessalonians 2:7b proves to be one of the most hotly debated verses in the New Testament regarding textual criticism, so too 1 Thessalonians 2:13–16 has generated almost endless discussion about Paul's attitude toward his Jewish kinspeople. Given the incendiary tone of this passage, some question whether it is possible Paul penned these words at all. For example, in 1982 Helmut Koester wrote the following: "The passage in 1 Thess 2:13–16, with its blatant anti-Judaic attitude, has been correctly identified as a later interpolation which takes up a Jewish tradition about the official leaders of the people as the murderers of the prophets and puts the death of Jesus as well as the experience of the church in that context."[96]

---

93. See McNeel, *Paul as Infant*, 39.

94. D. Marguerat is not alone in making the argument that, regardless of one's preferred reading here based on textual criticism, in the end the interpretation of Paul's point does not change substantially. Paul wishes, with either word, to underscore an apostolic attitude "de petitesse, des tendresse et de fragilité" [ET: "of smallness, tenderness, and fragility"]; see Marguerat, "Imiter l'apôtre, père et mère de la communauté (1 Th 2,1–12)," in *Not in the Word Alone*, ed. M. D. Hooker (Rome: Benedictina, 2003), 45.

95. It perhaps is worth noting that Plummer, in 1918, defended the νήπιοι reading and recognized the strong external support for it. He wrote: "There seems to be no sufficient reason for adopting the less strongly attested reading" (*A Commentary on St. Paul's First Epistle to the Thessalonians* [London: R. Scott, 1918], 23).

96. H. Koester, *Introduction to the New Testament* (Philadelphia: Fortress, 1982), 112–14; see similarly G. E. Okeke, "I Thessalonians 2.13–16: The Fate of the Unbelieving Jews," *NTS* 27 (1980): 127–36.

As far as I can tell, concerns about the origins and authorship of 1 Thessalonians 2:13–16 (or sometimes only 2:14–16) go back at least as far as 1847 with a comment by Albert Ritschl calling 2:13–16 a "textual gloss."[97] The prominent scholar Werner Kümmel expressed the same concern in 1962.[98] But the most thoroughgoing and influential case for distancing Paul from this text came from B. A. Pearson in his 1971 article, "1 Thessalonians 2:13–16: A Deutero-Pauline Interpolation."[99] Pearson defended his interpolation theory on three grounds. First, theologically this text seems out of character for Paul.[100] Second, an interpolation theory would make sense of the letter on literary grounds, insofar as 2:13–16 seems to be a digression or interruption between 2:12 and 2:17.[101] Finally, from a historical perspective, the condemnation and judgment of the Jewish people (2:16 in particular) seems to allude to the 70 CE destruction of the temple, but 1 Thessalonians was written significantly before that time.[102]

Pearson's arguments in favor of 2:13–16 as an interpolation were bolstered by further argumentation from D. Schmidt in 1983.[103] Schmidt set out to demonstrate that the content of 2:13–16 fits poorly into 1 Thessalonians overall, and also that Paul's rhetorical flow of argumentation, and that of 2:13–16 itself, appears to be a "conflation of Pauline expressions."[104] Ultimately Schmidt concludes that this passage simply does not fit the syntax and style of the first two chapters of 1 Thessalonians. In the late twentieth century there appeared to be some fresh energy around supporting this interpolation theory, for example as seen in Earl Richard's 1995 commentary.[105]

---

97. The comment by Ritschl appeared in the critical apparatus of the Nestle-Aland 1963 edition of the New Testament; see also appeal to Ritschl's note in P. Schmiedel, *Die Brief an die Thessalonicher und an die Korinther* (Freiburg: J. C. B. Mohr, 1892), 21; as cited in N. S. Murrell, "The Human Paul of the New Testament: Anti-Judaism in 1 Thess 2:14–16," *Eastern Great Lakes Biblical Society* 14 (1994): 170.

98. W. Kümmel, "Das literarische und geschichtliche Problem des ersten Thessalonicherbriefes," in *Neotestamentica et Patristica*, ed. W. C. van Unnik, NovTSup 6 (Leiden: Brill, 1962), 220–21; cf. E. Bammel, "Judenverfolgung und Naherwartung: Zur Eschatologie des ersten Thessalonicherbriefs," *ZTK* 56.3 (1959): 294–315.

99. Pearson, "Deutero-Pauline Interpolation," 79–94.

100. Pearson, "Deutero-Pauline Interpolation," 85.

101. Pearson, "Deutero-Pauline Interpolation," 88–91.

102. Pearson, "Deutero-Pauline Interpolation," 94.

103. Schmidt, "Linguistic Evidence for an Interpolation," 269–79.

104. Schmidt, "Linguistic Evidence for an Interpolation," 276.

105. Richard, *First and Second Thessalonians*, 119–27; Richard considers 2:14–16 to be non-Pauline. Around the time that Pearson was building his case, H. Boers published his "The Form Critical Study of Paul's Letters: 1 Thessalonians as a Case Study," *NTS* 22.2 (1975–76): 140–58. Boers argues that a structural study of the letter makes better sense *without* 2:13–16. Baarda later commented on a note in Nestle-Aland associated with H. Rodrigues, indicating that 2:15–16 was an interpolation;

Though labeling 2:13–16 (or 2:14–16) as an interpolation would certainly alleviate some of the tension felt by what seem to be anti-Jewish statements made in 1 Thessalonians, the vast majority of scholars in the last thirty years have largely rejected the argument that these verses came from someone other than Paul. Some have tried to weaken the incendiary tone of 2:16 by arguing that ἔφθασεν δὲ ἐπ᾽ αὐτοὺς ἡ ὀργὴ εἰς τέλος does not mean "the wrath of God has come upon them at last" but instead εἰς τέλος means "until the end." Thus the idea would not be that of permanence or finality but just the opposite, of temporality (bringing 2:16 into more alignment with the hopeful tone of Romans 9–11, particularly 11:25–26, 30–31).[106] Yet while this paints the text in a more positive light, it has not proven to be a convincing reading of 2:16 in its own context.

We now consider responses to 2:13–16 and especially explanations that take this passage as genuinely Pauline. We will use categories established by Pearson: *theological, literary,* and *historical.*

THEOLOGICAL CONCERNS: PAUL AND APOCALYPTIC

J. C. Hurd has perhaps offered the strongest case for rejecting the interpolation approach, especially by addressing the theological problems that Pearson, Koester, and others have with 1 Thessalonians 2:14–16.[107] To begin with, it should be noted that Hurd does sympathize with those who find Paul's words disturbing; indeed, they seem to contradict the message of Romans 9–11 in his opinion.[108] On the matter of Paul's view of Jews and Judaism, Hurd is quick to point to Philippians 3:4–7 where there is no whiff of animosity toward his "pre-conversion" experience in Judaism. When it comes to Pearson's arguments, Hurd gives the interpolation argument a fair hearing, even admitting Pearson "may be right."[109] Yet Hurd remains unconvinced that an interpolation approach can solve more problems than it creates. On the matter of this clever "editor" who supposedly inserted this passage, Hurd wonders, "Who is it who says unexpected things and

---

see T. Baarda, "1 Thess. 2:14–16. Rodrigues in 'Nestle-Aland,'" *Nederlands theologische tijdschrift* 39 (1985): 186–93.

106. Simpson rejects this approach. See J. W. Simpson, "The Problems Posed by 1 Thessalonians 2:15–16 and a Solution," *HBT* 12.1 (1990): 42–72.

107. J. C. Hurd, "Paul Ahead of His Time: 1 Thess. 2.13–16," in *Antijudaism in Early Christianity: Paul and the Gospels,* ed. P. Richardson and D. Granskou (Waterloo: Wilfrid Laurier University Press, 1986), 21–36.

108. Hurd, "Paul Ahead of His Time," 22.

109. Hurd, "Paul Ahead of His Time," 26.

sounds so much like Paul?"[110] Against Pearson and Schmidt, Hurd points out that there is demonstrable thematic overlap and consistency between 1 Thessalonians 1:2–10 and 2:13–16.[111]

When it comes to concerns that Paul was acting too hostile in his criticism of Jews, Hurd points to an idea that Paul seems to share with the Synoptic tradition that connects the persecution of Jesus (and his followers) to those Jews who persecuted the prophets (see Matt 23:29–37).[112] Yet the strongest case that Hurd makes in trying to make sense of 1 Thessalonians 2:13–16 involves an appeal to the "apocalyptic" nature of the letter.[113] Hurd refers to 2:13–16 as part of Paul's "apocalyptic logic, which is woven into the fabric of the whole letter."[114]

Karl Donfried has made a similar appeal to Paul's apocalyptic thought on this matter.[115] Donfried urges that Paul's apocalyptic perspective urges him to emphasize divine wrath in 2:13–16, but elsewhere, as in Romans 11, Paul has more to say on the matter. To put this matter in perspective, Donfried draws in J. C. Beker's notion of "contingency" and "coherence" in Paul. Different situations in Thessalonica and in Rome led Paul to different statements: "Only when the contingent situation of each Pauline audience is comprehended can the coherent theology of Paul be understood; only when the coherent theology of Paul is understood can the contingent situation of each Pauline letter be comprehended. The interpreter is invited to enter precisely into that hermeneutical circle."[116]

THEOLOGICAL CONCERNS: LET PAUL BE PAUL

Two important articles appeared in 1989 (Johnson) and 1995 (Murrell) that both pressed for reading 1 Thessalonians 2:14–15 theologically as a product of a first-century Paul. Nathaniel Murrell focused his attention on "The Human Paul of the New Testament."[117] Murrell expresses somewhat similar concerns as Hurd and Donfried, but he opens further the question about why we think Paul could *not* have written such a striking statement. Have we assumed and constructed an unrealistic image of Paul?

---

110. Hurd, "Paul Ahead of His Time," 26.
111. Hurd, "Paul Ahead of His Time," 29–30.
112. Hurd, "Paul Ahead of His Time," 23.
113. Hurd, "Paul Ahead of His Time," 33–34.
114. Hurd, "Paul Ahead of His Time," 35.
115. K. P. Donfried, "Paul and Judaism: 1 Thessalonians 2:13–16 as a Test Case," *Interpretation* 38.3 (1984): 242–53, especially p. 252.
116. Donfried, "Paul and Judaism," 253.
117. Murrell, "The Human Paul of the New Testament," 169–86.

Murrell comments, "Paul was no paragon of virtue, non-sexist, docile, early Christian theologian who could not make anti-Judaic statements."[118] Using a bit of creative imagination, Murrell remarks that we have so revised an artificial personality for Paul that "the demons in the book of Acts may cry out one day 'first-century Jesus and Paul I know, but who is this Paul of modern biblical scholarship?'"[119] Murrell reveals how tempting it is to excise 1 Thessalonians 2:15–16 from the letter despite the fact that in real life people say and do complicated and inexplicable things. Perhaps, Murrell wonders, there is an "uneasy and guilty conscience within Protestant Christianity for its complicity in anti-Semitism throughout the history of Christendom."[120]

Murrell encourages Paulinists to be more careful to read Paul on his own terms instead of simplifying him. Murrell does then attempt to explain Paul's surprising language. First, he wonders whether it is fair to label this passage as "anti-Semitic." After all, Paul focuses on *theological* concerns with these persecutors, not their race *per se*.[121] Second—and we will address this in more detail with Johnson's work below—Murrell notes the clearly hyperbolic nature of what Paul writes.[122] Still, in the end Murrell is most troubled by the way that Pearson and others sweep away this text; as far as Murrell is concerned, "The text reflects an irascible human Paul making a visceral response to a theological problem in a specific Jewish-Christian community."[123]

Luke Timothy Johnson has made a major contribution to this subject in a broader way in his important article "The New Testament's Slander and the Conventions of Ancient Polemic."[124] Johnson mentions a variety of relevant New Testament texts, including Matthew 23:1–39 and 1 Thessalonians 2:15–16. Johnson shares the same concern as we saw with Murrell, namely, that biblical scholars try too hard to ameliorate the impact of disturbing texts. Johnson warns against "solutions" that are "theologically motivated and . . . anachronistic."[125]

In order to put early Christian slander in context, Johnson notes that the persecution against this small religious group may have contributed to

---

118. Murrell, "The Human Paul of the New Testament," 177.
119. Murrell, "The Human Paul of the New Testament," 169.
120. Murrell, "The Human Paul of the New Testament," 172–73.
121. Murrell, "The Human Paul of the New Testament," 174.
122. Murrell, "The Human Paul of the New Testament," 183.
123. Murrell, "The Human Paul of the New Testament," 183.
124. L. T. Johnson, "The New Testament's Slander and the Conventions of Ancient Polemic," *JBL* 108.3 (1989): 419–41.
125. Johnson, "New Testament's Slander," 422.

the volume of their countercriticism. Early Christians were fighting for survival, and much effort in their writings was dedicated to in-group identity reinforcement.[126] Thus, even in the case of 1 Thessalonians 2:15–16, it is obvious how Paul was not addressing *Jews*, but rather talking about these Jews *to the Thessalonian believers.*

Without dismissing its hostile tone, Johnson does explain that NT writers appear to be following conventions of their own time for slanderous speech. Johnson offers as evidence a variety of philosophical rivalries in the Greco-Roman world, particularly between sophists and between orators. Johnson notes that polarizing language is extremely common, but "the polemic is not so much the rebuttal of the opponent as the edification of one's own school. Polemic was primarily for internal consumption."[127]

Furthermore, Johnson explains how Christians were not the only offenders. Rivalry between Jewish schools or groups was also common. So Johnson remarks, "Readers today hear the NT's polemic as inappropriate only because the other voices are silent."[128]

THEOLOGICAL CONCERNS: PAUL, JEWS, AND JUDAISM

Some scholars have pursued further the matter of Paul's disagreement with other Jews and inquired about *what* he was opposing.[129] Donald Hagner, for example, has offered a thoughtful discussion in "Paul's Quarrel with Judaism."[130] Similar to some of the scholars mentioned above, Hagner is eager to differentiate anti-Semitism (which presumes racial animosity) from "anti-Judaism," which for Hagner involves *theological* disagreement. Even then, Hagner does not think this is an appropriate label for early Christians and the New Testament writers, since "the Jewish Christians' response in the New Testament, including Paul, regarded Christianity as the fulfillment of Judaism."[131]

---

126. Johnson, "New Testament's Slander," 425.

127. Johnson, "New Testament's Slander," 433.

128. Johnson, "New Testament's Slander," 441. Quite similarly in argumentation, see I. Broer, "Antijudaismus im Neuen Testament? Versuch einer Annäherung anhand von zwei Texten (1 Thess 2,14–16 und Mt 27,24f.)," in *Salz der Erde*, ed. A. Vögtle, L. Overlinner, and P. Fiedler (Stuttgart: Katholisches Bibelwerk, 1991), 321–55; see also Broer, "'Der ganze Zorn ist schon über sie gekommen,'" in Collins, *Thessalonian Correspondence*, 137–59, for Broer's remarks on the interpolation theories for 1 Thess 2:14–16.

129. See T. L. Donaldson, *Jews and Anti-Judaism in the New Testament* (Waco, TX: Baylor University Press, 2010).

130. D. A. Hagner, "Paul's Quarrel with Judaism," in *Anti-Semitism and Early Christianity: Issues of Polemic and Faith*, ed. C. A. Evans and D. A. Hagner (Minneapolis: Fortress, 1993), 128–50.

131. Hagner, "Paul's Quarrel with Judaism," 129. In contrast, G. van Kooten proposes that early Christianity did *not* see itself as fulfilling Judaism, but rather Paul's anti-Jewish statements

When it comes to 1 Thessalonians 2:14–16, Hagner expresses the same concerns as Murrell, arguing that interpolation theories serve ostensibly to "keep Paul from saying what it seems he ought not to have said."[132] Hagner imagines that Paul was not playing the role of gentile slanderer of Jews; rather, the style of his polemic fits better a "Deuteronomistic-type judgment oracle directed against Jews in general."[133] This "polemical and emotional outburst," then, divulges the frustration and pain Paul experienced in face of the fact that many of his kinspeople, fellow Jews, stood opposed to the messianic good news that he heralded.[134]

Another consideration regarding the accusation of anti-Semitism against Paul involves how we translate 1 Thessalonians 2:14–15. Stanley Porter has examined the history of translation and interpretation of these verses with interest in the presence or absence in English of a comma after the word "Jews" at the end of 2:14.[135] Note these translations:

For you suffered the same things from your own countrymen as they did from the Jews, who killed both the Lord Jesus and the prophets, and drove us out. (RSV)

You suffered from your own people the same things those churches suffered from the Jews who killed both the Lord Jesus and the prophets, and also drove us out. (NIV 2011)

Porter talks about the presence of the comma in some translations as nonrestrictive, implying that Paul is condemning *all Jews* as those who

---

demonstrate that Christianity treated Judaism the same way they thought of "paganism." That is, early Christians treated Jewish religion as part of ancestral religious practices that should be discarded. For van Kooten to make his case, he must rely on what he calls a "universalizing tendency" of early Christianity, a case that I find difficult to prove. See G. H. van Kooten, "Broadening the New Perspective," in *Abraham, the Nations, and the Hagarites*, ed. M. Goodman, G. H. van Kooten, and J. T. A. G. M. van Ruiten (Leiden: Brill, 2010), 319–44.

132. Hagner, "Paul's Quarrel with Judaism," 131.

133. Hagner, "Paul's Quarrel with Judaism," 134.

134. See, rather similarly, the argument by T. Holtz, "The Judgment on the Jews and the Salvation of All Israel: 1 Thes 2,15–16 and Rom 11,25–26," in Collins, *Thessalonian Correspondence*, 284–94; and also R. Hoppe, "Der Topos Prophetenverfolgung bei Paulus," *NTS* 50.4 (2004): 535–49, where Hoppe portrays Paul within the persona and style of the persecuted prophet with a view toward Rom 11:1–10 and 1 Thess 2:13–16. See too the discussion by E. Stegemann in "Remarques sur la polemique antijudaique dans 1 Thessaloniciens 2,14–16," in *Le déchirement: juifs et chrétiens au premier siècle*, ed. D. Marguerat (Geneva: Labor et Fides, 1996), 99–112. Stegemann argues that Paul was not pronouncing an eternal judgment on all Jews but rather demonstrating that God would not let the persecutors go unpunished, just as he did not turn a blind eye to the persecuted prophets (see especially pp. 110–12).

135. S. E. Porter, "Translation, Exegesis, and 1 Thessalonians 2:14–15: Could a Comma Have Changed the Course of History?," *Bible Translator* 64.1 (2013): 82–98.

killed Jesus. The absence of a comma would circumscribe whom Paul is referring to, namely, *certain Jews* who do such things. Thus, the NLT glosses this as "for *some of the Jews* killed the prophets, and *some* even killed the Lord Jesus." Porter observes that prior to the end of the twentieth century, all major translations included a comma (indicating a nonrestrictive interpretation). Frank Gilliard made a case in a 1989 article that there should be *no comma* "so as to limit the Jews involved in the killing of Jesus and the further events related."[136] Porter supplements Gilliard's work by arguing that in the case of articular participles (τῶν Ἰουδαίων τῶν καὶ τὸν κύριον ἀποκτεινάντων Ἰησοῦν καὶ τοὺς προφήτας [1 Thess 2:14–15]) Paul had a strong, even incontrovertible, tendency to use them in a restrictive manner, thus making the comma unnecessary.[137]

LITERARY CONCERNS

What about the arguments of Pearson and Schmidt that posit an interpolation theory for 1 Thessalonians 2:13–16 on the basis of the way it serves as a "digression" from Paul's overall argumentation? Truth be told, most scholars today find form-critical theories highly subjective, so as to make them superfluous. Hurd had already commented on this in 1986, but the literary-rhetorical discussion has been picked up in an even stronger and more thorough way by Peter Wick.[138] Wick aims at reading this text as a unit within a particular rhetorical context rather than as a free-floating "idea" in Paul's mind. Wick attributes to Paul some level of skill in Greek rhetoric and posits that he crafted the chapters of 1 Thessalonians carefully. Based on his rhetorical analysis of 1 Thessalonians 1–2, Wick discerns that the master theme of 2:13–16 is not anti-Judaism but rather faith. Much in line with Luke Timothy Johnson's statements about slander and identity formation, Wick argues that Paul's primary interest was to strengthen the Thessalonians' faith.[139]

---

136. F. D. Gilliard, "The Problem of the Antisemitic Comma between 1 Thessalonians 2.14 and 15," *NTS* 35 (1989): 498–501. Porter laments the fact that, aside from Malherbe, commentators of 1–2 Thessalonians have largely ignored Gilliard's work.

137. See Porter, "Translation, Exegesis, and 1 Thessalonians 2:14–15," 86.

138. P. Wick, "Ist 1 Thess 2,13–16 antijüdisch? Der rhetorische Gesamtzusammenhang des Briefes als Interpretationshilfe für eine einzelne Perikope," *TZ* 50.1 (1994): 9–23.

139. He writes: "This paragraph, 1 Thess 2:13–16, incorporates 'faith' as a theme, and like the letter as a whole seeks to strengthen faith, to warn and to comfort. However, since it includes no note of warning, but only appreciation, even opening with a word of thanks, all the emphasis lies here clearly on comfort. This paragraph, interpreted so frequently as anti-Jewish polemic, actually aims to give the Thessalonians a word of comfort in their faith" (Wick, "Ist 1 Thess 2,13–16 antijudisch?," 19 [trans. mine]).

HISTORICAL CONCERNS

A major concern for interpreters of 1 Thessalonians 2:13–16 is the proper interpretation of the phrase "thus they have constantly been filling up the measure of their sins; but God's wrath has overtaken them at last" (2:16 NRSV). The past nature of the condemnation makes it seem as if the wrath of God has *already* overtaken the Jews in a visible and concrete manner. Thus Pearson and others argued that this passage seems to have the Jewish war and the destruction of the temple in view. Markus Bockmuehl has issued an important challenge to this assumption.[140] There has been some work in consideration of what *other* events Paul might have had in mind regarding these signs of trouble visited upon Jews. Bockmuehl imagines that Paul could have been referring to several different kinds of events and scenarios where Rome asserted its power against Jewish communities.

Bockmuehl makes a special case for a theory already put forward by a sixth-century writer named Malalas. Apparently Malalas made note of a Jewish persecution of the apostles and their followers that took place in 48/49.[141] We know that Jews suffered around that same period of time under procurator Ventidius Cumanus (see Josephus, *Ant.* 20.103–36). Cumanus executed many Jews, and Josephus notes that on this occasion "there was mourning henceforth instead of feasting" (*Ant.* 20.112 [L. H. Feldman, LCL]). Bockmuehl proposes that this very well could have been the event Paul had in mind, during the tenure of Cumanus, where "the violent and famished years after the death of Agrippa constituted a grave decline in Jewish fortune."[142]

NEW APPROACHES TO 1 THESSALONIANS 2:13–16

The proliferation of new exegetical methods and interdisciplinary approaches to the New Testament has opened fresh treatments of this troubling text. Robert Wortham approaches this passage with aid from social psychology and symbolic anthropology. He notes how prejudice may drive a person toward "strong feelings of inferiority."[143] The challenges and persecutions he faced may have driven Paul to such acerbic statements. Sarah Rollens examines 1 Thessalonians 2:14–16 from a social-scientific

---

140. M. N. A. Bockmuehl, "1 Thess 2:14–16 and the Church in Jerusalem," *TynBul* 52 (2001): 1–31.

141. Bockmuehl, "1 Thess 2:14–16 and the Church in Jerusalem," 23.

142. Bockmuehl, "1 Thess 2:14–16 and the Church in Jerusalem," 30.

143. R. A. Wortham, "The Problem of Anti-Judaism in 1 Thessalonians 2:14–16 and Related Pauline Texts," *BTB* 25.1 (1995): 36; cf. 43.

view.[144] Rollens draws from the concept of "invented tradition," which helps a group to concretize a unified identity and shared story. Paul draws the Thessalonians into a history of the faithful being persecuted and facing affliction.[145] Rollens reinforces the kind of conclusions found in the work of Johnson and Wick whereby Paul's intent was not to draw criticism toward an outside group *per se* but first and foremost to foster an in-group identity.[146]

CONCLUSION

As noted above, almost all interpreters of 1 Thessalonians in the last thirty years have found the interpolation theories of Pearson and Schmidt wanting. Some, like Murrell (and to some degree Wortham), have attempted to paint a more realistic, human portait of Paul, one where the apostle could have conceivably penned these words. Other scholars have tried to mitigate the impact of Paul's words through various avenues of study. Few scholars today who have studied Paul's letters carefully would conclude that he was "anti-Semitic," even if 1 Thessalonians 2:13–16 is still considered an uncomfortable text.

Paul's Vessel Metaphor (4:4)

Interpreters of Paul's letters are aware that the apostle's complex and thorny passages spark some of the liveliest discussions. First Thessalonians 4:4 has generated engagement after engagement in hopes of solving the mystery of the meanings of σκεῦος and κτάομαι in this context. The phrase in question is marked below.

³ Τοῦτο γάρ ἐστιν θέλημα τοῦ θεοῦ, ὁ ἁγιασμὸς ὑμῶν, ἀπέχεσθαι ὑμᾶς ἀπὸ τῆς πορνείας, ⁴ εἰδέναι ἕκαστον ὑμῶν τὸ ἑαυτοῦ σκεῦος κτᾶσθαι ἐν ἁγιασμῷ καὶ τιμῇ, ⁵ μὴ ἐν πάθει ἐπιθυμίας καθάπερ καὶ τὰ ἔθνη τὰ μὴ εἰδότα τὸν θεόν (1 Thess 4:3–5)

The RSV translates the underlined phrase as "that each one of you know how to take a wife for himself," while the NRSV reads "that each one of you know how to control your own body." These have tended to be the

---

144. S. E. Rollens, "Inventing Traditions in Thessalonica: The Appropriation of the Past in 1 Thess 2:14–16," *BTB* 46.3 (2016): 123–32.

145. Rollens, "Inventing Traditions in Thessalonica," 124.

146. Rollens, "Inventing Traditions in Thessalonica," 130.

two main options under consideration, namely, the "wife" interpretation and the "body" interpretation, though we will discuss other possibilities as well. Before going over the arguments for these views, it may be helpful to break down the challenges almost *every* word provides in the phrase εἰδέναι ἕκαστον ὑμῶν τὸ ἑαυτοῦ σκεῦος κτᾶσθαι.

εἰδέναι. Paul here proclaims that God's will for the Thessalonians is their sexual purity, which involves *knowing* how to do something. Why did Paul not simply comment that God's will is for them to *do* something (such as take a wife or control the body)? Why does he express it in terms of *knowing* how to do it?[147]

κτᾶσθαι. The word κτάομαι is not particularly rare, but this is the only place it occurs in the entire Pauline corpus. Furthermore, it appears six times in the New Testament outside of Paul (mostly in Luke-Acts).[148] The basic meaning of this word is "to acquire."[149] Thus, on the face of it Paul seems to be encouraging the Thessalonians to know how to "acquire your own vessel in holiness and honor." However, some have made the case that this verb could have a *durative* meaning, encouraging the translation "to possess" or "to control." One aspect of the debate, then, involves whether Paul could have meant "know how to *control* your own vessel [= body]."

σκεῦος. The meaning of σκεῦος is also debated. The noun clearly means "vessel," but it is obviously employed as a metaphor here. Paul had an interest in using σκεῦος metaphorically elsewhere in his letters, perhaps most famously in 2 Corinthians 4:7: "But we have this treasure in jars of clay [ἐν ὀστρακίνοις σκεύεσιν] to show that this all-surpassing power is from God and not from us." In Romans 9:21 where Paul raises the matter of God's wrath and mercy, he asks, "Has the potter no right to make from the same lump of clay one vessel [σκεῦος] for special use and another for ordinary use?" (NET). In both cases σκεῦος relates to the *person as a whole*, and one could naturally associate it with the human body formed by God; thus several scholars associate σκεῦος in 1 Thessalonians 4:4 with the body (σῶμα). Others, however, find this association unconvincing, largely because it is difficult to put κτάομαι and σκεῦος together in a sensible way (*how does one "acquire" a body?*).

ἑαυτοῦ. If the above challenges were not enough, we also have the use of ἑαυτοῦ here: "*Your own* vessel." Why would Paul not simply have said

---

147. See Weima, *1–2 Thessalonians*, 269.
148. Matt 10:9; Luke 18:12; 21:19; Acts 1:18; 8:20; 22:28.
149. L&N 57.58.

"your vessel" (τὸ σκεῦος ὑμῶν)? Is Paul implying that the Thessalonians were concerned more with acquiring *other* people's vessels? Needless to say, some find his choice of ἑαυτοῦ perplexing.

THE "WIFE" INTERPRETATION

Both the "wife" interpretation and the "body" interpretation (see below) have a long pedigree of advocacy. For the former, premodern proponents include Theodore of Mopsuestia, Augustine, and Aquinas. In terms of more modern scholars, we see this view endorsed by Frame, Collins, Baumert, Malherbe, and Witherington.[150] Several arguments are put forward to support this view.

"Taking a wife" and κτάομαι *in the LXX.* In the book of Ruth, we see κτάομαι twice used to refer to "taking" or "acquiring" a wife (Ruth 4:5, 10). Similarly, in Sirach 36:24 we have the proverb, "He who acquires a wife enters upon a possession [my trans.; ὁ κτώμενος γυναῖκα ἐνάρχεται κτήσεως]."

Wife as "vessel." If it is true that κτάομαι could be used in a kind of idiomatic phrase to refer to "taking a wife," then why does Paul use σκεῦος? The case is sometimes made that Jews could use σκεῦος metaphorically to refer to a wife. Although some have appealed to 1 Peter 3:7 where the wife is called the ἀσθενεστέρῳ σκεύει,[151] it is obvious from the comparative form of ἀσθενής that here *both* marriage partners are considered "vessels." Therefore, appeal tends to be made to the use of "vessel" language in rabbinic sources.[152] For example, b. Megillah 12b reads as follows:

> Some said: The Median women were the most beautiful; and some said: The Persian women are the most beautiful. Said Ahasuerus to them: The vessel that I use is neither Median nor Persian, but Chaldean. Do you wish to see her? They said to him: Yes, but only if she is naked.[153]

---

150. J. E. Frame, *A Critical and Exegetical Commentary on the Epistles of St. Paul to the Thessalonians* (New York: Scribner's, 1912); Collins, *Studies on the First Letter to the Thessalonians*; N. Baumert, "Brautwerbung—das einheitliche Thema von 1 Thess 4,3–8," in Collins, *Thessalonian Correspondence* (Leuven: University Press, 1990), 316–39; Malherbe, *Letters to the Thessalonians*, 226; Witherington, *Thessalonians*, 113–14; cf. especially O. L. Yarbrough, *Not Like the Gentiles: Marriage Rules in the Letters of Paul*, SBLDS 80 (Atlanta: Scholars Press, 1985); also T. Burke, *Family Matters: A Socio-Historical Study of Kinship Metaphors in 1 Thessalonians*, JSNTSup 247 (London: T&T Clark, 2003), 185–93.

151. Note how C. Maurer goes as far as arguing that 1 Pet 3:7 is influenced directly by Paul's statement in 1 Thess 4:4; Maurer, "σκεῦος," *TDNT* 7:367; see also H. Binder, "Paulus und die Thessalonicherbrief," in Collins, *Thessalonian Correspondence*, 87–93.

152. This kind of rabbinic evidence is put forth by Yarbrough, *Not Like the Gentiles*, 72–73.

153. As cited in J. E. Smith, "1 Thessalonians 4:4: Breaking the Impasse," *BBR* 11 (2001): 68–69.

1 Corinthians 7:2. In 1 Corinthians 7 Paul writes:

But because of cases of sexual immorality, each man should have his own wife and each woman her own husband. (7:2 NRSV)

διὰ δὲ τὰς πορνείας ἕκαστος τὴν ἑαυτοῦ γυναῖκα ἐχέτω καὶ ἑκάστη τὸν ἴδιον ἄνδρα ἐχέτω.

The parallels between 1 Corinthians 7:2 and 1 Thessalonians 4:4 are intriguing. In both we have the concern with πορνεία and the language of ἕκαστος and ἑαυτοῦ. Just a few verses later Paul addresses the matter of sex and that each marriage partner has "authority" over the body of the other and not his or her *own* body.[154]

Ingressive present form of κτάομαι. One of the linchpin arguments in favor of the "wife" view involves the form of κτάομαι. The present tense of κτάομαι, it is argued, clearly carries the ingressive meaning of "acquire," to take possession of something not already in one's possession. This makes very good sense of the idea of "taking" a woman to be a wife, but it hardly makes sense if σκεῦος means "body." Again, what would it mean for Paul to counsel the Thessalonians to know how to "acquire one's own body in holiness"?

THE "BODY" INTERPRETATION

As with the "wife" view, the "body" interpretation goes back many centuries, at least to Tertullian, Ambrosiaster, Theodoret, and Chrysostom. In the modern era it has been defended by Morris, Marxsen, Bruce, Marshall, Beale, Holmes, and Cousar.[155] The rationale for this interpretation tends to focus on the common metaphorical use of σκεῦος, though other factors enter the equation to a lesser degree as well.

σκεῦος *as body.* We already mentioned above how Paul could use σκεῦος to refer to the body (2 Cor 4:7; cf. v. 10). Body as vessel of *what*, though? In 2 Corinthians 4:7, the body is a vessel of that unique treasure

---

154. See Yarbrough, *Not Like the Gentiles*, 69.
155. L. Morris, *1 and 2 Thessalonians*, TNTC (Grand Rapids: Eerdmans, 1984), 121; Marxsen, *Thessalonicher*, 60–61; Bruce, *Thessalonians*; Marshall, *Thessalonians*, 108; G. K. Beale, *1–2 Thessalonians*, IVPNTC (Downers Grove, IL: InterVarsity Press, 2003), 116–19; Holmes, *Thessalonians*, 125–26; C. Cousar, *Reading Galatians, Philippians, and 1 Thessalonians* (Macon, GA: Smyth & Helwys, 2013), 220; cf. M. McGehee, "A Rejoinder to Two Recent Studies Dealing with 1 Thessalonians 4:4," *CBQ* 51 (1989): 82–89.

of the gospel of Jesus Christ. In the context of counsel on sexual purity in 1 Thessalonians 4, it could be that Paul was reminding the Thessalonians of how they were to treat their bodies with dignity and holiness as vessels *of the Holy Spirit*.[156]

Possible meanings of κτάομαι. Those who defend the "body" interpretation must make sense of the use of the present tense of κτάομαι. One approach has been to make a case that the present tense could be understood duratively as "to control." Jay Smith attempts to make such a case, pointing to examples from a variety of texts such as LXX Proverbs 1:14; Philo, *Moses* 1.160; and Luke 18:12. Unfortunately, in none of these cases is a durative reading of κτάομαι absolutely necessary, thus weakening Smith's case.[157] Still, that does not mean that the "body" interpretation would make no sense if one takes κτάομαι ingressively. It very well could be that Paul was intending something such as "know how to gain control over one's own vessel," the equivalent to our own colloquial "get ahold of yourself!"[158]

Arguments against the "wife" interpretation. Those who defend the "body" interpretation tend to favor this view largely because they find the "wife" view so specious. Several concerns tend to be put forward. First, how is it that one would know how to marry a woman "not in passionate lust" (1 Thess 4:5)? Second, in antiquity marriages were not self-determined by the groom but rather coordinated by the parents, especially the father. So why would Paul be encouraging the men to acquire wives to curb lust? Third, what would it mean for a man to acquire his "*own*" wife?[159]

OTHER APPROACHES

In the last couple of decades, other possible interpretations of 1 Thessalonians 4:4 have been proposed with varying levels of cogency. Jouette Bassler proposed the idea that Paul has in mind something similar to 1 Corinthians 7:36–38, what Bassler calls "spiritual marriages," acquiring

---

156. Smith points out how in Barnabas 7.3 believers are precisely called "the vessel of his Spirit"; see Smith, "Breaking the Impasse," 91.

157. See Smith, "Breaking the Impasse," 84–85. The one exception may be Luke 18:12: "I fast twice a week; I give a tenth of all my income" (NRSV). Here Luke writes ἀποδεκατῶ πάντα ὅσα κτῶμαι, which could mean "I give a tenth of whatever I *get*" or "I give a tenth of whatever I *have*." Most translations opt for the former (an ingressive nuance), but one point in favor of the more durative meaning is that the Vulgate reads, "decimas do omnium quae *possideo*."

158. See Beale, *1–2 Thessalonians*, 117: "Those not presently living holy lives must begin to do so, that is, take possession of their bodies and begin to control them and then continue to do so."

159. See Smith, "Breaking the Impasse," 76–79.

virgin partners for the purpose of honoring God. This view has not gained much traction.[160] Jennifer Glancy suggests that in 1 Thessalonians 4:4 "obtain a vessel" refers to the sexual use of slaves.[161] Again, this argument has little in its favor and would hardly have made sense of Paul's wider argument that believers in Jesus ought to have a strict sexual ethic and show self-mastery over passions.[162]

There has been much more support for the view that σκεῦος refers to the male sexual organ (the phallus). It is unclear to me where this view originated,[163] but it goes back at least to Karl Donfried, who tried to contextualize it in relation to pagan cults in Thessalonica. According to Donfried, "Both Antistius Vetus and Aelianus use the term 'σκεῦος' as referring to the *membrum virile* and given the strong phallic symbolism in the cults of Dionysus, Cabirus and Samothrace such a reference is hardly surprising."[164] Gordon Fee also finds this interpretation reasonable. Fee points to LXX 1 Samuel 21, where David inquires about bread, and all that is on hand is "holy bread." David reasons that it is okay for his men to take this bread since his men have refrained from sexual relations with women while on active duty; thus their vessels (τὰ σκεύη) are consecrated (1 Sam 21:5 LXX). Here to link sex and the "vessels" of men seems to point in the direction of the male sexual organ.[165] Ultimately Fee finds this reading such a convincing interpretation of 1 Thessalonians 4:4 because it can explain why Paul used a metaphor instead of simply writing "body" or "wife." Paul was employing a euphemism.[166]

Another lively point of dialogue involves a potentially parallel Hebrew text from the Dead Sea Scrolls. In 1997 Torleif Elgvin published an article on information from the Dead Sea Scrolls that might prove useful for the study of 1 Thessalonians 4:4. In particular he drew attention to Instruction

160. J. M. Bassler, "SKEUOS: A Modest Proposal for Illuminating Paul's Use of Metaphor in 1 Thessalonians 4:4," in *The Social World of the First Christians*, ed. L. M. White and O. L. Yarbrough (Minneapolis: Fortress, 1995), 53–66.

161. J. A. Glancy, *Slavery in Early Christianity* (Oxford: Oxford University Press, 2002), 61.

162. See K. B. Neutel, "Slaves Included? Sexual Regulations and Slave Participation in Two Ancient Religious Groups," in *Slaves and Religions in Graeco-Roman Antiquity and Modern Brazil*, ed. S. Hodkinson and D. Geary (Newcastle upon Tyne: Cambridge Scholars, 2012), 141n18.

163. Though see A. Koch, *Commentar über den ersten Brief des apostels Paulus an die Thessalonicher* (Berlin: L. Oehmigke's, 1855), 297.

164. K. P. Donfried, *Paul, Thessalonica, and Early Christianity*, 31.

165. Fee, *Thessalonians*, 149.

166. Fee, *Thessalonians*, 149. Wanamaker seems to combine the "body" and "phallus" view into one as he argues that Paul has in mind "the human body in its sexual aspect" (Wanamaker, *Thessalonians*, 152).

or Sapiental Work A (1Q26; 4Q415/416/417/418/418a/418c/423).[167] This second-century-BCE work, according to Elgvin, includes the phrase "do not dishonor the vessel of your bosom" (4Q416 col. 4; frg. 2 ii 21). Elgvin argues that the Hebrew word here for "bosom" tends to have a sexual connotation in the Old Testament.[168]

In the same text (4Q416), Elgvin notes the phrase "wife of your bosom," which he takes to mean "the wife you embrace in your bosom."[169] On the basis of these occurrences, Elgvin argues that "vessel" here appears to be a euphemism for the male sexual organ.[170] Thus he finds this to support the phallus view regarding 1 Thessalonians 4:4. He writes:

> The Hebrew sources demonstrate that the obvious meaning of *keli* as "sexual organ" in 1 Sam 21.6 was not forgotten. Not only does Sap. Work A testify to *keli* in the same sense, the story on Rabbi Judah, preserved in four different rabbinic sources, demonstrates that *keli* was used in the same sense in the late 2nd cent. AD and throughout the Talmudic period.[171]

Elgvin addresses the natural question of whether the Thessalonian believers would have picked up on what appears to be a Jewish expression. Though this issue is problematic, Elgvin does not consider it insurmountable—whether or not they had *already* encountered this sexual metaphor, they probably would have picked up the right idea in the context of Paul's letter.[172]

John Strugnell takes a different view than Elgvin regarding 4Q416. Strugnell argues that "vessel" here refers to the female vagina, and thus to the wife in general.[173] Menahem Kister adds another possibility, namely that the phrase in question has been wrongly transcribed by interpreters

---

167. See T. Elgvin, "'To Master His Own Vessel': 1 Thess 4.4 in Light of New Qumran Evidence," *NTS* 43 (1997): 604–19.

168. See Gen 16:5; Deut 13:7; 28:54, 56; 2 Sam 12:8; 1 Kgs 1:2; Prov 5:20; 6:27; Mic 7:5.

169. See Elgvin, "'To Master His Own Vessel,'" 606–7.

170. Elgvin, "'To Master His Own Vessel,'" 607; see too J. E. Smith, "Another Look at 4Q416 2ii.21, a Critical Parallel to First Thessalonians 4:4," *CBQ* 63 (2001): 499–504.

171. Elgvin, "'To Master His Own Vessel,'" 610–11.

172. M. Kister, "A Qumranic Parallel to 1 Thess 4:4? Reading and Interpretation of 4Q416 2 II 21," *DSD* 10.3 (2003): 365–70.

173. J. Strugnell and D. J. Harrington, eds., *Qumran Cave 4.XXIV: Sapiential Texts, Part 2. 4QInstruction: 415ff. With a Re-edition of 1Q26* (Oxford: Clarendon, 1999), 108. See also M. Konradt, "Εἰδέναι ἕκαστον ὑμῶν τὸ ἑαυτοῦ σκεῦος κτᾶσθαι . . . : zu Paulus' sexualethischer Weisung in 1 Thess 4,4f.," *ZNW* 92.1–2 (2001): 128–35: "A comparison of 4Q416 frag. 2 2,21 with 1 Thess 4:4 favors this 'wife' interpretation" (132 [trans. mine]).

and the key phrase reads, "And do not be disgraced by (living) not according to your prescribed portion."[174]

To sum up, at present the connection between 1 Thessalonians 4:4 and 4Q416 is intriguing but inconclusive. A few possibilities exist, yet the σκεῦος conundrum remains.

CONCLUSION

In the late twentieth century, it appears that there was about equal representation for the "wife" and the "body" views in commentaries. The 2001 article by Jay Smith, "1 Thessalonians 4:4: Breaking the Impasse," probably tipped the scales of scholarship in favor of the "body" reading, with openness to the male sexual-organ connotation. The "wife" view has become more troublesome, at the least because it treats women as an object at best and at worst a mere "container for semen."[175] Most translations also seem to be moving in the direction of the body or phallus interpretation, with the "your own body" gloss now the most common—see NIV 2011, NET ("his"), NLT ("his"), NRSV, and CEB.[176]

Quiet Lives, Working with Hands (4:11)

In 1 Thessalonians 4:1–12, a section of Paul's letter dedicated to instruction about living in a manner that is pleasing to God, we have the apostle's specific instruction regarding φιλαδελφία, "sibling-love." Paul commends the Thessalonians for their mutual love (vv. 9–10), but exhorts them to love one another even more and "to make it your ambition to lead a quiet life: You should mind your own business and work with your hands, just as we told you, so that your daily life may win the respect of outsiders and so that you will not be dependent on anybody" (vv. 11–12).

---

174. See Kister, "A Qumran Parallel," 367. For a helpful overview of the debate among Qumran scholars, see M. J. Goff, *4QInstruction* (Atlanta: SBL Press, 2013), 86–90. In the end, Goff finds the parallel with 4Q416 2 ii 21 helpful and illuminating for the study of 1 Thess 4:4. Goff urges that "vessel" in the Qumran text does appear to refer to "wife," thus strengthening the case for the "wife" interpretation; see Goff, *4QInstruction*, 90. For further discussion of 4Q416, see B. Wold, "Reading and Reconstructing 4Q416 2 II 21: Comments on Menahem Kister's Proposal," *DSD* 12 (2005): 205–11.

175. Bassler, "SKEUOS," 55; also J. Buckmann, "1 Thessalonians: Opposing Death by Building Community," in *Feminist Biblical Interpretation*, ed. L. Schottroff and M.-T. Wacker (Grand Rapids: Eerdmans, 2012), 810.

176. I found it somewhat unexpected, then, when Hurtado dismissed the "body" meaning (esp. the NRSV translation in particular), presuming that Paul was referring to a wife. As evidence, Hurtado refers to the "male-oriented nature of Paul's exhortation." Hurtado does not address the scholarship of the debate directly, so I am unsure he is aware that his view (vessel = wife) is much less popular now among scholars than it once was; see Hurtado, *Destroyer of the Gods*, 156.

Scholars are basically in agreement that the three matters of living quietly, minding one's business, and working with hands belong together and are somehow interrelated. Furthermore, virtually all agree that such advice is not simply generic Christian ethics but is driven by a concern for Christian integrity in view of the watchful eye of outsiders (see v. 12). Beyond that, however, there is major disagreement about what some of these exhortations mean (*What kind of "quiet"? What "business"? How literal is the reference to "hands"?*) and how they relate to other concerns the apostle expresses elsewhere in 1 Thessalonians. Before getting directly into the scholarly discussion, it behooves us to briefly examine the Greek text.

Παρακαλοῦμεν δὲ ὑμᾶς, ἀδελφοί, περισσεύειν μᾶλλον καὶ φιλοτιμεῖσθαι ἡσυχάζειν καὶ πράσσειν τὰ ἴδια καὶ ἐργάζεσθαι ταῖς [ἰδίαις] χερσὶν ὑμῶν, καθὼς ὑμῖν παρηγγείλαμεν (1 Thess 4:10b–11)

φιλοτιμεῖσθαι ἡσυχάζειν. It would have been rather obvious to Greek readers and auditors that these words can only be combined awkwardly. The verb φιλοτιμέομαι (Rom 15:20; 2 Cor 5:9), as Gene Green notes, does not simply mean "aspire" but played an important role vis-à-vis the honor-conscious, agonistic Greco-Roman culture. Green recounts how this verb appears with some regularity in inscriptions with the meaning "consider it an honor" or "act with a public spirit."[177] A good example of the socially conscious use of this verb comes from Philo who writes:

And why are we anxious for, and why do we vie with one another [σπουδάζομέν τε καὶ φιλοτιμούμεθα] in specimens of Doric, and Ionic, and Corinthian sculpture, and in all the refinements which luxurious men have devised in addition to the existing customs, adorning the capitals of their pillars? And why do we furnish our chambers for men and for women with golden adornments? Is it not all from our being influenced by vain opinion? (*Somn.* 2.55 [Yonge])[178]

Contrast that with the verb ἡσυχάζω, which carries a sense of living peacefully and with tranquility or serenity.[179] The key question is

---

177. G. L. Green, *The Letters to the Thessalonians*, PNTC (Grand Rapids: Eerdmans, 2002), 209, though Green himself does not think it necessarily *must* relate to benefaction.

178. Similarly see Philo, *Moses* 1.256.

179. Note how MM 281 recounts the use of the cognate ἡσύχιος in P.Oxy I. 129, "where a

what these words mean in combination: How does one "aspire" to live serenely?[180]

πράσσειν τὰ ἴδια. The simple translation of these words is straightforward: *attending to your own affairs*. Most scholars recognize the problem here is not laziness *per se* (i.e., doing *nothing*) but rather too much attention paid to the affairs of others and, as a result, the neglect of one's own affairs. Still, what are these "things" that are meant to be done?

ἐργάζεσθαι ταῖς [ἰδίαις] χερσὶν ὑμῶν. The idea of "working with hands" has led most scholars to the conclusion that most of the Thessalonian believers were of the artisan class, those that Paul could presume *had* manual labor for which they were responsible.[181] But if they were not working with their hands, what exactly were they doing that was so problematic? If 2 Thessalonians comes after 1 Thessalonians and is authentically Pauline (see pp. 197–220), then Paul's message did not take, and the problem worsened rather than improved, so much so that he had to reiterate an earlier teaching: "The one who is unwilling to work shall not eat" (2 Thess 3:10).

THE MYSTERY OF THE ἌΤΑΚΤΟΙ

To explain how theories related to the interpretation of 1 Thessalonians 4:11 have developed (and ensuing debates have played out), we must briefly mention the mystery of the ἄτακτοι—a reference to a group of people that emerges briefly in 1 Thessalonians 5:14 and becomes the subject of more significant discussion in 2 Thessalonians 3:6–15. Because most scholars believe this group does *not* occupy Paul's attention in the context of the situation behind 1 Thessalonians (and relates more directly to 2 Thess), we will only make brief mention of this problem here as it relates to 1 Thessalonians 5:14, with the expectation that a more thorough discussion will appear in the exegetical discussion of 2 Thessalonians 3:6, 11 (see pp. 257–64).

In 1 Thessalonians 5:14, Paul calls the Thessalonian brothers and sisters to "warn those who are ἀτάκτους, encourage the disheartened, help

---

father repudiates a betrothal because he wishes that his daughter 'should lead a peaceful and quiet life'—εἰρηνικὸν καὶ ἡσύχιον βίον διάξαι." Note too how it can be used of "rest" on the Sabbath as well (Luke 23:56).

180. Plummer cites a parallel from Epictetus: "Make a desperate effort on behalf of tranquillity (sic) of mind" (Arrian, *Epict. diss.* 2.16); see Plummer, *Thessalonians*, 65–66.

181. See Plummer, *Thessalonians*, 66; J. Murphy-O'Connor, *Paul: A Critical Life* (Oxford: Clarendon, 1996), 117; N. O. Miguez, *Practice of Hope* (Minneapolis: Fortress, 2012), 66–67; cf. P. Oakes, *Reading Romans in Pompeii* (Minneapolis: Fortress, 2009), 44.

the weak, be patient to everyone." This is the sole mention of these people, the NRSV rendering the term as "idlers" and the NET as "undisciplined" (NIV: "idle and disruptive"). We get a strong sense, when we combine this with what Paul writes in 4:11, that these people are those who did not work with their hands or mind their own business. But why? Until the end of the twentieth century, it was a rather natural presumption that these people were idle or loafers because they were caught up with eschatological fervor, essentially forsaking the regular order of life in anticipation of the end of the world. This "eschatological" view of the ἄτακτοι is well represented by commentators such as F. F. Bruce and Leon Morris.[182] Thus, Bruce refers to an "undue eschatological excitement" that "induced a restless tendency in some of the Thessalonian Christians and made them disinclined to attend to their ordinary business."[183] If it is the case that eschatological fervor led to such behavior, Paul's counsel in 4:11 would be this: *Don't get too wound up about end times and be sure to stay committed to good daily habits of work and self-sustainment, especially as a positive testimony to the productive behavior of Jesus-followers in society.*

In 1988, R. Russell challenged this "eschatological" approach to the ἄτακτοι (and consequently the interpretation of 1 Thess 4:11).[184] Russell argued that the ἄτακτοι presented a social problem that was not related to eschatological fervor. Members of lower status were attaching to benefactors and were relying on them for livelihood. In this situation, Paul was discouraging such clients from taking advantage of the hospitality of Christian patrons.[185] In this case, one could read 4:11 like this: *Carry out your work with your own hands and be responsible for your own affairs.*

NEWER APPROACHES AND READINGS OF 4:11

Since Russell's important article, a variety of other new readings of the situation behind 4:11 have emerged. We now consider a few of these.

Eschatology and Evangelism. By and large an "eschatological" view of the ἄτακτοι (generally, and in relation in particular to 1 Thess 4:11)

---

182. Bruce, *Thessalonians*, 175; Morris, *Thessalonians*, 9. See too Dobschütz, *Die Thessalonicher-Briefe*, 180–83; Rigaux, *Thessaloniciens*, 519–21.

183. Bruce, *Thessalonians*, 175.

184. R. Russell, "The Idle in 2 Thess 3.6–12: An Eschatological or a Social Problem?," *NTS* 34.1 (1988): 105–19.

185. See too B. W. Winter, "'If a Man Does Not Wish to Work . . .': A Cultural and Historical Setting for 2 Thessalonians 3:6–16," *TynBul* 40 (1989): 303–15; cf. Witherington, *Thessalonians*, 44, 121; Green, *Thessalonians*, 210.

has fallen out of favor in Thessalonian scholarship, but J. M. G. Barclay has offered a new kind of eschatological theory. His approach, however, does not insinuate that the ἄτακτοι were loafing or being lazy. Rather (see pp. 66–68), Barclay suggests that perhaps some of the Thessalonians became overzealous in their newfound faith, gave up on their regular (wage-earning) work, and instead engaged in extensive evangelism— perhaps a kind of rash "preaching" that could be harsh and off-putting.[186] Trevor Burke takes up Barclay's reading and expands on it. Burke considers the possibility that Thessalonian believers employed evangelistic methods that may have included "pouring scorn on non-Christians' morals and beliefs," and this tension would have been exacerbated by a reputation that the Christians had of not providing for their families.[187] In such a case, Paul might have been counseling the Thessalonians to cool down their Christian fanaticism and settle back down into their normal jobs, especially as a favorable witness to their nonbelieving neighbors who were observing their ostensibly "unproductive" lifestyle.[188]

Greco-Roman Philosophy and Work. Some scholars have devoted energy to explore Paul's encouragement to the Thessalonians to work with their hands. In Malherbe's view, Paul looked a lot like those itinerant philosophers who sought to make converts from among the working class.[189] As an example, Malherbe gives Socrates, who sometimes taught in workshops.[190] The first-century Roman Stoic Gaius Musonius Rufus encouraged manual labor, believing and teaching that "one should endure hardships, and suffer the pains of labor with his own body, rather than depend upon another for sustenance" (Musonius Rufus, *Fragment* 11).[191] Malherbe urges that this philosophical support of manual labor offers a stronger background for Paul's instruction than Jewish teaching.

---

186. See Barclay, "Conflict in Thessalonica," *CBQ* 55 (1993): 522–24.

187. See Burke, *Family Matters*, 207.

188. For my own response to Barclay's work, see p. 139.

189. Malherbe, *Paul and the Thessalonians*, 19–20. It is nevertheless important to remember that most elites resonated with the thoughts of Cicero who believed that the ideal was to pursue investments and occupations that led to a life of leisure. Cicero looked down upon "hired workmen whom we pay for mere manual labor, not for artistic skill; for in their case the very wage they receive is a pledge of their slavery" (*On Duties* 1.150–51 [Miller, LCL], as cited in N. Elliott and M. Reasoner, *Documents and Images for the Study of Paul* [Minneapolis: Fortress, 2010], 29–30). See also Hock, *Social Context*, 42–45; R. M. Grant, *Early Christianity and Society: Seven Studies* (San Francisco: Harper & Row, 1977), 74.

190. Diogenes Laertius, *Lives of Eminent Philosophers* 2.21, 122; Malherbe, *Paul and the Thessalonians*, 19; see too R. F. Hock, "Simon the Shoemaker as an Ideal Cynic," *GRBS* 17 (1976): 41–53.

191. Malherbe, *Paul and the Thessalonians*, 20.

Malherbe believes, however, that Paul differed from such work-approving philosophers in various ways. For example, while some philosophers promoted work, they often did not do any themselves! In contrast, Paul himself clearly plied a trade for all to see.[192] And it was not just to earn a living, but as a "demonstration of his self-giving and love for his converts."[193] This reinforced Paul's confidence that he could, in good conscience, encourage his converts to imitate him. Thus, Paul "made use of elements from the Greco-Roman philosophical moral tradition, but adapted them to express his theological understanding of his enterprise and to form communities of believers."[194]

Calvin Roetzel also relates contemporary philosophical perspectives to Paul's statement in 4:11, but instead of focusing on manual labor he gives attention to the notion of the "quiet" life. For this, he appeals to Philo.[195] For Philo, the quiet life was not about political quietism but a unique perspective on life offered by wisdom. Philo could advocate for the contemplative, tranquil life as "an eloquent silence coming from a simple reliance on God, a confident waiting on God by Abraham to provide an animal for the commanded sacrifice, or even the eschatological rest hovering over the land in the final days."[196]

Those like Malherbe and Roetzel who tend to read Paul's instructions in 1 Thessalonians 4:11 in light of Greco-Roman philosophers and moralists desire to properly contextualize the apostle. They also wish to argue that his teachings may not have been reactionary (at least not reactionary to eschatological laziness), but rather pedagogical, pertaining to the ideal of the good life—in Paul's case, the gospel life.[197]

Work and Greco-Roman Associations. Richard Ascough has opened a new contextual framework for understanding 1 Thessalonians 4:11. He argues that there is a link between the Thessalonian believing community

---

192. See A. J. Malherbe, "Paul: Hellenistic Philosopher or Christian Pastor," in Holladay et al., *Light from the Gentiles*, 1:200.

193. Malherbe, "Hellenistic Philosopher," 200.

194. Malherbe, "Hellenistic Philosopher," 201.

195. C. J. Roetzel, "Theodidaktoi and Handiwork in Philo and 1 Thessalonians," in *L'Apôtre Paul: personnalité, style et conception du ministère*, ed. A. Vanhoye (Leuven: Leuven University Press, 1986), 324–31.

196. See C. Roetzel, *Paul, a Jew on the Margins* (Louisville: Westminster John Knox, 2003), 29.

197. J. W. Thompson recognizes parallels between Paul and the moralists on this matter, but prefers to read Paul's instructions about work in light of *Jewish* ethical thought as demonstrated in places such as the Old Testament (e.g., Exod 20:9; Prov 6:6–11; 24:30–34; 28:19) and early Jewish literature (e.g., Sir 7:15; T. Iss. 5:1–3; Ps.-Phoc. 153–74); see J. W. Thompson, *Moral Formation according to Paul* (Grand Rapids: Baker, 2011), 82–83.

and Greco-Roman associations.[198] Partly based on Paul's reference to his own labor (1 Thess 2:9) and the command for the letter recipients to work with their hands, Ascough argues that the believers were manual laborers and that Paul was at the same social level.[199] Ascough explains that Paul's reminding the Thessalonians of his own faithful manual labor would not be well received if the Thessalonian community was comprised of elites.

Ascough devotes some attention to φιλοτιμέομαι in 1 Thessalonians 4:11 in view of his association theory. He points out that φιλοτιμέομαι (and its cognates) are found in association inscriptions related to competition for recognition and status within such guilds.[200] He writes, "It is most often used for the competition and rivalry for honor within the group itself."[201] According to Ascough, Paul was taking up such familiar language, not to encourage rivalry but rather to find value and honor in a peace-filled "community of mutual coexistence."[202] The notion of the quiet or tranquil life involves deference, not quietism.[203]

Callia Rulmu accepts Ascough's "association" theory and has taken it further, reading 1 Thessalonians in light of political circumstances in Roman Macedonia.[204] Rulmu believes that Paul's letter to the Thessalonians offered counsel that helped the believing community survive.

Rulmu begins by describing the precarious situation that associations experienced in the first-century Roman Empire. Despite Thessalonica demonstrating loyalty to Rome in the end (especially for the successful Octavian; see p. 48), Rulmu argues that Rome did not consider this city to represent its ideals.[205]

Furthermore, Thessalonica experienced economic depression in the first-century CE, where unemployment and "idleness" would have been rather common. Associations would have provided networks of support for lower-status workers. Like unions today, Greco-Roman associations could

---

198. See Ascough, *Paul's Macedonian Associations*; idem, *1 and 2 Thessalonians*; and idem, "The Thessalonian Christian Community as a Professional Voluntary Association," *JBL* 119.2 (2000): 311–28.

199. Ascough, "Thessalonian Christian Community," 314–15.

200. Ascough, "Thessalonian Christian Community," 321.

201. Ascough, "Thessalonian Christian Community," 321.

202. Ascough, "Thessalonian Christian Community," 322.

203. Ascough recounts how, in Greco-Roman associations, the group might enforce social control via fines or floggings—not so with Paul (Ascough, "Thessalonian Christian Community," 322).

204. C. Rulmu, "Between Ambition and Quietism: The Sociopolitical Background of 1 Thessalonians 4,9–12," *Biblica* 91.3 (2010): 393–417.

205. Rulmu, "Between Ambition and Quietism," 397.

be perceived as a strong political entity. Thus civic leaders (appointed by Rome) tended to stand in some tension with these guilds. Rulmu explains that in Paul's time, eastern provinces of the Roman Empire experienced power struggles between local native leadership and appointed Roman leadership.[206]

As an example, Rulmu offers Dio Chrysostom's speech before Tarsus. Apparently Dio refers to a guild of linen-workers who were mistreated by the populus and blamed for local unrest.

> At times the citizens are irritated by them and assert that they are a useless rabble and responsible for the tumult and disorder in Tarsus, while at other times they regard them as a part of the city and hold the opposite opinion of them. . . . Well, if you believe them to be detrimental to you and instigators of insurrection and confusion, you should expel them altogether and not admit them to your popular assemblies; but if on the other hand you regard them as being in some measure citizens . . . then surely it is not fitting to disenfranchise them or to cut them off from association with you (*Tarsica altera* [*Or.* 34] 21–22).[207]

To "strive to keep quiet" (1 Thess 4:11), then, Rulmu argues, relates to Paul's desire that the Christian community in Thessalonica maintain a positive civic reputation. Rulmu imagines that these believers would have been stuck in a kind of political tug-of-war. Local Greek leaders would have wanted their support, but there would have been nothing to gain from upsetting Roman rulers.[208] To encourage being *quiet* involves finding a third space separate from Roman patronage and local political alliances that could increase disharmony within and around them.[209] Thus Rulmu concludes, "This behavior would help them remain unnoticed by imperial authorities (Roman benefactors), city dwellers, and local politarchs (Greek patrons), and secure the association's continuance."[210]

---

206. Rulmu, "Between Ambition and Quietism," 411.
207. Rulmu, "Between Ambition and Quietism," 412.
208. See Rulmu, "Between Ambition and Quietism," 415.
209. Rulmu explains how Rome called for a "redistribution of the city's resources" as a way to frustrate "local oligarchic powers," and if the Thessalonian believers availed themselves of such resources, Paul may have worried that it might lead to retaliation from Greek patrons (Rulmu, "Between Ambition and Quietism," 416).
210. Rulmu, "Between Ambition and Quietism," 416.

CONCLUSION

Each of these approaches has something to commend it. The old assumptions about a connection to eschatological fervor would connect with that desire to gather together and simplify the problems that Paul was addressing in the letter (think Occam's razor). The drawback with the early-middle twentieth-century theories is that they seem to assume that Paul's main concern was with laziness. Yet if that were so, Paul could have used a number of different words to address that problem. Why instead do we have the language of ἄτακτοι?

The emerging sociological theories (e.g., Russell, Winter) recognize that it is possible for Paul to be addressing problems unrelated to eschatological enthusiasm. They were problems that would have been common to the Roman world and included the temptation to latch onto a patron and enter a race for honors. Nevertheless, I cannot imagine that Paul's advice would be unrelated to the volatile situation of this Thessalonian church (apparently under persecution, and a situation where some members of their community had recently died). Besides, we get the impression from the Pauline corpus that Paul was trying to live beyond heavy patronage ties, but could it be true that he rejected patronage *en toto*?

What about those who argue that Paul's thought is in line with the moral philosophers of his day? Most philosophers probably would have sided with the elite in eschewing manual labor, despite the advocacy of those few voices in favor of it. While it is helpful to know broader discussions in society about work, I find it unlikely that Paul had some intentional, direct connection to those conversations.

As for Ascough's association theory, supplemented by Rulmu, again, one can certainly applaud the desire to place Paul's letter in its ancient context. Ascough is a leading expert on the subject of Greco-Roman associations, and his body of work has illuminated the study of early Christianity. However, I think there is a temptation to want to make connections in light of perceived parallels. How significant it would be if discovered and translated inscriptions shed direct light on biblical texts! But it is important to note that the connections between associations and 1 Thessalonians are circumstantial. For example, "working with hands" does not prove that Paul assumed that the Thessalonians were artisans. Paul could simply be referring to one's own work (as in Wis 1:12). As for the phrase φιλοτιμεῖσθαι ἡσυχάζειν, it is important to recognize that both φιλοτιμέομαι and ἡσυχάζω are not uncommon words in ancient Greek literature, so it is unsurprising to find them (the former especially) in association inscriptions. Rulmu seems to get more specific, seeing Paul's advice as not just good counsel generally but a necessary response to the delicate economic and political situation that this Jesus-association found itself in at the time. Again, though, it is just a theory, with unclear connections to Greek politarchs on the right and Roman rulers on the left, as it were.

I am more open to Barclay's approach that imagines that, in light of recent circumstances, the Thessalonian believers forsook their work and engaged in radical evangelism. What seems highly likely to me is that the non-working Thessalonians were not lazy or loafing around waiting for the end times. They were doing *something*. For Barclay, that something was well intentioned, but in the end it marred their testimony to the gospel. Again, Barclay's theory is speculative. My major concern is that I would expect Paul to exhort them more gently *not* to hurt their testimony, and yet I assume he would be sure to still *encourage* their proclamation of the gospel, something he never does in this letter in any direct way.

My own perspective is that the recent deaths within the community happened as a result of local persecution, and perhaps it was communicated to these believing Thessalonians (by friends, relatives, and neighbors) that either the local deities were punishing or cursing them (if the persecutors were pagans) or that the God of Israel was punishing them (if the persecutors were Jews).

It is conceivable that the confusion over these deaths and the ongoing persecution may have led to a series of church meetings that set a priority of discerning the divine will (hence Paul's clarification of the will of God [1 Thess 4:3; 5:18]) and the discerning of spirits (5:19–21, where some Thessalonians may have gone in the *other* direction, eliminating spiritual discernment altogether).

"Peace and Security": A Roman Slogan? (5:3)

Throughout this chapter we have observed how interpretations of convoluted or difficult texts in 1 Thessalonians have morphed especially throughout the last few decades. This is especially true for 1 Thessalonians 5:3, where the reading of this text has taken a decided turn since 1985. Virtually all scholars now read this verse in a way that would not have been considered before. Let's begin with the text.

The opening verses of 1 Thessalonians 5 involve Paul's instruction regarding "times and seasons" in view of the day of the Lord (vv. 1–11 NRSV).

Paul portends the unexpected arrival of the Lord, like a thief in the night (v. 2). He warns the Thessalonians that some may say, "There is peace and security," but immediately they will be destroyed (5:3 NRSV).

> Now concerning the times and the seasons, brothers and sisters, you do not need to have anything written to you. For you yourselves know very well that the day of the Lord will come like a thief in the night. When they say, "There is peace and security," then sudden destruction will come upon them, as labor pains come upon a pregnant woman, and there will be no escape. (1 Thess 5:1–3 NRSV)

> Περὶ δὲ τῶν χρόνων καὶ τῶν καιρῶν, ἀδελφοί, οὐ χρείαν ἔχετε ὑμῖν γράφεσθαι, ² αὐτοὶ γὰρ ἀκριβῶς οἴδατε ὅτι ἡμέρα κυρίου ὡς κλέπτης ἐν νυκτὶ οὕτως ἔρχεται. ³ ὅταν λέγωσιν· εἰρήνη καὶ ἀσφάλεια, τότε αἰφνίδιος αὐτοῖς ἐφίσταται ὄλεθρος ὥσπερ ἡ ὠδὶν τῇ ἐν γαστρὶ ἐχούσῃ, καὶ οὐ μὴ ἐκφύγωσιν.

The origin of this phrase "peace and security" (5:3; NIV: "peace and safety") has been the subject of much interest throughout the modern period. Prior to the 1980s, it was common to read this in light of Old Testament allusions. F. F. Bruce, for example, points to the possibility that Paul was inspired by prophetic criticism of the proclamation of false peace. For instance, Jeremiah addresses the matter of corrupt leadership. Rather than trusted leaders looking out for the public's best interest, such charlatans say "peace, peace" even when there is no peace (Jer 6:14). Similarly, Ezekiel identifies false prophets who peddle false visions and deceptive divinations. They deceive the people with promises of "peace," but no such peace exists (Ezek 13:10). Wrath is coming on the people of Israel, and the Lord will break out against those false prophets (Ezek 13:16–23).[211] For most commentators, this appeal to the Old Testament background largely settled the matter.

"PEACE AND SECURITY" AS ROMAN POLITICAL SLOGAN

Toward the last quarter of the twentieth century, when New Testament scholarship took a stronger interest in the political dynamics of the Roman Empire,[212] several scholars detected a resonance with this phrase

---

211. See Bruce, *Thessalonians*, 110.
212. See E. Bammel, "Ein Beitrag zur paulinischen Staatsanschauung," *TLZ* (1960): 837–40; see further Hendrix, "Thessalonicans Honor Romans."

with the kind of propaganda publicized by Rome in relation to imperial pronouncements and promises of political stability and peace. Many would trace the influence of this reading to Klaus Wengst (*Pax Romana and the Peace of Jesus Christ*).[213] It was further reinforced by Donfried, Koester, Brocke, and Harrison.[214] In 2012, Jeffrey Weima wrote an extensive review and discussion of the major evidence in favor of this Roman slogan ("peace and security"), and also offered some reflection on why Paul would have referred to this motto.[215] Weima considers four categories of evidence for the "peace and security" theme in Roman (or pro-Roman) material: numismatic, monumental, inscriptional, and literary. We will offer here a brief review of Weima's strongest pieces of evidence for the Roman slogan or theme.

Numismatics. In this category, Weima identifies how peace (*pax*) appears on numerous imperial coins throughout the reigns of Octavian, Tiberius, Claudius, and Nero. According to Weima, this consistent emphasis reflects a "trajectory of imperial propaganda begun with Augustus and continued by others not just in the Julio-Claudian line but subsequent emperors as well—a trajectory of imperial propaganda whereby the Roman leaders used coins to market their rule as one that offered its citizens benefits of peace and security."[216] While Weima readily acknowledges that most coins of note focus on *pax* alone, there is some evidence that "security/safety" was treated as a deified Roman value as well (*Securitas*).[217]

Monuments. Weima discusses several monuments relevant to Roman peace. He describes a statue of Pompey (from Ilium) that bears this inscription: "Restoring peace and security on land and sea."[218] This is one of the most important pieces of Weima's evidence, because both words—

---

213. Klaus Wengst, *Pax Romana and the Peace of Jesus Christ* (London: SCM, 1987).

214. K. P. Donfried, "The Cults of Thessalonica and the Thessalonian Correspondence," *NTS* 31.3 (1995): 336–56; H. Koester, "Imperial Ideology and Paul's Eschatology in 1 Thessalonians," in *Paul and Empire*, ed. R. A. Horsley (Harrisburg, PA: Trinity Press International, 1997), 161–62; Brocke, *Thessaloniki*, 176–79; Harrison, *Paul and the Imperial Authorities*, 61–62; cf. H. Hendrix, "Archaeology and Eschatology at Thessalonica," in *The Future of Early Christianity: Essays in Honor of Helmut Koester*, ed. B. A. Pearson (Minneapolis: Fortress, 1991), 107–18; T. R. Neufeld, *Put on the Armour of God: The Divine Warrior from Isaiah to Ephesians* (Sheffield: Sheffield Academic Press, 1997), 81; Carter, *Roman Empire*, 89; L. Nasrallah, "Empire and Apocalypse in Thessaloniki," *JECS* 13.4 (2005): at 498–99.

215. J. Weima, "'Peace and Security' (1 Thess 5.3): Prophetic Warning or Political Propoganda?," *NTS* 58.3 (2012): 331–59.

216. Weima, "'Peace and Security' (1 Thess 5.3)," 340.

217. Weima, "'Peace and Security' (1 Thess 5.3)," 340.

218. ἀποκαθεστάκοτα δὲ [τὴν εἰρ]ήνην καὶ τὴν ἀσφάλειαν καὶ κατὰ γῆν καὶ κατὰ θάλασσαν; see Weima, "'Peace and Security' (1 Thess 5.3)," 341–42.

peace and security—*in Greek* are found here, just as they are in 1 Thessalonians 5:3. Weima also notes the Nicopolis monument commemorating the victory of Octavian, acclaiming his "peace acquired on land and sea" (*pax parta terra marique*).[219] And of course there is the Ara Pacis ("Altar of Peace"). Again, though, "security" is not necessarily prominent in the monument evidence, but Weima adds that the people of Praeneste had dual altars—one in honor of *Pax Augusta* and the other for *Securitas Augusta*.[220]

Inscriptions. Weima also finds the Roman inscriptional evidence to be significant. He begins with the *Res Gestae Divi Augusti* inscription that praises the recovery of peace ushered in by Augustus, especially through conquest and war.[221] There is also an important Syrian inscription that reads as follows: "The Lord Marcus Flavius Bonus, the most illustrious Comes and Dux of the first legion, has ruled over us in *peace* and given constant *peace* and *security* to travelers and to the people" (*OGIS* 613).[222] Similar to the case of the Pompey statue, here with the Syrian inscription we have the terms "peace" and "security" together.[223]

Literary. The last category that Weima considers involves literary texts. Weima offers Josephus as an example. Josephus narrates a decree from the people of Pergamum that reads as follows:

> In the presidency of Cratippus, on the first of the month Daisios, a decree of the magistrates. As the Romans in pursuance of the practices of their ancestors have accepted dangerous risks for the common safety [ἀσφάλεια] of all humankind and strive emulously to place their allies and friends in a state of happiness and lasting peace [εἰρήνη], the Jewish nation and their high priest Hyrcanus have sent as envoys to them . . . (*Ant.* 14.247–48)[224]

---

219. Weima, "'Peace and Security' (1 Thess 5.3)," 342–43; also L. D. Ginsberg, *Staging Memory, Staging Strife: Empire and Civil War in the Octavia* (Oxford: Oxford University Press, 2016), 71–72.

220. Weima, "'Peace and Security' (1 Thess 5.3)," 343; P. Zanker also notes that after the death of Augustus, the Praenestan people added another altar to these two, one for the deified emperor; see Zanker, *The Power of Images in the Age of Augustus* (Ann Arbor: University of Michigan Press, 1988), 307; cf. Harrison, *Paul and the Imperial Authorities*, 61.

221. Weima, "'Peace and Security' (1 Thess 5.3)," 349. Again, though, Weima notes that *securitas* is not prominent in this lengthy inscription (350).

222. Weima, "'Peace and Security' (1 Thess 5.3)," 352.

223. See Wengst, *Pax Romana*, 19; Harrison, *Paul and the Imperial Authorities*, 61.

224. Weima, "'Peace and Security' (1 Thess 5.3)," 353.

Elsewhere in *Antiquities* Josephus writes how Herod was praised for establishing peace [εἰρήνη] and "secure[ing] enjoyment" (ἀσφαλῆ . . . ἀπόλαυσιν; *Ant.* 14.160).

Weima also offers material from Roman historian Velleius Paterculus, who referred to the victories of general Lucius Piso (under Tiberius) against the Thracians. Piso was recognized for the restoration of *"security* to Asia and *peace* to Macedonia *(Asiae securitatem, Macedoniae pacem).*"[225] Weima finds a particularly important text in Plutarch's *Parallel Lives.* According to Plutarch, Mark Antony was duped by Parthian King Phraates, who offered the false promise of "peace and security."[226] Here, again, we find the phrase εἰρήνη καὶ ἀσφάλεια just as we find in 1 Thessalonians 5:3.

In summary, Weima has collected strong evidence in favor of demonstrating a peace and security Roman slogan was something that Paul was referring or alluding to in 1 Thessalonians 5:3. This argument, however, has not convinced everyone. Joel White wrote an important 2013 *New Testament Studies* article challenging the logic and evidence of Weima's work.[227] A major goal of White's work is breaking down the pattern and trajectory traced by Weima and others. While White does not intend to completely *refute* the slogan idea, he does seek to demonstrate that the evidence is not nearly as homogenous, prominent, or consistent as it may seem.

Numismatics. White points out that *securitas* does not appear on coins until the later period of Nero's reign, much later than Paul's writing of 1 Thessalonians.[228]

Pompey inscription (Ilium). While indeed this inscription refers to "peace and security," White argues that it simply dates too early (62 BCE) to be considered "Roman imperial propaganda" since the Roman principate was established decades later.

Praeneste altar inscription (near Rome). In terms of dating, White acknowledges that these altars come from the late Augustan period (at their original production). However, he urges that the simple fact of their existence, even their paired erection, does not supply proof of a Roman slogan.

---

225. Weima, "'Peace and Security' (1 Thess 5.3)," 354.
226. Weima, "'Peace and Security' (1 Thess 5.3)," 355.
227. Joel R. White, "'Peace and Security' (1 Thessalonians 5.3): Is It Really a Roman Slogan?," *NTS* 59 (2013): 382–95.
228. White, "'Peace and Security,'" 392. White readily admits, though, that the "*pax*-ideology" of Rome was easily identifiable with the Julio-Claudian emperors.

Res Gestae Divi Augusti. This text goes back to 13 BCE. White recognizes that this is a work in praise of Augustus and lauds the political "peace" brought about by his leadership. However, White argues that this is also a rather large inscription and never actually pairs "peace and security." In fact, in the original Latin text, the word *securitas* is not present at all.

Vellius Paterculus. Weima gave attention to several texts from Paterculus. White examines the phrase "security to Asia and peace to Macedonia" (*Historia Romana* 2.98.2). He argues that Paterculus is simply being descriptive, not purveying Roman propaganda. In 2.103.4–5, safety/welfare and peace do occur together, but not as a phrase that repeats or attests to a slogan. Rather, Paterculus lists a series of related words: "welfare, stillness, peace, tranquility."[229]

Syrian inscription. White is quick to point out that there is no specific mention of "peace and security." Yet I think White is too quick to downplay the fact that εἰρήνη and εἰρηνεύω do appear in close proximity to ἀσφαλίζω:

Ὁ κύριος Μ(ᾶρκος) Φλ(άβιος) Βόνος ὁ λαμπρ(ότατος) πρώτου τάγ(ματος) κόμ(ης) καὶ δού(ξ) ἄρξας ἡμ(ῶ)ν ἐν εἰρήνῃ καὶ τοὺς διοδεύοντας καὶ τὸ ἔθνος διὰ παντὸς εἰρηνεύεσθαι ἠσφαλίσατο.

I believe the more significant point that White makes regarding the Syrian inscription is that the inscription dates to the late fourth-century CE, marginally relevant "to the discussion of Roman imperial ideology three centuries earlier."[230]

A major conclusion for White is that a Roman emphasis on *securitas*, present in imperial literature toward the end of the first-century CE and beyond, should not be read *back* into older works. White explains that "it was only in Nero's later reign that the ideology of *securitas* was articulated, precisely due to the fact that the Roman upper classes were feeling increasingly insecure, and very much later still that Roman authors began to lend credence to the self-aggrandizing claims of Nero and his sycophants and wistfully long for the presumed Golden Age under Nero."[231]

---

229. See similarly Seneca, *Clem.* 1.19.8, where Roman rule is connected to "justice, peace, modesty, security, and dignity"; again, "Seneca seems to be drawing from a mental canon of stock virtues that Rome tended to attribute to its benevolent rule" (White, "'Peace and Security,'" 388).

230. White, "'Peace and Security,'" 391.

231. White, "'Peace and Security,'" 393–94.

CONCLUSION

The "Roman slogan" reading of 1 Thessalonians 5:3 has a few items in its favor. The words "peace" and "security" do appear in Roman propaganda, and the phrase fits Roman concerns to represent their leadership as politically supreme and protective. Thessalonica itself had shown a history of trying to curry favor with Rome.[232] However, for my part I have found that this "Roman slogan" approach to 1 Thessalonians 5:3 feels too academically trendy, and care has not been given to answer the question of *satisfaction*. What would be Paul's point of linking to this imperial context and background? Moreover, as we will discuss further below, very few scholars have tried to make sense of how such repeating of a Roman slogan fits into Paul's overall message in 1 Thessalonians in light of the exigencies that influenced Paul's writing of the letter. Before we address those matters, I wish to offer some points of critique against Weima's essay, beyond what White offers.

First, Weima has some concern to point out the oddity of Paul's statement "when they say, 'There is peace and security,'" arguing that this must be a "borrowed phrase" because Paul tends to use the term "peace" with a religious meaning rather than as a political term.[233] Yet is it really possible to separate a different *religious* meaning from a *political* one—especially in an environment where "religion" and "politics" were not neatly separable entities? Moreover, do we not see that Paul would be going beyond a "religious" meaning (whatever exactly that means) when he refers to God as "the God of peace" who will crush Satan under his feet (Rom 16:20)? Or, even within 1 Thessalonians, are we to imagine that when Paul calls the believers to be "at peace with each other," there is a narrowly *religious* meaning intended here, particularly separate from a social or political one (1 Thess 5:13)?

Secondly, while Weima is well intentioned for trying to find every relevant political source from the Roman world that mentions "peace" or "peace and security," it ends up weakening rather than strengthening his case because it simply reinforces what should be rather obvious: "peace" and "safety/security" are very common words and are not technical terms in and of themselves. Consider the analogy of the American police motto "to serve and protect." It might prove very difficult to demonstrate how various texts might be drawing from this motto because the phrase utilizes mundane words that are used frequently in varied contexts.

---

232. See above with Rulmu, "Between Ambition and Quietism"; see also pp. 51–53 above.
233. Weima, "Peace and Security,'" 331n1.

To take a few examples, Weima offers a selection from Plutarch, but this example is not really a helpful demonstration of a Roman slogan because the offer of security actually comes from a non-Roman (Phraates) toward Mark Antony. Weima recognizes this and portrays it as irony,[234] but it is more likely that these are just fitting words found in political or social discourses of alliance and collaboration. And what about Josephus? Indeed, Josephus does have related terminology pertaining to pro-Roman Herod, but Josephus also pairs the words in view of a generic sense of political safety (*J.W.* 4.596). We must recognize that "peace" and "safety" are simply going to come up in political discourse and consider the possibility that this is not a "slogan." For example, Philo writes about how God serves as the great king, the one who brings true security and peace, "for, in truth, God is the president of peace, but his subordinate ministers are the chiefs of war" (*Decalogue* 178 [Yonge]). Also, in the *Letter of Aristeas* we read about the wish that "Almighty God might preserve your kingdom in peace with honor, and that the translation of the holy law might prove advantageous to you and be carried out successfully" (45 [OPE]).

Yet the greatest concern I have with the "Roman slogan" interpretation of 1 Thessalonians 5:3 is the failure to integrate it with Paul's concerns in 1 Thessalonians and the Thessalonian situation. While some have connected Paul's words to a desire on his part to encourage the Thessalonians to negotiate their delicate political standing with Rome diplomatically, most interpreters simply wrest 1 Thessalonians 5:3 out of its context to explain Paul's language of "peace and safety/security" (as anti-imperial). Below are three reasons why I find the "Roman slogan" reading unfitting for a cogent reading of 1 Thessalonians.

First, if there is a deceptive promise of "peace and security" given to the Thessalonian believers, one would think that it somehow relates to the concern over recent deaths in the community (e.g., 1 Thess 4:13). However, if "peace and security" relates to Roman protection, it is unclear how this could come as some sort of comfort to the Thessalonian Christian community. Let us say that some Thessalonians died of natural causes (e.g., health problems). Who would promise "peace and security," and how could they stop such diseases or illnesses through such Roman peace? I find it likely that some Thessalonian believers died due to persecution. In that case, it would make even less sense for them to be offered Roman "peace and security."

---

234. See Weima, "'Peace and Security,'" 355.

Second, in 5:3 the main verb is third plural (λέγωσιν; *"they* say"), and it appears as if there are *particular* people in mind who are promising safety. Contrast this with other ways that you might have a more generic construction, as you find in (for example) Luke 21:9: *"When you hear of wars and uprisings, do not be frightened. These things must happen first, but the end will not come right away"* (cf. also Deut 13:12–15). The way that 1 Thessalonians 5:3 expresses the promise of "peace and safety," the subject of the verb appears to be known people, and thus the promise is not a free-floating "slogan." The nearest context of this verse is Paul's warning that all must be ready for the day of the Lord (1 Thess 5:2) and not act like those in the dark who are doomed for destruction (vv. 3–5). But are Romans, in Paul's view, destined for wrath? Nowhere does Paul consign the pro-Roman masses to such. More likely he is criticizing local persecutors (whether Jews or gentiles) who are troubling the Thessalonian believers, and Paul's judgment speech against them in 5:3 would play a similar role as 2:14–16 where he assures the Thessalonian believers that their oppressors will pay in the end for their sins.

My own inclination is that Bruce and others (including White) are closer to the best interpretation by imagining an echo in 5:3 of false promises proffered by counterfeit prophets and leaders in the Old Testament. In Thessalonica, let's imagine that gentile Godfearers were drawn away from the synagogue by Paul's gospel of Jesus. The synagogue leaders were upset with Paul and were vying for these gentiles' allegiance. When some people from the believing community died, the Jewish leaders found an opportunity to claim that the God of Israel was cursing them for their betrayal and apostasy. If these gentiles would come back to proper homage to the God of Israel, they would find "peace and security" from divine wrath. Paul's response is that these peddlers of false peace will be caught out in their scheming on the day of the Lord, a day that could come suddenly.

RECOMMENDED READING

Themes

Donfried, K. P., and I. H. Marshall. *Theology of the Shorter Pauline Letters*. NTT. Cambridge: Cambridge University Press, 1993.

Johnson, A. *1 and 2 Thessalonians*. THNT. Grand Rapids: Eerdmans, 2016.

Morris, L. *1, 2 Thessalonians*. Word Biblical Themes. Dallas: Word, 1989.

Interpretation

Given the varied nature of the passages under discussion, we will only offer here technical commentaries and similar resources.

Bruce, F. F. *1 and 2 Thessalonians.* WBC. Waco, TX: Word, 1982.

Fee, G. D. *The First and Second Letters to the Thessalonians.* NICNT. Grand Rapids: Eerdmans, 2009.

Malherbe, A. *The Letters to the Thessalonians.* AB. New York: Doubleday, 2000.

Nicholl, C. R. *From Hope to Despair in Thessalonica: Situating 1 and 2 Thessalonians.* SNTSMS 126. Cambridge: Cambridge University Press, 2004.

Wanamaker, C. A. *The Epistles to the Thessalonians.* NIGTC. Grand Rapids: Eerdmans, 1990.

Weima, J. A. D. *1–2 Thessalonians.* BECNT. Grand Rapids: Baker, 2014.

Weima, J. A. D., and S. E. Porter. *An Annotated Bibliography of 1 and 2 Thessalonians.* NTTS 26. Leiden: Brill, 1998.

CHAPTER 4

HISTORY OF INTERPRETATION OF 1 THESSALONIANS

In this chapter we will survey how 1 Thessalonians has been interpreted throughout the centuries. Due to the swell of academic research in the modern period, more attention will be given to the study of 1 Thessalonians in the twentieth and twenty-first centuries.

EARLY AND MEDIEVAL CHRISTIAN INTERPRETATION OF 1 THESSALONIANS

From the extant literature from the first few centuries of Christianity, we can see that theologians took much interest in this short Pauline letter. We will begin with the incidental references to 1 Thessalonians in this material and then look at the early theological commentaries dedicated specifically to 1 Thessalonians.

Apostolic Fathers

In the works of the Apostolic Fathers we see 1 Thessalonians is of interest particularly for the Didache, Ignatius (*To Polycarp*), and Polycarp (*To the Philippians*). Regarding the first item, the mention of the "sound of the trumpet" as a sign of the end times (Did. 16.6) may relate to 1 Thessalonians 4:16. Also, the Didache's note that apostles expect to be welcomed with respect commensurate to their authority may have been supported by Paul's comments in 1 Thessalonians 2:6–7 (see Did. 11.4).

As for Ignatius, in the introductory words of his letter to Polycarp he repeats Paul's exhortation to pray "without ceasing" (Ignatius: προσευχαῖς σχόλαζε ἀδιαλείπτοις [Ign. *Pol.* 1.3]; Paul: ἀδιαλείπτως προσεύχεσθε

[1 Thess 5:17]). For Polycarp, the connection to 1 Thessalonians is by no means certain, but it is worth mentioning that he connects the words faith, hope, and love, the same theological triad that appears in 1 Thessalonians 1:3 and 1 Corinthians 13:13 (see Pol. *Phil.* 3.2–3).

The Greek Fathers

In *Against Heresies*, Irenaeus describes the folly of those who flippantly presume that they can properly identify the antichrist. Irenaeus calls them false prophets who will lead others astray and themselves face judgment. Irenaeus goes on to quote 1 Thessalonians 5:3 in full (see Irenaeus, *Haer.* 5.30.2).

Clement of Alexandria is probably the Greek Father who engages the most with 1 Thessalonians (in the extant literature). Much of this interaction comes in the *Stromata* and *Paedagogus*. He quotes or alludes to several phrases or ideas from 1 Thessalonians 2 (2:4 in *Strom.* 7.104; 2:5 in *Strom.* 1.12; 2:6 in *Paed.* 1.40), 1 Thessalonians 4 (4:3 in *Strom.* 4.122; 4:9 in *Paed.* 1.55), and 1 Thessalonians 5 (5:6 in *Strom.* 4.210; 5:13 in *Paed.* 3.204).

As for Origen, we find two references to 1 Thessalonians 2:14–16. One is found in Origen's correspondence with Africanus concerning the story of Susanna. Defending the authenticity of this story, Origen accuses Jewish leaders of removing it from their sacred texts because they hope to eliminate any literature that might discredit them. In support of this notion, Origen cites 1 Thessalonians 2:14–15 (see *Ep. Afr.* 9). In Origen's commentary on Matthew he again cites this text, this time in relation to Matthew 13:57 where Jesus explains that a prophet has no honor in his own country (*Comm. Matt.* 10.18). In both texts it is interesting to note that Origen refers to this passage as specifically coming from Paul's "first epistle to the Thessalonians."

Latin Fathers

By far Tertullian's works contain the most references to 1 Thessalonians among the early church theologians (aside from actual commentaries). In *Against Marcion* Tertullian devotes a section of his fifth book to 1 Thessalonians, even pointing out that these "shorter" epistles deserve attention and that one can find value in them despite their brevity! Here Tertullian refers to the Jewish persecution of the prophets (1 Thess 2:15 in *Marc.* 5.15). He discusses how Paul condemns fornication (1 Thess 4:3 in *Marc.* 5.15; see too *Exh. cast.* 3). He also briefly summarizes Paul's eschatological teaching regarding those who are dead and alive in Christ who will meet the Lord in the clouds (1 Thess 4:15 in *Marc.* 5.15; cf. *Marc.* 5.931 and *De patientia* 85 regarding 1 Thess 4:13). Before turning to 2 Thessalonians, Tertullian gives extended attention to Paul's theological anthropology (1 Thess 5:23) whereby Tertullian reinforces the notion of three components of the person: body, soul, and spirit (*Marc.* 5.15).

Tertullian also quotes 1 Thessalonians in his *The Resurrection of the Flesh*. In chapter 24, Tertullian cites 1 Thessalonians 1:9–10 to demonstrate that Paul's eschatology presumed anticipation of resurrection (cf. also *Adv. Jud.* 13). Almost immediately he also cites 1 Thessalonians 3:13, observing that death is not the end. First Thessalonians 4:13–17 is quoted next to give detail of Paul's understanding of the events of the raising of the dead and those who are still alive (*Res.* 24). And, again in this same chapter, Tertullian cites 1 Thessalonians 5:1–3 to the effect that Christians ought not to waver or doubt in any of these matters lest they be deceived. Elsewhere Tertullian refers to Paul's principle that each one must work with his own hands (*Idol.* 27; see 1 Thess 4:11).

As for Cyprian, in his *Testimonies against the Jews*, he cites verbatim 1 Thessalonians 4:6 and 5:3 (*Test.* 12, lines 752 and 753 respectively). Augustine's use of 1 Thessalonians extends across many of his works, but it appears especially in *The City of God*. He makes incidental reference to Paul's teaching on Christian encouragement (1 Thess 3:7 in *Civ.* 3.8). He quotes 1 Thessalonians 4:4 in relation to the vice of lust (*Civ.* 14.16). He gives more sustained attention to the eschatological material of 1 Thessalonians. In *City of God* 20.20 Augustine devotes a whole section entitled, "What the Same Apostle [Paul] Taught in the First Epistle to the Thessalonians regarding the Resurrection of the Dead." Here he quotes 1 Thessalonians 4:13–16 and intersperses material from 1 Corinthians 15.[1] Later in book 20, Augustine cites 1 Thessalonians 4:17 in proof of the heavenly judgment of God through Jesus Christ (*Civ.* 20.24).

Twice Augustine appeals to 1 Thessalonians 5:5 to address matters pertaining to the meaning of creation, especially the formation of days, celestial entities, and cosmology (*Civ.* 11.7, 33). Finally, regarding ethics, Augustine approves of Paul's emphasis on the Christian work of donning the "breastplate of faith and love" (1 Thess 5:8; *Civ.* 3.26). In book 15,

---

1. In book 12, Augustine also refers briefly to 1 Thess 4:16, affirming that in the resurrection believers will be with the Lord forever (*Civ.* 12.13).

Augustine handles the matter of the destructive and divisive nature of sin and the contrastive generosity of the Christian. Citing 1 Thessalonians 5:14–15 in full, Augustine discusses the Christian duty to eschew revenge and persistent anger (*Civ.* 15.6).

Hippolytus of Rome gave some attention to 1 Thessalonians in his *Demonstratio de Christo et Antichristo.* He warns a certain "Theophilus" against eschatological heresies and expresses concern that Scripture be carefully consulted on such matters. Hippolytus cites 1 Thessalonians 4:13 and 17 verbatim (§66).

Summary of Key Themes in Incidental References

There is obviously substantial interest in 1 Thessalonians among the earliest Christian theologians in noncommentary Christian texts of the first few centuries. It should be no surprise that *eschatology* (particularly resurrection and judgment) receives sustained attention in these texts. Moral formation and the reinforcement of proper Christian behavior is another major theme that these theologians relate to 1 Thessalonians, including rejection of idols, control of passions, and honest labor. Remarkably early in the Christian tradition, the faith-hope-love Pauline triad became "quotable" and disseminated. We also notice that 1 Thessalonians 2:13–15 quickly became a text that (unfortunately) led early Christians to attack the perceived corruption and hostility of Jews and could be more generally used to point out the fate of heretics and opponents of Christianity.

Early Christian Commentaries on 1 Thessalonians

We know that a number of early Christian theologians wrote exegetical pieces on 1 Thessalonians, though some of this information comes to us indirectly or in incomplete form (e.g., Theodore of Mopsuestia and Severian of Gabala). What we *do* have is complete material from John Chrysostom and Theodoret of Cyrrhus.

Chrysostom's commentary on 1 Thessalonians comes in the form of eleven homilies. His approach to interpreting Scripture is rather like modern exegetical approaches. Nevertheless, Chrysostom has a clear pastoral interest and comments on 1 Thessalonians with a view toward Christian formation in doctrine, but ultimately he is interested in Christian virtue. Paul is often presented as the model or ideal of the virtuous believer. Throughout these homilies, Chrysostom spends considerable time addressing themes such as perseverance in the face of trials (and the importance of prayer in such circumstances), the virtues of love and true friendship, the honorable attitude of hard work, and the resistance to Satan and his temptations. When it comes to eschatology (1 Thessalonians 4–5), Chrysostom dedicates most of his eighth homily (a rather lengthy treatise) to the question of whether the divine threats of judgment are real or simply rhetorical to curb misbehavior. Chrysostom offers an astounding barrage of proofs from Scripture that punishments and judgments are indeed a reality to take seriously.

Chrysostom also gives sustained attention to Paul's concern for sexual purity (1 Thess 4). This reflection from Chrysostom aptly summarizes his zeal for his reader's moral formation:

> On this account Paul said, "even as the Gentiles who knew not God." Let us be ashamed, let us be afraid, if the Gentiles, that know not God, are often chaste. Let us turn for shame, when we are worse than they. It is easy to achieve chastity, if we will, if we withdraw ourselves from those things that are injurious, since it is not even easy to avoid fornication, if we will not. For what is [easier] than to walk in the market-place? But from the excess of laziness it is become difficult, not only in the case of women, but sometimes even in that of men. What is [easier] than to sleep? But we have made even this difficult. Many however of the rich toss themselves through a whole night, from their not waiting for the need of sleep, and then sleeping. And in short nothing is difficult, when men are willing; as nothing is easy, when they are unwilling; for we are masters of all these things.[2]

Theodore of Mopsuestia was a fourth- and fifth-century bishop and authored several biblical commentaries, including works on most of Paul's letters. What is striking about Theodore's study of 1 Thessalonians is his clear integration of Acts 16–17 and the preface to his textual remarks that states what he considered to be the background and overall purpose of the letter. What many ancient theologians tended to either skip or mention in a brief sentence or two, Theodore dwells on with considerable interest, namely, the exigencies that led to the letter itself. He writes:

---

2. Chrysostom, *Homilies on First Thessalonians*, Homily 5 (*NPNF*1 13:347).

Thus, he preached the teaching of true religion to the Thessalonians as well as in other cities. But since there were opponents indignant because of this, it came about that the apostle suffered many things in the city of the Thessalonians. There, too, those who believed in Christ endured many evils from their compatriots, so that blessed Paul was compelled to leave Thessalonica and set out for Athens. And since he feared for those who had believed, that they might perhaps be driven by the fury of the opponents to stray from the message he had set forth, he was compelled to send Timothy to them both to find out what had happened and to strengthen the souls of the faithful as much by his presence as by his admonition with sound exhortation that they should persevere in faith.[3]

Again, most of Theodore's expositional notes are rather straightforward, but worthy of note is a comment he makes pertaining to Paul's use of "we" in 1 Thessalonians 4:15: "When he said *we*, he does not mean himself or those who were at that time kept in the present life, but those faithful who will be living when the future resurrection takes place."[4] Interestingly in the fourth and fifth centuries of early Christianity there is already a need to explain the urgency of the biblical text regarding the parousia.

Theodoret of Cyrrhus was a disciple of Theodore of Mopsuestia. He wrote numerous theological works of various kinds, including many letters. He was also prolific in expositional writings. His commentaries on Paul are contained in a single work, his notes on the Pauline epistles being rather brief. Theodoret himself confessed his work to be dependent on the work of Chrysostom and Theodore.[5] In a manner similar to Chrysostom, Theodoret emphasizes the virtue and model behavior of Paul. One scholar has referred to his work on 1–2 Thessalonians as "dry, scholarly, and periphrastic."[6] His comments tend to be rather simple, drawing out the basic sense of the text. Once in a while he comments on what we think of as

---

3. See R. A. Greer, *Theodore of Mopsuestia: Commentary on the Minor Pauline Epistles* (Atlanta: SBL Press, 2010), 439.

4. Greer, *Theodore of Mopsuestia*, 477.

5. Interestingly, though, Theodoret departs from both Theodore and Chrysostom on the matter of σκεῦος in 1 Thess 4:4. Theodoret takes the "body" reading, not the "wife" reading; see A. Thiselton, *1 and 2 Thessalonians through the Centuries* (Oxford: Wiley-Blackwell, 2011), 55.

6. Peter Gorday, ed., *Colossians, 1–2 Thessalonians, 1–2 Timothy, Titus, Philemon*, ACCS (Downers Grove, IL: InterVarsity Press, 2000), xxi; see too the comments by R. N. Longenecker, *Paul, Apostle of Liberty*, 2nd ed. (Grand Rapids: Eerdmans, 2015), 289–90.

doctrinal matters (such as Christology related to 1 Thess 1:9–10), but more often his commentary takes a pastoral tone, encouraging imitation of the apostolic example. For example, regarding 1 Thessalonians 3:6 Theodoret writes, "He [Paul] cited three desirable things—faith, love and memory of their teacher: faith implies steadfastness and godliness, love the practice of virtue, and memory of their teacher and longing for him testify to their regard for the teaching."[7] Concerning 1 Thessalonians 5:8 and Paul's paraenetic military imagery, he explains, "Let faith in God, he is saying, and love of neighbor protect you in place of a breastplate; let hope of the promised salvation be for you an unbreakable headpiece."[8]

Several ancient commentators took special interest in Paul's brief mention of prophecy (1 Thess 5:19–20). Theodoret, though normally brief, offers an extended explanation of a more historical kind than one would expect in his work:

> Some commentators claim that even in the time of the apostles the devil raised up false prophets against the prophets, and that some people on account of the bogus prophets stopped even those who foretold the truth from prophesying. So he urges them not to put a stop to the charism of prophecy for the reason that those doing this are in effect extinguishing the splendor coming from there.[9]

"Ambrosiaster" is the name given to an otherwise unknown author of an ancient commentary on Paul's epistles. It is associated with the work of Ambrose, but this connection was put into question in the sixteenth century. Augustine ascribed this work to Hilary (Decimus Hilarianus Hilarius), but ultimately the author is unknown. Experts date this writing to the middle-to-late fourth century. This author interpreted 1–2 Thessalonians according to a rather plain reading, though he clearly expresses interest in formation and the "spiritual" dynamics of the text.[10] His comments on 1 Thessalonians are brief, usually simplifying what is stated in the text, repeating it in other words, or offering a brief explanation of a difficult statement.

---

7. R. C. Hill, *Theodoret: Commentary on the Letters of St. Paul*, vol. 2 (Brookline, MA: Holy Cross Orthodox Press, 2001), 115.

8. Hill, *Theodoret*, 119.

9. Hill, *Theodoret*, 120–21.

10. G. Bray, ed., *Ambrosiaster: Commentaries on Galatians–Philemon*, ACT (Downers Grove, IL: InterVarsity Press, 2009), xviii.

Ambrosiaster treated 1 Thessalonians 2:1–12 as Paul's comparison of his own ministry over and against "false apostles."[11] Regarding 1 Thessalonians 4:1–6, Ambrosiaster presents a concise summary of the purpose of the letter:

> Although Paul praises them throughout the letter, he nevertheless warns them not to be led astray into unlawful activities by some form of subtlety, and thereby incur the penalty which they have learned is the recompense of evil. They know that they will please God if they keep their bodies pure, but they must also deal honesty with their brethren so as not to become like the Gentiles and lose their entitlement to adoption.[12]

Pelagius produced several works, many of which are not extant. He wrote a commentary on Romans and a set of expositions on the Pauline letters. This latter work is referenced both by Marius Mercator and Augustine, though there is an odd history to its reception over the centuries. Regarding Pelagius's treatment of 1–2 Thessalonians, as Gorday observes, Pelagius's remarks are brief and his concern was with "practical, existential bearing of Paul's message, particularly as it pertains to the exercise of free will and moral seriousness in the life of faith."[13]

In the medieval period, two figures wrote influential theological works on Paul in the form of commentaries (among other works)—Peter Lombard and Thomas Aquinas. As for Lombard, he gave serious attention to Paul's letters in his writings. His commentary on Paul's letters became "an instant classic in its own sphere."[14] Aquinas was also interested in biblical commentary. The material from Aquinas we have now either comes from *reportationes* (lecture notes) or *ordinationes* (dictations). His study on 1 Thessalonians falls in the former category, probably coming from work done in the 1260s.[15] As Angus Paddison explains, Aquinas tended to use Scripture itself as the primary tool for making sense of 1 Thessalonians. Thus, "His fervent espousal of gaining meaning from Scripture by citing other parts of Scripture reveals that it was the canonically narrated history,

---

11. Bray, *Ambrosiaster*, 103.
12. Bray, *Ambrosiaster*, 107.
13. Gorday, *Colossians, 1–2 Thessalonians, 1–2 Timothy, Titus, Philemon*, xxiv.
14. M. L. Colish, *Studies in Scholasticism* (Burlington, VT: Ashgate, 2006), 71–72.
15. See Paddison, *Theological Hermeneutics and 1 Thessalonians*, 71.

and the canon's organic history within the tradition of the church, which held the interpretative authority."[16]

When it comes to Aquinas's work on 1 Thessalonians, Francesca Aran Murphy offers an insightful analysis of his work.[17] She notes how Aquinas takes an interest in such matters as Christian virtue (especially love and charity), true friendship, judgment, faith ("knowledge of God sustained by an act of God"), life in the church, and ecclesial leadership.

We can also mention here the importance in the medieval period of the *Glossa Ordinaria*, a resource used as a Vulgate companion that included textual notes from the church fathers as well as the main editor(s). In the twelfth century the *Glossa* was distributed widely throughout Europe. According to *Glossa* expert Lesley Smith, by the end of the twelfth century "numbers of [*Glossa*] manuscrupts outpaced production of manuscripts of the plain Bible text."[18] So dominant had the *Glossa* become that Smith states it had "become the Bible" for many centuries.[19] It is difficult to trace the authorship of the *Glossa* to one person; more likely it was compiled and edited by many. Smith attributes the Pauline portion to Anselm of Laon, but contributors of other portions may have included Gilbert of Auxerre, Alberic of Reims, and Ralph of Laon (and others).[20]

When it comes to the *Glossa* on Paul's letters, emphasis is placed on comments and notes by Ambrosiaster and Augustine, with intermittent reference to Chrysostom, Anselm, and a few others. Concerning 1–2 Thessalonians, the primary editorial glosses are brief and tend to be basic exegetical notes with an occasional bit of homiletical or ethical nuance. To be expected is the increase of comments related to the eschatological portions of the Thessalonian correspondence. It is clear that the author explicitly integrates material from Revelation and Daniel in his treatment of the parousia and the final judgment.

---

16. Paddison, *Theological Hermeneutics and 1 Thessalonians*, 78.

17. See F. A. Murphy, "Thomas' Commentaries on Philemon, 1 and 2 Thessalonians and Philippians," in *Aquinas on Scripture: An Introduction to His Biblical Commentaries*, ed. T. G. Weinandy, D. A. Keating, and J. P. Yocum (London: T&T Clark, 2005), 167–96.

18. L. Smith, *The Glossa Ordinaria: The Making of a Medieval Bible Commentary* (Leiden: Brill, 2009), 1.

19. Smith, *Glossa Ordinaria*, 1.

20. See Smith, *Glossa Ordinaria*, 32–33. Alternatively, M. S. Woodward argues that the Pauline portions are an abridgement of Peter of Lombard's *Collectanea in omnes divi Pauli apostoli epistolas*. See Woodward, *The Glossa Ordinaria on Romans* (Kalamazoo: Western Michigan University, 2011), ix–xvi.

THE INTERPRETATION OF 1 THESSALONIANS IN THE REFORMATION AND POST-REFORMATION PERIOD

Martin Luther

It is well known that Luther had a special interest in translating the Bible into German so that the common believer could read Scripture. He also prepared aids in studying and making sense of the Bible, including prefaces to each book, his preface to Romans taking on special importance for the Reformation.[21] Below is his brief statement about Paul's first epistle to the Thessalonians:

> This epistle St. Paul writes out of especial love and apostolic care. For in the first two chapters, he praises them because they have received the gospel from him with such earnestness as to be steadfast in it through affliction and persecution, and to have become a fair example of faith to all congregations everywhere, and, like Christ and his apostles, to have suffered persecution from the Jews, their own friends. So he had himself suffered and led a holy life when he was with them. Therefore he thanks God that his gospel has borne such fruit among them.
>
> In chapter 3, he shows the diligent care he takes, lest this labor of his and its praiseworthy beginning be brought to naught by the devil, with doctrines of men. Therefore he has sent Timothy to them to find this out, and he thanks God that things are still right among them; and he hopes that they may continue to grow. In chapter 4, he exhorts them to guard against sin and do good to one another. He also answers a question, which they had presented to him through Timothy, touching the resurrection of the dead, whether all would rise at once, or some after others. In chapter 5, he writes of the last day, how it shall come suddenly and quickly, and gives them some good directions for governing other people, and tells them what attitude they are to take toward the lives and teachings of others.[22]

---

21. See T. F. Lull, "Luther's Writings," in *The Cambridge Companion to Luther*, ed. D. M. McKim (Cambridge: Cambridge University Press, 2003), 47.

22. Martin Luther, *Word and Sacrament I*, ed. E. T. Bachmann, Luther's Works 35 (Philadelphia: Muhlenberg, 1960), 387.

John Calvin

John Calvin is known as a profound theologian and prolific writer. The first commentary he wrote was on Romans (1540), developed from Geneva lectures given between 1536 and 1538. Calvin explained in this Romans commentary that his intent was to be brief in explanation, and to focus on the author's intentions (*mens scriptoris*). As Wulfert Greef explains, Calvin believed that "an exegete should not allow himself to be guided by a passion for innovation or a desire to polemicize; he must not attack another nor seek to satisfy his own ambition."[23]

Calvin's commentaries on 1–2 Thessalonians (and Philemon) were published in 1551. His interpretation of these shorter epistles follows the same sort of grammatical-historical method as his expository work overall. Of course, one can see where and how Calvin takes special interest in particular parts of these letters. For example, when Paul mentions the Thessalonians' election (1:4), Calvin spends time discussing the matter of predestination. He picks this up again later with reference to Paul's prayer for their whole sanctification (1 Thess 5:23): "But if it is the part of God to renew the whole man, there is nothing left to free will. For if it had been our part to co-operate with God, Paul would have spoken thus—'May God aid or promote your sanctification.' But when he says, *sanctify you wholly*, he makes him the sole Author of the entire work."[24]

When it comes to eschatology, Calvin disputes the claim of Augustine that all must die before they have new life. Calvin urges that those left alive at the return of Christ will undergo a "sudden change" that will be like dying and rising again.[25] Calvin also puts to question the view of Origen and the "Chiliasts" who expected a specific thousand-year kingdom— Calvin calls this view "absurd."[26]

When it comes to the final exhortations and instructions of 1 Thessalonians 5, Calvin relates these to the work of pastors. Here Calvin contrasts the humility of the pastorate (where such men labor without concern for offices and status) with the pope who, according to Calvin, puts too much emphasis on rank and station. On the matter of prophecy (1 Thess 5:20),

---

23. W. Greef, *The Writings of John Calvin*, trans. L. D. Bierma (Louisville: Westminster John Knox, 2008), 76.

24. See John Calvin, *Commentaries on the Epistles of Paul the Apostle to the Philippians, Colossians, and Thessalonians*, trans. J. Pringle (Edinburgh: Calvin Translation Society, 1851), 309.

25. Calvin, *Philippians, Colossians, and Thessalonians*, 283–84.

26. Calvin, *Philippians, Colossians, and Thessalonians*, 284.

Calvin does not believe this refers to future prediction. Rather he argues that this pertains to the work of interpreting Scripture.

John Wesley

John Wesley offered both his own translation of as well as explanatory notes on the Bible.[27] In the preface to his translation, he explains how his concern was to follow the original Greek text closely. He encouraged each believer to begin their reading of Scripture by reciting this Anglican prayer in good faith: "Blessed Lord, who hast caused all holy Scriptures to be written for our learning, grant that we may in such wise hear them, read, mark, learn, and inwardly digest them, that by patience and comfort of thy holy Word, we may embrace, and ever hold fast the blessed hope of everlasting life, which thou hast given us in our Saviour Jesus Christ."[28]

Unlike Calvin, Wesley's notes are just that—brief notes for explanation and direction in the personal study of Scripture. Wesley did not want his comments to disrupt the goal of engaging deeply in Bible study. He was also mindful of not making his notes academic, lest he discourage average layreaders from utilizing the resource. His notes were published in 1754. As for 1 Thessalonians, Wesley's overall summary (brief as it is) follows Acts 17:1–10 closely. Wesley describes this epistle as demonstrating a "peculiar sweetness . . . unmixed with any sharpness or reproof."[29]

It is unsurprising that Wesley perked up at Paul's discussion of holiness and sanctification—the latter Wesley defines as "entire holiness of heart and life" (see note on 1 Thess 4:3).[30] Wesley offers a rather extensive note on prayer and thanksgiving in his comments on 5:16. He describes heartfelt and exuberant thanksgiving to God as "Christian perfection." He explains that prayer is the "breath of our spiritual life"—one should always pray "ever giving praise, whether in ease or pain, both for prosperity and for the greatest adversity. He blesses God for all things, looks on them as coming from him, and receives them only for his sake; not choosing nor refusing, liking or disliking, anything, but only as it is agreeable

27. See "John Wesley's Notes on the Bible," Wesley Center Online, http://wesley.nnu.edu/john-wesley/john-wesleys-notes-on-the-bible/.

28. "John Wesley's Notes on the Bible."

29. John Wesley, "Notes on St Paul's First Epistle to the Thessalonians," Wesley Center Online, http://wesley.nnu.edu/john-wesley/john-wesleys-notes-on-the-bible/notes-on-st-pauls-first-epistle-to-the-thessalonians/.

30. Wesley, "Notes on St Paul's First Epistle to the Thessalonians."

or disagreeable to his perfect will."[31] Wesley, like Calvin, explains that "prophesying" (5:20) has not to do with prediction but with preaching, and not "extraordinary gifts."[32]

John Owen and Jonathan Edwards

The English nonconformist church leader and theologian John Owen appealed to 1 Thessalonians in his writings, but not predominantly with interest in eschatology. Rather, he cited 1 Thessalonians in reference to such matters as true belief (1 Thess 1:5), responsivenes to the gospel message (2:13), and especially the work of the Holy Spirit in the Christian life (4:3; 5:19–23).[33]

Puritan theologian Jonathan Edwards is famous for his sermons on the wrath of God. And no doubt he cited 1 Thessalonians occasionally when the topic was damnation and judgment (see 1 Thess 2:16; 5:3).[34] But Edwards appealed also to 1 Thessalonians on the subject of comfort for the mourning (4:13–18).[35] In one case (pertaining to 4:14), he makes the following comment about the nature of the resurrection and the resurrected body:

> However the parts of the bodies of many are divided and scattered; however many have been burnt, and their bodies have been turned to ashes and smoke, and driven to the four winds; however many have been eaten of wild beasts, of the fowls of heaven, and the fishes of the sea; however many have consumed away upon the face of the earth, and great part of their bodies have ascended in exhalations; yet the all-wise and all-powerful God can immediately bring every part to his part again.[36]

Edwards also found inspiration in the caring nature of Paul in 1 Thessalonians (2:6–7). As a sidenote to a biblical exposition of Luke 1:35 and Mary's care for young Jesus, Edwards appeals to the nuturing ministry of believers toward one another: "The care that a tender mother has for her

---

31. Wesley, "Notes on St Paul's First Epistle to the Thessalonians."
32. Wesley, "Notes on St Paul's First Epistle to the Thessalonians."
33. See W. H. Goold, ed., *The Works of John Owen* (Edinburgh: Banner of Truth, 1965).
34. Jonathan Edwards, *The Works of Jonathan Edwards* (Peabody, MA: Hendrickson, 1998), 2:122, 823.
35. Edwards, *Works*, 2:625, 889, 893, 898.
36. Edwards, *Works*, 2:195.

infant, is a very lively image of the love that a Christian ought to have of grace in the heart."[37]

Summary

As many have recognized, biblical interpretation in the Reformation period was influenced by the Renaissance, even if the Protestant Reformers can still be called "precritical" exegetes. As McKim observes, while the Reformers continued the medieval interest in the theological and doctrinal teachings of biblical texts, there was clearly a developing interest and engagement with rhetoric, philology, and ancient historical contextualization among the Reformers.[38]

MODERN-ERA INTERPRETATION (1800–1985) OF 1 THESSALONIANS AND THE "RAPTURE" DOCTRINE

It should come as no surprise that biblical commentaries continued to be produced in the academy in the post-Reformation period through the modern era. We see substantial research interest in 1–2 Thessalonians increase especially in the late nineteenth century onward. Significant works around the turn of the twentieth century came from scholars such as C. J. Ellicot, J. Eadie, G. Lünemann, W. Bornemann, G. Findlay, G. Milligan, A. Schlatter, J. E. Frame, and A. Plummer.[39]

What is particularly impressive is how many of these commentators had a mastery of not only Greek (Attic and Koine) but also Latin, Syriac, Coptic, Aramaic, and Hebrew. And many too were well acquainted with contemporaneous comparative literature whether of Hellenistic Judaism, early rabbinic literature, or even texts from non-Jewish ("pagan") Greek literature.[40]

---

37. Edwards, *Works*, 2:788.

38. See D. McKim, *Historical Handbook of the Major Biblical Interpreters* (Downers Grove, IL: InterVarsity Press, 1998), 130.

39. C. J. Ellicot, *A Critical and Grammatical Commentary on St Paul's Epistle to the Thessalonians* (Andover: W. F. Draper, 1864); J. A. Eadie, *A Commentary on the Greek Text of the Epistles of Paul to the Thessalonians* (London: Macmillan, 1877); G. Lünemann, *Kritisch exegetisches Handbuch über die Briefe an die Thessalonicher*, KEK 10 (Göttingen: Vandenhoeck & Ruprecht, 1878); W. Bornemann, *Die Thessalonicherbriefe* (Göttingen: Vandenhoeck & Ruprecht, 1894); G. Findlay, *The Epistles to the Thessalonians* (Cambridge: Cambridge University Press, 1894); Milligan, *Thessalonians*; A. Schlatter, *Die Briefe an die Thessalonicher und Philipper* (Stuttgart: Vereinsbuchhandlung, 1910); Frame, *Thessalonians*; Plummer, *Thessalonians*.

40. A basic overview of the history of research can be found in Hughes, "Thessalonians, First and Second Letters," 111–16.

In 1987, Wolfgang Trilling offered a deeply insightful analysis of academic scholarship during this time period under the title "Die beiden Briefe des Apostels Paulus an die Thessalonicher: Eine Forschungsübersicht."[41] We can hardly do better than to defer to his learned adumbration of key scholarship and developments in the study of 1 Thessalonians in this time period.

Trilling's study devotes a major section to the nineteenth century. Trilling begins with the massive influence of F. C. Baur (1792–1860), noting how much subsequent scholarship even into the middle of the twentieth century was largely interactive with or reactive to Baur's perspective on Paul's life and formation. According to Trilling, Baur gave little value to 1–2 Thessalonians in regard to understanding the historical Paul—Baur considered it largely insignificant from a doctrinal standpoint (with the possible exception of 1 Thess 4:13–18). Baur believed that the emphasis on the parousia in 1 Thessalonians was derived from 1 Corinthians 15:51. Baur also criticized the unpauline nature of the Jewish polemic in 1 Thessalonians (2:14–16). Thus, he argued against the authenticity of 1 Thessalonians, placing its writing into the period of 70–130 CE.[42]

After briefly surveying the agenda-setting work of Baur, Trilling addressed the perspective of some Dutch scholars in the nineteenth century who took Baur's Hegelian approach even further, arguing that 1 Thessalonians attests to the development of Christianity in the second century, particularly as a synthesis of Jewish ideas and Greek philosophy. In this construction, a Jewish messianic movement came first, followed by a second phase drawing influence from Greek "humanistic thought."[43] Trilling found such Hegelian formulations deeply flawed and problematic because they began deductively with a particular philosophy or theory and suppressed the exegetical work.[44]

Next Trilling addresses the important work of W. Wrede (1859–1906), particularly pertaining to his scholarship on 2 Thessalonians. We will therefore save this discussion for chapter six.

Then Trilling examines Thessalonian scholarship of the early twentieth

---

41. W. Trilling, "Die beiden Briefe des Apostels Paulus an die Thessalonicher: Eine Forschungsübersicht," *ANRW* 25.4:3365–403.

42. See M. Bauspiess, C. Landmesser, and D. Lincicum, *Ferdinand Christian Baur and the History of Early Christianity* (Oxford: Oxford University Press, 2017), 90; cf. 248.

43. Trilling, "Die beiden Briefe," 3373–74 (trans. mine).

44. "One should also note the dangers of an exegesis pressed into the straightjacket of what is in the end but a philosophical concept" (Trilling, "Die beiden Briefe," 3374 [trans. mine]).

century, particularly the work of D. W. Lütgert and W. Hadorn.[45] Trilling explains that if Baur believed that Paul's primary concern was to defend a law-free gospel, Lütgert wanted to build on this and refine it. Lütgert posited that Paul fought against both nomism (related to Judaism) and also radical antinomianism. Regarding 1 Thessalonians in particular, Trilling explains that Lütgert detected gnostic opponents; thus 1 Thessalonians 2:3–6 and 4:1 were reacting against libertinism.[46] On reflection, Trilling understands Lütgert's work as influential, since in the early twentieth century the subject of early gnosticism was a hot topic and theories proliferated regarding so-called libertine movements in early Christianity.

Hadorn also believed that 1 Thessalonians was not a text originating from the middle of the first century. Yet he defended the authenticity of both 1 and 2 Thessalonians. As Trilling recounts, Hadorn wrote that "if this is fake, then nothing is authentic in the New Testament."[47] Hadorn, comparing 1 Corinthians to 1 Thessalonians, found numerous comparisons (such as literary connections, as well as the presence and problem of "enthusiasts" in both contexts) such that he argued for Paul's writing of 1 Thessalonians to be during his third missionary journey.

Much discussion and debate has obviously surrounded the topic of early Christian eschatology, and on this matter there has been much interest in 1 Thessalonians. Thus, we here turn to discuss the development of and debate over the so-called "rapture" doctrine and how 1 Thessalonians has played a part in this discussion.

Prior to 1830, almost all Christian theologians assumed that the return of Christ and the resurrection of believers served as parts of the same eschatological event. The idea of the "rapture" divided these end-time happenings into separable events: Christ would first come for Christians and take them out of the world. After a "great tribulation," Christ would return a second time to snatch away new believers and to defeat the antichrist, so ushering in a thousand-year reign.[48]

The rapture doctrine can be traced back to the very early nineteenth

---

45. D. W. Lütgert, *Die Vollkommenen in Philippi und die Enthusiasten in Thessalonich*, BFCT 13 (Gütersloh: Bertelsmann, 1909); W. Hadorn, "Die Abfassung der Thessalonicherbriefe auf der dritten Missionsreise und der Kanon des Marcion," *ZNW* 19 (1919–20): 67–72.

46. See Trilling, "Die beiden Briefe," 3377–78.

47. See Trilling, "Die beiden Briefe," 3379 (trans. mine).

48. See Y. M. Gillihan, "Rapture," in *Encyclopedia of Millennialism and Millennial Movements*, ed. R. Landes (New York: Routledge, 2000), 347. As Gillihan notes, the scenario I have described is a distinctively premillennial perspective—postmillennial and amillennial views do exist that accommodate the rapture doctrine, but the premillennial perspective is by far the most popular

century, with the rising popularity of the premillennial perspective. Plymouth Brethren leader John Nelson Darby is credited with popularizing the rapture doctrine in his teaching on dispensational theology with a view toward futurist premillennial eschatology. Darby spread this teaching in America during trips in the middle-to-late nineteenth century. The rapture doctrine became further disseminated through the *Scofield Reference Bible* (1909). Throughout the twentieth century the rapture doctrine was supported by dispensationalist institutions such as Moody Bible Institute and Dallas Theological Seminary.[49]

The English word *rapture* comes from the Latin verb *rapio* found in the Vulgate translation of 1 Thessalonians 4:17, where Paul notes that at the return of Christ believers will be "caught up."

ἔπειτα ἡμεῖς οἱ ζῶντες οἱ περιλειπόμενοι ἅμα σὺν αὐτοῖς ἁρπαγησόμεθα ἐν νεφέλαις εἰς ἀπάντησιν τοῦ κυρίου εἰς ἀέρα (1 Thess 4:17)

deinde nos qui vivimus qui relinquimur simul rapiemur cum illis in nubibus obviam Domino in aera (Vulgate)

Many academic commentaries from the modern era ignored the rapture doctrine completely (e.g., Findlay, Milligan, Frame, Plummer[50]), leaving "theological debates" to ecclesial literature. In 1922 Princeton professor C. R. Erdman addressed the rapture doctrine in his *The Return of Christ* monograph. Erdman explained how the New Testament (even 1–2 Thessalonians) does not set out a clear picture of the end-time events. The eschatological discourses of Paul, Jesus (in the Synoptics), and Revelation are meant to stir up in the believer a sense of comfort, vigilance, and courage.[51] In 1956, George Ladd wrote a lengthy refutation of the rapture doctrine entitled *The Blessed Hope: A Biblical Study of the Second Advent and the Rapture.*[52]

---

view today; see further A. Hultberg, ed., *Three Views on the Rapture: Pretribulation, Prewrath, and Posttribulation* (Grand Rapids: Zondervan, 1996).

49. For a historical perspective on the development of the rapture doctrine, see B. Rossing, *The Rapture Exposed* (Boulder, CO: Westview, 2004), especially ch. 2, "The Invention of the Rapture," 19–46.

50. Plummer does use the word "rapture" to describe the act of being "caught up" (1 Thess 4:17), but he clearly does not imply any technical doctrine (*Thessalonians*, 77; see also Frame, *Thessalonians*, 175–76).

51. See C. R. Erdman, *The Return of Christ* (New York: George H. Doran, 1922), 53–55.

52. G. E. Ladd, *The Blessed Hope: A Biblical Study of the Second Advent and the Rapture* (Grand Rapids: Eerdmans, 1956).

Non-Academic Uses of 1 Thessalonians

One prominent way that 1 Thessalonians influenced church and society in this modern period was through the composition of hymns. In 1832 Margaret Mackay wrote "Asleep in Jesus, Blessed Sleep," inspired by Mackay's visit to a cemetery where the words "sleeping in Jesus" were carved on a tombstone (Devonshire, England). Mackay was moved by the peaceful atmosphere of this burial place. It was simple and serene, quiet and solemn.

1. Asleep, in Jesus! Blessed sleep,
From which none ever wakes to weep;
A calm and undisturbed repose,
Unbroken by the last of foes.

2. Asleep in Jesus! Oh, how sweet
To be for such a slumber meet,
With holy confidence to sing
That death has lost his venomed sting!

3. Asleep in Jesus! Peaceful rest,
Whose waking is supremely blest
No fear, no woe, shall dim that hour
That manifests the Savior's power.

4. Asleep In Jesus! Oh, for me
May such a blissful refuge be!
Securely shall my ashes lie
And wait the summons from on high.[53]

Scottish poet James Montgomery is known as a popular hymn-writer of the nineteenth century and authored his "Forever with the Lord" in 1835. This work was also inspired by 1 Thessalonians 4:16–17.

1. Forever with the Lord!
Amen! so let it be.
Life from the dead is in that word,
'Tis immortality.

---

53. M. Mackay, "Asleep in Jesus! Blesssed Sleep (1832)," in *The Handbook to the Lutheran Hymnal* (St. Louis: Concordia, 1942), 416; see www.ccel.org/a/anonymous/luth_hymnal/tlh587.htm (public domain).

2. Here in the body pent,
Absent from Him, I roam,
Yet nightly pitch my moving tent
A day's march nearer home.

3. My Father's house on high,
Home of my soul, how near
At times to faith's foreseeing eye
Thy golden gates appear!

4. Ah, then my spirit faints
To reach the land I love,
The bright inheritance of saints,
Jerusalem above!

5. Forever with the Lord!
O Father, 'tis Thy will.
The promise of that faithful word
E'en here to me fulfil.

6. Be Thou at my right hand,
Then can I never fail.
Uphold Thou me, and I shall stand;
Fight Thou, and I'll prevail.

7. So when my dying breath
Shall set my spirit free,
By death I shall escape from death
To endless life with Thee.

8. Knowing as I am known,
How shall I love that word
And oft repeat before the throne,
"Forever with the Lord!"[54]

---

54. James Montgomery, "For ever with the Lord," Hymnary.org, https://hymnary.org/text/forever_with_the_lord_amen_so_let_it_be?extended=true (public domain).

Other hymns related to key themes and texts from 1 Thessalonians include, "Great God What Do I See and Hear?" (William Collyer, 1802; 1 Thess 4:16–17), "Holy Ghost with Light Divine" (Andrew Reed, 1817; 1 Thess 5:23), and "My Soul Be On Thy Guard" (George Heath, 1781; 1 Thess 5:6). Perhaps the most well-known piece of art that pertains to 1 Thessalonians is Dore's *St. Paul Preaching to the Thessalonians:*

Gustave Dore, *St. Paul Preaching to the Thessalonians* (wood carving, 1865; public domain).

Modern Interpretation (1950–1985)

Two scholars offer a helpful understanding of the key conversations in the study of 1 Thessalonians in this period—Trilling (already noted above) and R. F. Collins in his "Recent Scholarship on Paul's First Letter to the Thessalonians."[55] We will begin with Trilling's examination of (mostly)

---

55. R. F. Collins, "Recent Scholarship on Paul's First Letter to the Thessalonians," in *Studies on the First Letter to the Thessalonians,* 3–75.

European scholarship and then turn to Collins's work that includes more Anglophone work.

Trilling gives significant attention to the influential work of W. Schmithals in this period.[56] Schmithals proposed a rather eloborate deconstruction of 1–2 Thessalonians and a four-letter reconstruction:

Letter A: 2 Thessalonians 1:1–12; 3:6–16
Letter B: 1 Thessalonians 1:1–2:12; 4:3–5:28
Letter C: 2 Thessalonians 2:13–14; 2:1–12; 2:15–3:5; 3:17ff.
Letter D: 1 Thessalonians 2:13–4:2

As one can see, Schmithals favors a reconstruction that imagines movement from more serious problems, pressures, and tensions to resolution.[57] Trilling finds Schmithals theory unconvincing but remains intrigued by his "history-of-religion theory."[58]

Another significant twentieth-century figure that Trilling addresses is Alfred Suhl.[59] Like Hadorn and Schmithals, Suhl was also interested in breaking the situational analysis of 1 Thessalonians away from a presumed Acts 17:1–10 coordination. Suhl found this alignment unnecessary and problematic, as he discovered and defended clues in 1 Thessalonians that better tie it to a later period than the original founding of the Thessalonian church.[60] Trilling also briefly mentions the work of A. Roosen, who argued that 1 Thessalonians was written in two stages, chapters 1–3 after the report from Timothy, and chapters 4–5 later in 51 CE as new information about the Thessalonian community came to Paul's attention.[61]

Collins nicely supplements Trilling's reflections on this period of scholarship. On the subject of the ordering of 1–2 Thessalonians, he highlights the work of R. Gregson, who advocated for the priority of 2 Thessalonians.[62]

---

56. See W. Schmithals, "Die Thessalonicherbriefe als Briefkompositionen," in *Zeit und Geschichte: Dankesgabe an Rudolf Bultmann zum 80 Geburtstag,* ed. E. Dinkler and H. Thyen (Tübingen: Mohr Siebeck, 1964), 295–315; idem, *Paulus und die Gnostiker: Untersuchungen zu den kleinen Paulusbriefen* (Hamburg: Herbert Reich, Evangelischer Verlag, 1965), 89–157.

57. Trilling, "Die beiden Briefe," 3381. Like Hadorn, Schmithals also favors a perspective that sets these letters within Paul's third missionary journey.

58. Trilling, "Die beiden Briefe," 3382 (trans. mine). Overall, Trilling found Schmithals work to be specious, though one wonders whether Trilling could not entertain the notion that the historical Paul himself had a hand in the writing of 2 Thessalonians.

59. See A. Suhl, *Paulus und seine Briefe: Ein Beitrag zur paulinischen Chronologie,* SNT 11 (Gütersloh: Gütersloher Verlagshaus Mohn, 1975).

60. See Trilling, "Die beiden Briefe," 3384; see also Collins, "Recent Research," 11–12.

61. A. Roosen, *De Brieven van Paulus aan de Tessalonicenzen* (Rome: Roermond, 1971).

62. R. Gregson, "A Solution to the Problems of the Thessalonian Epistles," *EvQ* 38 (1966):

On questions about the literary unity of 1 Thessalonians, Collins notes the radical work of Fuchs, who questioned the authenticity of 1 Thessalonians 2:1–10.[63] Fuchs apparently also found dubious 1 Thessalonians 2:13–16 and 5:1–11.

Collins furthermore identifies the growing interest in the middle-to-late twentieth century in Paul and Jewish apocalypticism. This relates in obvious ways to 1 Thessalonians.[64] On the historical situation behind the Thessalonian epistles, Collins observes that few studies of significance have been devoted to this.[65] He found much more promising insight coming from archaeological study of Thessalonica.[66] In terms of social history, Collins praised the work of Malherbe and Hock.

WHAT ARE THEY SAYING ABOUT 1 THESSALONIANS NOW? (1985-2017)

This brings us to the present period of 1985–2017. In chapter two we gave extensive attention to the influential work of Robert Jewett, John Barclay, Todd D. Still, Richard Ascough, Karl Donfried, and Abraham Malherbe.[67] Here we will consider more concisely other resources and works of note that pertain to the study of 1 Thessalonians in the last three decades.

Reference Works and Collections

In 1990, Raymond F. Collins compiled and edited papers from a conference (the thirty-eighth *Colloquium Biblicum Lovaniense*, August 1988),

---

76–80; also R. Thurston, "The Relationship between the Thessalonian Epistles," *ExpTim* 85 (1973–74): 52–56.

63. See Collins, "Recent Research," 13; E. Fuchs, "Meditation über 1 Thess 1,2–10," *Göttinger Predigtmediationen* 18 (1963–64): 299–303; cf. G. Friedrich, *Die erste Brief an die Thessalonicher*, NTD 8 (Göttingen: Vandenhoeck & Ruprecht, 1976), 203–51.

64. See also the work of A. F. J. Klijn and J. Plevnik: Klijn, "1 Thess 4,13–18 and Its Background in Apocalyptic Literature," in *Paul and Paulinism: Essays in Honour of C. K. Barrett*, ed. M. D. Hooker and S. G. Wilson (London: SPCK, 1982), 67–73; Plevnik, "The Parousia as Implication of Christ's Resurrection: An Exegesis of 1 Thess 4:13–18," in *Word and Spirit: Essays in Honor of David Michael Stanley*, ed. J. Plevnik (Willowdale: Regis College, 1975), 199–277.

65. Collins, "Recent Research," 33–34; he briefly mentions the modest contribution of M. Unger, "Historical Research and the Church at Thessalonica," *BibSac* 119 (1962): 38–44.

66. See P. Rossano, "Note archaeologiche sulla antica Tessalonica," *Revista Bíblica* 6 (1958): 242–47, for notes on archaeological insights, religions in Thessalonica, and information about the Roman imperial cult; cf. also W. Elliger, *Paulus in Griechenland: Philippi, Thessaloniki, Athen, Korinth* (Stuttgart: Katholisches Bibelwerk, 1978), 78–116.

67. See pp. 63–83 above.

later published under the title *The Thessalonian Correspondence*.[68] The volume is divided into four parts: the first on Paul's proclamation, the second on the text of 1 Thessalonians, the third on topics in 1 Thessalonians, and the last part on 2 Thessalonians. This collection boasts the work of several experts on 1–2 Thessalonians, including K. Donfried, F. W. Hughes, T. Holtz, G. P. Carras, M. J. J. Menken, H. Koester, R. Jewett, and E. Krentz.

In 1998, Jeffrey Weima and Stanley Porter published an indispensable resource called *An Annotated Bibliography of 1 and 2 Thessalonians*.[69] This reference volume covers over one-thousand bibliographic references pertaining to the Thessalonian correspondence, "including virtually all relevant works written in the twentieth century." The book is divided into four main sections: "Commentaries and Other Materials Related to 1 and 2 Thessalonians" (part 1), "Special Topics Related to 1 and 2 Thessalonians" (part 2), "Exegetical Treatments of 1 Thessalonians" (part 3), and "Exegetical Treatments of 2 Thessalonians" (part 4). Annotations range anywhere from a sentence or two to a long paragraph. For those of us whose German, French, Spanish, Danish, and Italian are "rusty" (or nonexistent!), this book is priceless. Note that, because the book was published in 1998, one will obviously not find comments on twenty-first-century scholarship.[70]

Another important essay collection is *The Thessalonians Debate*, edited by Karl Donfried and Johannes Beutler (2000).[71] This publication comes from the "Thessalonian Correspondence Seminar" of the *Studiorum Novi Testamenti Societas* (SNTS). Sharing of papers and research took place in 1995 and 1996 and continued through 1998. The issue in question concerns the interpretation of 1 Thessalonians 2:1–12, whether one reads a defensive tone in Paul's writing, and what, if anything, should be made of this for understanding the situation and Paul's overall response to that situation.

More recently, a multi-contributor study was done on the history of Thessalonica called *From Roman to Early Christian Thessalonikē*, edited

---

68. R. F. Collins, ed., *The Thessalonian Correspondence*, BETL 87 (Louvain: Leuven University Press, 1990).

69. J. A. D. Weima and S. E. Porter, *An Annotated Bibliography of 1 and 2 Thessalonians*, NTTS 26 (Leiden: Brill, 1998).

70. Impressively, I did find several works discussed that were published in 1997 *and even* 1998!

71. Donfried and Beutler, *Thessalonians Debate*.

by L. Nasrallah, C. Bakirtzis, and S. Friesen (2010).[72] This wide-ranging volume gathers experts in history, religion, and archaeology to examine the social, political, and religious contexts and environments of Thessalonica through Greek, Roman, and early Christian periods. Contributors include P. Nigdelis, R. Ascough, H. Koester, T. Stefanidou-Tiveriou, and C. Bakirtzis.[73]

Important Monographs and Commentaries

While, generally speaking, the individual contributions of R. F. Collins fall into the 1970s and 1980s, it is worthwhile to observe his influence in this section due to the publication of a collection of his essays under the title *Studies on the First Letter to the Thessalonians* (1984).[74] Collins's collection on 1 Thessalonians contains several seminal essays, including "The State of the Discipline: Recent Scholarship on the First Letter to the Thessalonians"; "The Text and Its Provenance: The Text of the Epistles to the Thessalonians in Nestle-Aland 26"; "Apropos the Integrity of 1 Thess"; "The Theology of Paul's First Letter to the Thessalonians"; and "The Church of the Thessalonians."

Mikael Tellbe published another significant monograph in 2001, called *Paul between Synagogue and State*.[75] Tellbe takes interest in the web of connections between Jews, Christians, and pagans in the first century. His overarching argument is that the early Christians were seeking sociopolitical legitimacy in their wider world. Interactions and tensions with Jews and civic authorities reinforced a particular Christian self-understanding. He states his thesis as follows:

> To reconstruct the interactions between Christians, Jews, and civic authorities in this tripartite relation shaped by the self-understanding and identity of the Christian communities of 1 Thessalonians, Romans, and Philippians.[76]

---

72. L. Nasrallah, C. Bakirtzis, and S. J. Friesen, eds., *From Roman to Early Christian Thessalonikē: Studies in Religion and Archaeology* (Cambridge: Harvard University Press, 2010).

73. Included in this volume is an essay by M. Johnson-DeBaufre which pushes back against Ascough's proposal that the Thessalonian church was all male ("'Gazing upon the Invisible': Archaeology, Historiography, and the Elusive Women of 1 Thessalonians," 73–108).

74. Collins, *Studies on the First Letter to the Thessalonians*.

75. Mikael Tellbe, *Paul between Synagogue and State: Christians, Jews, and Civic Authorities in 1 Thessalonians, Romans, and Philippians*, ConBNT 34 (Stockholm: Almqvist & Wiksell, 2001).

76. Tellbe, *Paul between Synagogue and State*, 4 (original italics removed).

In terms of methods and assumptions, Tellbe takes a largely historical approach to studying this topic, and regarding sources he draws both from Paul's letters as well as Acts.[77] Tellbe recognizes that Luke had his own theological concerns and that they shape his narrative to some degree. However, Tellbe argues that interpreters of Acts must find a way to push beyond a simplistic fact-versus-fiction dichotomy. Tellbe follows Hengel in identifying Acts as a historical monograph and desires to use Acts wherever it is useful, taking for granted both "the historiographical function and the theological-rhetorical conception" of Acts.[78] With this in mind, he lays out his method of incorporating as much historical information on Paul's ministry from Acts as possible.[79]

In the second chapter of his book, Tellbe examines the status of Judaism with Rome and the relationship of Jews with Rome. Jews benefited from a unique status that permitted their religious traditions, but that does not mean tensions never emerged.[80] In the next several chapters, Tellbe turns respectively to 1 Thessalonians, Romans, and Philippians, though we will only give attention to his treatment of 1 Thessalonians. In chapter three Tellbe discusses the background and history of Roman Thessalonica, the (presumed) Jewish presence in the city, and the development of the Christian community. When it comes to the situation that led to Paul's letter, Tellbe emphasizes the problem of persecution.[81] While Tellbe does find support in Acts 17 for this, he also makes a case from 1 Thessalonians itself. First, looking at 1 Thessalonians 2:15b, he reasons that the statement "drove us out" refers to Jews running Paul out of Thessalonica.[82] Connecting that to 2:17a, he reads the situation as a sudden and unexpected "banishment" from Thessalonica. This all helps to make sense of 2:14–15 and why he spends so much time and energy explaining the harsh behavior of some persecuting Jews.[83] Yet *why* did these Jews afflict the Thessalonian believers? Tellbe makes the educated guess that they did not

---

77. See Tellbe, *Paul between Synagogue and State*, 11.
78. Tellbe, *Paul between Synagogue and State*, 16.
79. See Tellbe, *Paul between Synagogue and State*, 18. He still expresses a self-consciously critical method where, if Acts and Paul's letter "disagree," he defers to Paul's letter (18).
80. See Tellbe, *Paul between Synagogue and State*, 63.
81. So his summary statement: "*In 1 Thessalonians Paul is not so much concerned to rebuke and correct an over realized eschatology or to curtail some radicals within the community as much as to comfort and encourage a group of distressed believers by presenting a sound eschatology that aims at reviving their hope and reinforcing their identity*" (104, emphasis original).
82. See Tellbe, *Paul between Synagogue and State*, 107.
83. Tellbe, *Paul between Synagogue and State*, 107–8, 113.

like the way Paul was redefining the people of God through his so-called gospel. Tellbe goes even further to make a case that these Jews judged and presented (to the Thessalonian believers) the case that Paul was a "false Jewish prophet."[84]

Tellbe adds to this historical sketch the possible motive of persecution by Jews out of concern that Paul's message would create troublesome backlash from civic authorities: "The Thessalonian Jews probably reacted as loyal clients of the Roman emperor. Consequently they interpreted Paul's missionary activities as a threat to their own stable and privileged status, and in order to openly dissociate themselves from their religious rivals they turned the matter into a public case."[85]

Some have critiqued the idea that Jews were opposing the Jesus-group in Thessalonica; one issue is the size of the Jewish community. Were they a sizable enough group to cause that much trouble for Paul and his converts? Also, would they not worry about how it might look if Jews of a city harassed gentiles? Tellbe responds to these concerns by stating that it very well may have been that Jews instigated gentile opposition to the Jesus community.[86]

In the latter part of his chapter on 1 Thessalonians, Tellbe dives deeper into the political dimensions of the Thessalonian situation. He argues that opponents of Paul and his ministry would have found it beneficial to make Paul an enemy of Rome by presenting the apostles as "a group of itinerant political revolutionaries" whose ideas were "seditious and illicit."[87] Thus, persecution would have not only come because of religious concerns from Jews but also because of political concerns of the Thessalonian people in general who wanted to show solidarity with Caesar. In particular, Tellbe pits Pauline eschatology against Roman imperial ideology: "The Thessalonian believers are encouraged to put their hope neither in imperial propaganda nor in being citizens of a Greek *civitas libera* but in the day of the coming of their heavenly Lord."[88]

Tellbe has been lauded for thinking about the situation behind Paul's letters in ways that are multidimensional, drawing together politics, religion, and culture. He has tried to hold together how Paul's ministry

---

84. Tellbe, *Paul between Synagogue and State*, 109.
85. Tellbe, *Paul between Synagogue and State*, 110–11.
86. Tellbe, *Paul between Synagogue and State*, 114.
87. Tellbe, *Paul between Synagogue and State*, 123.
88. Tellbe, *Paul between Synagogue and State*, 139. Tellbe carefully explains that Paul does not explicitly challenge Rome. He promotes a mood of peace and generosity toward outsiders (139).

simultaneously offended Jews and gentiles—sometimes for similar reasons, but also for different reasons as well. The common critique of Tellbe's work is his use of Acts 17:1–9.[89] Among the scholars we survey in this chapter, Tellbe (perhaps along with Weima) ranks as among those who most allow Acts to fill in the gaps in the reconstruction of the Thessalonian situation. On the one hand, Tellbe could be criticized for accepting *too* much of Luke's account; on the other hand, the proof of the pudding is in the eating, and scholars need to assess how *strong* of a reading he offers based on whether his reconstruction can put all the pieces (or the *most* pieces) from Acts and 1 Thessalonians together into a sensible scenario.

We have already noted Weima's coedited *Annotated Bibliography of 1 and 2 Thessalonians* (with Stanley Porter, see above). Here we will take a closer look at Weima's direct contributions on the Thessalonian correspondence. In 1994 Weima published his doctoral dissertation under the title *Neglected Endings: The Significance of the Pauline Letter Closings.*[90] While Weima's study included 1–2 Thessalonians, he also treated several other Pauline letters. Within a couple of years, though, Weima narrowed his research focus to 1–2 Thessalonians. He published the bibliography in 1998, contributed to *The Thessalonians Debate* (edited by Donfried and Beutler [2000]), and has published numerous journal articles. In 2002, he published a short commentary on 1–2 Thessalonians in the *Zondervan Illustrated Bible Background Commentary.*[91] His career of scholarship on 1–2 Thessalonians was able to be brought together in his 2014 commentary, and our summary of Weima's interpretation of the Thessalonian situation will refer to this work only.[92]

In terms of sources, Weima appeals both to the Pauline letters (1–2 Thessalonians) as well as Acts. How does Weima respond to the common objection that Acts is a weak historical source? First, he questions the

---

89. Ascough is critical of Tellbe's "undefended" use of Acts; see R. S. Ascough, review of *Paul between Synagogue and State*, by M. Tellbe, *JBL* 122.4 (2003): 772; also G. M. Smiga, review of *Paul between Synagogue and State*, by M. Tellbe, *CBQ* 64.2 (2002): 396: "Many will balk at treating Acts as such a robust historical source" (396); Peter Oakes—though he recognizes the problem with using Acts without significant explanation—finds "a certain coherence of view" in his reconstruction that attempts to bring together 1 Thess and Acts; see Oakes, review of *Paul between Synagogue and State*, by M. Tellbe, *BibInt* 12.3 (2004): 341.

90. J. A. D. Weima, *Neglected Endings: The Significance of the Pauline Letter Closings*, JSNTSup 101 (Sheffield: JSOT Press, 1994).

91. *1 & 2 Thessalonians, 1 & 2 Timothy, Titus*, ZIBBC (Grand Rapids: Zondervan, 2002), cowritten with S. M. Baugh covering the Pastoral Epistles.

92. J. A. D. Weima, *1–2 Thessalonians*, BECNT (Grand Rapids: Baker, 2014); on the Thessalonian situation specifically see pp. 23–39.

logic of demoting Acts on the basis of it being a "third-person" account. Second, Weima addresses the purported discrepancies between 1 Thessalonians and Acts 17:1–9. Weima admits that "Luke selected, omitted, and arranged the events in his description of Paul's mission-founding visit to Thessalonica to better fit the larger interests and themes at work in his book as a whole."[93] This acknowledgment not withstanding, Weima finds many points of agreement between Paul's letter and Luke's narrative.[94] Furthermore, Weima appeals to corroboration from other ancient sources that strengthen the case for Luke's historical accuracy and thus the overall reliability of his account. He offers the example of Luke's mention of the "politarchs" (17:6; NIV: "city officials"), once believed to be a mistake by Luke but now proven accurate by evidence from inscriptions.[95] Thus, Weima takes Luke's information more or less at face value.

Drawing from Acts 17, then, Weima imagines that Paul did indeed preach in the synagogue in Thessalonica, though the simple narrative in Acts leaves open the timeframe, and Weima believes Paul had a "post-synagogue ministry" there.[96] Paul would have stayed in Thessalonica long enough for the new church there to be comprised largely of gentiles. He would have had to be there to receive support from the Philippians (Phil 4:15–16). Furthermore, in 1 Thessalonians he refers to plying his trade, and that also would have taken time (2:9). Weima furthermore adds that there appears to be some form of leadership in the church, and it would have required some time to raise up and train such believers (5:12–13).[97]

Returning to the ethnic makeup of the church, Weima (as many others) takes 1 Thessalonians 1:9 to imply that the church was comprised largely of pagan converts.[98] These pagans would not have heard Paul's gospel in the synagogue, Weima assumes. So where did they meet Paul? Weima surmises that the most probable context would be "the semiprivate setting of a workshop" while he plied his trade.[99]

---

93. Weima, *1–2 Thessalonians*, 24.
94. Here Weima relies on the work of R. Riesner, *Paul's Early Period: Chronology, Mission Strategy, Theology*, 366–67.
95. Weima, *1–2 Thessalonians*, 24.
96. Weima, *1–2 Thessalonians*, 26.
97. But Weima leaves open the possibility that Timothy trained them (1 Thess 3:1–5).
98. See Weima, *1–2 Thessalonians*, 28–29.
99. Weima, *1–2 Thessalonians*, 29. Weima imagines that perhaps the workshop was owned by none other than Jason, "a wealthy Jew converted to the Christian faith during Paul's three weeks of preaching in the synagogue" (29). Weima numbers also among the possible believing community members Secundus and Demas (Weima, *1–2 Thessalonians*, 30).

When it comes to the persecution of and opposition to the believers in Thessalonica, Weima discusses the controversy over the interpretation of συμφυλέτης in 2:14. He resists the popular view that συμφυλέτης refers to ethnicity (i.e., gentiles only). Rather, he takes it more in a *geographic* sense, "referring to all the inhabitants of Thessalonica: the vast majority of them would have been Gentiles, but some would have been Jews" (here agreeing essentially with Acts 17:5–9).[100] Again, taking seriously that Paul won some converts from the synagogue, opposition came from some Jewish leaders, eventually leading to Paul's flight from the city. Furthermore, Weima affirms Luke's account that has Jews inciting gentiles to harass the believers as well. Weima appeals to a similar situation according to Plutarch involving "men who were of low birth and had lately been slaves but who were hanging around the marketplace [ἀγοραῖος—the same term used in Luke's account in Acts 17:5] and able to gather a mob and force all issues by means of solicitations and shouting" (*Aem.* 38.4).[101]

Weima underscores the *political* dimensions of how the Thessalonian populace was offended by Paul and his colleagues. They were accused of "disturbing the peace," and this would have been especially a sensitive matter in the Roman Thessalonica that worked hard to be a favored city of the empire.[102]

What situation and exigencies led to Paul's writing of 1 Thessalonians? Again, Weima combines information from Acts and Paul's letter. Timothy reported to Paul both good news of their ongoing faith but also problems, including the need for holiness (in sexual conduct), interrelational problems in the community, questions and concerns about dead and living believers in view of the return of Christ, the treatment of leaders, troubled members (5:14–18), and the nature of prophecy (5:19–22).[103] Weima proposes that Paul wrote 1 Thessalonians in 50/51 CE from Corinth.

One of the key factors in Weima's own interpretation of 1 Thessalonians is his argument that 2:1–12 is indeed a personal defense of Paul's character and ministry. Thanks in some part to the work of Malherbe, it has become increasingly common to buck the traditional view that 2:1–12

---

100. See Weima, *1–2 Thessalonians*, 30–31.
101. See Weima, *1–2 Thessalonians*, 31.
102. On pp. 32–34, Weima offers some helpful analysis of what the charges may have entailed related to opposing the "decrees of Caesar" (Acts 17:7). It could refer to treason, "Jewish messianic agitation," violation of the "oath of loyalty to Caesar," or illegal predictions of a "change of ruler" (33). Of these options, Weima finds the last one most likely (33–34).
103. Weima, *1–2 Thessalonians*, 38.

is "defensive." Malherbe argues that Paul was following a kind of philosophical convention whereby he set himself up as an example to follow. Weima recognizes the mimetic advantages of 2:1–12, but nevertheless understands there to be a defensive or apologetic function that presumes criticism from the Thessalonians.[104] Some of his more significant arguments include the rare invocation of the divine testimony in 2:5, 10, and the sheer frequency of antithetical statements in 2:1–6.[105]

In the end, Weima's interpretation of the Thessalonian situation is rather traditional, but the thoroughness of his argumentation (and rebuttals to other readings) means that in the future new proposals will have to reckon with his work.

RECOMMENDED READING

Collins, R. F. "Recent Scholarship on Paul's First Letter to the Thessalonians." Pages 3–75 in *Studies on the First Letter to the Thessalonians*. BETL 66. Leuven: Leuven University Press, 1984.

Gorday, P. J., ed. *Colossians, 1–2 Thessalonians, 1–2 Timothy, Titus, Philemon*. ACCS. Downers Grove, IL: InterVarsity Press, 2000.

Thiselton, A. C. *1 and 2 Thessalonians through the Centuries*. Oxford: Wiley-Blackwell, 2011.

Trilling, W. "Die beiden Briefe des Apostels Paulus an die Thessalonicher: Eine Forschungsübersicht." *ANRW* 25.4:3365–403. Part 2, *Principat*, 25.4. Edited by H. Temporini and W. Haase. New York: de Gruyter, 1989.

Weima, J. A. D., and S. E. Porter. *An Annotated Bibliography of 1 and 2 Thessalonians*. NTTS 26. Leiden: Brill, 1998.

---

104. See J. Weima, "An Apology for the Apologetic Function of 1 Thessalonians 2:1–12," *JSNT* 68 (1997): 73–99; cf. idem, "The Function of 1 Thessalonians 2:1–12 and the Use of Rhetorical Criticism: A Response to Otto Merk," in Donfried and Beutler, *Thessalonian Debate*, 114–31. In Weima's commentary, see pp. 120–58 (esp. 120–25).

105. See Weima, *1–2 Thessalonians*, 122–23.

2 THESSALONIANS

CHAPTER 5

TEXT OF 2 THESSALONIANS

In this chapter we will examine major text-critical issues, matters pertaining to the integrity of 2 Thessalonians, a brief discussion of authorship and date (with a much longer treatment of pseudepigraphy and situation theories covered in chapter six), and then key textual features such as the genre, style, and structure of the letter.

TEXTUAL WITNESSES AND SIGNIFICANT TEXT-CRITICAL CONCERNS

Textual Witnesses

For 2 Thessalonians, the consistently cited witnesses of the NA[28] text are as follows:

PAPYRI

$\mathfrak{P}^{30}$: 1:1–2
$\mathfrak{P}^{92}$: 1:4–5, 11–12

MAJUSCULES

א (01): Pauline corpus
A (02): Pauline corpus
B (03): Pauline corpus
D (06): Pauline corpus
F (010): Pauline corpus
G (012): Pauline corpus
I (016): only 2 Thessalonians 1:1–3, 10–11; 2:5–8, 14–17; 3:8–10
K (018): Pauline corpus

L (020): Pauline corpus
P (025): 2 Thessalonians
Ψ (044): Pauline corpus
0111: only 2 Thessalonians 1:1–2:2
0278: partial Pauline corpus; all of 2 Thessalonians

MINUSCULES

33: Pauline corpus
81: Pauline corpus
104: Pauline corpus
365: Pauline corpus
630: Pauline corpus
1175: Pauline corpus
1241: Pauline corpus
1505: Pauline corpus
1506: partial Pauline corpus; all of 2 Thessalonians
1739: Pauline corpus
1881: Pauline corpus
2464: Pauline corpus

LECTIONARIES

Both complete:
l 249: Pauline corpus
l 846: Pauline corpus

Major Textual Variants in 2 Thessalonians[1]

There are nine verses in 2 Thessalonians with textual-variant considerations worth discussion here.

1:2 θεοῦ πατρὸς [ἡμῶν] καὶ κυρίου

Textual critics are unsure regarding whether the ἡμῶν here is original. Both readings claim significant support from external evidence, hence the UBS committee's {C} rating and the bracketing in the text. In terms of internal evidence, Metzger considers both the possibility that copyists dropped ἡμῶν for "stylistic reasons" (to avoid repetition from v. 1 [πατρὶ

---

1. Again, for the latest discussion of the practice of textual criticism, see Ehrman and Holmes, *Text of the New Testament in Contemporary Research*; cf. Wachtel and Holmes, *Textual History of the Greek New Testament*.

ἡμῶν]), or alternatively it may have been added by copyists to conform to known Pauline convention.[2]

2:3 ὁ ἄνθρωπος τῆς ἀνομίας

Some mss (e.g., A D F G K L P Ψ; Vulgate) here read ὁ ἄνθρωπος τῆς ἁμαρτίας ("of sin"). Despite the impressive external support, most likely scribes substituted ἁμαρτία for ἀνομία, as the latter is less common in Paul.

2:4 καθίσαι

Here ὡς θεόν appears before καθίσαι in several mss (e.g., D[2] K L 0278 630 1175 1241). Other mss (1984 1985) have ὡς θεόν after καθίσαι.[3] In all likelihood, ὡς θεόν was added for clarification, and it is unlikely (if original) that it would be intentionally omitted subsequently.

2:8 ὁ κύριος [Ἰησοῦς]

Witnesses for the readings that omit or include Ἰησοῦς are both strong.[4] Metzger considers the possibility (in favor of original omission) that Ἰησοῦς was included by "pious scribes"; or (in favor of original inclusion) the Ἰησοῦς may have dropped by accident or perhaps to harmonize the text with LXX Isaiah 11:4.[5]

2:13 ἀπαρχήν

As noted in chapter one of this book (pp. 21–22), 1 Thessalonians contains what is considered to be one of the most contentious and fascinating text-critical issues in the New Testament. While 2 Thessalonians does not have an equivalent controversial variant, 2:13 is noteworthy nonetheless. There is significant support for the reading ἀπ᾽ ἀρχῆς ("God chose you *from the beginning*" [cf. NET]; ℵ D K L Ψ). Metzger gives favor to ἀπαρχήν (B F G[gr] P 33 81) due to the rarity of the prepositional phrase ἀπ᾽ ἀρχῆς in Paul, and more importantly due to the tendency for Paul to use ἀρχή with the meaning "power" rather than "beginning."[6] Furthermore, Metzger urges, ἀπαρχή appears several times in Paul. None of these arguments, however, offer cogent proofs for ἀπαρχήν. The best

---

2. See Metzger, *Textual Commentary*, 567; cf. Omanson, *Textual Guide to the Greek New Testament*, 430.
3. Cf. Metzger, *Textual Commentary*, 567.
4. See Comfort, *Commentary on the Manuscripts*, 359.
5. Metzger, *Textual Commentary*, 568.
6. The SBLGNT prefers ἀπαρχήν while the THGNT prefers ἀπ᾽ ἀρχῆς.

argument Metzger presents involves evidence from elsewhere in the New Testament (Rom 16:5; Rev 14:4), where it is clear that scribes changed ἀπαρχήν to ἀπ᾽ ἀρχῆς.[7]

2:16 [ὁ] θεὸς ὁ πατὴρ ἡμῶν
Here some manuscripts read ὁ θεὸς καὶ πατήρ ἡμῶν (e.g., A), others have ὁ θεὸς πατήρ ἡμῶν (e.g., א[b]). Metzger is uncertain whether the initial article in this phrase is original.[8]

3:6 παρελάβοσαν
One well-attested reading here has παρέλαβον (א[c] D[c] K L P et al.). The reading παρελάβοσαν is also strong (א* A 33 88 1827 et al.). The difference is one of dialectic preference.

3:16 τρόπῳ
Some witnesses read τόπῳ here (A* D* F G 33), but τρόπῳ boasts stronger manuscript support (א A[c] B D[c] K L P Ψ et al.). Probably certain scribes preferred τόπῳ in conformity to traditional Pauline expression (e.g., 1 Cor 1:2; 1 Thess 1:8).[9]

3:18 ὑμῶν
Some witnesses include ἀμήν at the close of the letter, though the support for its omission is formidable (א* B 6 33 1739 1881 et al.). Additionally, it is interesting to note the variety of subscriptions for 2 Thessalonians, including πρὸς Θεσσαλονίκεις β ἐπληρώθη (D) and πρὸς Θεσσαλονίκεις β ἐγράφη ἀπὸ Ἀθηνῶν (A B[c] K P 31), and τοῦ ἁγίου ἀποστόλου Παύλου πρὸς Θεσσαλονίκεις δευτέρα· ἐγράφη ἀπὸ Ἀθηνῶν (L).[10]

AUTHORSHIP, DATE, AND LITERARY INTEGRITY

When it comes to the authorship and dating of 2 Thessalonians, there is a long history of debate about the authenticity of this letter, which naturally

---

7. See Metzger, *Textual Commentary*, 568. Wanamaker seems to support ἀπαρχήν because it is the more difficult reading (Wanamaker, *Thessalonians*, 266). Comfort remains undecided (*Commentary on the Manuscripts*, 358).
8. Metzger, *Textual Commentary*, 568.
9. Metzger, *Textual Commentary*, 569.
10. Metzger, *Textual Commentary*, 570.

affects questions regarding the historical situation and composition date. We will give extensive attention to this matter in the next chapter (chapter six), but to set up the discussion we appeal briefly to an illuminating article by Paul Foster called "Who Wrote 2 Thessalonians? A Fresh Look at an Old Problem."[11] Foster observes that scholars today are mostly settled into a comfortable consensus about the authorship of the Pauline corpus. There are seven undisputed letters (1 Thessalonians, Galatians, 1 Corinthians, 2 Corinthians, Romans, Philippians, Philemon) and six disputed letters (2 Thessalonians, Colossians, Ephesians, 1 Timothy, 2 Timothy, Titus).[12] One could divide the matter even more finely by labelling 2 Thessalonians, Colossians, and Ephesians as "deutero-Pauline" and the Pastorals as "trito-Pauline."[13] Foster notes, however, that in the twenty-first century we are seeing the lines blur between these categories. Depending on the scholar in question, 2 Thessalonians and Colossians seem to hover between "authentic" and "deutero-." As part of the research for this article, Foster surveyed the opinion of scholars gathered at the 2011 British New Testament Conference (with over one-hundred New Testament scholars participating). When it came to opinions about the authorship of 2 Thessalonians, 63 scholars (out of 111) believed Paul was the author, 13 believed he was not the author, and 35 were "uncertain."[14] The largest category of votes was in favor of Pauline authorship, but admittedly the survey comes from one region (namely, the United Kingdom). We are seeing a time when scholarship is largely divided on the authorship (and, correspondingly, dating) question. Those who consider 2 Thessalonians to be written by Paul argue that it was written only a short time after 1 Thessalonians and should probably be dated to 50 or 51 CE.[15] Those who imagine that a pseudepigrapher is responsible for 2 Thessalonians tend to date the letter to the last quarter of the first century; others still consider whether it might have been composed in the early second century.[16]

---

11. Paul Foster, "Who Wrote 2 Thessalonians? A Fresh Look at an Old Problem," *JSNT* 35.2 (2012): 150–75.

12. Foster, "Who Wrote 2 Thessalonians?," 1–2.

13. Foster, "Who Wrote 2 Thessalonians?," 2; see Wischmeyer, *Paul*, 3, 307.

14. See Foster, "Who Wrote 2 Thessalonians?," 19.

15. There is also the possibility that 2 Thess predates 1 Thess; see Wanamaker, *Thessalonians*, 37–45.

16. See esp. M. J. J. Menken, *2 Thessalonians*, NTR (New York: Routledge, 1994), 65–66; Boring, *1 and 2 Thessalonians*, 222. Raymond Brown explains that if 2 Thess is pseudonymous, it would probably date to the end of the first century "when increased apocalyptic fervor was manifest" (*Introduction to the New Testament* [Garden City, NY: Doubleday, 1997], 591).

When it comes to the literary integrity of 2 Thessalonians, almost *no* modern scholar argues that this is a composite letter or that it contains interpolations. As was discussed on page 169, Schmithals proposed that what we have now as 2 Thessalonians is actually more than one letter. Again, no one today follows Schmithals's partitions. Ernest Best expressed openness to composite theories, finding the placement of 2:13 awkward (for example).[17] But even Best admits that one is best served by interpreting 2 Thessalonians in the final form, the only form we have access to today.[18]

LETTER FEATURES

Genre

Because of 2 Thessalonians's junior status compared to the longer and presumably earlier 1 Thessalonians, there are far fewer discussions in scholarship of the genre of 2 Thessalonians. Nevertheless, the same concerns apply to 2 Thessalonians as 1 Thessalonians regarding whether one should approach it in terms of *epistolary* analysis or *rhetorical* conventions (see pp. 34–35 above). Regarding the former, Jeffrey Weima argues in favor of reading 2 Thessalonians *as a letter*; while he does not categorize 2 Thessalonians as a particular letter type, his structural outline of 2 Thessalonians (as a letter) hints at his reading of 2 Thessalonians as primarily a letter of consolation (1:1–2:17) and exhortation (3:1–15). Similarly, Malherbe is interested in the genre of 2 Thessalonians, preferring an epistolary framework over a rhetorical one; he urges that 2 Thessalonians ought not to be labeled rigidly as *one* type of letter (from the categories that were presumed in ancient Greek usage). For example, as Wanamaker considers the possible "fit" for 2 Thessalonians in terms of letter types (drawing from Stower's categories), he considers it most probable that it be considered a "letter of advice."[19] Malherbe argues instead that 2 Thessalonians bears a "mixed type" that has broader interests in exhortation.[20]

---

17. Best, *Thessalonians*, 49.
18. Best, *Thessalonians*, 49.
19. See Wanamaker, *Thessalonians*, 48; cf. Stowers, *Letter Writing*, 107f. According to Stowers, a letter of advice gives direction and counsel (sometimes at the behest of particular questions) and need not always presume authoritative commands (108).
20. See Malherbe, *Thessalonians*, 361. Similarly see Green, *Thessalonians*, 72.

Another way to interpret 2 Thessalonians is in relation to rhetorical categories, specifically the species of deliberative, judicial, or epideictic rhetoric (see pp. 31–33 above). Frank W. Hughes, Robert Jewett, and George Kennedy all consider 2 Thessalonians to be deliberative, as the author's apparent purpose was for the audience to rethink their understanding of the final events of history.[21] So also Ben Witherington, a major advocate for reading Paul's letters within an ancient rhetorical framework, classifies 2 Thessalonians as deliberative, referring to it as demonstrating "the rhetoric of advice and consent, the rhetoric that deals with what is coming in the future, the rhetoric which seeks a change of belief and practice in the audience."[22] Menken has labeled 2 Thessalonians an "advisory letter" (which focuses on exhortation) and observes how this epistolary classification has "affinities with deliberative rhetoric."[23]

Style

According to George Milligan, 2 Thessalonians fits the Greek writing style of 1 Thessalonians quite closely, whether it is in regard to "drawn out sentences" (1:6ff.; 2:8ff.), frequent ellipses (1:3, 9; 2:7; 3:6), how Paul might "go off" at a word (2:10), the inversion of metaphors (2:4), or the overall intensity of feeling demonstrated in the text.[24] Malherbe also offers comments on the style of 2 Thessalonians. Both Thessalonian letters have about the same number of *hapax legomena* relative to the size of the overall text.[25] In terms of potential stylistic differences, Malherbe noticed that 2 Thessalonians carries a more Septuagintal ring, but he wonders

---

21. F. W. Hughes, *Early Christian Rhetoric and 2 Thessalonians*, JSNTSup 30 (Sheffield: JSOT Press, 1989), 55; Hughes writes: "2 Thessalonians is an intentionally worked-out document of deliberative rhetoric with a clear goal: to refute those who say 'whether by spirit or *logos* or a letter from us, that the Day of the Lord has come'" (73); see also Jewett, *Thessalonian Correspondence*, 82; Kennedy, *New Testament Interpretation through Rhetorical Criticism*, 144; for a wider discussion of this, see Wanamaker, *Thessalonians*, 48. See also K. P. Donfried, "2 Thessalonians and the Church of Thessalonica," in *Paul, Thessalonica, and Early Christianity* (London: T&T Clark, 2002), 50.

22. Witherington, *Thessalonians*, 30.

23. Menken, *2 Thessalonians*, 21; similarly see Furnish, *1–2 Thessalonians*, 127–28.

24. Milligan, *Thessalonians*, lvi. This is not the place to engage thoroughly in the contentious matter of what to make of the "copycat" nature of 2 Thess in relation to 1 Thess (see pp. 202–7 below); nevertheless, Milligan does *not* find this close literary/stylistic connection a point in favor of pseudepigraphical dependence. Rather, he believes that a scenario makes sense where Paul, who "had evidently not the pen of a ready writer," was simply not that skilled at varying up his style. The same thoughts and phrases, Milligan surmises, that filled his head as he waited for Timothy to return (regarding 1 Thess) were still in his memory "and have risen almost unconsciously to his lips, as he dictated his second letter to the same Church so shortly afterwards" (lvi).

25. Malherbe, *Thessalonians*, 365.

whether this may simply be due to the "apocalyptic elements" in the first two chapters.[26]

Style discussions often take an interest in authorship, comparing the style of 1 Thessalonians to 2 Thessalonians. Menken rehearses the analysis of Trilling: in 2 Thessalonians there are several examples of parallelisms (e.g., 1:10; 2:8, 12), exaggerated language (e.g., 3:16), doubling up of substantives (e.g., 2:8, 13), and repetition of keywords (such as "oppress/ion").[27] In the middle of the twentieth century, with the rise of computers, there was much interest in seeing how these machines might crunch the data of the Pauline corpus and help to analyze the Pauline style. Unfortunately, the results from various studies were inconclusive at best, and sometimes contradictory. Andrew Morton and James McLeman presented their findings in *Christianity in the Computer Age*.[28] From their study they concluded that Romans, 1–2 Corinthians, Galatians, and Philippians had the same style, but 1–2 Thessalonians were not determined to be authentically Pauline. However, their study suggested that the same person that wrote 1 Thessalonians also penned 2 Thessalonians. K. Grayston and G. Herdan conducted a "statistical linguistics" analysis of Paul's letters and found that both 1 and 2 Thessalonians bore the same style as the *Hauptbriefe*.[29] In G. K. Barr's "scalometry" analysis, he found that 2 Thessalonians had an extraordinarily long second sentence (over 158 words), but this did not amount to a technical difference of "style" as much as a by-product of the author dwelling on a key theme of the letter at its opening, the subject of "the judgement at Christ's coming."[30]

Structure

The discussion that relates to the literary structure of 2 Thessalonians also parallels the scholarship on 1 Thessalonians (for reference, see pp. 34–35 above). As Weima helpfully notes, scholars tend to orient their

---

26. Malherbe, *Thessalonians*, 365.

27. See Menken, *2 Thessalonians*, 32; cf. W. Trilling, *Untersuchungen zum zweiten Thessalonischerbrief* (Leipzig: St. Benno, 1972), 48–65.

28. A. Q. Morton and J. McLeman, *Christianity in the Computer Age* (New York: Harper & Row, 1964).

29. K. Grayston and G. Herdan, "The Authorship of the Pastorals in the Light of Statistical Linguistics," *NTS* 6 (1959): 1–15.

30. G. K. Barr, *Scalometry and the Pauline Epistles*, JSNTSup 261 (London: T&T Clark, 2004), 86. See also the results of A. Kenny who analyzed 99 stylistic elements in Paul's letters and came to the conclusion that 2 Thess showed as much coherence with a prototypical Pauline letter as 1 Thess (and even more than 1 Cor) in *A Stylometric Study of the New Testament* (Oxford: Clarendon, 1986), 95–100.

structural analysis in terms of genre, some reading 2 Thessalonians in light of *rhetorical* categories, others in view of *epistolary* analysis, and others still with a generic or thematic approach. Virtually all scholars agree that 2 Thessalonians 1:1–2 serves as the prescript or opening and 3:16–18 the closing. The weightier considerations concern the material between these.

For a good example of a rhetorical structuring of 2 Thessalonians, one might turn to Jewett, who offers a rather simple breakdown. He labels 1:1–12 as 2 Thessalonians's *exordium*, then the *partitio* (2:1–2), followed by the *probatio* (2:3–3:5). The *exhortatio* comes next (3:6–15), with the *peroratio* at the end (3:16–18).[31] Charles Wanamaker also provides a rhetorical analysis with epistolary bookends, though he breaks the middle portions of 2 Thessalonians up differently than Jewett. For Wanamaker, the *probatio* (2:3–15) transitions to a *peroratio* (2:16–17).[32]

Weima is an advocate for reading all of Paul's letters, including 2 Thessalonians, primarily as *letters* and thus develops his structure via epistolary analysis. In practice, his outline is rather basic: after the letter opening (1:1–12), Paul offers a "thanksgiving" (1:3–12). Chapter two is comprised of a main set of teaching intended to give comfort concerning the day of the Lord (2:1–17). Then comes "exhortations about the rebellious idlers" (3:1–15), with the epistolary closing at the end.[33] The simple structure proposed by Menken is almost identical to Weima's.[34]

Fee's commentary is an example of a thematic approach to structure, but again his outline is nearly identical to Weima and Menken. What is distinctive about Fee's structure is the focus on 2 Thessalonians's addressing of *three issues* in the letter. The first issue pertains to persecution (1:3–10). The second issue involves "the 'when' of the day of the Lord" (2:1–17). Finally, the author handles the concerns surrounding "the disruptive-idlers" (3:1–15).[35]

---

31. See Jewett, *Thessalonian Correspondence*, 225.

32. See Wanamaker, *Thessalonians*, 50. Wanamaker argues that because 2 Thess is deliberative and 1 Thess is not, there are some key structural differences. For example, deliberative rhetoric does not include a major narration.

33. Weima, *1–2 Thessalonians*, 55–56. The structural proposal by E. Reinmuth is even simpler. Reinmuth works with two main portions; "Erster Briefteil [First Letter Section]" (1:1–2:17) and "Zweiter Briefteil [Second Letter Section]" (3:1–18); see E. Reinmuth, "Der zweite Brief an die Thessalonicher," in *Die Briefe an die Philipper, Thessalonicher und an Philemon*, ed. N. Walter, E. Reinmuth, and P. Lampe, NTD 8/2 (Göttingen: Vandenhoeck & Ruprecht, 1998), 159–204.

34. See Menken, *2 Thessalonians*. See also, similarly, P.-G. Müller, who works with the three primary categories of Briefeingang [letter introduction] (1:1–12), Briefkorpus [letter body] (2:1–3:13), and Briefschluss [letter ending] (3:14–18); see *Der Erste und Zweite Brief an die Thessalonicher*, Regensburger Neues Testament (Regensburg: Pustet, 2001).

35. Fee, *Thessalonians*, passim.

Malherbe has what is certainly one of the more complex structural analyses (with more thematic interests). In Malherbe's outline, 2 Thessalonians cycles between thanksgiving and exhortation. The letter begins with thanksgiving (1:3–12), then exhortation (2:1–12), then another thanksgiving statement (2:13–14), and another hortatory section (2:15–3:5), followed by commands related to the disorderly (3:6–15), and the conclusion (3:16–18).[36]

Despite the differences between these various structures and their methodological perspectives, in the end the sectional breaks are mostly agreed upon (and fit the artificial chapter divisions), with Malherbe as the outlier.[37]

Sources and Influences on 2 Thessalonians

As explained in chapter one (p. 36), it is uncommon today to examine Pauline texts with a specific interest in determining separate sources on which the text is dependent. However, in the specific case of 2 Thessalonians, it appears to be a more direct and pressing matter. For over one-hundred years, scholars have noticed remarkable similarities in structure, phrasing, and style between 2 Thessalonians and 1 Thessalonians. This seems to go beyond the normal way that several letters from the same person (like Paul) bear that author's personality and style. It seems as if 2 Thessalonians *copies* from 1 Thessalonians extensively, which thus serves in some way as a foundational source. This led Wrede, for example, to argue in 1903 that the copycat feature points in favor of treating 2 Thessalonians as pseudonymous (again, we will tackle the authorship question in detail in chapter six).[38] Others have found it possible to imagine that Paul, having retained a copy of 1 Thessalonians, had reason to draw directly from that letter as he wrote 2 Thessalonians.[39] Below is the presentation offered by Boring with dependence on Wrede, marking out the similar passages between 2 Thessalonians and 1 Thessalonians.[40]

---

36. Malherbe, *Thessalonians*, 356–60.
37. See the appended outline comparison for more information (p. 196).
38. W. Wrede, *Die Echtheit des zweiten Thessalonicherbriefes* (Leipzig: Henrich, 1903); cf. G. Hollmann, "Die Unechtheit des zweiten Thessalonicherbriefs," *ZNW* 5 (1904): 28–38; see Trilling, *Untersuchungen*.
39. See J. Wrzól, *Die Echtheit des zweiten Thessalonicherbriefes*, Biblische Studien 19.4 (Freiburg: Herder, 1916).
40. As cited in Boring, *1 and 2 Thessalonians*, 211; see also Menken, *2 Thessalonians*, 37–38; Furnish, *1–2 Thessalonians*, 132.

Similar Passages between
2 Thessalonians and 1 Thessalonians

2 THESSALONIANS	1 THESSALONIANS
1:1–2	1:1
1:3–2:17	1:2–3:13
2:13–15 (general similarities)	2:13–3:10
2:16–17	3:11–13
3:1–15 (general similarities)	4:1–5:22
3:16–18	5:22–28
3:16	5:23–24
3:17	5:26
3:18	5:28

Here we may briefly draw attention to a few examples to demonstrate this ostensible dependence.

2 Thessalonians 1:1 Παῦλος καὶ Σιλουανὸς καὶ Τιμόθεος τῇ ἐκκλησίᾳ Θεσσαλονικέων ἐν θεῷ πατρὶ ἡμῶν καὶ κυρίῳ Ἰησοῦ Χριστῷ, ² χάρις ὑμῖν καὶ εἰρήνη ἀπὸ θεοῦ πατρὸς [ἡμῶν] καὶ κυρίου Ἰησοῦ Χριστοῦ.

1 Thessalonians 1:1 Παῦλος καὶ Σιλουανὸς καὶ Τιμόθεος τῇ ἐκκλησίᾳ Θεσσαλονικέων ἐν θεῷ πατρὶ καὶ κυρίῳ Ἰησοῦ Χριστῷ, χάρις ὑμῖν καὶ εἰρήνη.

In the Pauline corpus, there is no verbatim overlap that covers as many words between two letters as we see here. Further, in both 2 Thessalonians and 1 Thessalonians we have the collocation of faith-love-endurance:

2 Thessalonians 1:3–4 Εὐχαριστεῖν ὀφείλομεν τῷ θεῷ πάντοτε περὶ ὑμῶν, ἀδελφοί, καθὼς ἄξιόν ἐστιν, ὅτι ὑπεραυξάνει ἡ πίστις ὑμῶν καὶ πλεονάζει ἡ ἀγάπη ἑνὸς ἑκάστου πάντων ὑμῶν εἰς ἀλλήλους, ⁴ ὥστε αὐτοὺς ἡμᾶς ἐν ὑμῖν ἐγκαυχᾶσθαι ἐν ταῖς ἐκκλησίαις τοῦ θεοῦ ὑπὲρ τῆς ὑπομονῆς ὑμῶν καὶ πίστεως ἐν πᾶσιν τοῖς διωγμοῖς ὑμῶν καὶ ταῖς θλίψεσιν αἷς ἀνέχεσθε

1 Thessalonians 1:3 μνημονεύοντες ὑμῶν τοῦ ἔργου τῆς πίστεως καὶ τοῦ κόπου τῆς ἀγάπης καὶ τῆς ὑπομονῆς τῆς ἐλπίδος τοῦ κυρίου ἡμῶν Ἰησοῦ Χριστοῦ ἔμπροσθεν τοῦ θεοῦ καὶ πατρὸς ἡμῶν

Perhaps the most unusual link between 2 Thessalonians and 1 Thessalonians is the use of the verb κατευθύνω, a word that appears nowhere else in Paul beyond the Thessalonian correspondence, and only once in the NT outside of Paul (Luke 1:79). In 2 Thessalonians 3:5 we read ὁ δὲ κύριος κατευθύναι ὑμῶν τὰς καρδίας εἰς τὴν ἀγάπην τοῦ θεοῦ καὶ εἰς τὴν ὑπομονὴν τοῦ Χριστοῦ. The focus is on the wish-prayer that the Lord would direct the Thessalonians' hearts. In 1 Thessalonians 3:11 Paul writes, αὐτὸς δὲ ὁ θεὸς καὶ πατὴρ ἡμῶν καὶ ὁ κύριος ἡμῶν Ἰησοῦς κατευθύναι τὴν ὁδὸν ἡμῶν πρὸς ὑμᾶς. Again, this is in the context of a wish-prayer, and we have that same rare use of the optative, but here the hope is that God would direct the apostles toward the Thessalonians. The similarities appear to be more than coincidental, but the different messages render problematic any simple conclusion that Paul was depending on the first letter to (essentially) repeat his concerns in the second letter. Whatever the interpreter surmises, we are confronted with a text (2 Thess) that must surely depend in some way on 1 Thessalonians, but not always in a verbatim manner, at least not in this case.[41]

As with 1 Thessalonians, it behooves us to consider the Old Testament as a source for 2 Thessalonians, or perhaps more properly as a significant influence. Again, as with 1 Thessalonians, 2 Thessalonians does not quote any Old Testament text verbatim, but scholars have made several claims regarding connections between 2 Thessalonians and a particular Old Testament text. For example, Roger Aus treats 2 Thessalonians 1–2 as an interpretation of Isaiah 66.[42] Jeffrey Weima considers it likely that we find in 2 Thessalonians 1:8a a strong allusion to Isaiah 66:15:[43]

---

41. Compare Boring's conclusion: "(1) Paul wrote both letters, so a personal, pastoral, or psychological explanation for his compositional procedure must be found; or (2) a later author wrote 2 Thessalonians and consciously imitated 1 Thessalonians, closely following the form of his template, but elaborating its content in terms of his own agenda" (211); see Furnish, *1–2 Thessalonians*, 132.

42. R. Aus, "The Relevance of Isaiah 66.7 to Revelation 12 and 2 Thessalonians 1," *ZNW* 67 (1976): 252–68; also R. Aus, "God's Plan and God's Power: Isaiah 66 and the Restraining Factors of 2 Thess 2:6–7," *JBL* 96 (1977): 537–53; see also S. G. Brown, "The Intertextuality of Isaiah 66.17 and 2 Thessalonians 2.7: A Solution to the 'Restrainer' Problem," in *Paul and the Scriptures of Israel*, ed. C. A. Evans and J. A. Sanders (Sheffield: JSOT Press, 1993), 254–77.

43. Weima, "1–2 Thessalonians," 883–84.

Isaiah 66:15 ἰδοὺ γὰρ κύριος ὡς πῦρ ἥξει καὶ ὡς καταιγὶς τὰ ἅρματα αὐτοῦ ἀποδοῦναι ἐν θυμῷ ἐκδίκησιν καὶ ἀποσκορακισμὸν ἐν φλογὶ πυρός

2 Thessalonians 1:7b–8 ἐν τῇ ἀποκαλύψει τοῦ κυρίου Ἰησοῦ ἀπ᾽ οὐρανοῦ μετ᾽ ἀγγέλων δυνάμεως αὐτοῦ ἐν πυρὶ φλογός, διδόντος ἐκδίκησιν τοῖς μὴ εἰδόσιν θεὸν καὶ τοῖς μὴ ὑπακούουσιν τῷ εὐαγγελίῳ τοῦ κυρίου ἡμῶν Ἰησοῦ

Notice here not only the shared language of the fiery flame but also that of giving or recompense (ἀποδίδωμι; δίδωμι) and the mutual emphasis on vengeance (ἐκδίκησις). When 2 Thessalonians refers to "the glory of his [the Lord's] strength" (1:9 NET), this may come from the same phrase often repeated in Isaiah 2 (vv. 10, 19, 21).[44]

As we consider 2 Thessalonians 2, we enter into the murky waters of trying to identify the specific influences on the "day of the Lord" language and apocalyptic imagery in this section. We will not engage into the tedium of discussing every possible "echo," but rather we will address the traditions and major texts that relate to key concepts and phrases in 2 Thessalonians 2:1–17.

Man of lawlessness (2:3). Here Weima points to texts like LXX Psalm 88:23 and LXX Isaiah 57:3–4, which refer to this idiom in generic ways.[45]

"Who opposes and exalts himself above every so-called god or object of worship" (2:4 NRSV). There appears to be an echo here of Daniel 11:36, where it is said of an ambitious king "he will be enraged and will be exalted over every god" (11:36 NETS).[46] Gordon Fee also argues in favor of a connection to Ezekiel 28:2 where the king of Tyre proclaims about himself, "I am a god; I sit on the throne of a god."[47]

"Whom the Lord Jesus will overthrow with the breath of his mouth" (2:8). Most scholars consider self-evident the link to Isaiah 11:4: "He shall administer justice to a humble one and convict the humble ones of the

---

44. See Keesmaat, "In the Face of the Empire," 182–212; cf. C. C. Newman, "Resurrection as Glory: Divine Presence and Christian Origins," in *The Resurrection: An Interdisciplinary Symposium on the Resurrection of Jesus*, ed. S. T. Davis et al. (Oxford: Oxford University Press, 1997), 76. This observation was made by Tertullian: "[Paul in 2 Thess 1:9] uses the words of Isaiah" (*Against Marcion* 5.16, as cited in S. McKinion, ed., *Isaiah 1–39*, ACCS [Downers Grove, IL: InterVarsity Press, 2014], 29).

45. Weima, "1–2 Thessalonians," 887; cf. Malherbe, *Thessalonians*, 419.

46. See Malherbe, *Thessalonians*, 420.

47. Fee, *Thessalonians*, 283; cf. Gaventa, *First and Second Thessalonians*, 112.

earth, and he shall strike the earth with the word of his mouth, and with breath through his lips he shall do away with the impious" (NETS).[48]

A final consideration is 2 Thessalonians 3:5, as I have argued previously that there are interesting linguistic and thematic parallels with LXX Psalm 77:8. In both texts we find the motif of hearts being directly rightly. LXX Psalm 77 (78), like 2 Thessalonians as a whole, shows special concern for the fidelity and trust of God's people in the Lord.[49]

Finally, in this section we have opportunity to briefly mention the importance of 2 Thessalonians's appeal to prior teachings and traditions. Thus, 2:15: "So then, brothers and sisters, stand firm and hold fast to the teachings we passed on to you, whether by word of mouth or by letter"; and 3:6: "In the name of the Lord Jesus Christ, we command you, brothers and sisters, to keep away from every believer who is idle and disruptive and does not live according to the teaching you received from us." Both texts are clear that the traditions being reinforced to the Thessalonians are ones introduced by Paul, but they also clue us into the fact that the passing down of traditions was important and open up the possibility that the apostles had particular traditions that they felt necessary to transmit and support.[50]

RECOMMENDED READING

Textual Criticism and 2 Thessalonians

Comfort, P. W. *A Commentary on Textual Additions to the New Testament.* Grand Rapids: Kregel, 2017.

———. *A Commentary on the Manuscripts and Text of the New Testament.* Grand Rapids: Kregel, 2015.

Ehrman, B. D., and M. W. Holmes, eds. *The Text of the New Testament in Contemporary Research: Essays on the Status Quaestionis.* 2nd ed. NTTSD 42. Leiden: Brill, 2013.

Metzger, B. M. *A Textual Commentary on the Greek New Testament.* 2nd ed. Stuttgart: German Bible Society, 1994.

---

48. See Weima, "1–2 Thessalonians," 887; Richard, *First and Second Thessalonians,* 332; cf. D. Frayer-Griggs, *Saved through Fire: The Fiery Ordeal in New Testament Eschatology* (Eugene, OR: Wipf & Stock, 2016), 129. For the influence of Isaiah 11:4 on a variety of NT texts, see D. D. Hannah, "Isaiah within Judaism of the Second Temple Period," in *Isaiah in the New Testament,* ed. S. Moyise and M. J. J. Menken (London: T&T Clark, 2005), 15–16.

49. See N. K. Gupta, "An Apocalyptic Reading of Psalm 78 in 2 Thessalonians 3," *JSNT* 31.2 (2008): 179–94.

50. See G. Strecker, *Theology of the New Testament* (Berlin: de Gruyter, 2014), 602; cf. R. P. Martin, *New Testament Foundations,* vol. 2 (Grand Rapids: Eerdmans, 1994), 285.

Royse, J. R. "The Early Text of Paul (and Hebrews)." Pages 175–203 in *The Early Text of the New Testament*. Edited by Charles E. Hill and Michael J. Kruger. Oxford: Oxford University Press, 2012.

Authorship and Date

Campbell, D. A. "Locating the Thessalonian Correspondence." Pages 190–253 in *Framing Paul: An Epistolary Biography*. Grand Rapids: Eerdmans, 2014.

Wrede, W. *The Authenticity of the Second Letter to the Thessalonians*. Translated by R. Rhea. Eugene, OR: Wipf & Stock, 2017. Original German volume: *Die Echtheit des zweiten Thessalonicherbriefes*. TU 9/2. Leipzig: C. J. Henrich, 1903.

Sources

Weima, J. A. D. "1–2 Thessalonians." Pages 871–90 in *Commentary on the New Testament Use of the Old Testament*. Edited by G. K. Beale and D. A. Carson. Grand Rapids: Baker, 2007.

APPENDIX

	WANAMAKER	MALHERBE	JEWETT*	MENKEN	WEIMA**	FEE
1:1-2	Epistolary Prescript	Address	Exordium (1:1-12)	Prescript (1:1-2)	Letter Opening (1:1-2)	Thanksgiving and Prayer (1:1-12)
1:3-12	Exordium	**Thanksgiving and Exhortation (1:3-2:12):** Thanksgiving Proper (1:3-12)		Proem (1:3-12)	Thanksgiving (1:3-12)	[First Issue 1:3-10]: The problem of persecutors
2:1-2	*Partitio*	**Thanksgiving and Exhortation (1:3-2:12):** Exhortation (2:1-12)	*Partitio* (2:1-2)	Letter Body (2:1-17)	Comfort concerning the day of the Lord (2:1-17)	The Second Issue: The "when" of the day of the Lord (2:1-17)
2:3-15	*Probatio*	**Thanksgiving and Exhortation (2:13-3:5):** Thanksgiving Period Proper (2:13-14) **Thanksgiving and Exhortation (2:13-3:5):** Exhortation (2:15-3:5): Admonition (2:15)	*Probatio* (2:3-3:5)			
2:16-17	*Peroratio*	**Thanksgiving and Exhortation (2:13-3:5):** Exhortation (2:15-3:5): Prayer for Encouragement (2:16-17)				
3:1-15	**Exhortatio**	**Thanksgiving and Exhortation (2:13-3:5):** Exhortation (2:15-3:5): request for prayer (3:1-2); the faithfulness of God (3:3-4); prayer for faithfulness (3:5) **Commands (3:6-15)**	*Exhortatio* (3:6-15)	Exhortation (3:1-15)	Exhortations about the Rebellious Idlers (3:1-15)	The Third Issue: About the Disruptive Idle (3:1-15)
3:16-18	Epistolary Closing	Conclusion (3:16-18)	*Peroratio* (3:16-18)	Letter Closing (3:16-18)	Letter Closing (3:16-18)	Concluding Matters (3:16-18).

* See Jewett, *Thessalonian Correspondence*, 225.

** Other epistolary structure theories are analyzed by Jewett including those of J. A. Bailey, J. C. Hurd, G. Krodel, and R. J. Peterson; see Jewett, *Thessalonian Correspondence*, 224 (chart five).

CHAPTER 6

BACKGROUND, SITUATION, AND DATE OF 2 THESSALONIANS

INTRODUCTION

In the previous chapter, we already had reason to briefly introduce the matter of the contested authorship of 2 Thessalonians in scholarship. Second Thessalonians is considered one of the disputed letters within the Pauline corpus. Still, this simply means that the matter is part of an ongoing debate, and few scholars confidently consign it to a "deutero-Pauline" category the way many scholars do, for example, 1 Timothy and Titus. Occasionally you will find someone who considers the issue insignificant altogether—*Why bother arguing over authorship at all? How much does it affect interpretation?*[1] Stanley Porter argues that discernment of the author is hermeneutically fundamental. He posits that

> the implications of falsely attributed authorship are significant. In a discipline that has typically been concerned with issues of history, to assign a particular text to an incorrect historical milieu wreaks havoc upon interpretation. Furthermore, a discipline often grounded in certain theological and ethical pursuits must take care to fairly weigh the ramifications of literary forgery upon such issues as canon, theology, authority, and, ultimately, truth.[2]

---

1. S. Fowl does not dismiss the importance of historical study, but he does question the ability of scholars to discern authorial intent and then to read a text in light of that assumed intent. See his comments in *Ephesians*, NTL (Louisville: Westminster John Knox, 2012), 9–27.

2. S. E. Porter, "On Pauline Pseudepigraphy: An Introduction," in *Paul and Pseudepigraphy*, ed. S. E. Porter and G. P. Fewster, PAST (Leiden: Brill, 2013), 2. See too idem, "Pauline Authorship and the Pastoral Epistles: Implications for Canon," *BBR* 5 (1995): 105–23. See also C. Spinks, *The Bible*

In chapter five we noted the study conducted by Paul Foster regarding opinions about authorship of various Pauline letters, including 2 Thessalonians.[3] A larger group of (mostly) British scholars showed more confidence in labeling 2 Thessalonians as authentic than those who believed it was pseudonymous. Still, there were many who simply could not commit to either view confidently.[4]

Yet it is important that we have a panoramic perspective on this matter. Hanna Roose, for example, explains that "German scholars almost unanimously view 2 Thessalonians as a pseudepigraph."[5] Foster seems to be correct that in the UK (and to some degree in the US) the previous consensus about 2 Thessalonians is eroding, perhaps not toward authenticity but toward a kind of agnosticism.[6] In his *Paul and the Faithfulness of God*, N. T. Wright addresses at length the question regarding what "sources" to use when studying the historical Paul. Wright points to widespread agreement on the authenticity of the undisputed (seven) letters.[7] Wright believes it is time to revisit the status of Ephesians, Colossians, and 2 Thessalonians.[8] Wright labels the lingering dismissal of these as a "matter of fashion and prejudice."[9] Because the guild treated these as dubious, they were demoted in importance. Wright also argues that scholarly resistance to Ephesians, Colossians, and 2 Thessalonians has something to do with viewing these

---

and the Crisis of Meaning: Debates on the Theological Intepretation of Scripture (London: T&T Clark, 2007), 110–11.

3. Foster, "Who Wrote 2 Thessalonians?," 150–75.

4. See p. 185 above.

5. H. Roose, "'A Letter as by Us': Intentional Ambiguity in 2 Thessalonians 2.2," *JSNT* 29 (2006): 109n6. Among English-speaking scholars, she says, "The authorship of 2 Thessalonians is a truly open question"; she cites here G. S. Holland, "'A Letter Supposed from Us': A Contribution to the Discussion about the Authorship of 2 Thessalonians," in Collins, *Thessalonian Correspondence*, 402. For a relatively recent example, see E. Reinmuth, "Die zweite Brief an die Thessalonicher," 159–204; otherwise, see U. Schnelle, *Einleitung in das Neue Testament*, 5th ed. (Göttingen: Vandenhoeck & Ruprecht, 2005), 372. A. G. Van Aarde boldly states, "By the early eighties the hypothesis [of pseudonymity] had acquired the characteristic of 'scientific certainty'"; see "The Second Letter to the Thessalonians Re-Read as Pseudepigraph," *HTS* 56.1 (2000): 122.

6. Note, e.g., how D. Horrell claims *agnosticism* regarding 1 Peter's authorship (*1 Peter*, NTG [London: T&T Clark, 2008], 20–23). See too the work of J. C. Hurd. Hurd was given the task by the Seminar on the Thessalonian Correspondence (Annual Meeting of the Society of Biblical Literature, 1983) of defending the authenticity of 2 Thessalonians. He did so (with Krentz on the opposite side), but Hurd voices this caveat: "We do, of course, benefit from the fact that the answer to our present question is real, i.e., either Paul [did] or did not write this letter. History, however, has left us with insufficient evidence to achieve anything near consensus, much less certainty, on the authenticity of 2 Thessalonians." See J. C. Hurd, "Concerning the Authenticity of 2 Thessalonians," in *The Earlier Letters of Paul—And Other Letters* (New York: Peter Lang, 1998), 135–61.

7. N. T. Wright, *Paul and the Faithfulness of God* (Minneapolis: Fortress, 2013), 56.

8. Wright, *Paul and the Faithfulness of God*, 56.

9. Wright, *Paul and the Faithfulness of God*, 58; cf. also Campbell, *Framing Paul*.

texts as doctrinaire and authoritarian, elements that irritate some scholars and taint their image of a maverick and charismatic Paul. Thus, Wright has called for a kind of reset of the Pauline corpus, approaching the texts within that library afresh to see again whether they all belong to the historical Paul. Specifically with respect to 2 Thessalonians, Wright believes that it tends to be labeled un-Pauline because of the unusual dimensions of apocalyptic discourse in 2:1–12. Wright believes that because so many scholars are interested now in the "apocalyptic Paul," there should be much more openness to seeing 2 Thessalonians as authentic. He claims, "It would be ironic now, with interest running high in Paul as both an apocalypticist and a political thinker, if we continued to rule out of consideration, largely for reasons of scholarly tradition and fashion, a letter where both themes play key roles."[10]

Gordon Fee offers an American (evangelical) perspective on the authorship of 2 Thessalonians: "The writing of a commentary on this letter in and of itself tends to push one toward authenticity regarding authorship, so that there has been only one significant commentary in English over the past century and a half that has tried to make sense of this letter as a forgery."[11] His reference to an outlier here is directed at Earl Richard (1995), but we can also include Menken (1996). To my knowledge, Karl Donfried is completing the ICC volume on 1–2 Thessalonians and will defend (a form of) Pauline authorship. Helmut Koester was working on the Hermeneia volume of 1–2 Thessalonians, but he passed away in 2016. He would have argued *against* Pauline authorship of 2 Thessalonians, but the commentary project has now been passed to AnneMarie Luijendijk.[12]

We will give focused attention to the development of thought on the authorship of 2 Thessalonians in the early modern period later on pages 273–80, but here it will suffice to give a very brief overview. We do not find scholarly articulation of a position that doubts that the apostle Paul wrote 2 Thessalonians until the eighteenth century.[13] The first full-scale

---

10. Wright, *Paul and the Faithfulness of God*, 61.

11. Fee, *Thessalonians*, 237. Fee's word "significant" is obviously subjective; Thompson notes the 1978 commentary by G. Krodel that argued for pseudonymity (see below); see T. Thompson, "A Stone that *Still* Won't Fit: An Introductory and Editorial Note for Edgar Krentz's 'A Stone that Will Not Fit,'" in *Pseudepigraphie und Verfasserfiktion in frühchristlichen Briefen*, ed. J. Frey et al., WUNT 256 (Tübingen: Mohr Siebeck, 2009), 433; cf. G. Krodel, "2 Thessalonians," in *Ephesians, Colossians, 2 Thessalonians, and the Pastoral Epistles*, Proclamation (Philadelphia: Fortress, 1978), 73–96.

12. It appears, though, that the volume will only be on 1 Thess.

13. See D. W. MacDougall, *The Authenticity of 2 Thessalonians* (Milton Keynes: Paternoster, 2016), 1.

argument for pseudonymity came from William Wrede in the early twentieth century.[14] According to Howard Marshall, until the 1970s most (Anglophone?) scholars held to Pauline authorship of 2 Thessalonians.[15] After that time, more studies were devoted to the subject, and the pseudonymity position found stronger grounding and drew wider favor.[16]

Below we will outline the contemporary state of the discussion of the authorship of 2 Thessalonians with main arguments for and against authenticity, and arguments for and against pseudonymity. After that we will consider what the proposed "situational" scenarios could be in the case of authenticity, and then in the case of pseudonymity. The matter of the dating will also briefly be considered.

Modern Methodology of Authorship Analysis

While individual scholars have developed their own criteria for determining authorship on New Testament texts, overall the guild of biblical scholarship has functioned in this area mostly on an accumulation of impressions and relative evidence. All of this is to say that there is no agreed upon set of proofs one way or the other. Those who decide in favor of pseudonymity—especially with a text like 2 Thessalonians—do so on the basis of cumulative clues and evidence, admittedly so in most cases.[17]

In 2013 I published an article reviewing what I call "the hermeneutics of authorship analysis," using Colossians as a case study, though the discussion runs nearly parallel with 2 Thessalonians.[18] In that study of mostly late twentieth-century and early twenty-first-century scholarship, I noted that five factors seemed to be particularly important in the determination of authorship.

Language. This feature includes analysis of the text's style and syntax of verbal expressions.

Logic. Logic considers the thought patterns and process of argumentation found in the text.

Theology. This includes major categories such as Christology, ecclesiology, and eschatology—the text in question tends to be compared in these areas with the theology of the undisputed letters.

---

14. Wrede, *Die Echtheit des zweiten Thessalonicherbriefes.*
15. Marshall, *1 and 2 Thessalonians*, 29.
16. See J. A. Bailey, "Who Wrote II Thessalonians?," *NTS* 25 (1978–79): 131–45.
17. See N. Richardson, *Paul's Language about God*, JSNTSup (Sheffield: Sheffield Academic Press, 1994), 330; Bailey, "Who Wrote II Thessalonians?," 131–45.
18. N. K. Gupta, "What Is in a Name? The Hermeneutics of Authorship Analysis concerning Colossians," *CBR* 11 (2013): 196–217.

Historical plausibility. Here is considered the question, *Does this text "fit" into the assumed time period, or are there clues that it was actually written at a later time?*

Pseudonymous-authorship currency/acceptability. In the last fifty years, the study of ancient Jewish and Christian (and pagan) pseudonymous texts has grown exponentially. While in times past a certain stigma (deceit, trickery) may have been fixed to the notion of pseudonymity, today the practice of ancient pseudepigraphy, especially within Judaism, was considered to be somewhat conventional. How this convention relates to certain Pauline letters is a major crux in this discussion.

To these traditional factors in the study of Pauline pseudonymity, we could also add more contemporary considerations.

The meaning of "authorship." In the matter of pseudonymity, scholars conventionally ask whether Paul *wrote* such and such a letter. Truth be told, the verb "to write" itself can be an ambiguous one. Charles Talbert carried out a study of Cicero's *Letters to Atticus* and discerned five ways that he refers to "authorship" in one way or another:[19]

1. Authorship as writing in one's own hand (2.23.1)
2. Authorship as writing by dictation (4.16.1)
3. Authorship as collaboration in writing (11.5)
4. Authorship as authorizing someone else to write (3.1.5)
5. Authorship "as if" by the putative author (6.6).

We must be willing to expand our horizons of what "authorship" means when it comes to studying Paul's letters.[20]

Reception history and patristic testimony. Another critical factor in the study of pseudonymity is reception history and patristic testimony, a consideration often ignored but gaining interest in recent years. This includes early conversations about canonical status.[21]

Pseudonymous "tells." Especially when it comes to 2 Thessalonians, scholars have an interest in detecting occasions where a pseudepigrapher has tried too hard to appear as if he is the named author, such that this

---

19. C. H. Talbert, *Ephesians and Colossians*, Paideia (Grand Rapids: Baker, 2007), 8.
20. See too E. R. Richards, *The Secretary in the Letters of Paul*, WUNT 2/42 (Tübingen: Mohr Siebeck, 1991), 23–53.
21. Consider the attention D. C. Allison gives to this in his *A Critical and Exegetical Commentary on James*, ICC (London: Bloomsbury, 2013).

"gives away" his false identity. This would be comparable to when someone bluffing in a card game has a certain tell that proves that they are
lying—perhaps someone bluffing might raise the bet as a trick or smile as
if holding sure-bet cards.

In our discussion of the debate of the authorship of 2 Thessalonians
below, we will give attention to these features, though not necessarily in
the exact wording or order presented above.

Literary Dependence

As noted in the previous chapter (chapter five), one of the primary reasons that many scholars believe that Paul did *not* write 2 Thessalonians is
due to its remarkable similarities with 1 Thessalonians.[22] While one might
find similarities naturally to lead to a decision in favor of authenticity,
there is so much verbatim and formal overlap between 2 Thessalonians and
1 Thessalonians that it can seem less like someone was writing *another* letter
and more like someone was *cutting and pasting* from one letter (1 Thess) to
another (2 Thess). Years before Raymond Brown raised this very question:
"Why would Paul copy himself in this almost mechanical way?"[23]

Edgar Krentz offers this comprehensive summary of the remarkable
literary and structural parallels between 1 and 2 Thessalonians:

> The salutation in the two letters is almost identical, describing the
> recipients as "the church of the Thessalonians," naming the inhab-
> itants rather than the city, as Paul does elsewhere (1 Thess 1:1;
> 2 Thess 1:1). Both letters begin with a long thanksgiving. Both also
> have thanksgivings for the Thessalonians in the middle of the letter
> body (Krodel [1978: 77] speaks of "two thanksgivings"), a feature
> found in no other Pauline letter. The letter body in each closes with a
> request to God expressed by a volitive optative (each uses the optative
> verb form στηρίξαι and the phrase ὑμῶν τὰς καρδίας as direct object,
> a combination found nowhere else in Paul). Each letter concludes the
> paraenetic section with a request that the "God [Lord] of peace" do
> something (1 Thess 5:23–24; 2 Thess 3:16). Both include petitions
> that use the verb κατευθῦναι (though in different contexts, 1 Thess
> 3:11; 2 Thess 3:5), found nowhere else in Paul. Both letters describe

---

22. See MacDougall, *Authenticity of 2 Thessalonians*, 8–11, 215–52.
23. R. E. Brown, *Introduction to the New Testament* (Garden City, NY: Doubleday, 1997), 592.

the situation of the Thessalonians in the context of the opening thanksgiving (1 Thess 1:6–10; 2 Thess 1:4–6). Their structure, as Bailey makes clear, is similar.[24]

Neither letter identifies Paul as an apostle in the prescript. Both letters describe Paul's manual labor in Thessalonica in similar wording (1 Thess 2:9; 2 Thess 3:8) and urge the Thessalonians to imitate him in doing manual labor (1 Thess 4:11; 2 Thess 3:12) in quietness or tranquility (ἡσυχάζω/ἡσυχία). They use the same form of appeal (ἐρωτῶμεν [δὲ] ὑμᾶς; 1 Thess 4:1; 2 Thess 2:1), a locution that occurs elsewhere in Paul's letters only in Philippians 4:3. Both have extensive sections dealing with matters of eschatology (1 Thess 4:13–5:11; 2 Thess 1:6–2:12), though the one in 2 Thessalonians appears in the opening thanksgiving and forms the body of the letter, while the one in 1 Thessalonians occurs in the paraenesis. Both letters use motifs and expressions that do not occur elsewhere in Paul.[25]

So noticeable are these parallels that Philip Esler urges that "supporters of authenticity . . . need to explain what had happened that induced Paul to write a second letter to Thessalonica using language and structure so similar to that in 1 Thessalonians."[26] That is, for some who press that 2 Thessalonians is pseudonymous, this feature alone is worthy of deciding against authenticity.

Of course, in the end many scholars still argue for authenticity despite these similarities and overlappings.[27] Leon Morris, for example, takes the opposite perspective on the seemingly copycat features of 2 Thessalonians. He reasons that only Paul *himself* could produce such a text that is as close to 1 Thessalonians while still having its own distinct message. Morris explains that "a forger would have to be imbued with the very mind of Paul to have produced such a work."[28]

Howard Marshall also recognizes the unique literary overlap between 1 and 2 Thessalonians, but responds to this by urging that it very well may

24. E. M. Krentz, "Thessalonians, First and Second Epistles to the: 2 Thessalonians," *ABD* 6:518; see Bailey, "Who Wrote II Thessalonians?"

25. Krentz, "Thessalonians," *ABD* 6:518, and idem, "A Stone that Will Not Fit," in Frey et al., *Pseudepigraphie und Verfasserfiktion*, 456–63; see also Richard, *First and Second Thessalonians*, 21; Marshall, *Thessalonians*, 29; R. F. Collins gives special attention to the appearance of two thanksgivings in each letter; see his *Letters that Paul Did Not Write* (Wilmington, DE: Glazier, 1988), 219.

26. P. E. Esler, "2 Thessalonians," in *The Oxford Bible Commentary*, ed. J. Barton and J. Muddiman (Oxford: Oxford University Press, 2001), 1213–19.

27. See Nicholl, *From Hope to Despair*, 4–8.

28. Morris, *Thessalonians*, 23.

have been that a short time passed between the writing of the first letter and the second, and Paul felt compelled to repeat much of what he already wrote.[29] For Marshall, there is also the problem that we are dealing with a small sample of Pauline writings for comparison. He argues, "We have, therefore, no accepted 'control' against which to gauge the significance of the similarities in structure between 1 and 2 Th. It would certainly seem that we have no evidence which would enable us to say that because the general structure of 2 Th. is so close to that of 1 Th. it must be an imitation by a pseudonymous author."[30]

Gordon Fee makes the case that the problem of the so-called "copycat" style of 2 Thessalonians is superficial and does not stand up when the details are examined closely. Fee notes that both letters contain thanksgiving sections and place them in parallel sections, but the subjects of each "are without an even remotely close relationship to one another (Paul's past relationships with the Thessalonians; and the fact that their persecutors are headed for divine judgment)."[31] Fee finds it highly unlikely that a forger could accomplish this.[32] Fee also picks up a concern similar to Morris's statement noted above, namely, that this forger would have been apparently *too* acqainted with Pauline style. Fee gives the example of the use of ἀδελφός—2 Thessalonians's use is so much like 1 Thessalonians and unlike other Pauline letters. How could a forger, writing in the late first century with (probably) access to and acquaintance with a larger Pauline corpus, tailor this usage so approximately to 1 Thessalonians?[33] Fee concludes that it seems unimaginable that a forger would be so careful to "think Paul's thoughts after him" stylistically while apparently deviating so far from Paul's theology.

J. C. Hurd has added the important argument that there are places even in the undisputed Pauline letters where we see Paul mimicking the structure and themes of something he has already written. As an example, Hurd offers the many literary parallels between Galatians 5:13–25 and Romans 8:2–10. Below I reproduce some of the connections that Hurd identifies (e.g., freedom, flesh, law, fulfillment, walking, spirit).[34]

---

29. Marshall, *Thessalonians*, 30–31; see similarly Beale, *1–2 Thessalonians*, 31.
30. Marshall, *Thessalonians*, 31.
31. Fee, *Thessalonians*, 239.
32. Fee, *Thessalonians*, 239; see too Hurd, "Concerning the Authenticity of 2 Thessalonians," 140–41.
33. Fee, *Thessalonians*, 239.
34. Hurd, "Concerning the Authenticity of 2 Thessalonians," 139–41.

GALATIANS 5:13–25	ROMANS 8:2–10
[13] You, my brothers and sisters, were called to be **free**. But do not use your freedom to indulge the **flesh**; rather, serve one another humbly in love. [14] For the entire **law** is **fulfilled** in keeping this one command: "Love your neighbor as yourself." [15] If you bite and devour each other, watch out or you will be destroyed by each other. [16] So I say, **walk** by the **Spirit**, and you will not gratify the desires of the **flesh**. [17] For the **flesh** desires what is contrary to the **Spirit**, and the **Spirit** what is contrary to the **flesh**. They are in conflict with each other, so that you are not to do whatever you want. [18] But if you are led by the **Spirit**, you are not under the law. [19] The acts of the **flesh** are obvious: sexual immorality, impurity and debauchery; [20] idolatry and witchcraft; hatred, discord, jealousy, fits of rage, selfish ambition, dissensions, factions [21] and envy; drunkenness, orgies, and the like. I warn you, as I did before, that those who live like this will not inherit the kingdom of God. [22] But the fruit of the **Spirit** is love, joy, peace, forbearance, kindness, goodness, faithfulness, [23] gentleness and self-control. Against such things there is no **law**. [24] Those who belong to **Christ** Jesus have crucified the **flesh** with its passions and desires. [25] Since we live by the **Spirit**, let us keep in step with the **Spirit**.	[2] because through Christ Jesus the law of the Spirit who gives life has set you **free** from the **law** of sin and death. [3] For what the law was powerless to do because it was weakened by the **flesh**, God did by sending his own Son in the likeness of sinful **flesh** to be a sin offering. And so he condemned sin in the flesh,[4] in order that the righteous requirement of the **law** might be [fulfilled] in us, who do not live according to the **flesh** but according to the **Spirit**. [5] Those who live according to the **flesh** have their minds set on what the **flesh** desires; but those who live in accordance with the **Spirit** have their minds set on what the **Spirit** desires. [6] The mind governed by the **flesh** is death, but the mind governed by the **Spirit** is life and peace. [7] The mind governed by the **flesh** is hostile to God; it does not submit to God's **law**, nor can it do so. [8] Those who are in the realm of the **flesh** cannot please God. [9] You, however, are not in the realm of the **flesh** but are in the realm of the **Spirit**, if indeed the **Spirit** of God lives in you. And if anyone does not have the **Spirit** of Christ, they do not belong to Christ.[10] But if **Christ** is in you, then even though your body is subject to death because of sin, the **Spirit** gives life because of righteousness.

On the matter of the literary dependence of 2 Thessalonians on 1 Thessalonians, the jury is clearly still out. Those who argue for pseudepigraphal copying have made a strong case.[35] There is an unusual structural and verbatim reemployment of 1 Thessalonians in 2 Thessalonians. This certainly could point in the direction of a forger who borrowed heavily

---

35. Krentz states matter-of-factly, "Wrede's argument still stands. It has been reinforced by subsequent detailed investigation, not overturned. It is a powerful argument for the non-Pauline origin of Second Thessalonians" ("Stone," 463).

from 1 Thessalonians. At the same time, it cannot be a decisive factor because there could be a host of reasons why Paul might have reused portions of his earlier letter or perhaps authorized someone else to do so (see below pp. 217–19).

Tone

It has been long observed that the tone of 2 Thessalonians differs substantially from 1 Thessalonians.[36] As Furnish comments, "The tone of 2 Thessalonians is impersonal and formal. Unlike 1 Thessalonians, with its many familial images, its expressions of affection, and its patient counsels, this letter has an official, even authoritarian aspect: thanksgiving is presented as an *obligation* (1:3; 2:13); *commands* are issued (3:6–12); what the letter says must be *obeyed*."[37] Similarly, Linda McKinnish Bridges labels 1 Thessalonians "personal and deeply affective, focusing on compassion and encouragement," while she considers 2 Thessalonians "sharp, precise, and lacking in affection."[38] Raymond Collins finds this difference determinative: "Were the two letters to have been written by the apostle himself, he would have had to change his attitude toward the Thessalonian Christians rather radically in a very short space of time—a few months at most."[39]

Alternatively, Howard Marshall represents what is probably the majority perspective on the issue of "tone" in comparisons of 1–2 Thessalonians:

> It is surely time that the myth of the cold tone of the letter was exploded. Granted that it is not as full of personal references as 1 Thessalonians nor was written on such a crest of emotion, it is nevertheless by no means cold in tone. The claim that "we ought to give thanks as is fitting" (1:3) is a cold and formal expression is quite unfounded (cf. Phil. 1:7). The personal concern of the author for the readers shines through the letter.[40]

---

36. See MacDougall, *Authenticity of 2 Thessalonians*, 9.
37. Furnish, *1–2 Thessalonians*, 132; see also Richard, *First and Second Thessalonians*, 24.
38. Bridges, *1 & 2 Thessalonians*, 195.
39. Collins, *Letters that Paul Did Not Write*, 223.
40. Marshall, *Thessalonians*, 34. Similarly see comments by Malherbe who urges that on this matter differences between the two letters have been exaggerated especially once a label of "pseudonymous" is placed on 2 Thess. Malherbe considers the tone to vary based on the goals of the text and that each letter by Paul will inevitably have its unique features (*Thessalonians*, 376); similarly Murphy-O'Connor, *Paul: A Critical Life*, 110.

Ben Witherington focuses on the rhetorical dimensions of 2 Thessalonians. He considers it deliberative discourse, and thus the tone is based on this factor primarily.[41]

The element of tone is continuing to play a smaller role in the discernment of authorship of 2 Thessalonians in the twenty-first century for precisely the reasons noted above, that there could be a number of factors at play that could affect the tone of a letter beyond simply a difference of writer.

Pauline Style

Literary dependence, addressed above, has to do with the unusual similarities between 1 and 2 Thessalonians. But there is also the question of *stylistic* differences. Many have observed that 2 Thessalonians uses several unusual vocabulary words.[42] But almost all scholars today put little stock in the "vocabulary" argument. As R. Wayne Stacy has observed, "The problem with this line of argument is that, proportionately speaking, Paul employs a similar number of unique words in 1 Thessalonians."[43]

The more pressing matter is how the author communicates in general, that is, the writing style. Vocabulary can change from one text to the next based on the subject matter. But writing style is a kind of *signature* or *thumbprint* feature, something that one does that is simply part of that person's way of writing.[44] Brown notes that earlier on in 2 Thessalonians the author writes in sentences that are long and complex compared to 1 Thessalonians; he also observes a less personal writing style overall.[45] Earl Richard points out the use of simple theological phrases in 2 Thessalonians, phrases that do not seem to be the way the apostle Paul himself writes, such as "good hope" and "eternal comfort."[46] Krentz, building on

---

41. Witherington, *Thessalonians*, 29.

42. See Frame, *Thessalonians*, 28–37; Rigaux, *Thessaloniciens*, 80–85; Boring, *1 and 2 Thessalonians*, 217–18. Boring does not consider unusual vocabulary to be a decisive factor, but it still points in the direction of "deuteropauline authorship." He makes special note of not only *hapax legomena*, but also how common Pauline words are used in 2 Thess in unusual ways, such as πίστις, ἀγάπη, and πνεῦμα; see Boring, *1 and 2 Thessalonians*, 217; cf. G. S. Holland, *The Tradition That You Received from Us: 2 Thessalonians in the Pauline Tradition* (Tübingen: Mohr Siebeck, 1988), 87–88.

43. R. W. Stacy, "Introduction to the Thessalonian Correspondence," *RevExp* 96 (1999): 178. Similarly, Krentz concludes that comparing vocabulary adds nothing significant to the authorship debate ("Stone," 444).

44. Krentz argues that 1 Thess bears a "hellenistic character," while 2 Thess has more of a semitic style ("Stone," 469).

45. Brown, *Introduction*, 593.

46. Richard, *First and Second Thessalonians*, 22.

the work of Frame and Trilling, offers a long list of peculiar phrases in 2 Thessalonians, presenting nearly twenty of them.[47]

Christina Kreinecker conducted a study of how the author of 2 Thessalonians makes requests with special interest in the verbs ἐρωτάω, παρακαλέω, and παραγγέλλω.[48] Kreinecker compares the use of these verbs in 2 Thessalonians to both material from the documentary papyri and 1 Thessalonians. She concludes that 1 Thessalonians follows the patterns of use of ἐρωτάω found in the documentary papyri, but 2 Thessalonians does not.[49] Specifically with regard to παραγγέλλω, Kreinecker found that the documentary papyri do not show evidence that this verb was used in Paul's time to "express requests for interpersonal relationships or communal life" (as she believes 2 Thess does).[50] She also found the combination of παρακαλέω and παραγγέλλω (2 Thess 3:12) unattested in the documentary papyri.[51] In the conclusion to her overall study, she explains that 2 Thessalonians offers an unprecedented style, one not found at all in the documentary papyri.[52] Thus she wonders, "How is it possible that a letter writer of the first century CE broke with conventions of his time?"[53] She explains this by hypothesizing that a forger failed to imitate Paul, missing the fact that such stylistic differences would be noticeably different from someone coming from a later time.

As mentioned above, the matter of style differences is critically important for the concerns regarding authorship of 2 Thessalonians. Those who continue to lean in favor of authenticity, however, have not found the stylistic concerns to be insurmountable. Marshall raises the matter of method. He argues that there are no agreed upon tools to determine style consistency or coherence. He urges that "much depends on subjective judgments as to what a given author may or may not do."[54] Marshall wrote this many years before Kreinecker's essay, and certainly Kreinecker has

---

47. Krentz, "Stone," 445–46.

48. C. M. Kreinecker, "The Imitation Hypothesis: Pseudepigraphic Remarks on 2 Thessalonians with Help from Documentary Papyri," in Porter and Fewster, *Paul and Pseudepigraphy*, 197–219. See also M. Ernst who compared 2 Thess stylistically to standards of ancient rhetoric and found 2 Thess to be pseudonymous (*Distanzierte Unpersönlichkeit: Analyse von Sprache und Stil des zweiten Thessalonicherbriefes im Vergleich mit paulinischen Texten* [Salzburg: Institut für Neutestamentliche Bibelwissenschaft, 1998]).

49. Kreinecker, "Imitation Hypothesis," 205–6.

50. Kreinecker, "Imitation Hypothesis," 215.

51. Kreinecker, "Imitation Hypothesis," 215.

52. Kreinecker, "Imitation Hypothesis," 216.

53. Kreinecker, "Imitation Hypothesis," 217.

54. Marshall, *Thessalonians*, 32; similarly, see Hurd, "Concerning the Authenticity of 2 Thessalonians," 138–39.

invested much in developing a critical method with the documentary papyri an important pool of stylistic information. It is interesting to note, however, that in the same volume where we find Kreinecker's essay that judges on stylistic reasons *against* authenticity, we also have Andrew Pitts's essay, which offers a different perspective on style. Pitts addresses the issue of style and authorship through the lens of *register*. Much like Marshall, Pitts has noted how "style variation" arguments have lacked methodological sophistication. Pitts defines *register* as "contexts for language varieties ranging from literary genres to social situations."[55] Pitts notes how even style might change for the same author based on "audience design."[56] He explains that expecting the exact same style from one discourse to another is rather rigid, even with an assumption of the same audience. Overall, Pitts concludes that the corpus of Paul's letters is simply too small of a sample and the register too varied. He writes, "With Paul, we are necessarily measuring possible responses to a complex of variables, in addition to genre, that we cannot isolate from one another."[57]

I find that style is more of a significant factor in the determinination of authorship than literary dependence. In some ways the writer of 2 Thessalonians does not write like the Paul of 1 Thessalonians. The problems of methodology and sample, however, should not be underestimated.[58] An important case study in this matter comes from Harold Hoehner.[59] He wrote a clever essay entitled, "Did Paul Write Galatians?"[60] Hoehner did not sincerely set out to question the authenticity of Galatians. Rather, he demonstrates how one could make a case that a forger wrote Galatians, using the same kinds of arguments that scholars use against Ephesians, 2 Thessalonians, and the Pastoral Epistles. He concludes, "Personally, I think we are using a double standard. We apply these rules to the disputed

---

55. A. W. Pitts, "Style and Pseudonymity in Pauline Scholarship: A Register Based Configuration," in Porter and Fewster, *Paul and Pseudepigraphy*, 117.

56. Pitts, "Style and Pseudonymity in Pauline Scholarship," 117.

57. Pitts, "Style and Pseudonymity in Pauline Scholarship," 152.

58. So J. D. G. Dunn writes, "Given the diversity of Paul's undisputed letters, the arguments claimed to be decisive for the latter position are quite surprising, since they seem to depend on a rather wooden use of word- and style-statistics and an unwillingness either to allow sufficiently for different situations calling forth different responses or to accept that Paul could have so written. The cooler reality is that there are no decisive stylistic reasons against attributing the letter to Paul, bearing in mind the changed circumstances presupposed in 2 Thessalonians" (*Beginning from Jerusalem*, 714). See also Jewett, *Thessalonian Correspondence*, 3–18.

59. In the following discussion, I draw significantly from my article, "What Is in a Name?," 213–14.

60. Hoehner, "Did Paul Write Galatians?," 150–69.

books of Paul but not the *Hauptbriefe*. . . . The critics do not allow the flexibility that is allowed within the *Hauptbriefe*."[61]

Historical Implausibility

This factor has a special concern to determine whether there are clues or features of 2 Thessalonians that place it at a later date, too late to be considered genuinely Pauline. Three issues have been raised in this respect for 2 Thessalonians. The first is the note regarding a possible forged letter:

> Concerning the coming of our Lord Jesus Christ and our being gathered to him, we ask you, brothers and sisters, not to become easily unsettled or alarmed by the teaching allegedly from us [ὡς δι' ἡμῶν]—whether by a prophecy or by word of mouth or by letter— asserting that the day of the Lord has already come. (2 Thess 2:1–2)

The phrase ὡς δι' ἡμῶν is ambiguous, but it appears to open the possibility that a forgery was circulating.[62] Some have made the case that it is unlikely for Paul at such an early period of Christianity to be concerned with a forgery of his own letters—something that would more likely happen at the end of the first century with the notoriety of his letters.[63] Of course it is not clear that this text is directly addressing forgery. It could simply be hypothetical, as in "even from us."

Another issue pertaining to historical plausibility involves 2 Thessalonians's use of the language of traditions and the passing down of Christian teaching (e.g., 2 Thess 2:15; 3:6).[64] This kind of formalistic language bears close resemblance to what we see in the Pastoral Epistles.[65] This is potentially a noteworthy consideration, but it ought to be taken into consideration that Paul could talk about Christian tradition

---

61. Hoehner, "Did Paul Write Galatians?," 169. Fee makes this intruiging throw-away comment buried in a footnote in his commentary (regarding 2 Thess 2:13 and resonances with Deut 33:12, the Benjamin blessing): "Paul has used the exact language of the blessing of Benjamin from Deut 33:12, Paul's own family 'crest,' as it were. How could a forger have known and done this? And to have done so by luck would seem to border on one chance in several billion" (*Thessalonians*, 239n5).

62. On the phrase ὡς δι' ἡμῶν, note H. Roose who sees the ambiguity as an intentional forgery strategy; "'A Letter as by Us,'" 107–24.

63. Note the discussion in Gaventa, *First and Second Thessalonians*, 93. See also Becker who wonders whether the letter in question was an actual Pauline letter (not 1 Thess, and now no longer extant). See E.-M. Becker, "'Ὡς δι' ἡμῶν in 2 Thess 2.2 als Hinweis auf einem verlorenen Brief," *NTS* 55.1 (2009): 55–72.

64. See MacDougall, *Authenticity of 2 Thessalonians*, 5–6.

65. See Brown, *Introduction*, 594.

on occasion as demonstrated in the undisputed letters (Rom 6:17; 16:17; 1 Cor 11:2).

Perhaps the most interesting case for historical implausibility relates to the description of the man of lawlessness in 2 Thessalonians 2:1–12. Several features of this text have pointed scholars toward the notion that here the author imagines a type of Nero. Pertaining to the language of ὁ ἄνθρωπος τῆς ἀνομίας (v. 3), it is often pointed out that Nero was known to be "utterly lawless."[66] As for ὁ υἱὸς τῆς ἀπωλείας (v. 3), Dio Cassius commented, "Nero set his heart on accomplishing what had doubtless always been his desire, namely to make an end of the whole city and realm during his lifetime."[67] The evil figure mentioned in 2 Thessalonians is also described as challenging deities and claiming occupation of the temple (vv. 3–4). Nero famously disrespected almost all cults (Suetonius, *Nero* 56). Nero died in 68 CE, but some believed that he did not actually perish but went into hiding in the East, thus the tradition of a "Nero *Redivivus*."[68] If 2 Thessalonians uses this Nero Redivivus motif in the portrayal of the man of lawlessness, this affects the question of dating 2 Thessalonians. For 2 Thessalonians 2:1–12 to be taking up the Nero Redivivus motif, the letter would have to be written *after* 68 CE, after the purported death of Nero.[69]

While the suggested connections between Nero and 2 Thessalonians's man of lawlessness are intriguing, at the end of the day they are circumstantial.[70] Moreover, Marshall observes that if 2 Thessalonians is a forgery written in the late first century, then Jerusalem would have been destroyed, and it would hardly have made sense to refer to this Nero Redivivus as someone taking over the Jewish temple.[71] Menken, however, offers a potential response to this: "The mention of the temple in 2.4 has to be explained as part of the fiction created by the pseudonymous author, who knew very well that the temple still stood during Paul's apostolic career."[72]

---

66. G. H. van Kooten, "'Wrath Will Drip in the Plains of Macedonia': Expectations of Nero's Return in the Egyptian Sibylline Oracles (Book 5), 2 Thessalonians, and Ancient Historical Writings," in *The Wisdom of Egypt: Jewish, Early Christian, and Gnostic Essays in Honour of Gerard P. Luttikhuizen*, ed. A. Hilhorst and G. H. van Kooten (Leiden: Brill, 2005), 188.

67. Dio Cassius, *Roman History* 62.16; as cited in van Kooten, "'Wrath Will Drip,'" 189–90.

68. As van Kooten explains, Nero was astonishingly young when he died, only thirty years old ("'Wrath Will Drip,'" 180 [citing Dio Cassius, *Roman History* 61.3.1]).

69. Menken, *2 Thessalonians*, 107.

70. P. J. Achtemeier, J. B. Green, and M. M. Thompson, *The New Testament: Its Literature and Theology* (Grand Rapids: Eerdmans, 2001), 444.

71. See Marshall, *Thessalonians*, 191.

72. Menken, *2 Thessalonians*, 107.

Again, historical implausibility is *in theory* one of the most "objective" factors that could rule out authenticity. In the case of 2 Thessalonians, we do not seem to have irrefutible evidence of instances of historical implausibility; hence its authenticity is considered "dubious," and the letter is not fully rejected by most scholars.

Theological Differences

Perhaps one of the most long-lasting arguments against the authenticity of 2 Thessalonians regards what appear to be theological differences when compared to 1 Thessalonians.[73] The main concern in this area relates to eschatological teaching and perspective. To put it simply, 1 Thessalonians represents the day of the Lord as coming suddenly. Second Thessalonians, alternatively, teaches that there are a series of events that must take place *before* the day of the Lord will arrive.[74] Bridges explains it this way: "The author of 2 Thessalonians establishes a precise eschatological timetable, which suggests that either Paul has changed his mind from the time of writing the first letter or the letter is not from Paul."[75] She observes a sharp change from 1 Thessalonians. As far as her reading is concerned, with 2 Thessalonians "the motion slows; the action shifts into low gear. The author of 2 Thessalonians states that a series of selected events must first take place before the end. The list is long, systematic, and highly descriptive, using stock imagery from the world of apocalyptic language."[76]

Colin Nicholl wrote a cogent dissertation that sought to provide a compelling explanation for the eschatological teaching in 2 Thessalonians and also to validate the genuine Pauline authorship of 2 Thessalonians in the process.[77] His argument on this point is that *if* a situation could be considered that could account for both sets of eschatological teachings, this "theological differences" issue would be a nonfactor.[78] Nicholl's reconstruction is as follows. Regarding the situation of 1 Thessalonians, Nicholl argues that the Thessalonian believers were "deeply perturbed" by the deaths of fellow believers. They believed these departed believers

---

73. See MacDougall, *Authenticity of 2 Thessalonians*, 1–4; also A. G. Van Aarde, "The Second Letter to the Thessalonians Re-Read as Pseudepigraph," 105–7.

74. Collins, *Letters that Paul Did Not Write*, 221; Krentz notes that even when Paul takes up apocalyptic eschatological language, he does not focus on any sort of "time calculation devices"; this only appears in 2 Thess 2:1–12 (Krentz, "Stone," 464–65).

75. Bridges, *1 & 2 Thessalonians*, 196.

76. Bridges, *1 & 2 Thessalonians*, 196.

77. Nicholl, *From Hope to Despair*.

78. Nicholl, *From Hope to Despair*, 8–9.

could not participate in the salvation of the parousia.[79] The deaths were treated as signs of divine displeasure and wrath. As one considers the (potentially) related situation behind 2 Thessalonians, Nicholl posits that these Thessalonian believers fell into despair, believing "the parousia had passed them by."[80] Nicholl hypothesizes (based on 2 Thess 2:2) that Paul himself did not really know what led the Thessalonians down the road of hopelessness. It could be chalked up to "an immature and probably young and predominantly Gentile community having difficulties processing Jewish eschatological notions."[81] Ultimately, then, Nicholl interprets the Thessalonian correspondence as reflective of "two stages of the *same single* crisis."[82] Thus, Nicholl refers to 2 Thessalonians as a kind of *addendum* to 1 Thessalonians.[83]

While appeal to "eschatological differences" in the evaluation of authorship is a long-held consideration, many Thessalonian scholars find this line of concern largely subjective. Two types of refutations tend to be given by those who discount this ostensible contrast of eschatological perspective. First, some have argued that the same kind of paradox appears in the Synoptic eschatological discourses. F. F. Bruce observes that Jesus's eschatological teaching contains a similar diversity of eschatological perspectives as we see in the Thessalonian correspondence.[84] He notes that certain Q-influenced texts refer to the "suddenness of Noah's flood or the destruction of Sodom and Gomorrah (Luke 17:26–30)." On the other hand, in Mark we see that "wars and rumors of wars" will be rife, but "the end is not yet."[85] The Markan Jesus explains that "'the gospel must first be preached to all the nations,' and not until the abomination of desolation is seen 'standing where he ought not' will the Son of Man come (Mark 13:7, 10, 14, 26)."[86] Bruce reasons that Luke and Matthew do not see a contradiction in eschatological perspective. Luke himself includes both the tone of suddenness and a set series of events in two separate sections of his Gospel (Luke 17:22–37; 21:5–36). Matthew has them both within a single eschatological discourse (Matt 24:1–51).[87]

---

79. Nicholl, *From Hope to Despair*, 183.
80. Nicholl, *From Hope to Despair*, 185.
81. Nicholl, *From Hope to Despair*, 186.
82. Nicholl, *From Hope to Despair*, 188.
83. Nicholl, *From Hope to Despair*, 195; cf. 206.
84. See Bruce, *Thessalonians*, xlii. For a similar perspective, see Shogren, *Thessalonians*, 29.
85. Bruce, *Thessalonians*, xlii.
86. Bruce, *Thessalonians*, xlii-xliii.
87. Bruce, *Thessalonians*, xliii.

Another line of criticism that rejects the presumed contradictory eschatological perspectives of 1–2 Thessalonians relates to Jewish apocalyptic thought in general. Leon Morris makes the general observation that apocalypses commonly communicate the immediacy and suddenness of the end along with the expectation of certain "preparatory signs."[88] John Barclay probably says it best:

> Apocalypticists are notoriously slippery characters. Many apocalyptic works present conflicting scenarios of the end and inconsistent theses concerning signs of its imminence. That Paul should write both of these apocalyptic passages, and do so within a short space of time, is by no means impossible; why should his apocalyptic statements be any more consistent than his varied remarks about the law?[89]

The "theological differences" factor turns out to be a rather small and subjective criticism when it comes to determining authorship of 2 Thessalonians.[90] As Barclay notes, having two texts offer differing, even divergent, views does not rule out Pauline authorship, at least not when it involves the messy and often convoluted matter of final eschatology and apocalyptic traditions. Even with these caveats taken into consideration, Nicholl has offered a rather compelling theory about the development of the situation in Thessalonica that *could* lead to such different eschatological teaching as we see in 1 and 2 Thessalonians.

Patristic Testimony and Canonical Inclusion

Sometimes we can detect hesitation or concern about the canonicity of a biblical book in the patristic period (e.g., concerning James).[91] The situation is rather different for 2 Thessalonians. This letter is included within the Pauline epistles section of the Muratorian canon, and Eusebius does not designate it as one of those texts that is under dispute. Therefore, this factor strongly favors authenticity.[92] Sometimes modern scholars make the mistaken assumption that precritical scholars were not capable of or interested in detecting forgeries. But Bruce Metzger argues that

---

88. Morris, *Thessalonians*, 21.
89. Barclay, "Conflict in Thessalonica," 525.
90. While Krentz finds this issue pressing, he only devotes a few pages to it ("Stone," 464–67).
91. See Allison, *James*, 99–109.
92. See MacDougall, *Authenticity of 2 Thessalonians*, 31–62; cf. Hurd, "Concerning the Authenticity of 2 Thessalonians," 137.

there is evidence to the contrary. He offers the case of Dionysus, bishop of Alexandria, who questioned the Johannine authorship of Revelation based on peculiarities of its style of vocabulary.[93] Armin Baum argues that the church fathers, such as Tertullian and Jerome, were keenly concerned with authorship claims and suspicious of pseudonymous works.[94] Again, regarding the authorship of 2 Thessalonians, no one really questioned its Pauline authenticity until relatively recently in history.

In terms of patristic use of 2 Thessalonians in nonbiblical texts (see pp. 266–70), we find that Irenaeus quotes or strongly alludes to 2 Thessalonians extensively, and especially portions of 2 Thessalonians 2 are cited in a wide variety of early Christian works, such as the *Constitutions of the Holy Apostles*, the *Didache*, and Hippolytus's *De antichristo*.[95]

MacDougall has made much of Polycarp's use of 2 Thessalonians in particular. In Polycarp's *To the Philippians* he uses the language of "do not regard such men as enemies," highly reminiscent of 2 Thessalonians 3:15.[96] In another place (Pol. *Phil.* 11.3), MacDougall argues for another use of 2 Thessalonians by Polycarp, particularly the language of "he boasts in all the church" (2 Thess 1:4).[97] If Polycarp's work can be dated to about 90 CE (as MacDougall suggests), this would strictly limit *when* a forger was writing—one could not responsibly imagine 2 Thessalonians written in the last decade of the first century or later.[98] Suffice it to say here that patristic testimony does not seem in any way to support a case for pseudonymity.

Pseudonymous "Tells"

The final factor in the determination of genuine authorship that we will discuss is something I call pseudonymous "tells." These are clues in a text where the forger seems to be overcompensating or trying *too* hard to look genuine, and thus the reader might find here evidence that the

---

93. See B. M. Metzger, "Literary Forgeries and Canonical Pseudepigrapha," *JBL* 91.1 (1972): 13.

94. See A. Baum, *Pseudepigraphie und literarische Fälschung im frühen Christentum: mit ausgewählten Quellentexten samt deutscher Übersetzung*, WUNT 2/138 (Tübingen: Mohr Siebeck, 2001); cf. idem, "Authorship and Pseudepigraphy in Early Christian Literature: A Translation of the Most Important Source Texts and An Annotated Bibliography," in Porter and Fewster, *Paul and Pseudepigraphy*, 11–64.

95. G. Green makes the stunning, though defensible, statement that "the external evidence in favor of [2 Thessalonians's] authenticity is even stronger than that of 1 Thessalonians" (*Thessalonians*, 59). See also Morris, *Thessalonians*, 20; Brown, *Introduction*, 595.

96. MacDougall, *Authenticity of 2 Thessalonians*, 37–38; also K. Berding, *Polycarp and Paul: An Analysis of Their Literary and Theological Relationship in Light of Polycarp's Use of Biblical and Extra-Biblical Literature* (Leiden: Brill, 2002), 112–13.

97. MacDougall, *Authenticity of 2 Thessalonians*, 39.

98. MacDougall, *Authenticity of 2 Thessalonians*, 254. For a response and refutation of perceived usage of 2 Thess in Polycarp, see Menken, *2 Thessalonians*, 65–66.

document is a forgery.[99] As far as 2 Thessalonians is concerned, such a tell appears in 3:17: "I, Paul, write this greeting in my own hand, which is the distinguishing mark in all my letters. This is how I write."[100] Again, some take this to be a forger's indiscreet effort to establish his credibility *as Paul*.[101] And so Krentz's famous conclusion: "The author of Second Thessalonians doth protest too much, methinks."[102] Trilling picks up on the language of *every letter*, hinting at a forger's knowledge of a whole Pauline corpus.[103]

Those who still consider 2 Thessalonians authentic do not consider 3:17 a serious problem.[104] For example, J. Duff reasons that if a forger did try such a strategy to reinforce his genuineness, it would be risky—what if the readers did in fact have access to the autograph of 1 Thessalonians or to other genuine Pauline letters for that matter?[105] Paul Foster offers a more thoroughgoing critique of using 3:17 as evidence of forgery. He first observes the verbatim match between 3:17 and 1 Corinthians 16:21 (cf. Col 4:18). It would seem, then, that a forger would have had to have learned of this Pauline feature from 1 Corinthians.[106] In this case, the forger would only really have knowledge of one such case. The forger would be taking an unusual liberty to claim that this is *always* Paul's practice, especially if whatever access he had to Pauline letters was through copies (in someone else's handwriting).[107] Furthermore, there are no clear indicators that

99. See M. Rist, "Pseudepigraphy and the Early Christians," in *Studies in New Testament and Early Christian Literature*, ed. D. E. Aune (Leiden: Brill, 1972), 77; C. Rothschild, *Hebrews as Pseudepigraphon: The History and Significance of the Pauline Attribution of Hebrews* (Tübingen: Mohr Siebeck, 2012), 151.

100. See B. D. Ehrman, *Forgery and Counter-Forgery: The Use of Literary Deceit in Early Christian Polemics* (Oxford: Oxford University Press, 2014), 127; M. M. Mitchell, "1–2 Thessalonians," in *The Cambridge Companion to St Paul*, ed. J. D. G. Dunn (Cambridge: Cambridge University Press, 2003), 60.

101. See Best, *Thessalonians*, 50.

102. Krentz, "Stone," 469; similarly see Collins, *Letters That Paul Did Not Write*, 223; W. Trilling, *Der zweite Brief an die Thessalonicher*, EKKNT 14 (Zürich: Benzinger/Neukirchen, 1980), 158; Richard, *First and Second Thessalonians*, 394; Menken, *2 Thessalonians*, 35–36.

103. See Trilling, *Der zweite Brief*, 159; cf. W. Marxsen, *Der zweite Thessalonicherbrief* (Zürich: TVZ, 1982), 104–5.

104. For example, classicist S. Reece notes the prevalence of epistolary postscripts in ancient Greco-Roman letters, even to authenticate a text. He gives the example of an extant letter: "Plato to Dionysius Tyrant of Syracuse. Do well. Let the beginning of my letter to you serve at the same time as a sign that it is from me." See S. Reece, *Paul's Large Letters: Paul's Autographic Subscriptions in the Light of Ancient Epistolary Conventions*, LNTS (London: T&T Clark, 2016), 51–52.

105. J. Duff, "A Reconsideration of Pseudepigraphy in Early Christianity" (PhD diss., Oxford University, 1998), 214; cf. Hurd, "Concerning the Authenticity of 2 Thessalonians," 158–59.

106. Foster, "Who Wrote 2 Thessalonians?," 165–66.

107. Foster, "Who Wrote 2 Thessalonians?," 166. See also B. J. Oropeza, *Jews, Gentiles, and the Opponents of Paul* (Eugene, OR: Wipf & Stock, 2012), 37.

2 Thessalonians was literarily influenced by any Pauline text other than 1 Thessalonians, which would be odd if the forger were writing in the late first or second century.[108] Those who consider 2 Thessalonians genuine argue that it makes more sense that Paul was himself verifying the authenticity of this letter in view of possible previous forgeries (hence 2:2).[109] Donfried also adds that Paul may have regularly concluded his letters with a personal section written by hand—perhaps he even did so when writing 1 Thessalonians 5:27. But in 2 Thessalonians 3:17 he has reason to draw particular attention to this authentication.[110]

This factor has become more significant over the last few decades as the study of ancient forgery develops and analysis of pseudepigraphal documents becomes more sophisticated. There are a few peculiarities that raise potential flags in this area for 2 Thessalonians—such as the obvious literary dependence and the autograph notation in 3:17. Still, these factors are far from foolproof. Historical implausibility is much more of an objective consideration than the detection of pseudonymous tells.

Mediated Authorship

At the beginning of this chapter, we introduced the notion that we must break out of simplistic assumptions about what "authorship" means. Scholars tend to presume either that Paul put pen to paper or that someone else (usually a "forger") did. But as we learn from Cicero's letters, there is room for other possibilities in Paul's time (see p. 201 above). Regarding 2 Thessalonians, many scholars also seem stuck in the binary of "Paul" or "not Paul." Yet a few scholars have considered the intriguing possibility of a *third* option—it is conceivable that a colleague of Paul wrote 2 Thessalonians on Paul's behalf.[111] Karl Donfried is the scholar usually

---

108. See MacDougall, *Authenticity of 2 Thessalonians*, 29.

109. Green, *Thessalonians*, 61. Hurd posits that Paul's comment is not retrospective (this is what I *have* always done) but prospective: *starting now* this is how you can know if the letter is trustworthy ("Concerning the Authenticity of 2 Thessalonians," 159).

110. K. P. Donfried, "Issues of Authorship in the Pauline Corpus: Rethinking the Relationship Between 1 and 2 Thessalonians," in *2 Thessalonians and Pauline Eschatology*, ed. C. Tuckett and C. Breytenbach (Leuven: Peeters, 2013), 109–110.

111. See Witherington, *Thessalonians*, 10. Ascough shows openness to this possibility, but leans in favor of pseudonymity (*Paul's Macedonian Associations*, 165n15). Still also shows openness, but prefers authenticity (*Conflict at Thessalonica*, 58). Reece offers this reflection in consideration of the scribe as a primary "author" of the letter particularly in this case of 2 Thess: "Categorizations of Colossians and 2 Thessalonians, for example, as later pseudepigrapha on stylistic and linguistic grounds, are perhaps overly hasty. We should entertain the possibility that Paul was simply relying more heavily on his scribes in these letters. In this light Paul's insistence that he is writing a final

associated with this theory.[112] Donfried admits that 2 Thessalonians does not seem to be written in Paul's personal style, and he finds the problem of the literary dependence on 1 Thessalonians serious enough to rule out Pauline authorship "in the technical sense."[113] And yet Donfried believes that 2 Thessalonians makes the most sense as a letter that responds to developing and escalating problems in Thessalonica within a short time after 1 Thessalonians. Given that Timothy and Silvanus are mentioned in 2 Thessalonians 1:1, Donfried surmises that one of these Pauline companions could have written the letter.

Donfried considers Timothy the more likely option of the two. Timothy was a known apostle to the Thessalonians (1 Thess 2:6), he spent significant time in Macedonia (1 Cor 4:17; 16:10–11), and he appears as an associate of Paul in 2 Corinthians, Philippians, and Philemon.[114] If this were the case, Timothy would be leveraging Paul's apostolic authority to call the Thessalonians to adhere to the teachings they received from Paul. As Donfried explains, "Certainly a letter from Timothy alone would not carry the same weight or be as effective in refuting distortions directed primarily at Paul."[115]

Paul Foster is among the few scholars who have interacted the most with this theory.[116] His critique is strong:

> It is basically the traditional view, with the caveat that Timothy wrote independently of Paul's guidance, but nonetheless managed to articulate Pauline teachings in a more Pauline way than the apostle himself. The second epistle is still written to the Thessalonians, very shortly after the first, and its purpose was to correct misperceptions concerning eschatological teaching. Along the way, Timothy provided a robust defence of the apostolic authority, which Paul did not do in the first letter.[117]

---

greeting in his own hand at the end of Colossians and 2 Thessalonians could be regarded as his stamp of approval on two letters that were perhaps crafted largely by his scribes" (*Paul's Large Letters*, 207).

112. See K. P. Donfried, "2 Thessalonians and the Church of Thessalonica," 49–68; also cf. idem, "Issues of Authorship in the Pauline Corpus," 107–8. J. D. G. Dunn addresses this possibility, as well as the idea that the letter secretary played a stronger role in the structure and style of the letter (*Beginning from Jerusalem*, 714).

113. Donfried, "2 Thessalonians and the Church of Thessalonica," 53.

114. Donfried, "2 Thessalonians and the Church of Thessalonica," 54.

115. Donfried, "2 Thessalonians and the Church of Thessalonica," 56.

116. Cf. Collins, *Letters that Paul Did Not Write*, 215–16.

117. Foster, "Who Wrote 2 Thessalonians?," 167. Similarly, MacDougall states: "This solution does not explain the literary relationship of 2 Thessalonians to 1 Thessalonians. Both letters claim

As far as Foster is concerned, little is gained or explained by this theory, and we still have the problem of the apostolic autograph (2 Thess 3:17).

I am probably more optimistic about this possibility regarding the authorship of 2 Thessalonians than Foster and Collins. In my reading, it would explain the literary-dependence issue, and it makes good sense of the strong appeal to previous teachings and traditions as well.

Conclusion

It appears to me that the case against the authenticity of 2 Thessalonians is rather weak.[118] Then again, among the disputed Paulines, 2 Thessalonians is considered by scholars more likely to be written by Paul than the Pastoral Epistles. A century ago, many factors including unique vocabulary, peculiar turns of phrase, and differences of theology served as primary argumentative planks to make a case of pseudonymity for 2 Thessalonians. Today only the last of these seems to hold up, and yet even then concerns over theological "inconsistency" appear to be overplayed. The most peculiar aspect of 2 Thessalonians is the unusual literary dependence on 1 Thessalonians—something we do not see elsewhere in the undisputed letters of Paul to this degree, though we do not have a large sampling to begin with (compared to, e.g., our extant library from Philo). Furthermore, the possible detection of pseudonymous tells (e.g., 3:17) does not decide decisively in favor of pseudonymity, but certainly this is a curious statement from Paul, and we are at a disadvantage for not being able to check the original autographs as 2 Thessalonians intended that the readers do.

A major consideration in the discussion of the authorship of 2 Thessalonians concerns the kind of setting that would be required to make sense of 2 Thessalonians as a forgery from the late first century (or early second). John Barclay makes this important comment:

> The chief problem [with the pseudonymity theory regarding 2 Thessalonians] is the difficulty in constructing a convincing *Sitz im Leben*

---

the exact same authorship—Paul, Silas, and Timothy—and therefore to say that Timothy or Silas had a greater hand in one epistle than the other is merely speculation. It is hard to believe that two close associates of Paul could be so different in theological outlook and presentation, as some have claimed" (*Authenticity of 2 Thessalonians*, 17).

118. It is rather common for skeptics to urge that the argument against authenticity is cumulative; however, Nicholl refutes this approach handily: "Several pieces of uncompelling evidence do not combine to make a strong case, for cumulative doubt must also be taken into account" (*From Hope to Despair*, 214).

for the letter. Second Thessalonians presupposes that its recipients are undergoing fierce persecution (1:4–9), that there is a serious problem of those in their midst who will not work (3:6–13), and that there are some who claim that "the day of the Lord is here" (2:2). This limited range of topics and the specific character of the topics do not support Wolfgang Trilling's thesis that the document is more a general tract than a letter; in comparison with Ephesians, or even with the Pastorals, it appears to be closely tied to a specific situation.[119]

Until those who label 2 Thessalonians a forgery are able to construct a convincing scenario that would necessitate such a pseudepigraphal letter, it seems more responsible to treat this text as a genuine Pauline letter, warts and all.

DATE

If 2 Thessalonians is treated as authentically written by Paul, almost all scholars date it closely to the time of Paul's first letter to the Thessalonians.[120] The reason is that there seems to be a quick development in the situation that Paul wished to address. Jewett treats the similarities in terms of "argument and vocabulary" between the two letters as an indicator that the second letter probably followed the first within a matter of weeks (he guesses five to seven weeks).[121] For Jewett this is further supported by the unique inclusion of both Timothy and Silvanus in the prescript of both letters (1 Thess 1:1; 2 Thess 1:1); in no other Pauline letter are both of these included in the prescript.[122]

For those who consider 2 Thessalonians pseudonymous, hypothesizing a precise year is tricky. As Furnish notes, "Neither Paul's associates and supporters nor his detractors and opponents would have had reason

---

119. Barclay, "Conflict in Thessalonica," 526. Similarly, Donfried claims: "It is difficult to imagine a setting where a letter specifically addressed to the Thessalonians by Paul would be relevant and convincing to a non-Thessalonian church some thirty or more years after the apostle's death" (K. P. Donfried and I. H. Marshall, *The Theology of the Shorter Pauline Letters*, NTT [Cambridge: Cambridge University Press, 1993], 132).

120. As noted above, because 2 Thess refers to the possibility of the man of lawlessness positioning himself in the seat of authority and honor in the (Jerusalem) temple, this seems to many scholars to be an important indicator that the letter could not have been written after 70 CE.

121. Jewett, *Thessalonian Correspondence*, 59–60.

122. Note that in 2 Cor 1:19 both Silvanus and Timothy are *mentioned*, but not treated as cosenders.

to produce a letter in his name while he was still alive."[123] Thus, it makes best sense to imagine a forger writing *after* the apostle's demise; hence the setting of a date range around 80–120 CE.[124] Again, some have refuted this by pointing to the assumption of the standing Jerusalem temple in 2:4, but Furnish (and others) reason that this detail is "part of the fiction created by the post-Pauline writer; it is understandable that he would adopt the time frame of the apostle's ministry."[125]

SITUATION

In part the determination of the situation behind 2 Thessalonians depends on whether one considers the letter to be written by Paul just after the writing of 1 Thessalonians or to be a pseudonymous letter written later (toward the end of the first century). Still, from a study of the letter itself, most scholars believe that clues emerge that point to reasons why the letter was written. There appear to be three major concerns addressed in 2 Thessalonians. The first is the reality of ongoing and severe persecution that the recipients were enduring.[126] So we read how these believers are commended for their "perseverance and faith in all the persecutions and trials you are enduring" (2 Thess 1:4). A second major concern involves further teaching on eschatology and the day of the Lord in light of confusion; they ought "not to become easily unsettled or alarmed by the teaching allegedly from us—whether by a prophecy or by word of mouth or by letter—asserting that the day of the Lord has already come" (2:2). This verse and 2:3a seem to indicate that there may have been false teaching at the root of this misunderstanding. Finally, there is the extended discussion of the problem of the ἄτακτοι in 2 Thessalonians 3:6–15. The Thessalonians are told to distance themselves from such people (v. 6), the importance of work is reinforced (v. 10), and the ἄτακτοι themselves are told to "settle down and earn the food they eat" (v. 12). While they are to be admonished, they are not to be ousted (v. 15). First, we will consider

---

123. Furnish, *1–2 Thessalonians*, 139.

124. F. Laub argues that the presumption of the delay of the parousia plays a factor in deciding that 2 Thess is written later in the first century; see Laub, *1 und 2 Thessalonicher* (Würzburg: Echter, 1985), 40.

125. Furnish, *1–2 Thessalonians*, 139; see too Menken, *2 Thessalonians*, 65–66.

126. Among those scholars who consider 2 Thess pseudonymous, not all of them consider this factor to be "real" to the forger's concerns; see below, pp. 226–28.

scholarly theories about the situation that gave rise to these developments (and the letter's corresponding teachings) if 2 Thessalonians is authentic. Then we will examine theories about these matters if the letter is deemed pseudonymous (and beyond the lifetime of Paul).

Persecution

While both 1 and 2 Thessalonians seem to reveal that the letter recipients were suffering persecution, the matter seems significantly more explicit in light of 2 Thessalonians 1:5–10.[127] What Paul seeks to do in this passage, then, is "to reassure these beleaguered believers that their persecutors have their own divinely appointed destiny."[128] Second Thessalonians uses θλῖψις and διωγμός to describe the suffering of the Thessalonians in 1:4. Todd Still relates these to "external strife."[129] Still explains that it is not likely to be a state-enforced persecution. Thus, even the word "persecution" could be misleading. Still's tentative suggestion is that the Thessalonians were subject to "verbal abuse."[130] Still also mentions the probability of strained and tense social relations with neighbors and community members.[131] Some scholars argue that the persecution did carry a political element—believers were criticized for not giving due respect to political authorities, such as the emperor.[132]

Eschatology

The more central concern of the letter pertains to the author's eschatological teaching. The teaching appears to be the attempt to clarify a misunderstanding: "Concerning the coming of our Lord Jesus Christ and our being gathered to him, we ask you, brothers and sisters, not to become easily unsettled or alarmed by the teaching allegedly from us—whether by a prophecy or by word of mouth or by letter—asserting that the day of

---

127. So Donfried: "Without question powerful dynamics have altered the situation in Thessalonica since the writing of 1 Thessalonians. Paul especially (note the 'I' language in 1 Thess 3,5) is sufficiently concerned about the 'persecutions' [θλίψεσιν] that they are suffering that he sends Timothy to them. . . . The situation confronted by the writers of 2 Thessalonians had advanced considerably in terms of its negative consequences, provoked undoubtedly by more intense and systematic persecution, and, as a result, a far more uncompromising and forceful language was required" (Donfried, "Issues of Authorship," 101).

128. Fee, *Thessalonians*, 241; see too Marshall, *Thessalonians*, 23.

129. Still, *Conflict at Thessalonica*, 212.

130. Still, *Conflict at Thessalonica*, 213.

131. Using social-scientific criticism, Still observes how the Thessalonian believers would have been treated by their community as a "dangerously deviant minority" (*Conflict at Thessalonica*, 215).

132. See Witherington, *Thessalonians*, 42; cf. Donfried, *Paul, Thessalonica, and Early Christianity*, 46–48.

the Lord has already come" (2:1–2). After that, 2 Thessalonians offers a consideration of a series of events that must transpire before such a day is fully present.

It is unclear what "the day of the Lord has already come" means here. Nicholl presents several options that various scholars have proposed. It might mean that the day is very close.[133] It could also mean that certain happenings were interpreted by the Thessalonians as "messianic woes" linked with the day of the Lord (as in Dan 12:1b).[134] Yet if the idea was that the day of the Lord was *coming soon*, Nicholl wonders why 2 Thessalonians did not use ἐγγίζω.[135] Nicholl argues it is most plausible to assume that the Thessalonians believed the day of the Lord had *already* come (along with the parousia), and that this was due to received information (hence 2 Thess 2:2–3a). That is, they received some news or teaching about the arrival of the day of the Lord that caused dread and anxiety: "Rather than being enthused and positively excited, they were disoriented and terrified, needing stabilising and reassurance" as if falling into the cold shadow of divine wrath.[136] They came to believe that "salvation must somehow have bypassed them."[137]

If something like this were the case, 2 Thessalonians 2:1–12 offered the comfort that the day of the Lord had not yet arrived and certain events would come first, namely, "the revelation of a rebellious person who is at present restrained from appearing; once he has been revealed, the Lord will also appear and destroy him. Those who follow the rebel will come under condemnation, but the readers are God's people and will be saved, provided that they hold fast to the gospel as they have been taught it."[138]

Jewett approaches 1–2 Thessalonians from the perspective of a "millenarian" model. A millenarian perspective, as Jewett defines it (building on the work of Yonina Talmon) expects "the total transformation of this world to occur in connection with a cataclysm in the near future."[139] Jewett argues that the strains caused by political powerlessness and colonial exploitation

---

133. Nicholl, *From Hope to Despair*, 116; Dobschütz, *Die Thessalonicher-Briefe*, 267–68; more recently L. J. E. Peerbolte, *The Antecedents of Antichrist* (Leiden: Brill, 1996), 73–74.

134. Nicholl, *From Hope to Despair*, 116; see U. B. Müller, "Apocalyptic Currents," in *Christian Beginnings*, ed. J. Becker, trans. A. S. Kidder and R. Krauss (Louisville: Westminster John Knox, 1993), 307.

135. Nicholl, *From Hope to Despair*, 117.

136. Nicholl, *From Hope to Despair*, 131.

137. Nicholl, *From Hope to Despair*, 142.

138. Marshall, *Thessalonians*, 23.

139. Jewett, *Thessalonian Correspondence*, 161.

in Thessalonica in the first century created conditions that gave rise to millenarianism. For these Thessalonian believers, Jewett reasons that

> the expectation of a returning Cabirus who would aid the poor and defend them against their oppressors was transformed and revitalized in the new and more compelling form of Christ who was present in the congregation as their redeemer and the source of their ecstasy, and who was also proclaimed as coming again in wrath against the wicked.[140]

Jewett hypothesizes that Paul wrote 1 Thessalonians to reassure and comfort the Thessalonian believers in light of doubts and stress caused by persecution in light of their eschatological expectations. According to Jewett, Paul's (first) letter had the opposite effect—instead of calming their fears and concerns, it fueled them further.[141]

> They refused to return to their normal occupations or to curtail their ecstatic activities as suggested by the letter. They rejected the interventions of the congregational leaders that were suggested in 1 Thessalonians, increasing their commitment to countercultural activities. In this situation of deepening radicalism, the ecstatic message was suddenly proclaimed by the ἄτακτοι that the day of the Lord had arrived. For some reason Paul's teaching and letter as well as the ecstatic spirit of the radicals were used to support the legitimacy of this exciting claim of millenarian inauguration (2 Thess 2:2). What had hitherto been merely implicit in the activities of the radicals was now stated in final form: the millenium had come. Paul responds in irritation and disbelief to this incredible report by writing 2 Thessalonians, whose rhetoric centers on a refutation of the false new doctrine, and whose tone is vastly different from 1 Thessalonians.[142]

Jewett ought to be commended for a theory of the situation behind 2 Thessalonians that tries to integrate all pieces of information from

---

140. Jewett, *Thessalonian Correspondence*, 165–66.

141. Donfried also considers it possible that 2 Thess was necessitated because of a misunderstanding of the teachings in 1 Thess. How could the Thessalonian readers have arrived at this erroneous understanding? Donfried conjectures that it could have been due to "inattentive listening, deliberate intent or as a result of the increased pressure produced by intensified persecution" ("Issues of Authorship," 107).

142. Jewett, *Thessalonian Correspondence*, 177.

1–2 Thessalonians and what we know of the history and social and political contexts of Roman Thessalonica, but in the end this perspective requires quite a bit of speculation about the previous beliefs of the Thessalonians and the concerns of the ἄτακτοι.[143]

John Barclay offers another contextual scenario to explain the exigencies that gave rise to 2 Thessalonians. He observes that due to the way that Paul referred to the day of the Lord and the parousia in 1 Thessalonians 4:13–18 and 5:1–11, it is possible that the Thessalonian believers did not fully understand the relationship between these events. The Thessalonians may have interpreted signs of "sudden destruction" related to the day of the Lord without directly associating this with the return of the Lord. As far as the "trigger" for this belief in the arrival of the day of the Lord, Barclay observes that Tacitus considered the year 51 CE "particularly ill omened, with prodigies such as repeated earthquakes and a famine."[144] Whether the Thessalonians witnessed and gave meaning to *these* events is not determinative for Barclay. He explains that "a fevered apocalyptic imagination can interpret almost any unusual event as an eschatological moment, and divine wrath can explain many types of calamity. The tendency of early Christians to find signs of the end in such events as wars, famines, earthquakes, and astronomical phenomena is well demonstrated by Mark 13 and the Apocalypse."[145]

Barclay hypothesizes that the Thessalonian believers interpreted a local disaster as evidence of divine wrath marking the day of the Lord. Some may have taken comfort in the impending end, but others would have been troubled. In his second letter, Paul aims to redress a problematic "imbalance" in the church. Barclay considers it possible that 2 Thessalonians 2:1–3 points to "some spurious word of prophecy. Or even a spurious letter in his name."[146] The outlining of eschatological events in 2:1–12 is meant to cool their knee-jerk reaction. As Donfried cogently explains about this text, apocalyptic language as we find in 2 Thessalonians is intended

---

143. So Barclay writes, "Not only does this hypothesis assume far more than we presently know about economic conditions in Thessalonica and the obscure cult of Cabirus, it also appears to be based on the false assumption that an apocalyptic ideology is necessarily founded on economic deprivation or fostered by it" ("Conflict in Thessalonica," 519–20).

144. Barclay, "Conflict in Thessalonica," 528; cf. Tacitus, *Ann.* 12.43 (but, Barclay notes, this might only refer to Rome).

145. Barclay, "Conflict in Thessalonica," 528.

146. Barclay, "Conflict in Thessalonica," 528.

to offer comfort and encouragement to the struggling and harrassed Thessalonian believers. The justice of God and his plan for execution, although locked in the mystery of God, is the foundation of consolation for those who find themselves in the midst of violent persecution.[147]

The ἄτακτοι

In 1 Thessalonians 5:14, Paul makes mention of certain ἄτακτοι, those whom the church ought to correct. This bare reference in the letter is peculiar given that this terminology is rather rare, but all the same it seems to be mentioned in passing in Paul's final exhortations. However, a whole section of the end of 2 Thessalonians appears to be devoted to these same people (2 Thess 3:6–15). Clearly the problem of the ἄτακτοι did not go away; in fact it appears to have worsened. We will reserve a major discussion of these ἄτακτοι for the next chapter (see pp. 257–64), but here we will briefly comment that scholars disagree as to whether the eschatological problems are directly related to the nonworking attitude of the ἄτακτοι. That is, are these two separate issues in the letter, or are they directly related? Were the ἄτακτοι idle due to beliefs about the end of the ages? Scholars are not in agreement on this, though few would separate these issues entirely.

PSEUDONYMOUS SITUATIONAL ANALYSIS

One of the main reasons why many scholars do not favor a perspective that 2 Thessalonians is pseudonymous is due to the difficulty of constructing a scenario that would give rise to the letter—especially given that nearly all scholars supporting pseudonymity of 2 Thessalonians presume it would have been written in the late first century after Paul's death and separated by decades from the situation behind 1 Thessalonians.[148]

Howard Marshall (who argues for authenticity) presents what appears to be the scenario that must be imagined by those who believe that 2 Thessalonians is pseudonymous:

---

147. Donfried, "Issues of Authorship," 104; Hurd, "Concerning the Authenticity of 2 Thessalonians," 157–61.

148. Thus Morris's question: "What possible motive could the forger have had? Unless the letter is written to meet the genuine need of the Thessalonian church there seems no point to it" (*Thessalonians*, 20).

An unknown author wrote this letter to deal with a group of apocalyptic enthusiasts who were claiming Paul's authority for their belief
in the imminence of the parousia; he sought to quench their views
by himself assuming the mask of Paul and insisting on the delay
of the parousia. His very insistence on the authenticity of his letter
(2 Th. 3:17) betrays its authenticity; letters falsely ascribed to Paul
are unlikely to have circulated during his lifetime.[149]

Trevor Thompson, who argues strongly for pseudonymity, confesses
that reconstructing a situation behind 2 Thessalonians is almost futile.
If 2 Thessalonians is a late first-century forgery, we learn nothing from
the prescript—neither the authors are real nor even the addressees.[150] The
letter is a "literary fable," so the interpreter must be cautious about mirror
reading and situational reconstruction.[151] The reader is confronted with a
series of complicated hermeneutical questions:

Where if anywhere in the text does the identity of the actual author
emerge from behind the mask of the ascribed authors and their narrated context? Do the historical reminiscences and past experiences of
the ascribed authors resonate with the real experiences of the actual
author? If so, to what extent and how would we know? Was there an
actual persecution against Christians raging among perceived readers
(1:4–10)?[152]

Thompson's final, in this case perhaps rhetorical, question is methodologically sobering: "In terms of reconstructing a *Sitz im Leben* through

---

149. Marshall, *Thessalonians*, 30. Similarly, Furnish (who considers 2 Thess pseudonymous)
explains that many churches of the late first century would have been candidates for needing such a
letter of encouragement. That is, numerous Christian communities "were experiencing the hostility
of unbelievers, perplexed about the end-time, and troubled by disorderly conduct within their own
community" (*1–2 Thessalonians*, 140). In terms of the *region* of the (real) recipients, Furnish admits
that there are no internal clues in the letter. Furnish surmises that it would make sense to guess Asia
Minor since this would have been a hub for the collection of Paul's letters in the late first century.
Furthermore, Christians there suffered severe persecution under Domitian (81–96 CE). See Furnish,
1–2 Thessalonians, 140.

150. T. Thompson, "As If Genuine: Interpreting the Pseudepigraphic Second Thessalonians,"
in *Pseudepigraphie und Verfasserfiktion in frühchristlichen Briefen*, ed. J. Frey et al., WUNT 246
(Tübingen: Mohr Siebeck, 2009), 471.

151. Thompson, "As If Genuine," 471–72; similarly Van Aarde, "The Second Letter to the
Thessalonians Re-Read as Pseudepigraph," 107.

152. Thompson, "As If Genuine," 488.

the window of 2 Thessalonians, does deception ever end and truth begin?"[153] In the end, Thompson calls for a "rigorous hermeneutical model" that can manage these convoluted dimensions of situational reconstruction when examining a pseudepigraphon.[154]

Menken, while not naive to these complexities, is somewhat optimistic about the potential of drawing out the situation—or at least key aspects of the situation behind 2 Thessalonians (presuming it is pseudonymous). Menken treats the sender and recipients as fictional ("a literary expedient").[155] He believes that 2 Thessalonians still functions *as a letter*, that is, a text written by a particular sender to address concerns with a particular recipient group. In that sense, it is not a general theological essay. Menken hypothesizes that two concerns are behind this letter. Some believers thought the day of the Lord had arrived, and the author sought to condemn this notion as false. Menken also argues that the problem with nonworking, disorderly people was also real.[156]

Menken insists that the author of 2 Thessalonians was not trying to reject 1 Thessalonians. He considered his letter to be "an authentic reinterpretation of 1 Thessalonians in a situation in which some people considered this letter as a confirmation of their conviction that the day of the Lord had arrived."[157] That is, "the attribution of the reinterpretation to the person [Paul] at the origin of the tradition [1 Thessalonians] is tantamount to the assertion that the reinterpreting text is an authentic application of the authoritative tradition to a new situation."[158]

At the end of the day, all that can legitimately be asserted about the context of the letter if it is pseudonymous is that the situation called for corrective teaching on eschatological matters, specifically refuting the notion (however it developed) that the day of the Lord had arrived.

---

153. Thompson, "As If Genuine," 488.
154. Thompson, "As If Genuine," 488.
155. Menken, *2 Thessalonians*, 15.
156. Menken, *2 Thessalonians*, 15. Van Aarde tries to set out a case for a situation behind 2 Thessalonians involving false teaching related to Sadducean beliefs (that there is no "after-life" or final judgment). As evidence, Van Aarde points to comparative texts such as rabbinic texts that seem to refute the Sadducean perspective. When Van Aarde re-reads 2 Thessalonians from this perspective, he argues that 2 Thessalonians 2:4 alludes to "the Sadducean temple authorities" and the Roman administration is the "restrainer"; see Van Aarde, "The Second Letter to the Thessalonians Re-Read as Pseudepigraph," 135–36.
157. Menken, *2 Thessalonians*, 43. Somewhat similarly, see E. Cuvillier, "Vérité et historicité de la fiction littéraire. La seconde épître aux thessaloniciens comme pseudépigraphe," *Études théologiques et religieuses* 88.4 (2013): 515–28.
158. Menken, *2 Thessalonians*, 43; i.e., "2 Thessalonians can be considered as a reinterpretation of the eschatological teaching of 1 Thessalonians" (43).

CONCLUSION

The issues of background, situation, and date in the case of 2 Thessalonians are far more convoluted than they are for 1 Thessalonians. Much hinges on the determination of authorship. In terms of how scholars analyze the Pauline corpus, 2 Thessalonians is rather lightly disputed, and today the matter seems less of an open-and-shut case than it did perhaps a quarter of a century ago. Most Anglophone scholars either judge 2 Thessalonians to be authentic or are on the fence on the matter, though there are several scholars who are firm in their view of pseudonymity (e.g., Furnish, Boring, Krentz). German scholarship is much more settled against authenticity. While criteria such as unique vocabulary, theological differences/contradictions, and historical implausibility do not seem today to be major factors, the issues of style, literary dependence, and pseudonymous tells appear to remain significant.

As for date, those who consider 2 Thessalonians genuine almost all place it very close to the time of the writing of 1 Thessalonians, even within weeks. If it is pseudonymous, scholars propose a range of about 80–120 CE.

In terms of situation, Nicholl, Donfried, and Jewett have offered detailed discussions of the possible events and developments in life and thought that may have given rise to 2 Thessalonians. For all of these, amplified persecution and confusion over eschatological teaching seem to be at play, as well as other contextual factors. These scholars have found a way to make sense of 2 Thessalonians as a genuine second letter to the Thessalonians from the apostle Paul. For those who consider 2 Thessalonians pseudonymous, the matter of "situation" is far more complicated and the context far more elusive. Many such scholars assume that historical details in the letter could easily be fictional, though it appears that the most crucial matter is the need to clarify certain eschatological concerns. In the next chapter we will zoom in and consider several exegetical problems in 2 Thessalonians in more detail.

RECOMMENDED READING

Collins, R. F. *Letters that Paul Did Not Write: The Epistle to the Hebrews and Pauline Pseudepigrapha*. Wilmington, DE: Glazier, 1988.

Foster, P. "Who Wrote 2 Thessalonians? A Fresh Look at an Old Problem." *JSNT* 35.2 (2012): 150–75.

Gupta, N. K. "What Is in a Name? The Hermeneutics of Authorship Analysis concerning Colossians." *CBR* 11 (2013): 196–217.

Hurd, J. C. "Concerning the Authenticity of 2 Thessalonians." Pages 135–61 in *The Earlier Letters of Paul—And Other Letters*. New York: Peter Lang, 1998.

Krentz, E. "A Stone That Will Not Fit: The Non-Pauline Authorship of 2 Thessalonians." Pages 456–63 in *Pseudepigraphie und Verfasserfiktion in frühchristlichen Briefen*. Edited by J. Frey et al. WUNT 256. Tübingen: Mohr Siebeck, 2009.

MacDougall, D. W. *The Authenticity of 2 Thessalonians*. Paternoster Biblical Monographs Series. Milton Keynes: Paternoster, 2016.

Roose, H. "'A Letter as by Us': Intentional Ambiguity in 2 Thessalonians 2.2." *JSNT* 29 (2006): 107–24.

Wrede, W. *Die Echtheit des zweiten Thessalonicherbriefes*. TU 9/2. Leipzig: C. J. Henrich, 1903.

CHAPTER 7

THEMES AND INTERPRETATION OF 2 THESSALONIANS

THEMES

Second Thessalonians is a short letter and, as already discussed in chapter five, it mimics many structural, linguistic, and topical features of 1 Thessalonians. Thus, it should be no surprise that 2 Thessalonians also contains several similar themes as 1 Thessalonians.[1] We will review some of these shared themes briefly and then consider further a few themes more specific to 2 Thessalonians.[2]

Themes Shared with 1 Thessalonians

One of the most striking features of 1 Thessalonians is the heavy emphasis on spiritual kinship in the community of faith,[3] as well as some sense of Pauline spiritual parentage (1 Thess 2:7). While in 2 Thessalonians this theme is not as pronounced as the earlier letter, it is still clearly present and should be observed as distinctive of Paul's way of shaping the Thessalonians' shared identity as ἀδελφοί (see 2 Thess 1:3; 2:1, 13, 15;

---

1. E. M. Boring states rather matter-of-factly, "Second Thessalonians introduces no new topics or themes but is entirely devoted to three themes taken from 1 Thessalonians: persecution, eschatology, and the 'disorderly'"; see Boring, *1 and 2 Thessalonians*, 211. Only on the flattest reading of 2 Thess would one believe this text offers only a rehearsal of 1 Thess. We will make a case below that certain key themes, such as dignity and honor, are rather pronounced in 2 Thess, enough so to classify them as *distinctive* themes of the letter.

2. There are few resources that examine themes of 2 Thessalonians *per se*, but see Morris, *1, 2 Thessalonians*. The way Morris's book is designed, the themes are not particular to either 1 or 2 Thess, but shared. The six themes that Morris covers are "the living and true God," "Jesus Christ our Lord," "the last things," "the defeat of evil," "the Christian family," and "the Christian life." Probably the most concentrated attention that Morris gives to 2 Thess pertains to chapter four, "The Defeat of Evil," for obvious reasons (see 63–76).

3. See Hellerman, "Brothers and Friends in Philippi," 15–25; cf. also Aasgaard, *My Beloved Brothers and Sisters*; and Burke, *Family Matters*.

3:1, 6, 13). As with 1 Thessalonians, 2 Thessalonians seeks to underscore the close bond that the community has with one another through Jesus Christ, that they should care for one another as family, that they should listen to Paul as one of their brethren, and that they ought to feel confident and hopeful about the divine judgment as members of God's own family (see 2 Thess 1:6–7).

Another repeated theme in 2 Thessalonians is anticipation of the day of the Lord and the final events of the current age. This is considered the core of 2 Thessalonians, especially as it relates to fears about the mistaken Thessalonian belief that "the day of the Lord has already come" (2:2). Paul offers further clarification about the events and signs that will accompany this time and comforts the Thessalonians by reassuring them that those evil and pernicious forces that will plague humanity will not thwart God's plans and cannot ultimately penetrate his protection of his people (2:8, 14).[4]

Just as the subject of faith, belief, and works was emphasized in 1 Thessalonians (1 Thess 1:3, 8; 2:13; 3:2–10; 5:8), so too in 2 Thessalonians. Previously Paul commended the Thessalonians for their "work of faith" (1 Thess 1:3 NRSV); in the second epistle he encourages them in view of their "steadfastness and faith [ὑπὲρ τῆς ὑπομονῆς ὑμῶν καὶ πίστεως] during all your persecutions and the afflictions that you are enduring" (2 Thess 1:4 NRSV). When it comes to those who are glorified in the day of the Lord, Paul identifies these as those who have dared to *believe* the truth of the gospel (1:10). What 1 and 2 Thessalonians share, then, is a profound symbiosis between faith and work(s) that mark out the life of the follower of Jesus.[5] See below for further discussion of the theme of work and orderliness in 2 Thessalonians (p. 236).

Finally, 2 Thessalonians also picks up the emphasis that Paul places on hope in the Lord. In chapter two, Paul shares about the gift of "eternal encouragement and good hope" that the Thessalonians have graciously been given through Jesus Christ and God the Father (2:16). This theme of hope also appears in 1:5 and 1:11–12, where Paul talks about the role that suffering plays in preparing the believer for the future kingdom and glory. Below we will consider themes that are more specific to 2 Thessalonians.

---

4. On this topic in 2 Thess, see R. Aus, "Comfort in Judgment: The Use of Day of the Lord and Theophany Traditions in Second Thessalonians 1" (PhD diss., Yale University, 1971); M. Aernie, *Forensic Language and the Day of the Lord Motif in Second Thessalonians 1 and the Effects on the Meaning of the Text* (Eugene, OR: Wipf & Stock, 2010).

5. A helpful recent treatment of this subject can be found in Bates, *Salvation by Allegiance Alone*.

Dignity and Honor

As noted in the previous chapter, scholars have long observed how 2 Thessalonians carries a more serious tone, which some consider to be a signal that this cannot be the same author as of 1 Thessalonians, which offers a warmer, more personal tone. We have already addressed the authorship question and will not repeat those arguments here (see pp. 197–220), but the solemn tone of 2 Thessalonians is worthy of note. It need not imply either less affection from the author or a different author altogether. Rather, there may have been *rhetorical* reasons why the author set a different mood, namely, to give the text a liturgical flavor with the interest in reinforcing a sense of dignity and honor in service to and honor of the Lord. Paul writes:

> We ought always to thank God for you, brothers and sisters, and rightly so, because your faith is growing more and more, and the love all of you have for one another is increasing. (2 Thess 1:3)

Closely related to discussion of honor and dignity is that of glory and glorification, and 2 Thessalonians has plenty to say about this. That is, on the day of the Lord evildoers and the enemies of God will be separated from the presence of the Lord and "from the glory of his might" (1:9–10). Believers will further add to the glory of the Lord (1:12). And they themselves will finally be glorified as those whom God has called his own (2:13–14). For Paul, this reality is a call to sobriety, maturity, and responses to affliction that are in keeping with their calling and membership in the kingdom.

Roger Aus considers the possibility that Paul was using a liturgical tone here that we find in other Jewish texts of the time, such as in Philo. Philo called for a sacrifice of praise in view of the blessed life, as each one "has as his bounden duty to requite God, who has been the pilot of his voyage . . . with hymns, and songs, and prayers, and also sacrifices, and all other imaginable tokens of gratitude in a holy manner; all which things taken together have received the one comprehensive name of praise" (*Spec.* 1.224).[6]

We find similarities as well with early Christian texts like the *Hermas Similitudes*. In one section an angel shares with Hermas about the

---

6. R. Aus, "Liturgical Background of the Necessity and Propriety of Giving Thanks according to 2 Thess 1:3," *JBL* 92.3 (1973): 433–34.

blessings and honor bestowed on martyrs: "All who once suffered for the name of the Lord are honorable before God; and all these the sins were remitted, because they suffered for the name of the Son of God" (Herm. Sim. 9.28.3 [*ANF* 2:52]). The angel goes on to explain that when these faithful believers were brought to trial, they did not renounce their faith, but "suffered cheerfully." Such are held in great honor because they did not doubt (9.28.4). The angel then warns Hermas that suffering can either lead to doubt or deeper faith: "And ye who suffer for His name ought to glorify God, because He deemed you worthy to bear His name" (9.28.5).[7] We can see, from this perspective, how 2 Thessalonians may be establishing an atmosphere where suffering believers could reenvision their afflictions as part of a solemn testimony to the glory of God as they lived obedient lives and demonstrated a resilient faith.

Truth and Deception

It should come as no surprise that truth and deception comprise a major theme of 2 Thessalonians, a letter where Paul warns the Thessalonians not to believe rumors that the day of the Lord has already come. This is obviously a major emphasis of chapter two, where the author gives further instruction about how the end events will play out and the signs for which to be on the lookout. For our purposes here, we may focus on the way Paul draws out the problem of deception in the last days. First, the lawless one is considered a deceiver (2 Thess 2:8–9). Yet there is every reason to believe that while *Paul* knows him to be unrighteous, many will align with him. Why? Because he will have certain credentials and proofs that seemingly authenticate his leadership. He will conduct all manner of false miracles, "false" here meaning that while he may have supernatural acts, they do not *genuinely* attest to his true (anti-God) identity (2:9). This deceiver will fool those who are perishing and lead them to their demise (2:10–12).

When Paul then tells the Thessalonians to "stand firm and hold fast to the teachings we passed on to you," he exhorts them to have their full wits about them so that they do not fall into deception as well (2:15). They are expected to have spiritual discernment, but Paul especially points them to adherence to apostolic teaching for their own safety.

---

7. See further Gupta, *Thessalonians*, 120–21.

Justice and Peace

The next themes are those of justice and peace. Beginning with the former, we may observe that 2 Thessalonians spends considerable time reinforcing the notion that God is a God of justice who will, as it were, ensure that truth and justice win out in the end. Thus Paul writes to the Thessalonians that ultimately, despite the unfairness of the present age in their experience, God will relieve the afflicted and trouble the afflictors (2 Thess 1:6–7). So God is known as the God of vengeance (1:8; cf. NRSV), not because he is naturally wrathful and belligerent but because justice must prevail. It is for this reason too that the lawless one must be annihilated, because the coming age must be free from the power of such unrighteousness and injustice (2:8).

Paul also emphasizes the theme of peace in this letter. Bassler has written an important essay on peace as a leitmotif of 2 Thessalonians, even if the word technically only appears in the prescript (1:2) and postscript (3:16). Bassler observes that 2 Thessalonians clearly is concerned with giving comfort to a troubled community (so 1:5–10). While 2 Thessalonians is often remembered for its teachings on divine warfare and wrath, Bassler rightly points out that the primary rhetorical concern of 2 Thessalonians is "the promise of peace/rest to the afflicted saints."[8] She continues, "Though the Lord Jesus will prove to be an agent of terrible vengeance for those who have persecuted the church, he will be a 'Lord of peace' for the faithful, granting them the eschatological peace of the kingdom of God, which includes most concretely *rest* from their present tribulations."[9]

When it comes to 2:1–3:5, Bassler urges that here too, despite bewildering apocalyptic scenarios, 2 Thessalonians is concerned with bringing a sense of calm and reassurance about these matters. While the journey to the eschatological age will be bumpy, peace will prevail. Bassler's final summary is instructive:

> In every instance [i.e., section of the letter] a peaceful attitude or existence is contrasted with a state of disorder or turmoil, whether inflicted from without or experienced within the minds and the social

---

8. J. M. Bassler, "Peace in All Ways: Theology in the Thessalonian Letters," in *Pauline Theology 1: Thessalonians, Philippians, Galatians, Philemon*, ed. J. M. Bassler (Minneapolis: Fortress, 1991), 77.
9. Bassler, "Peace in All Ways," 77–78.

world of the community's members. Peace is a significant component of all Pauline letters, but rarely does it appear with such structural and thematic clarity as in this letter.[10]

Cooperation, Orderliness, and Work

Our last themes are found especially in 2 Thessalonians 3:6–15, where the letter refers to a group within the church who are "idle and disruptive" (3:6), refusing to work and instead acting as "busybodies" (3:11). While there have been some translations and interpreters that have implied or stated that the problem here is one of laziness, in fact Paul does not put the matter in such a way. The problem is not that these troublemakers are doing *nothing* but rather that they refuse to work and intentionally behave in a counterproductive way. What exactly they may have been up to we will address at length below (pp. 257–63); suffice it to say here that Paul shows concern with the impact on the believing community (3:8) and the expectation that all will equally devote themselves to honest labor. Honest work should be carried out in a spirit of quietness (i.e., work for the sake of productive labor) and independence (i.e., with a view toward self-dependence when possible; 3:12).

It ought to be pointed out that Paul was not condemning the down-trodden, the weak, those down on their luck *per se*. He especially refers here to those who *refused* to work (3:14). Paul encouraged the Thessalonians to function as a healthy community, with each person (as able) participating in honest labor for the sake of the community's overall welfare.[11]

INTERPRETATION OF 2 THESSALONIANS

In the study of 2 Thessalonians, we could identify a host of exegetical concerns to examine, but to allow for some measure of depth, we will limit our purview to five key issues.

Evidence of God's Righteous Judgment? (1:5)

Early in the first chapter of 2 Thessalonians the reader is presented with an interpretive problem. After Paul offers his greetings and thanksgiving

---

10. Bassler, "Peace in All Ways," 79–80.
11. For scholarship on the subject of "work" in Paul, see the earlier discussion on pp. 98–100.

to God (1:1–3), he goes on to express his "boast" in their endurance and faith in the face of hardships and persecution (1:4). Then he writes:

> All this is evidence that God's judgment is right, and as a result you will be counted worthy of the kingdom of God, for which you are suffering. (1:5)

> ἔνδειγμα τῆς δικαίας κρίσεως τοῦ θεοῦ εἰς τὸ καταξιωθῆναι ὑμᾶς τῆς βασιλείας τοῦ θεοῦ, ὑπὲρ ἧς καὶ πάσχετε

The overall point is clear—their suffering is not hopeless but rather a means to glory. And in the end the afflictors will face justice (1:6). Still, the wording of 1:5 is somewhat perplexing as it leaves open the referent of "evidence" (ἔνδειγμα). What is the evidence? The answer to this question helps to interpret how such evidence relates to the righteous judgment of God. To begin to answer these questions and address these issues, we must go back to 1:4 to determine the referent of ἔνδειγμα. Wanamaker cogently lays out the options. The term refers to:

1. The Thessalonian believers' endurance and faith (in general)
2. "The persecution and affliction that they experience"
3. Their endurance and faith "in the face of persecution and affliction"[12]

Given these options, most interpreters prefer option (3).[13] This view would understand that the Thessalonian believers' perseverance is a sign especially of the protective and sustaining work of God. Despite the overall popularity of this view, Wanamaker demurs. He finds it more likely

---

12. See Wanamaker, *Thessalonians*, 220. Witherington entertains (and prefers) a fourth option, to take ἔνδειγμα not as anaphoric (pointing to evidence already mentioned, i.e., in 1:4), but as cataphoric, identifying the "evidence" with what comes in 1:6–10 "where a theology of recompense is enunciated in a way similar to what we find in Luke 16:25" (Witherington, *Thessalonians*, 192). Nicholl offers another option, preferring to read this as their sufferings being "proof that just judgment will yet come" (*From Hope to Despair*, 149). While Nicholl's thinking is on the right track, with a view toward being counted worthy of the kingdom (1:5b), his reading would expect a word like "guarantee" or "promise." The interpretation that I offer is a variation of this view, but without that sense of reading κρίσις as especially pertaining to *future* judgment. Similar to Nicholl, see Hughes, *Early Christian Rhetoric and 2 Thessalonians*, 54.

13. So Bruce, *Thessalonians*, 149; Richard, *First and Second Thessalonians*, 305; Malherbe, *Thessalonians*, 395; Beale, *1–2 Thessalonians*, 183.

that the flow of verses 4–5 lead to the second interpretation.[14] Following the work of Bassler, Wanamaker points to a Jewish tradition that viewed sufferings as present "chastisement" for the pious to prove their faith.[15] Psalms of Solomon tends to be cited in support:

> For the Lord spares his pious ones, and blots out their errors by his chastening. For the life of the righteous will be forever; but sinners will be taken away into destruction, and their memorial will be found no more. But upon the pious is the mercy of the Lord, and upon them that fear him his mercy. (Pss. Sol. 13:10–12 [OPE])

Also, a similar sentiment is found in Genesis Rabbah 33.1:

> [God] deals strictly with the righteous, calling them to account for the few wrongs which they commit in this world, in order to lavish bliss upon and give them a goodly reward in the world to come; he grants ease to the wicked and rewards them for the few good deeds which they have performed in this world in order to punish them in the future world.[16]

Again, not everyone is convinced that Paul was trying to follow this same line of thought in 2 Thessalonians. Beverly Gaventa, for instance, shows concern that reading ἔνδειγμα as the sufferings themselves could lead to a dangerous view of God: "Shall I measure my standing with God by my misfortunes (since God is punishing me now and will reward me later)?"[17]

At the end of the day, the interpretation that will be most satisfying will explain why Paul focuses here on the language of God's righteous (or just) judgment (τῆς δικαίας κρίσεως τοῦ θεοῦ). For my part, the way this verse is worded gives the sense of an *apologia*, as if Paul felt the need to defend the way God operates and handles the affairs of mortals.

---

14. Other scholars who prefer this view include Rigaux, *Thessaloniciens*, 620, and J. M. Bassler, "The Enigmatic Sign: 2 Thessalonians 1:5," *CBQ* 46 (1984): 496–510; cf. also Menken, *2 Thessalonians*, 85–86.

15. Wanamaker, *Thessalonians*, 222. Green points to 1 Pet 1:7 as a potential parallel to support this view (*Thessalonians*, 285).

16. See Talbert, *Learning through Suffering*, 15.

17. Gaventa, *First and Second Thessalonians*, 102–3; see also Shogren, *Thessalonians*, 249, for a similar criticism.

Paul's concern, it would seem, is to reassure the Thessalonian believers that what is transpiring presently in their midst fits into the sovereign plan of God. In my judgment, it makes most sense that Paul was trying to put their afflictions into perspective, that is, view (2) above. But how does he accomplish this?

Let us focus on the word "judgment" (κρίσις), a relatively rare word in the New Testament, and here one of the only appearances in the Pauline corpus (the other coming in 1 Tim 5:24). While it is common for κρίσις to take a negative value (judgment = condemnation), especially as a semitechnical term for the final judgment of condemnation for the wicked, it can also carry a more neutral meaning, as in "I trust the teacher's *judgment*."[18] We have previously discussed the possibility that some people who had persuasive influence over the believing community in Thessalonica (friends, neighbors, etc.) tried to convince them that the difficulties they were facing were indicators of divine wrath (i.e., "judgment"; hence 2 Thess 2:2). Paul's response in 2 Thessalonians 1:4–5 would be that the trials that they are facing are not unrelated to God and do indeed involve his κρίσις (judgment), but Paul wanted to reframe their experience in light of the *positive* meaning of κρίσις—he had *deemed it right and appropriate* to allow his Thessalonian people to face persecution, just as he showed Paul how much Paul must suffer for God's name (Acts 9:16; cf. 5:41). If this reading is correct, here is an imaginative paraphrase that captures Paul's rhetorical intentions:

> You Thessalonians are suffering and wonder, "Is God (the God of Jesus Christ) in control, and if so why am I being punished?" I say to you, God is in control, and he is acting in accordance with his good pleasure and attentive to your situation with deep concern. The afflictions you are suffering are not a negative reflection of your condemnation but rather a privilege such that he would let you represent his kingdom and trusts you to rise above the persecution in faithfulness and hope.[19]

Paul operates here with a kind of reversal hermeneutic, trying to deconstruct a view that interprets their trials as divine wrath and instead

---

18. See, e.g., Sir 25:4; 33:13; Matt 12:18; John 5:30; 7:24; Acts 8:33.
19. See Gupta, *Thessalonians*, 124.

reframing their experience as a carefully considered plan of discipleship and kingdom representation such that through perseverance and faithfulness they would be refined in alignment with the kingdom.

The Day of the Lord Has Come? (2:2)

As noted beforehand, the heart of 2 Thessalonians involves further teaching from Paul regarding concerns about the "day of the Lord" (see 2:2–3). The rest of 2 Thessalonians 2 is largely devoted to outlining intervening occurrences that will precede that final day. All of this is straightforward enough. What is confusing is the precise meaning of the statement "that the day of the Lord has already come" (ὅτι ἐνέστηκεν ἡ ἡμέρα τοῦ κυρίου). The natural question a modern reader might have is, *If the day of the Lord had come, wouldn't it have been incontrovertably clear?* What sorts of statements or signs would have convinced some Thessalonian believers that this day had arrived?[20] Before engaging directly with 2 Thessalonians 2:2, we will briefly review the background and origin of the day-of-the-Lord concept as well as how it is referenced in 1 Thessalonians.

Specific references in the Old Testament to the day of the Lord are found in the prophetic books (esp. Isaiah, Ezekiel, Joel, Amos, and Zephaniah). It is presented as a day of judgment and of destruction for the wicked: "Wail, for the day of the Lᴏʀᴅ is near" (Isa 13:6). It will be "cruel, with wrath and fierce anger, to make the earth a desolation, and to destroy its sinners from it" (13:9 NRSV; cf. Ezek 30:3; Amos 5:18).[21] It is unclear how this judgment-day concept developed, but one theory is that it comes from Israel's "holy war" experiences.[22] Such conflict-oriented events were major turning points in history and often led either to capture and destruction or freedom and victory.[23]

The apostle Paul periodically refers to the day of the Lord. In Romans

---

20. The verb used here is ἐνίστημι and has the simple meaning "be present" or "arrive." It is not a particularly common word in the NT (7x) or the LXX for that matter (13x, mostly in 1–4 Macc).

21. See Y. Hoffmann, "The Day of the Lord as a Concept and a Term in the Prophetic Literature," *ZAW* 83 (1987): 37–50; also J. Plevnik, *Paul and the Parousia*, 12–39, which includes discussion of the OT pseudepigrapha as well.

22. "Day of the Lord," *DBI* 196.

23. As an important contribution to the background of this, cf. E. Adams, "The 'Coming of God' Tradition and Its Influence on New Testament Parousia Texts," in *Biblical Traditions in Transmission: Essays in Honour of Michael A. Knibb*, ed. C. Hempel and J. Lieu, JSJSup 111 (Leiden: Brill, 2006), 1–19. In brief, Adams argues that the tradition of the coming of God develops within the Old Testament and Jewish tradition, becoming increasingly future oriented and ultimately apocalyptic. He examines the "eschatologization" of this tradition as present in Isa 66:15–16 and Zech 14. Adams also shows how this "coming" takes on a cosmic dimension and comes to be associated with a "radical transformation of the cosmos" (6).

he refers to this as the "day of God's wrath" (Rom 2:5; cf. 2:16; 1 Cor 5:5). As for believers, while Paul did not view this as a day of condemnation for them, he still presumed that because it is a day of reckoning, it ought to be anticipated with preparation, sobriety, and even reverential fear (1 Cor 1:8; 3:13; 2 Cor 1:14; Phil 1:10; 2:16).

In 1 Thessalonians Paul gives attention to the day of the Lord in chapter five. He repeats the idea that "the day of the Lord will come like a thief in the night" (1 Thess 5:2; cf. 5:4). While these are the only occasions where he explicitly uses the word "day" to refer to the day of the Lord, it is reasonable to link it here to the way Paul refers to the parousia.[24] In 1 Thessalonians Paul uses parousia language often (2:19; 3:13; 4:15; 5:23). He writes, "According to the Lord's word, we tell you that we who are still alive, who are left until the coming of the Lord, will certainly not precede those who have fallen asleep" (1 Thess 4:15). His primary concern in 1 Thessalonians is to call the Thessalonians to vigilance in their faith and hope that the departed will not be dishonored or forgotten.

Let us revisit now 2 Thessalonians 2:2. Paul warns the Thessalonians to disregard any message to the effect that the day of the Lord ἐνέστηκεν. As L. J. L. Peerbolte observes, this verb could imply present reality ("has already come") or imminent reality ("is about to come").[25] Peerbolte argues that this does not refer to a present reality because this would mean the end of the world, something which clearly had *not* happened already. Instead, Peerbolte reasons that it must refer to a *future* coming.[26] However, most Thessalonian scholars do not adopt this future reading of 2:2 but prefer the present-reality interpretation. When it comes to ἐνίστημι in its Pauline usage, the verb carries the idea of something being present or in the "now" time (Rom 8:38; 1 Cor 3:22). In 2 Timothy this verb is used in the future tense to refer to "distressing times" to come (2 Tim 3:1). One would expect then that if the statement about the day of the Lord in 2 Thessalonians 2:2 was meant to be future oriented, it would have been in the future tense. Yet in such a case other verbs may have been more fitting (such as μέλλω or ἐγγίζω[27]).[28]

---

24. On the matter of whether the day of the Lord and the parousia are coterminous for Paul, Plevnik answers in the affirmative, pointing to shared language and imagery in 1 Cor 4:1–5 and Rom 13:12. He also notes how Matt 24:27 refers to the *coming* of the Son of Man, while the parallel text Luke 17:24 reads "the *day* of the Son of Man"; see Plevnik, *Paul and the Parousia*, 11.

25. Peerbolte, *Antecedents of Antichrist*, 73.

26. See Peerbolte, *Antecedents of Antichrist*, 73–74.

27. See Nicholl, *Hope to Despair*, 116–17.

28. Menken (and many others) add the important conceptual point that the author of 2 Thess

We are therefore left to consider the meaning of 2 Thessalonians 2:2 in light of the Thessalonians' assumption that the day of the Lord was somehow already present. Dale Allison opens up the possibility that this statement might mean that the Thessalonians in some way spiritualized the day of the Lord, such that they believed the end had come (and gone, as it were; see 2 Tim 2:17–18 for a possible comparable teaching).[29] Similarly, Karl Donfried has proposed that 2 Thessalonians 2:2 might refer to a "spiritualized, almost gnostic-like, understanding, namely, that there will not be any future, physical coming of the Lord, much like the problem described in 1 Cor. 15:12–18."[30] He goes on to explain that this misunderstanding may have developed because gentile believers had trouble making full sense of Paul's eschatological teaching.[31] The problem with this "overrealized" theory is that it does not seem to fit the Thessalonian situation and how Paul responds to that situation overall. In a context where the believers have an overrealized and overspiritualized perspective, there tends to be an air of confidence and libertinism. But 2 Thessalonians is written to a persecuted and suffering community, and Paul's overall message is one of comfort and reassurance, not corrective teaching *per se*.[32]

An important question to ask regarding 2 Thessalonians 2:2 is *why* the Thessalonians came to believe the day of the Lord had come. Of course, Paul mentions the idea that they might have received some kind of news, whether through a letter or perhaps through a prophecy. Jewett holds that the Thessalonians had been persuaded by a prophetic oracle.[33] Similarly, Menken observes (with a glance at the apocalyptic teachings in the Synoptics) that believers taught that the end times would be marked by the appearance of false prophets.[34] Furthermore, Menken notes that there would be false messianic claimants; he gives testimonies from Josephus that demonstrate such incidents.

---

would not have been so exercised by this problematic belief if they had simply thought the day of the Lord was coming *soon*. Indeed, that is what 1 Thess communicated (Menken, *2 Thessalonians*, 98).

29. D. C. Allison, "Day of the Lord," *NIDB* 2:46.

30. See Donfried, "2 Thessalonians and the Church of Thessalonica," 57. As further evidence in favor of his theory, Donfried notes the "spirit" language in 2 Thess 2:2, 15 and the mentioning of the "restrainer" (2:6, 7) as what seems to be a spiritual entity (58).

31. Donfried, "2 Thessalonians and the Church of Thessalonica," 57.

32. See J. M. G. Barclay, "Thessalonica and Corinth: Social Contrasts in Pauline Christianity," *JSNT* 15.47 (1992): 49–74.

33. Jewett, *Thessalonian Correspondence*, 100–101, 178.

34. Menken, *2 Thessalonians*, 101.

At this time there came to Jerusalem from Egypt a man who declared
that he was a prophet and advised the masses of the common people
to go out with him to the mountain called the Mount of Olives. . . .
For he asserted that he wished to demonstrate from there that at
his command Jerusalem's walls would fall down, through which he
promised to provide them an entrance into the city. (*Ant.* 20.169
[Feldman, LCL])

There too may have been other "signals" that led the Thessalonians
to believe that the day of the Lord had arrived, or at least the *beginnings*
of these final events had been inaugurated. John Barclay considers the
possibility that the Thessalonians were predisposed to be on the lookout
for signs for the day of the Lord and perhaps *mis*interpreted surrounding
events as such omens. In particular, Barclay notes how Tacitus considered
the years 51–52 to be "particularly ill-omened, with prodigies such as
repeated earthquakes and a famine."[35] Could it be that these happenings
led to this eschatological assumption? Barclay finds this possibility "tan-
talizing," but in reality "a fevered apocalyptic imagination can interpret
almost any unusual event as an eschatological moment, and divine wrath
can explain many types of calamity."[36]

The present-oriented reading of 2 Thessalonians 2:2 is most sensible
and also the most popular interpretation. It is nevertheless unlikely that
the Thessalonians believed that the day of the Lord had *come and gone*, as
it were. As Menken rightly reasons, the parousia "should be such a public
event, perceptible to everybody, leaving no room for doubt."[37] More likely,
they came to believe that the dawning of the day of the Lord had arrived,
probably accompanied by various "signs," including fresh prophecies (i.e.,
oracles), physical omens perhaps, increased persecution, etc. Colin Nicholl
hastens to add that 2 Thessalonians 2:2–3 seem to imply that this notion of
the appearance of the end times did not seem to bring the Thessalonians a
sense of comfort, hope, or reassurance but quite the opposite. It seemed to
be terrifying, "undermining the essence of their Christian hope."[38] I would
also add my own theory here that one could align this with the notion that
Jewish leaders in Thessalonica—upset that some of their Godfearers had

---

35. Barclay, "Conflict in Thessalonica," 527–28.
36. Barclay, "Conflict in Thessalonica," 528.
37. Menken, *2 Thessalonians*, 99.
38. See Nicholl, *From Hope to Despair*, 131.

abandoned the synagogue to honor Christ exclusively—may have played a role in perpetuating the notion that divine wrath was breaking out against these Thessalonian Jesus followers.[39]

Who is the Man of Lawlessness? (2:3)

The figure of the man of lawlessness is one of the most memorable features of 2 Thessalonians.[40] He appears to be more than one who disregards the law or way of God; he could be better understood as the "anti-law one." He is "anti-law" insofar as he stands against God, his commandments, and his ways. He is also called "the son of destruction" (ESV; NET). Most scholars and translators take this to mean he is destined for destruction (cf. NIV; NRSV), but it makes good sense to see this language as comprehensive. It refers to someone who is anti-law and anti-God; destruction follows wherever he goes, and his own demise is inevitable.

In the Christian tradition, it is common to see the man of lawlessness associated with the antichrist, though we will not venture into the Johannine literature to consider this matter in detail, as most scholars believe it does not help us to interpret 2 Thessalonians directly. More pertinent is the question of the identity of this man of lawlessness (or the major factors behind how Paul crafts his portrayal of this figure). Sigve Tonstad recently defended the idea that the man of lawlessness could in fact be Satan. Tonstad first notes the use of the definite article with the various titles for the man of lawlessness.[41] Furthermore, he considers the kinds of things claimed about this figure, such grandiose aspirations and accomplishments that it would appear that he is "not a peripheral, occasional, or local manifestation of evil but the real thing," the essence of evil itself.[42] Most scholars, however, take the evidence of 2:9 at face value where Paul claims that the "lawless one" will appear through Satan's workings, aligned with Satan but distinct from him nonetheless.[43]

When it comes to how Paul constructs and depicts this figure, the overwhelming tendency is to identify the man of lawlessness with a

---

39. An important implication here is that Jews felt a sense of competition for supporters or converts with early (Jewish) Christians.

40. In the next chapter we will give more focused attention to how writers throughout the ages have associated this figure with various contemporary leaders.

41. Nicholl, *From Hope to Despair*, 139.

42. Nicholl, *From Hope to Despair*, 139.

43. See especially J. Weima, "The Slaying of Satan's Superman and the Sure Salvation of the Saints," *CTJ* 41 (2006): 80; cf. also R. Hamerton-Kelly, *Politics and Apocalypse* (East Lansing: Michigan State University Press, 2007).

formative archetype. Paul does not specifically identify the lawless one, but the language he uses for him is reminiscent of notorious enemies in Israel's past. As Dunn aptly explains,

> the expectation is the wholly Jewish one of an archetypal opponent in whom the final rebellion of the nations against the one God will come to its eschatological crisis—wholly of a piece with the expectation of Mark 13.14, with its deliberate echo of the same Syrian crisis (which sparked off the Maccabean rebellion) to which Daniel 11.31 and 12.11 allude and which likewise provided the archetype of the final rebellion against God and his people.[44]

As Dunn observes, some features of 2 Thessalonians's man of lawlessness are influenced by Old Testament texts and types. Psalm 89:22 refers to a generic enemy and "a son of lawlessness" (NETS; LXX 88:23: υἱὸς ἀνομίας). Similarly, Isaiah 57:3 warns the wayward among Israel to repent: "But as for you, draw near here, you lawless sons, you offspring of adulterers and of a whore" (NETS; LXX: ὑμεῖς δὲ προσαγάγετε ὧδε υἱοὶ ἄνομοι σπέρμα μοιχῶν καὶ πόρνης).

In terms of the divine pretensions of the man of lawlessness, it has long been observed how what 2 Thessalonians states parallels texts like Ezekiel 28:1–2 and Isaiah 14:13–14:[45]

> The word of the LORD came to me: "Son of man, say to the ruler of Tyre, 'This is what the Sovereign LORD says:
>
> > "In the pride of your heart
> >   you say, 'I am a god;
> > I sit on the throne of a god
> >   in the heart of the seas.'
> > But you are a mere mortal and not a god,
> >   though you think you are as wise as a god.""" (Ezek 28:1–2)

> You [king of Babylon] said in your heart,
>   "I will ascend to the heavens;

---

44. J. D. G. Dunn, "Deutero-Pauline Letters," in *Early Christian Thought in Its Jewish Context*, ed. J. M. G. Barclay (Cambridge: Cambridge University Press, 1996), 132.

45. See Harrison, *Paul and the Imperial Authorities*, 85.

I will raise my throne
above the stars of God;
I will sit enthroned on the mount of assembly,
on the utmost heights of Mount Zaphon.
I will ascend above the tops of the clouds;
I will make myself like the Most High." (Isa 14:13–14)

A key archetype for the man of lawlessness is Antiochus IV Epiphanes, and scholars point to Daniel 11:36 in particular (as Dunn did in the above quote): "The king will do as he pleases. He will exalt and magnify himself above every god and will say unheard-of things against the God of gods. He will be successful until the time of wrath is completed, for what has been determined must take place."[46] James Harrison adds evidence from 2 Maccabees to strengthen the case for a connection between the man of lawlessness and Antiochus IV. Second Maccabees narrates a bloodthirsty rampage by Antiochus where he commanded the slaughter of over eighty thousand Jews including children (2 Macc 5:11–14). After that, he raided the Jewish temple and desecrated it (2 Macc 5:15–16). Antiochus took pride in this unholy act (5:17).[47] Robert Gundry articulates a common perspective on the Antiochus archetype for the man of lawlessness: "He models the man of lawlessness after Antiochus Epiphanes, amalgamates him with the ruler of Tyre, and christianizes this already hybrid figure by giving him the characteristics of the false christs and false prophets predicted in the dominical tradition underlying the Olivet Discourse."[48]

Another probable archetype for the man of lawlessness is Pompey, who also profaned the temple.[49] According to Psalms of Solomon 17:11–15, Pompey is called "the lawless one [ὁ ἄνομος]," an enemy, and one who corrupted God's holy house. Similar to 2 Maccabees's portrayal of Antiochus IV, Pompey here is depicted as a murderer, dispensing "glorious wrath" (17:12).[50] What Wanamanker finds particularly resonant about this model

---

46. See A. Y. Collins, "The Transformation of Paul's Apocalyptic Ideas in the First Two Centuries," in *Revealed Wisdom: Studies in Apocalyptic in Honour of Christopher Rowland*, ed. J. Ashton (Leiden: Brill, 2014), 148; see also M. Karrer, "Der zweite Thessalonicherbrief und Gottes Widersacher," *HBT* 29.2 (2007): 119.

47. The text reads: καὶ ἐμετεωρίζετο τὴν διάνοιαν ὁ Ἀντίοχος. One could add the relevant information from 2 Macc 9:8, which describe Antiochus's pretensions to supernatural power.

48. R. H. Gundry, *The Old Is Better: New Testament Essays in Support of Traditional Interpretations* (Tübingen: Mohr Siebeck, 2005), 313.

49. See Richard, *First and Second Thessalonians*, 245.

50. Harrison, *Paul and the Imperial Authorities*, 76.

is how Pompey's actions led some Jews to flee and hide but many others to fall into depravity and apostasy:

> There was none among [Israel] that perform righteousness and jus-
> tice. From the chief of them to the least (of them) all were sinful. The
> king was a transgressor, and the judge disobedient, and the people
> (were) in sin. Behold, O Lord, and raise up to them their king, the
> son of David, at the time in which you choose, O God, that he may
> reign over Israel your servant (Pss. Sol. 17:19b–21 [OPE]).[51]

From 37–41 CE, Caligula was emperor. According to a variety of ancient sources, Caligula desecrated the Jewish temple, attempting to erect a statue of himself there (Josephus, *Ant.* 18.257–309; *J.W.* 2.184–203) with an inscription reading "Gaius 'the new Zeus made manifest'" (Philo, *Legat.* 346 [Colson, LCL]).[52] Martin Karrer find this archetype partic-ularly influential and compelling. He sees Caligula as the catalyst and model from which the man of lawlessness figure is apocalypticized: "The density of the parallels means that we cannot entirely rule out influence of the Caligula allusion in the portrayal in 2 Thessalonians. Of course, this allusion has morphed into a mythical expectation, heightened even more by apocalyptic dualism."[53] Mention can also briefly be made of scholarly interest in connections between the man of lawlessness of 2 Thessalo-nians and the emperor Nero. This matter was also discussed in chapter six regarding the dating of 2 Thessalonians. Nero was emperor from 54–68 CE, so many find it doubtful that Nero could serve as an antecedent arche-type for 2 Thessalonians if it was written by Paul. Briefly, we can repeat that after Nero's death rumors spread that he did not actually die, but rather fled to Parthia and was expected to return (hence Nero *redivivus*). Based on the Sibylline Oracles 5.29–34, G. van Kooten has argued that

---

51. See Wanamaker, *Thessalonians*, 245.

52. See S. R. Llewelyn et al., eds., *New Documents Illustrating Early Christianity*, vol. 10 (Grand Rapids: Eerdmans, 2012), 74; cf. also M. Reasoner, *Roman Imperial Texts: A Sourcebook* (Minneapolis: Fortress, 2013), 61–66. Apparently Caligula was determined to establish himself as *synnaos*, "divine companion of the Jewish god, in the Jerusalem Temple." See M. Bernett, "Roman Imperial Cult in the Galilee," in *Religion, Ethnicity, and Identity in Ancient Galilee: A Region in Transition*, ed. J. Zangenberg, H. W. Attridge, and D. B. Martin, WUNT 210 (Tübingen: Mohr Siebeck, 2012), 348. For a helpful and extensive treatment of the source material recounting the Caligula sacrilege and its impact on early Judaism and the early church, see N. H. Taylor, "Caligula, the Church of Antioch and the Gentile Mission," *Religion and Theology* 7.1 (2000): 1–23.

53. Karrer, "Der zweite Thessalonicherbrief," 123 (trans. mine).

the connections between the image of Nero and the man of lawlessness are too strong to ignore.[54] If 2 Thessalonians was written later in the first century, this indeed is a possibility, but there are enough resonant archetypal figures that it is unlikely that the man of lawlessness is based primarily on Nero in any case.[55] James Harrison summarizes what is probably the consensus scholarly view on the identity-construction of 2 Thessalonians's man of lawlessness: "In the variegated traditions of Second Temple Judaism the figure of the 'lawless one' emerges as an amalgam of Antiochus IV 'Epiphanes,' Nicanor, the 'Wicked Priest,' Pompey, and Caligula, each of whom defiled (or attempted to defile) the Jerusalem Temple."[56]

An important question raised about the man of lawlessness is whether Paul (or the author) and the letter recipients would have considered him a human figure (described in grandiose terms) or a superhuman entity, and whether this passage in general should be taken figuratively or literally. This relates closely to current discussions about the nature of apocalyptic discourse. N. T. Wright has argued that imagery of cosmic destruction in early Jewish and early Christian apocalyptic discourse ought not always to be taken literally, but points to political upheaval.[57] Recently Edward Adams has challenged Wright's view, arguing instead that there is evidence and reason to suggest that readers (and writers) would naturally have presumed real "cosmic catastrophe."[58] It is difficult to referee this discussion, because both views seem to have strong points in their favor, and ultimately the final answer is unclear.

Howard Marshall argues that Paul does not present the man of lawlessness as particularly superhuman in essence or action. He writes, "A man taking his seat on a throne in a temple and producing counterfeit miracles that take people in is perfectly conceivable, and such things have

---

54. See G. H. van Kooten, "'Wrath Will Drip,'" 177–215.

55. See Menken, *2 Thessalonians*, 107.

56. Harrison, *Paul and the Imperial Authorities*, 85.

57. See N. T. Wright, *New Testament and the People of God* (Minneapolis: Fortress, 1992), 321; also N. T. Wright, "Putting Paul Together Again: Toward a Synthesis of Pauline Theology," in *Pauline Theology*, ed. J. Bassler (Minneapolis: Fortress, 1991), 211; see also T. D. Still, "Eschatology in the Thessalonian Letters," *RevExp* 96.2 (1999): 195–210: "My inclination is to take this text [2 Thess 2:3–10] as well as other ancient texts cast in an apocalyptic hue as figurative" (201). He shows hesitation in this, however, as he notes that different audiences might take the language differently.

58. E. Adams, *The Stars Will Fall from Heaven*, LNTS 347 (London: T&T Clark, 2007); see too D. C. Allison, "Jesus and the Victory of Apocalyptic," in *Jesus and the Restoration of Israel: A Critical Assessment of N. T. Wright's Jesus and the Victory of God*, ed. C. C. Newman (Downers Grove, IL: InterVarsity Press, 1999), 126–42. D. Frayer-Griggs tends to side with Adams and Allison on this; see Frayer-Griggs, *Saved through Fire*, 22–23.

happened."[59] As a counterperspective, we might turn to Best's reflections on the man of lawlessness. Best argues that the man of lawlessness is portrayed as the archenemy of God, a formidable opponent. While Best acknowledges parallels with Antiochus, Pompey, and Caligula, he also points to the clear connection to what Jews called the "abomination of desolation."[60] This, especially when considering apocalyptic thought, pushes the man-of-lawlessness figure to the mythical level in Best's view.[61]

I personally find it doubtful that Paul had in mind a singular precursor, whether Antiochus, Pompey, Caligula, or anyone else. Certainly the description of the man of lawlessness would call to mind such despots, but the reader would do a disservice to the interpretation of 2 Thessalonians 2:3–10 by limiting the profile of the man of lawlessness. As far as the right way to read the man of lawlessness within apocalyptic discourse, I lean toward the notion that this figure is expected by the author (and most readers) to be a human like Caligula, who aspired to prove his supremacy even within the divine realm. As far as how one ought to take the apocalyptic imagery of the narrative of the man of lawlessness, Malherbe's reflection is apropos:

> What is enigmatic to the modern reader was known to Paul's readers, and his reminders of what they were told or knew show that he was not informing them of details about the eschatological drama, but rather speaking to them as a person with inside knowledge of the mystery. The apocalyptic images confirm them in what they already know, which thus performs a pastoral function when the readers are confronted by false teachers. They are surrounded by evil, and although the Anti-God is not yet present, the evil of the future is already at work proleptically. Paul will be explicit in his exhortations and prayers for their stability, but he already acts pastorally in laying out the apocalyptic scheme. It is important to remember this function of what is said, even when the meaning of the details eludes us.[62]

---

59. Marshall, *New Testament Theology*, 247.
60. Best, *Thessalonians*, 289.
61. Similarly, see Wanamaker, *Thessalonians*, 248.
62. Malherbe, *Thessalonians*, 432. For an insightful essay on the man of lawlessness in 2 Thess, see A. Johnson, "Paul's 'Anti-Christology' in 2 Thess 2:3–12 in Canonical Context," *JTI* 8.1 (2014): 125–43.

Who (or What) is the Restrainer? (2:6–7)

In the study of the Thessalonian correspondence, the modern interpreter faces few issues more confounding than the determination of the meaning and identity of τὸ κατέχον (the restraining influence) and ὁ κατέχων (the "restrainer"). There appear to be two major obstacles to understanding what 2 Thessalonians is saying in 2:6–7. First, we have the overall challenge of the cryptic nature of apocalyptic discourse. The author obviously sought to comfort and reassure the Thessalonians in light of fears regarding the day of the Lord (2:2), and part of his response is to outline how certain eschatological events will unfold. Yet the language he uses to describe these events and the characters involved is highly poetic, defying any attempt at historical precision. First, he mentions "the rebellion" and then relates this to the appearance of the "man of lawlessness" (2:3). He then backs up to give this reminder to the Thessalonians: "And you know what is now restraining him, so that he may be revealed when his time comes. For the mystery of lawlessness is already at work, but only until the one who now restrains it is removed" (2:6–7 NRSV). Again, we are not privy to names and dates of any of these matters. Clearly Paul claims to have already taught the Thessalonians on this subject, though we cannot know what kind of information they received. Did they have a name to go with the restainer? Or the man of lawlessness?

The second major obstacle we face is the terminology itself. The verb κατέχω is rather mundane. It carries the sense of holding or containing. This can be extended to mean "restrain" or "detain." For example, in the book of Tobit the father Tobit is concerned about his son Tobias, who has not yet returned from a trip. Tobit wonders, "Perhaps he has been detained [κατεσχέθη] there?" (Tob 10:2 Sinaiticus).

There are numerous occurences of κατέχω in the New Testament, including several appearances in Paul's letters. In Romans, Paul talks about the *suppression* of truth by the depraved (Rom 1:18), and the way the law once *restrained* (i.e., held captive) believers (7:6). In 1–2 Corinthians reference is made to *possession* of property (1 Cor 7:30; 2 Cor 6:10) and *adherence* to tradition (1 Cor 11:2; 15:2). In Philemon, Paul mentions wanting to *retain* the service of Onesimus (Phlm 13). And in 1 Thessalonians, Paul tells the Thessalonians to *hold on tightly* to what is good (1 Thess 5:21). So κατέχω is not a term restrictively used in apocalyptic discourse.[63]

---

63. The verb κατέχω does not appear in Rev; in Daniel it is found in chapter seven, but only in

In 2 Thessalonians 2:6–7, Paul gives it a kind of technical sense by referring to it as an entity that holds onto the man of lawlessness. The man of lawlessness is eventually free to operate, once the restrainer is out of the equation, so to speak.

Again, the identity and nature of the restrainer and the restraining situation is left rather vague in 2 Thessalonians, as also is the set of circumstances that *remove* the restrainer.[64] If the restrainer is viewed as a *good* force, this means that it has served the role of stopping the man of lawlessness and fails to keep him in check. If the restrainer is viewed as an *evil* force, it supports the man of lawlessness but has held it at bay until the right time. The word κατέχω alone is not decisive in this matter; instead, scholars have relied on the context of 2 Thessalonians and this text in relation to other biblical and extrabiblical texts to consider the most persuasive interpretive options.

We now turn to consider the unfolding and ongoing academic discussion and debate regarding the restrainer.[65] We will outline this discussion with three categories in mind: restrainer as Roman Empire, restrainer as Paul, and restrainer as a spiritual power (whether God or an angel).[66]

RESTRAINER AS THE ROMAN EMPIRE

The view with the longest history is the one that connects the restrainer to the Roman Empire, especially to the positive impact of Roman efficiency and justice. For example, John Wesley makes this comment in his "Explanatory Notes": "The power of the Roman emperors," what keeps the "son of perdition" at bay, is the successive "potentate" coming after Rome, that is, "the emperors, heathen or Christian; the kings, Goths or Lombards;

---

the sense of the holy people coming to *possess* the kingdom (Dan 7:18–22); see Malherbe, *Thessalonians*, 433.

64. One peculiar feature of this text is the way that Paul refers to *the restraining thing* (neuter) in 2:6, and then *the restraining man* (masculine) in 2:7. It would appear then that he switches from referring to an event or phenomenon involving the holding back of the man of lawlessness to then go on to speak of the restrainer in more personal terms. Why Paul would do this is not clear.

65. For a helpful overview, see P. Metzger, *Katechon: II Thess 2,1–12 im Horizont apokalyptischen Denkens* (Berlin: de Gruyter, 2005), 15–48.

66. It is worth mentioning here at the outset that Boring posits that the author of 2 Thess did not have a specific figure or entity in mind, choosing instead to offer a "provocatively obscure" reference. The point was not to identify a named restrainer but rather to expose the ongoing battle between good and evil. Indeed, "The restraining power will not hold back the final revelation of evil forever. God will remove this restraining force, and the eschatological drama will begin" (Boring, *1 and 2 Thessalonians*, 276–78, quote from p. 278). See also L. J. L. Peerbolte, "The κατέχον/κατέχων of 2 Thess. 2:6–7," *NovT* 49.2 (1997): 138–50.

the Carolingian or German emperors."[67] F. F. Bruce also finds this view appealing, as he points back to Tertullian: "What is this but the Roman state, whose removal when it has been divided among ten kings will bring an Antichrist?" (cf. *De resurrectione carnis* 24).[68] With respect to Paul's view of the positive work of the government, Bruce appeals to Romans 13:3–4. Paul's ministry benefited from fair trials (cf. Acts 18:12–17) and overall sensible judgment. So Bruce considers it possible that τὸ κατέχον refers to the Roman Empire, and ὁ κατέχων refers to the emperor in particular. So Bruce interprets 2 Thessalonians 2:6–7 in this way: "He knew that Roman rule would not last forever, and that its benevolent neutrality could not be counted on indefinitely, but in the present situation a welcome curb was placed on the forces of lawlessness."[69] Earl Richard offers a similar perspective, treating 2 Thessalonians (as well as Romans and 1 Peter) as representative of an early Christian view that considered the positive dimensions of government, operating according to a "divinely instituted principle of order, the organs of statecraft which keep the forces of chaos at bay."[70] David Williams offers a more generic version of this view (similar to Wesley), considering the possibility that Paul had in mind not Rome *per se* but "the principle of law and order, of which Roman rule was but one instance and of which there have been many others."[71]

RESTRAINER AS PAUL

One view popular in the middle of the twentieth century was that Paul was referring to *himself* as the restrainer. Because this view has not been affirmed by many in the last few decades, we will not go into all the points for and against this interpretation, but it is at least worth noting.

---

67. Wesley's Explanatory Notes; see www.ccel.org/ccel/wesley/notes.i.xv.iii.html.

68. Bruce, *Thessalonians*, 171.

69. Bruce, *Thessalonians*, 172.

70. Richard, *First and Second Thessalonians*, 352; cf. Richard's excursus on the interpretation of the restrainer (340).

71. D. J. Williams, *1 and 2 Thessalonians*, NIBC (Peabody, MA: Hendrickson, 1999), 127. Interestingly, J. Munck dismisses this possibility out of hand, as it is "out of the question that a Christian of the first century can have taken such a positive attitude toward imperial Rome, which was held in Christian apocalyptic thought to be the incarnation of Antichrist" (*Paul and the Salvation of Mankind*, trans. F. Clarke [London: SCM, 1959], 37). P. Metzger argues that the restrainer is indeed the Roman Empire, but does not see this as a positive entity that helps the church *per se* (*Katechon*, 15–47). Similarly, Krodel describes the restrainer and the restraining activity as "the all-encompassing religious-political claims of society"; Krodel does not interpret this as a benevolent force that restrains, but more as an antecedent to ὁ ἄνομος (G. Krodel, "The 'Religious Power of Lawlessness' (*Katechon*) as Precursor of the 'Lawless One' (*Anomos*) 2 Thess 2:6–7," *Currents in Theology and Missions* 17.6 (1990): 446.

As far as I can tell, Oscar Cullmann was the first to make this proposal in modern scholarship.[72] This was also taken up by Munck.[73] Munck follows Cullmann in arguing that Paul believed the parousia would not come before the completion of the preaching of the Gospel to the gentiles.[74] In the last thirty years, however, this view has not attracted support among scholars. First, it is unclear why Paul would be so cryptic about his own ministry. Second, even if Paul were calling himself the restrainer, he would then be predicting his own demise (i.e., being "taken out of the way"). Yet as Terence Donaldson points out, Paul expected to live until the parousia.[75]

RESTRAINER AS GOD

Some interpreters have advocated for understanding the restrainer in terms of divine action. One obstacle to adopting this view would be making sense of the restrainer being removed—what could this mean (2:7)? Furthermore, one might wonder why God would release the man of lawlessness in any case. Malherbe nevertheless argues that this view is possible in view of Jewish thought where God is understood as the proto-logical agent and the one who moves all of history.[76] In the 1970s, Roger Aus argued that Paul's inspiration for the language of the restrainer came from Isaiah 66:9 and the use of the Hebrew verb עצר.

> [5] Hear the word of the LORD, you who tremble at his word: Your own people who hate you and reject you for my name's sake have said, "Let the LORD be glorified, so that we may see your joy"; but it is they who shall be put to shame. [6] Listen, an uproar from the city! A voice from the temple! The voice of the LORD, dealing retribution to his enemies!
>
> [7] Before she was in labor she gave birth; before her pain came upon her she delivered a son. [8] Who has heard of such a thing? Who has seen such things? Shall a land be born in one day? Shall a nation

---

72. O. Cullmann, "'Le caractère eschatologique du devoir missionnaire et de la conscience apostolique de S. Paul," *RHPR* 16 (1936): 210–45.

73. See Munck, *Paul and the Salvation of Mankind*, 36–42.

74. See Munck, *Paul and the Salvation of Mankind*, 38; Munck tries to align this view of 2 Thess 2 with Mark 13 and Matt 24 (pp. 38–39).

75. T. L. Donaldson, *Paul and the Gentiles: Remapping the Apostle's Convictional World* (Minneapolis: Fortress, 1997), 229.

76. Malherbe, *Thessalonians*, 433. Rarely is there any interest among biblical scholars in parallels from the Greco-Roman world on this matter, but in passing Malherbe makes mention of Plutarch's *On the Delay of the Final Judgment* (433).

be delivered in one moment? Yet as soon as Zion was in labor she delivered her children. ⁹ Shall I open the womb and not deliver? says the LORD; shall I, the one who delivers, shut [עָצַר] the womb? says your God.

¹⁰ Rejoice with Jerusalem, and be glad for her, all you who love her; rejoice with her in joy, all you who mourn over her—¹¹ that you may nurse and be satisfied from her consoling breast; that you may drink deeply with delight from her glorious bosom. ¹² For thus says the LORD: I will extend prosperity to her like a river, and the wealth of the nations like an overflowing stream; and you shall nurse and be carried on her arm, and dandled on her knees. ¹³ As a mother comforts her child, so I will comfort you; you shall be comforted in Jerusalem. ¹⁴ You shall see, and your heart shall rejoice; your bodies shall flourish like the grass; and it shall be known that the hand of the LORD is with his servants, and his indignation is against his enemies. (Isa 66:5–14 NRSV)

While the Septuagint does not use κατέχω here, Aus argues that the Hebrew verb עָצַר aligns with the meaning of κατέχω and refers in Isaiah 66:9 to the idea of God restoring Israel in the use of the imagery of "restraining" childbirth.[77] Furthemore, Aus sees a connection between the hostile attitude of the man of lawlessness and the mention of "enemies" in Isaiah 66:6.[78] He also sees a link to the temple language in Isaiah 66:6. Similar to Cullmann and Munck, Aus (via intertextual links to Isaiah 66) considers "that which is restraining" (2 Thess 2:6) to be the gentile mission.[79] But for Aus the restrainer is not Paul but God himself who alone "determines the course of events."[80] As further evidence, Aus observes how 2 Thessalonians itself posits that God will delude those who reject the truth (2:10).[81] What about the matter of the restrainer being "removed"?

---

77. See Aus, "God's Plan and God's Power," 537–53. The LXX reads differently than the Hebrew: ἰδοὺ ἐγὼ γεννῶσαν καὶ στεῖραν ἐποίησα; "See, was it not I who made the woman who gives birth and the one who is barren?" (NETS).

78. Aus, "God's Plan and God's Power," 539.

79. Aus, "God's Plan and God's Power," 540.

80. Aus, "God's Plan and God's Power," 546.

81. See too Hughes, *Early Christian Rhetoric and 2 Thessalonians*, 60: "It seems logical (insofar as apocalyptic is logical) that God should be the one to restrain someone who is given supernatural power by the Evil One. The activity of restraining in 2.6–7 is perhaps also explained by 2.11–12 where it is clear that God is behind the scenes as the planner and executor of apocalyptic events."

Aus argues that the subject here is not the restrainer but rather the *mystery* of lawlessness.

> The mystery of lawlessness is to be active until its mysterious aspect is removed or disappears. That is, evil or lawlessness has not yet reached its peak. Only then, when it is most intense and apparent to all, will God cease his restraining, the Messiah will come, and the decisive battle between the lawless one and the Lord Jesus will take place.[82]

The idea that the restrainer is God merits consideration for some of the reasons Aus and others have provided.[83] However, few scholars follow Aus's approach, which relies on intertextual links to Isaiah 66. Wanamaker states that Aus's Isaianic reading of 2 Thessalonians 2:6–7 is "more ingenious than credible."[84]

RESTRAINER AS AN ANGEL

While some have argued that the restrainer is God, there is strong support, especially in more recent years, for the idea that the restrainer is an (arch)angel.[85] In 2000 Colin Nicholl made a thorough case in favor of identifying the restrainer with Jewish tradition regarding the archangel Michael.[86] First, Nicholl identifies the numerous places where Michael is mentioned in Jewish tradition to highlight his prominence. For example, 1 Enoch 20 lists protective angels including Uriel, Raphael, Saraqael, Gabriel, Remiel, and Michael, the last one being "he that is set over the best part of mankind and over chaos" (20:4 [*APOT* 2:201]). Nicholl describes Michael as the chief angel given the task of protecting Israel, often portrayed as central to events surrounding the eschaton.[87]

---

82. Aus, "God's Plan and God's Power," 551.

83. S. K. Tonstad has argued for the identification of the restrainer with God based on textual connections to Isa 14:12–20 and Hab 2:3; see "The Restrainer Removed: A Truly Alarming Thought (2 Thess 2:1–12)," *HBT* 29.2 (2007): 133–51. Note also that C. E. Powell advocates for identifying the restrainer with the Holy Spirit, partly with appeal to advocacy from early Christians such as Severian of Gabala, Theodore of Mopsuestia, and Theodoret ("The Identity of the 'Restrainer' in 2 Thessalonians 2:6–7," *BibSac* 154 [1997]: 320–32).

84. Wanamaker, *Thessalonians*, 251. Brown also advocates for reading 2 Thess 2:6–7 in the light of Isa 66, but urges that Aus was focusing in the wrong place. Instead, Brown presses for a link to Isa 66:17 "which depicts false worshippers led by a shaman or wizard who fully conforms to our view of the τὸ κατέχον or ὁ κατέχων" (Brown, "The Intertextuality of Isaiah 66.17 and 2 Thessalonians 2.7," 269.

85. Marshall, *1 and 2 Thessalonians*, 199–200; Menken, *2 Thessalonians*, 113.

86. C. Nicholl, "Michael, the Restrainer Removed (2 Thess 2:6–7)," *JTS* 51.1 (2000): 27–53.

87. Nicholl, "Michael, the Restrainer Removed," 33–34; see e.g., T. Levi 5:5–6; 1QM

Nicholl begins with 2 Thessalonians 2:4's reliance on Daniel 11:36–37 and the overall vision of a great battle (Dan 10:1). Here Michael serves to oppose the power of evil. Daniel is told of the hostility of the prince of Persia and how Michael was dispatched to keep this king from causing problems (10:11–14). In terms of Michael's work as a "restrainer," Nicholl appeals to the magical papyri where on one occasion κατέχω is used to describe Michael's resistance to the devil.[88]

When it comes to the *removal* of this angelic restrainer, Nicholl explains that this happens in God's foreordained timing to allow for an "unequalled tribulation" that will test God's people.[89] This scenario explains the masculine ὁ κατέχων, but what about τὸ κατέχον? Nicholl imagines this could refer to the will of God or perhaps the army of heaven.[90] Ultimately he believes that the masculine and neuter terms need not be neatly separated and most likely refer to the same thing. That is, Paul could refer in the masculine form to Michael and in the neuter to Michael's activities (making the grammatical gender differences superfluous).[91]

CONCLUSION

There is much about 2 Thessalonians that will remain a mystery to modern readers who are not privy to information and assumptions that Paul (presumably) already shared with the original letter recipients. The topic of the restrainer has been vigorously debated and argued for centuries, mostly based on impressions and hunches. Those theories that have searched for scriptural links that can explain the language of restraining seem to be on more solid ground in terms of evidence, although Aus's appeal to Isaiah 66 has not convinced many interpreters today. Much more appealing is Nicholl's identification of the restrainer with the archangel Michael, a figure prominent in Daniel 10–12 (a text that certainly influenced 2 Thess overall) and important to Jewish apocalyptic tradition in general. While the restrainer conundrum is not considered "solved," still

---

9:14–16. So Nicholl explains, "This pre-eminence of Michael in contemporary Jewish thought, especially as *archistrategos*, opponent of Satan and protector of God's people, renders him an especially plausible candidate for the role of 'restrainer'" (35).

88. Nicholl, "Michael, the Restrainer Removed," 39–40.

89. Nicholl, "Michael, the Restrainer Removed," 50.

90. Nicholl, "Michael, the Restrainer Removed," 51.

91. Nicholl, "Michael, the Restrainer Removed," 51–52. Weima has found Nicholl's argumentation persuasive, especially the resonances with Dan 10–12. See Weima's helpful excursus on this subject, *1–2 Thessalonians*, 567–77, and on Michael in particular see pp. 574–77; cf. also Shogren, *Thessalonians*, 287–88.

the archangel Michael theory appears to be the one that satisfies the most exegetical problems.

The ἄτακτοι: *Meaning and Situations*

While the restrainer discussion is one of the more perplexing issues in the study of 2 Thessalonians, the issue of the ἄτακτοι seems to be more important, because it both takes up more space in the letter (3:6–15) and appears to be a driving concern of the letter itself, a social problem that Paul is eager to resolve. The adjective ἄτακτος does not occur in this section, but the adverb ἀτάκτως does (twice: vv. 6, 11) and so does the verb ἀτακτέω (v. 7), describing the people with whom Paul is concerned. Paul offers a stern and clear warning for believers to distance themselves from these ἄτακτοι (v. 6). Not only are they bad examples but they seem to be causing community conflict (v. 12), not least by undermining the teachings of Paul (v. 14). They are not to be ousted (v. 15), but Paul is urgently concerned for this problem to be resolved immediately.

We will note the unusual nature of this language and its debated meanings in 2 Thessalonians 3:6–15 in a moment. Here it is important to observe the adjective ἄτακτος employed in 1 Thessalonians 5:14 where Paul seems to make passing reference to a need for admonishment for certain "idle" or "unruly" people. We chose to not discuss this matter in relation to 1 Thessalonians because the matter is given little space or attention in 1 Thessalonians itself. Still, there must be some connection between 1 Thessalonians and 2 Thessalonians on this matter. It is the consensus of Thessalonian scholarship that the ἄτακτοι appear as a problem in the situation that gave rise to 1 Thessalonians, but either it was a small problem or Paul failed to understand its gravity or potential impact. In any case, it grows to become a major thorn in the community's flesh by the time 2 Thessalonians was written.

The ἀτακτ- word group occurs rarely in the New Testament. It is only found in 1 Thessalonians 5:14 and 2 Thessalonians 3:6, 7, 11. Moreover, it only occurs once in the LXX (see below). Its basic meaning is clear. The root τακτ* means "order" or "arrangement." When the negative prefix is added (α-), it obviously means "disorder." For example, note Proverbs 30:27 LXX: "The grasshopper is without a king; yet they march orderly [εὐτάκτως] at the command of one" (NETS). The cognate τάγμα can be found in 1 Corinthians 15:23 to refer to eschatological events happening in their proper order.

This word group is often found in military situations. Josephus, for example, refers to a scenario where a group of soldiers were spooked and left their trenches in a state of disorder (ἄτακτοι), losing both their focus and any hope of victory (*Ant.* 15.150; cf. *J.W.* 1.382; 2.517; 3.113; 6.255). Philo uses this word group in reference to alignment and cooperation. In a discourse where he sets out to demonstrate that the soul (and reason) are necessary to keep the body on track, so he offers this illustration: "If a charioteer in the contest of the horse-race were to quit his chariot, is it not inevitable that the course of the free horses would be disorderly and irregular [ἄτακτον καὶ πλημμελῆ]?" (*Det.* 141; cf. *Agr.* 74).

Ceslas Spicq notes that the τακτ- word group is sometimes found in philosophical texts that link disorderliness to "passions" and moral instability (see T. Naph. 2.9).[92] Spicq also quotes Diodorus Siculus who compares the unrestrained with animals: "Settling down into an *unruly* and beastlike life and go[ing] out to various pastures at random."[93] It is this nuance of ἄτακτος that inspires Spicq to imagine that when Paul exhorts the ἄτακτοι, he is calling out those who

> free themselves from the rule of community life. One thinks of sins against brotherly love, a propensity to favor discord, a refusal to accept the customs or discipline of the church. Certain "troubled" ones seem particularly stormy, befuddled types who disturb the peace. At any rate, "their walk is not in line" (Gal 2:14). They are "culpable" and probably stubborn.[94]

Spicq follows a certain interpretation of the τακτ- word group that presumes that these ἄτακτοι were consciously, willfully, even deviously rebellious. This is plausible, but it is certainly not the only possibility. Moulton and Milligan observe the common use of the τακτ- word group in relation to apprentices who must sign a contract that will curtail delinquency.[95] When it comes to this language in 1–2 Thessalonians, we can start with the basic sense that the ἀτακτ- word group refers to some sense of disorder or disarray, as also suggested in the one appearance in the LXX:

---

92. C. Spicq, "ἀτακτέω," *TLNT* 1:224–25.
93. Diodorus Siculus, *Bibliotheca historica* 1.8.1; *TLNT* 1:225.
94. *TLNT* 1:226.
95. MM 89–90; see P.Oxy II 275, P.Oxy IV 725.

Those women who had recently been arrayed for marriage abandoned the bridal chambers prepared for wedded union, and, neglecting proper modesty, in a disorderly [ἄτακτον] rush flocked together in the city. (3 Macc 1:19 NRSV)

We will now turn to scholarly scenarios regarding what this language means in the context of 2 Thessalonians, particularly situations where certain ἄτακτοι have become a cause for concern in the community and needed to be called out in 2 Thessalonians.[96]

THE IDLE AND THE END OF THE WORLD

One of the most popular theories throughout history has been that it was eschatological anticipation of the end of the world that led these ἄτακτοι to forsake normal labor.[97] Howard Marshall, while recognizing that one can only guess at the underlying situation, finds it plausible that some gave up on work due to the belief that the final judgment was imminent, and thus work was futile.[98] They acted in view of an *imminent eschatology*, the anticipation of a soon-coming, but still future parousia.

Another possibility would involve an *overrealized eschatology*; such a view is proposed by G. K. Beale. Beale theorizes that some stopped their work because they believed that the final age had *already* come, perhaps in a spiritual way. With that mentality, they became convinced that work was not necessary because they had entered a kind of eternal Sabbath rest. As Beale explains, "Some of the readers apparently believed that the pains associated with work (and work itself) had ceased because of the last Adam's final coming and their 'spiritual' experience of final resurrection."[99] Similarly, Menken proposes that some believed that they were living in a kind of new Eden age and did not fall under the labor expectation

---

96. We will focus primarily on the scholarly theories of those who consider 2 Thess Pauline (and not a late first-century forgery), because under the assumption of authenticity contextual theories tend to be more detailed and argued more thoroughly. Put the other way around, when 2 Thess is considered a forgery and its historical situation (largely) a fabrication, then situational theories pertaining to 2 Thess 3:6–15 especially tend to be speculative. It ought to be noted that most scholars adhering to pseudonymity treat this passage as a rhetorical strategy that reinforces apostolic tradition. E.g., see Y. Redalie, "Work with One's Hands," in *Paul and the Heritage of Israel*, ed. D. P. Moessner et al. (London: Bloomsbury, 2012), 282–89; M. Crüsemann, "'Wer nicht arbeiten will, soll auch nicht essen': Sozialgeschichtliche Beobachtungen zu 2 Thess 3,6–13," in *Essen und Trinken in der Bibel*, ed. M. Geiger et al. (Gütersloh: Gütersloher, 2009), 212–23; for a helpful methodological discussion, see Boring, *1 and 2 Thessalonians*, 296–97.

97. See Best, *Thessalonians*, 334; see too Bruce, *Thessalonians*, 209.

98. Marshall, *Thessalonians*, 219.

99. Beale, *1–2 Thessalonians*, 251.

mentioned in Genesis 3:17–19, because that former expectation had been annulled.[100]

The advantage of and attraction to these eschatologically centered approaches is that they try to integrate the ἄτακτοι problem with the main concern of 2 Thessalonians, which is fear regarding the day of the Lord (2 Thess 2:2). But many scholars find it strange that Paul does not directly link the ἄτακτοι problem to eschatological expectation or enthusiasm. Therefore, while it could be related, it is also conceivable that it is a separate problem.

(NON-)WORK AND PATRONAGE

While eschatological-centered approaches have been most popular in Thessalonian scholarship throughout history, in 1988 Ronald Russell challenged this perspective and argued in favor of a more socially oriented origin and context for the development of these nonworking believers. Russell argued that certain social and economic factors could have been at work.[101] He imagines that the scenario could have involved poorer members of the community depending on the more well-to-do, perhaps due to limited employment opportunities.[102]

Not long after Russell's publication, Bruce Winter furthered this sociological approach.[103] Winter appreciated that Russell pointed to patronage as the context for the ἄτακτοι issue, but Winter offers more detailed information about the patron-client relationship and what sort of circumstances may have led to the ἄτακτοι situation in Thessalonica. He imagines it possible that nonworking clients were bound up with the concerns of their benefactors and so did not do their own duty for the civic good by being self-sufficient and also "seek[ing] the welfare of their city by having the wherewithal to do good to others."[104] In view of this scenario, how should we understand Paul's concern that these ἄτακτοι are

---

100. See Menken, *2 Thessalonians*, 130–41.

101. Russell, "The Idle in 2 Thess 3:6–12," *NTS* 34 (1988): 105–19.

102. See Russell, "The Idle in 2 Thess 3:6–12," 108, 112. In the early and middle twentieth century there was consideration of whether some had rejected work because of a general cultural disdain toward manual labor, but this theory has been thoroughly debunked; only elites presented such a view, but the believers in Thessalonica would have been laborers themselves with no such assumptions. For an example of scholarship supporting such a theory see W. Bienert, *Die Arbeit nach der Lehre der Bibel. Eine Grundlegung evangelischer Socialethik* (Stuttgart: Evangelisches Verlagswerk, 1954), 270–72. For a refutation, see Winter, "'If a Man Does Not Wish to Work,'" 304–5.

103. Winter, "'If a Man Does Not Wish to Work,'" 303–15.

104. Winter, "'If a Man Does Not Wish to Work,'" 314. A helpful exegetical discussion, reliant on Winter, can be found in Witherington, *Thessalonians*, 247–49.

"busybodies"? Gene Green argues that the issue is not laziness, gossip, or neighborhood meddling. Rather, the issue is "the involvement of the clients in public assembly where they supported the causes of their patrons, entangling themselves in issues that were properly none of their concern. At issue is their political participation in favor of their patron."[105]

DISORDER IN THE ASSOCIATION

Richard Ascough has argued that the Thessalonian believing community was probably a voluntary association that mass converted to following Jesus. Thus they continued to operate like an association as a Jesus community. In relation to 1 Thessalonians 5:14 and the reference to certain ἄτακτοι, Ascough believes that this language can be understood in such a context.[106] He notes that there is inscriptional evidence that voluntary associations had to deal with "disorderly behavior" and managed these incidents with fines and other penalties. Association members could cause disturbances such as fights, interruptions, and harm toward others, incidents that occurred not infrequently during communal meals and celebrations. From this perspetive, Ascough argues, these disorderly men were not usurping leadership but rather distracted the community during worship.[107] Paul was not promoting traditional association punishments in such circumstances but instead encouraged more gentle and affirming rebuke.[108]

Ascough's appeal to the context of the voluntary association is intriguing but thus far difficult to prove. If Ascough is right about the Thessalonian church deriving from a single guild, then his comments about the use of the ἄτακτ- word group could well be true. However, it should be noted that this terminology is found in wide-ranging social scenarios.

ITINERANT EVANGELISTS

In the early 1990s, J. M. G. Barclay offered his own scenario that could account for these ἄτακτοι. Influenced by a proposal first made by E. von Dobschütz,[109] Barclay imagines that some Thessalonians gave up on their normal work to engage in intensive evangelism. Barclay writes,

---

105. Green, *Thessalonians*, 351.
106. See Ascough, "Thessalonian Christian Community," 318–19.
107. See R. S. Ascough, "Of Memories and Meals: Greco-Roman Associations and the Early Jesus-Group at Thessalonikē," in Narallah, Bakirtzis, and Friesen, *From Roman to Early Christian Thessalonikē*, 60.
108. Ascough, "Of Memories and Meals," 60–61.
109. Dobschütz, *Die Thessalonicher-Briefe*, 180.

"For those whose faith is under attack, a natural reaction is to affirm their faith all the more loudly; if non-believers criticize their failure to worship the gods, they, the believers, become all the more insistent in the scorn they heap on worthless idols."[110]

Barclay reasons that these fervent evangelists may have expected their community to support them financially. Paul responded to this by arguing that these ἄτακτοι ought to respect gainful labor. While Barclay paints an impressive picture of how apocalyptic pressure and fervor could create unique problems, it is unclear how these ἄτακτοι could be called "busybodies."

SELF-APPOINTED APOSTLES

Some have offered the possibility that these Thessalonian ἄτακτοι were not lazy, busy, or misguided but rather *defiant*, establishing their own power as local leaders. Robert Jewett, for example, argues that these were "obstinate resisters of authority" who gave up normal employment and expected community financial support. Here they claimed for themselves "something like apostolic privilege in demanding such support."[111] Gary Shogren affirms Jewett's approach and establishes the following points.

First, Paul's concern over a proper work ethic has to do with ministry leadership and an irreproachable reputation. This makes sense of why he appeals to his own example of independent ministry. Second, the early church clearly dealt with false apostles on a regular basis. We will return to this point in a moment. Third, this hypothesis would make sense of the naming of the ἄτακτοι as "busybodies," those who meddle, in this case who presume to have a say over the lives and decisions of others.[112]

In the Didache we find a striking example of how the church warned against false apostles:

Act toward the apostles and prophets as the gospel decrees. Let every apostle who comes to you be welcomed as the Lord. But he should not remain more than a day. If he must, he may stay one more. But if he stays three days, he is a false prophet. When an apostle leaves, he should take nothing except bread, until he arrives at his night's lodging. If he asks for money, he is a false prophet.[113]

---

110. Barclay, "Conflict in Thessalonica," 522.
111. Jewett, *Thessalonian Correspondence*, 105.
112. See Shogren, *Thessalonians*, 331–35.
113. Didache 11:3–6; translation from M. A. Powell, *Introducing the New Testament* (Grand

David deSilva also finds this type of scenario attractive in view of 2 Thessalonians. He explains that in both situations, warnings are made "to cut down on the abuses of local church support by wandering spiritualists. They might have been the self-appointed spiritual directors of the community who gave up their mundane occupations to devote themselves full-time to regulating the lives (i.e., meddling, being busybodies) of their less spiritual brothers and sisters."[114]

Again, the ἄτακτοι passage in 2 Thessalonians 3:6–15 is one of the most difficult texts in the New Testament insofar as scholars are unsure of what to make of this language, how to relate it to other parts of 2 Thessalonians, and what to presume to be the underlying problems in Thessalonica. Many have taken it for granted that eschatological concerns fueled the abandonment of work for one reason or another. Some today still advocate for this kind of interpretation. Others, however, believe that there is no reason to presume that the abandonment of work is directly related to concerns or beliefs about the day of the Lord. Could it be that the ἄτακτοι situation developed from local economic and social concerns?

My own inkling is that, while we ought to understand better the social reality of middle-first-century Thessalonica, it makes the most sense to interpret the actions of the ἄτακτοι in light of central eschatological concerns in the community. Thus, I am more persuaded by the last view, one that imagines these ἄτακτοι as self-appointed "apostles." It explains Paul's concern over the preservation of Christian tradition, the apostolic example of self-sufficiency, the concern over meddling, and the overall need for reproof.

CONCLUSION

Second Thessalonians has not received the scholarly interest and attention that has been paid to 1 Thessalonians in last century, and thus the exegetical discussions are not as widespread or deep. This paucity of scholarship can probably be attributed to several factors. For one, this letter is one of

---

Rapids: Baker, 2009), 394. The Didache is an early Christian text that probably came into existence in the late first century or early second century CE. See too warnings against false teachers and prophets in Jude 5–16 and 2 Pet 2:1–22.

114. David deSilva mentions this as one possibility, but he does not explicitly commit to this theory (*An Introduction to the New Testament* [Downers Grove, IL: InterVarsity Press, 2004], 549). See too Holland, *Tradition That You Received from Us*, 82.

the shortest texts in the Pauline corpus. Moreover, 2 Thessalonians clearly rehearses many themes and ideas from 1 Thessalonians. Yet perhaps the most significant reason for this relative lack of interest in 2 Thessalonians can be associated with the conclusion of many scholars that this letter is pseudonymous. To some degree we have seen the tide turning toward more attention to 2 Thessalonians in the last couple of decades, almost certainly because of the fresh interest in apocalypticism in early Judaism and early Christianity. Furthermore, we can also trace the developments in biblical scholarship regarding forgery and pseudonymity in antiquity, which has implications for 2 Thessalonians.

When it comes to the key discussions related to the text of 2 Thessalonians, the identity and background of the man of lawlessness and restrainer figures always pique interest and curiosity; however, it is clear that the more weighty subjects concern the meaning of "the day of the Lord has already come" (2:2) and the problem concerning the ἄτακτοι (3:6–15). Both subjects shed light on the socio-historical situation behind this letter.[115]

RECOMMENDED READING

Themes

Bassler, J. M. "Peace in All Ways: Theology in the Thessalonian Letters: A Response to R. Jewett, E. Krentz, and E. Richard." Pages 71–85 in *Pauline Theology, Volume 1: 1 Thessalonians, Philippians, Galatians, Philemon*. Edited by Jouette M. Bassler. Minneapolis: Fortress, 1991.

Donfried, K. P., and I. H. Marshall. *Theology of the Shorter Pauline Letters*. NTT. Cambridge: Cambridge University Press, 1993.

Johnson, A. *1 and 2 Thessalonians*. THNT. Grand Rapids: Eerdmans, 2016.

Interpretation

Barclay, J. M. G. "Conflict in Thessalonica." *CBQ* 55 (1993): 512–30.

Bruce, F. F. *1 and 2 Thessalonians*. WBC. Waco, TX: Word, 1982.

Holland, G. S. *The Tradition That You Received from Us: 2 Thessalonians in the Pauline Tradition*. Hermeneutische Untersuchungen zur Theologie 24. Tübingen: Mohr Siebeck, 1986.

Jewett, R. *The Thessalonian Correspondence: Pauline Rhetoric and Millenarian Piety*. Philadelphia: Fortress, 1986.

---

115. See T. Nicklas, "'Der Tag des Herrn ist schon da' (2 Thess 2:2b): ein Schlüsselproblem zum Verständnis des 2. Thessalonicherbriefs," *HTS* 71.1 (2015): 1–10.

Malherbe, A. J. *The Letters to the Thessalonians*. AB. New York: Doubleday, 2000.

Menken, M. J. J. *2 Thessalonians*. NTR. New York: Routledge, 1994.

Nicholl, C. R. *From Hope to Despair in Thessalonica: Situating 1 and 2 Thessalonians*. SNTSMS 126. Cambridge: Cambridge University Press, 2004.

Russell, R. "The Idle in 2 Thess 3:6–12: An Eschatological or a Social Problem?" *NTS* 34 (1988): 105–19.

Weima, J. A. D., and S. E. Porter. *An Annotated Bibliography of 1 and 2 Thessalonians*. NTTS 26. Leiden: Brill, 1998.

CHAPTER 8

HISTORY OF INTERPRETATION OF 2 THESSALONIANS

INTRODUCTION

The history of the interpretation of 2 Thessalonians must be studied together with that of 1 Thessalonians. Especially from the second century until the Enlightenment, these two letters were read and interpreted in relation to one another. While we will cover 2 Thessalonians more briefly than we did 1 Thessalonians, we will follow the same basic pattern of examining early Christian and patristic theologians, then the Reformation, and finally trends in the modern era of scholarship.

EARLY CHRISTIAN AND PATRISTIC INTERPRETATION

Incidental References to 2 Thessalonians

A wide variety of early theologians gave attention to 2 Thessalonians, often with appeal to snippets as certain relevant themes or topics made this epistle useful for illustration or argumentation. Five theologians appear to have taken special interest in 2 Thessalonians for one reason or another: Irenaeus, Tertullian, Origen, Lactantius, and Augustine. Four trends are apparent when we examine these theologians' appeals to 2 Thessalonians. First, they are drawn to the explicit and vivid depictions of the end times and the powerful emergence and ultimate defeat of the man of lawlessness, often referred to as the "antichrist" in these early texts.[1] Second, they tend to harmonize eschatological material in 2 Thessalonians 1–2

---

1. See, e.g., Hippolytus's *Demonstratio de Christo et Antichristo.*

with material from texts like Daniel, Matthew 24, and Revelation. Third, 2 Thessalonians often appears in polemical and anti-heretical texts such as Irenaeus's *Against Heresies* and Origen's *Against Celsus.*

Most of the time, these early theologians focused on the second chapter of 2 Thessalonians, with some further appeals to 1:5–10.[2] Once in a while a particularly important doctrinal statement or moral exhortation might be cited from 2 Thessalonians,[3] but the only place where further weight was given pertains to the ἄτακτοι and the matter of honest and community-honoring work.[4]

Early Christian Commentaries

The same early theologians who wrote commentaries on 1 Thessalonians also did so for 2 Thessalonians. Theodoret of Cyrus's commentary is short, less than ten pages, and consists of straightforward textual explanation.[5] Theodoret describes 2 Thessalonians as a letter concerned with "instruction on consummation."[6] As expected he dwells on 2 Thessalonians 2 and the material related to the antichrist.[7] He posits that the antichrist is not portrayed as a supernatural being but a mere man. He includes a careful discussion of the restrainer. As far as Theodoret is concerned, the restrainer is not the Roman Empire, but more likely some form of divine control.[8] As for the "mystery of lawlessness," Theodoret disagrees with those who identify this as Nero; rather, he believes that Paul had in mind heresies that have infected churches.[9]

Theodore of Mopsuestia wrote a much longer commentary on 2 Thessalonians.[10] He gives ample attention to its background and situation. Theodore underscores a context where Paul intended to give perspective and encouragement to beleagured believers as they persevered in the face of increasingly taxing trials.[11] Theodore imagines a scenario where a heresy

---

2. See Irenaeus, *Haer.* 4.400, 499, 502; 5.25; Tertullian, *Marc.* 5.731–38; *Scorp.* 93; *Res.* 170; Origen, *Cels.* 2.115; 3.36; 6.45, 236; Lactantius, *Inst.* 7.17.4; *Epit.* 66.7–8; Augustine, *Letter* 199; *Grat.* 42.21; *Civ.* 20.12–19.

3. Augustine had a fondness for 2 Thess 3:1–2, where Paul asks the Thessalonians to pray for his ministry; he also repeatedly referred to the statement "not all have faith" (3:2). See *C. Jul.* 6.24.80; *Grat.* 25.13; *Homily* 127.8; 175.1; 265.2.

4. Tertullian, *Pud.* 18.11; *Marc.* 5.16.7

5. Hill, *Theodoret.*

6. Hill, *Theodoret,* 127.

7. Hill, *Theodoret,* 128–29.

8. Hill, *Theodoret,* 128–29.

9. Hill, *Theodoret,* 129.

10. Greer, *Theodore of Mopsuestia.*

11. Greer, *Theodore of Mopsuestia,* 495.

spread by false teachers from the outside has been assimilated into parts of the church. Furthemore, the ἄτακτοι have become a larger problem.[12] So Paul wrote 2 Thessalonians as a powerful word of encouragement: "He writes this second letter first [of all] to praise them because they had not been conquered in struggling against all the attacks of their adversaries."[13]

Theodore slows down in 2 Thessalonians 2 to address eschatological matters with more care. In relation to 2:2–4, Theodore explains that Paul felt the need to remind the Thessalonians that the end would not happen before the antichrist comes.[14] Theodore denies the possibility that the antichrist described here is Satan (based on 2 Thess 2:9). As for the ἄτακτοι, Theodore points out that Paul was not trying to say that Christian leaders must work (in manual labor) for their pay; in 1 Corinthians 9 Paul notes how Jesus made a provision that gospel laborers could expect material support from the church. Instead, Paul was admonishing the idle, he who "by living idly stirs up the life of other people inquisitively."[15] One of Theodore's concluding insights from his commentary is in reference to 2 Thessalonians 3:13 (ὑμεῖς δέ, ἀδελφοί, μὴ ἐγκακήσητε καλοποιοῦντες):

> [P]ursue your own work and do not abandon good work because of
> the wickedness of others. Even though those people are perverse in
> their own purpose, you will have an appropriate reward because of
> your purpose in supplying their needs.[16]

Ambrosiaster's commentary on 2 Thessalonians is, like Theodoret's, rather brief. In his preliminary statement, he notes that 2 Thessalonians addresses the key topics of "destruction of the Roman Empire, the appearance of the antichrist, the condemnation and the tribulation of some of the brethren."[17] In his interpretation of chapter two, he shows awareness of differing theological views on hell and takes Paul's statement in 2:9 to reinforce the idea of ongoing conscious torment of the wicked.[18] He also believes that Paul's eschatological statements in 2 Thessalonians predict the demise of Rome, which subsequently would be restored by the anti-

---

12. Greer, *Theodore of Mopsuestia*, 495.
13. Greer, *Theodore of Mopsuestia*, 495.
14. Greer, *Theodore of Mopsuestia*, 505.
15. Greer, *Theodore of Mopsuestia*, 519.
16. Greer, *Theodore of Mopsuestia*, 521.
17. Bray, *Ambrosiaster*, 113.
18. Bray, *Ambrosiaster*, 114.

christ.[19] Furthermore, Ambrosiaster associated the "mystery of lawlessness with the persecution and evil work initiated by Nero, but carried on in the nefarious work of Diocletian and Julian."[20]

I would be remiss not to address Chrysostom's homilies on 2 Thessalonians. In his first homily on 2 Thessalonians, Chrysostom engages with the eschatological concerns that the Thessalonians were facing, namely, the idea that "the resurrection was already past."[21] Chrysostom takes this to mean that the Thessalonians came to believe there was no future final judgment or punishment, that the Thessalonians had been duped by a false teaching they believed came from Paul. The apostle then offers in this second letter a corrective teaching with the purpose of freeing them from "childish fables and from old women's fooleries."[22] In his second homily, Chrysostom reflects on the apocalyptic tone of 2 Thessalonians and its statements on final judgment.[23] In his third homily he talks about the man of lawlessness, presuming him to be a mortal.[24] Homily four makes reference to Nero as a "type of Antichrist," the famous emperor presuming himself to be divine.[25] In his last homily on 2 Thessalonians, Chrysostom waxes about the final exhortations of Paul's short letter, affirming support for the poor with generous alms, caring for those "who are not able to support themselves by the work of their own hands."[26]

In the medieval period, Thomas Aquinas wrote a commentary on 2 Thessalonians, but unfortunately for many years there was no English translation. Francesca Aran Murphy and Morton Gauld created their own translation but have not made it public.[27] More recently, Jeremy Holmes produced his own translation of Aquinas's "Lectures on 2 Thessalonians."[28] Our discussion here will be based on Holmes's translation.

In Aquinas's first lecture, he addresses the purpose and introduction of the letter, especially the apostle's concern for the Thessalonians' twisted beliefs about the end.[29] Aquinas stops to dwell on the language of

19. Bray, *Ambrosiaster*, 114.
20. Bray, *Ambrosiaster*, 115.
21. See www.ccel.org/ccel/schaff/npnf113.toc.html.
22. Chrysostom, *Homilies on Second Thessalonians*, Homily 1 (*NPNF*1 13:378).
23. Chrysostom, *Homilies on Second Thessalonians*, Homily 2 (*NPNF*1 13:380–84).
24. Chrysostom, *Homilies on Second Thessalonians*, Homily 3 (*NPNF*1 13:386).
25. Chrysostom, *Homilies on Second Thessalonians*, Homily 4 (*NPNF*1 13:389).
26. Chrysostom, *Homilies on Second Thessalonians*, Homily 5 (*NPNF*1 13:394).
27. See Murphy, "Thomas' Commentaries," 168.
28. J. Holmes, "Lectures on 2 Thessalonians: A New Translation," *Letter & Spirit* 5 (2009): 211–38.
29. Holmes, "Lectures on 2 Thessalonians," 213.

"faith" and "charity" (or love) in 2 Thessalonians 1. According to Aquinas, faith for Paul is a divine gift "through which God dwells in us."[30] Christians move through various stages from knowledge to devotion to *inhaesio* ("adherence").[31] As for charity, Aquinas notes how this is a distinguishing mark of the Christian life, because God himself is charity (1 John 4:16).

Commenting on 2 Thessalonians 1, Aquinas instructs concerning the formative role of trials and tribulations. For the wicked they serve the purpose of instilling fear, while for the righteous they serve to "increase merit," a notion he supports by appeal to Paul's comment that suffering serves to make one worthy of the kingdom.[32]

In his second lecture, Aquinas develops his understanding of the nature of divine punishment and reward. He comments that 2 Thessalonians 2 relates to "what will happen in the future as regards the dangers to the Church that will arise during the time of the Antichrist."[33] Aquinas writes at length on curiosities related to the rebellion and the antichrist. Regarding the former, he addresses the question of timing: Why did this not happen under the Roman Empire? He answers by saying that Pope Leo taught that the rebellion does not involve a "temporal" revolt but rather a "spiritual" one.[34] Aquinas similarly addresses the idea that the man of lawlessness will take seat in the "temple." Which one? The Jerusalem temple had been gone for many centuries, Aquinas acknowledges. He notes that some scholars believe that 2 Thessalonians presumes (and thus predicts) the temple's rebuilding. Others take the reference to "temple" to be metaphorical—i.e., the church.[35]

We have introduced the medieval *Glossa Ordinaria* in chapter four (p. 157) with an interest in its treatment of the Thessalonian correspondence. Here we will just add that 2 Thessalonians is given significant attention; so much so that Kevin L. Hughes comments that it "provides the most thorough treatment of the letter in the commentary tradition thus far."[36]

---

30. Holmes, "Lectures on 2 Thessalonians," 214.
31. Holmes, "Lectures on 2 Thessalonians," 214.
32. Here Aquinas cited in support Luke 24:26 and Rom 8:17.
33. Holmes, "Lectures on 2 Thessalonians," 219.
34. Holmes, "Lectures on 2 Thessalonians," 222.
35. Holmes, "Lectures on 2 Thessalonians," 223.
36. K. L. Hughes, *Constructing Antichrist: Paul, Biblical Commentary, and the Development of Doctrine in the Early Middle Ages* (Washington, DC: Catholic University of America Press, 2005), 222.

REFORMATION ERA

Luther's preface to 2 Thessalonians is brief, and we can easily cite it here:

> In the First Epistle, Paul had solved for the Thessalonians the question of the Last Day, telling them that it would come quickly, as a thief in the night. Now it is wont to happen that one question always gives birth to another, because of misunderstanding; and so the Thessalonians understood that the Last Day was already close at hand. Thereupon, Paul writes this epistle and explains himself. In chapter 1, he comforts them with the eternal reward that will come to their faith and their patience in afflictions of every kind, and with the punishment that will come to their persecutors in eternal pain. In chapter 2, he teaches that before the Last Day, the Roman Empire must pass away and Antichrist rise up before God in the Church and seduce the unbelieving world with false doctrines and signs until Christ shall come and destroy him by His glorious advent, first slaying him with spiritual preaching. In chapter 3, he gives some admonitions, especially that they shall rebuke the idlers, who will not support themselves by their own labor, and if they will not reform, that they shall avoid them; and this is a hard rebuke to the clergy of today.[37]

In this concise statement, it is difficult to ascertain much about how Luther interpreted 2 Thessalonians, except that he believed Paul wrote about the demise of the Roman Empire. We have one extant sermon where Luther preached on 2 Thessalonians 1:3–10.[38] In this sermon, he places special emphasis on how Christians should think about suffering. He observes that from a carnal perspective, Christians appear to be "wretched, tormented, persecuted, unhappy people" because they experience such affliction. Even they themselves may sometimes feel abandoned by God, "for he allows them to remain prostrate under the weight of the cross," and others seemingly live enjoyable and rewarding lives.[39] But 2 Thessalonians teaches that God has promised a great hope for his people. He promises to reward them for their endurance. He writes:

---

37. See www.stepbible.org/?q=version=Luther%7Creference=2Thess.2.9.
38. See J. N. Lenker, *The Precious and Sacred Writings of Martin Luther* (Minneapolis: Lutheran in All Lands, 1903).
39. See Lenker, *Precious and Sacred Writings of Martin Luther*, 381.

O beloved Christians, regard your sufferings as dear and precious. Think not God is angry with you, or has forgotten you, because he allows you to endure these things. They are your great help and comfort, for they show God will be a righteous judge, will richly bless you and avenge you upon your persecutors. Yes, therein you have unfailing assurance. You may rejoice, and console yourselves, believing without a shadow of a doubt that you belong to the kingdom of God, and have been made worthy of it, because you suffer for its sake.[40]

John Calvin's commentary on 2 Thessalonians is, as one expects, detailed, lengthy, and technical. Like Luther, Calvin was fascinated with the theological problem of the suffering of the righteous. Calvin sees 2 Thessalonians 1:5–10 as teaching that the wicked ought not to be insolent in thinking that their occasional prosperity is a signal of divine pleasure.[41] As for the righteous, Calvin understands Paul to be giving them comfort by teaching that God the "just Judge will one day restore peace to the miserable, who are now unjustly harrassed."[42]

Calvin was also careful to explain (regarding 2 Thess 1:5) that Paul claims the benefit of suffering for the kingdom, not that trials *earn* salvation. Believers, Calvin notes, are "polished under God's anvil, inasmuch as, by afflictions, they are taught to renounce the world and to aim at God's heavenly kingdom."[43]

When it comes to the material in 2 Thessalonians 2, Calvin hypothesizes about the historical situation—it well could be that some Thessalonians who received Paul's earlier teachings on the future "were disposed to indulge curiosity" and to speculate "unseasonably" about the exact timing.[44] As for the antichrist, Calvin dismisses immediately any reading related to a return of Nero. In fact, Calvin discourages interpreting Paul's man of lawlessness as a specific individual, although he then immediately tips his hat to the evils of the pope, who has seemingly taken up residence in "God's Temple" in the seat of honor.[45] Rather, the antichrist is an agent of an evil kingdom with representatives in every age.[46]

---

40. Lenker, *Precious and Sacred Writings of Martin Luther*, 382.
41. See John Calvin, *Commentaries on the Epistles of Paul the Apostle to the Philippians, Colossians, and Thessalonians*, trans. J. Pringle (Edinburgh: Calvin Translation Society, 1851), 313.
42. Calvin, *Commentaries on the Epistles of Paul*, 313.
43. Calvin, *Commentaries on the Epistles of Paul*, 314.
44. Calvin, *Commentaries on the Epistles of Paul*, 232.
45. Calvin, *Commentaries on the Epistles of Paul*, 327; cf. too 331.
46. Calvin, *Commentaries on the Epistles of Paul*, 333.

Who or what is the restrainer? Calvin understands that God is in control, and he can see fit to afflict his people for a set period, but ultimately he plans for their redemption.[47]

John Wesley wrote several short notes on 2 Thessalonians. He gave extra attention to Paul's language of "everlasting destruction" (2 Thess 1:9). His view was that the punishment of the wicked is endless because their resistance to God is persistent, "sin and its punishment running parallel throughout eternity itself."[48] This requires the wicked to be separated from God with no hope.

Wesley also treated more extensively the eschatological rebellion (2 Thess 2:3). Wesley saw beginning signs of this apostasy even in the first century, though the antichrist was yet to come. Like Calvin, Wesley highlights the wiles of the pope, whom he calls "the man of sin," doomed to perish eternally himself. Wesley found particularly unsettling (and telling) the pope's use and acceptance of the titles "Most Holy Lord" and "Most Holy Father." For Wesley, this was tantamount to declaring himself divine.[49]

As for the restrainer (see previous chapter, pp. 250–57), Wesley was clear that Paul was referring to the Roman emperor and, by extension, the rule of Rome itself. But across time this is understood by Wesley as "the emperors, heathen or Christian; the kings, Goths or Lombards; the Carolingian or German emperors."[50]

MODERN ERA[51]

2 Thessalonians and the "Delay of the Parousia"

According to Albert Schweitzer, Jesus himself believed the parousia would happen immediately, but it did not.[52] A school of thought exists,

---

47. Calvin, *Commentaries on the Epistles of Paul*, 334.

48. John Wesley, "Notes on St Paul's Second Epistle to the Thessalonians," Wesley Center Online, http://wesley.nnu.edu/john-wesley/john-wesleys-notes-on-the-bible/notes-on-st-pauls-second-epistle-to-the-thessalonians/#Chapter+I.

49. Wesley, "Notes on St Paul's Second Epistle to the Thessalonians."

50. Wesley, "Notes on St Paul's Second Epistle to the Thessalonians."

51. One could easily spend time on how 2 Thess has been used in the development and defense of the rapture doctrine, but we will assume that the discussion in chapter four sufficiently explains the matter in view of the Thessalonian correspondence.

52. See A. Schweitzer, "The Solution of Thoroughgoing Eschatology," in *The Historical Jesus in Recent Research*, ed. J. D. G. Dunn and S. McKnight (Winona Lake, IN: Eisenbrauns, 2005), 6–49; cf. also M. Werner, *The Formation of Christian Dogma* (London: Black, 1957).

popular especially at the beginning of the twentieth century, that treated certain New Testament texts or books as reactionary toward this so-called "delay of the parousia." One of the prime texts of interest has been 2 Peter 3:8–9:

> [8] But do not forget this one thing, dear friends: With the Lord a day is like a thousand years, and a thousand years are like a day. [9] The Lord is not slow in keeping his promise, as some understand slowness. Instead he is patient with you, not wanting anyone to perish, but everyone to come to repentance.

This text has appeared to some like an *apologia* for the nonappearance of the Lord. Thus, the early Christians tended either to press toward an eschatology that was realized in spiritual experiences (e.g., Eph), or to justify the "delay" by emphasis placed on certain crucial intervening events (e.g., 2 Thess). Norman Perrin serves as a model for this approach to the New Testament; regarding 2 Thessalonians Perrin wrote:

> By now Jesus should have come on the clouds of heaven to judge the world, but he had not done so. The Paulinist who wrote 2 Thessalonians meets this problem just as his teacher had, and hence virtually repeats 1 Thessalonians, which he clearly knows well and obviously regards as a tract for his own time and as an answer to the problem he and his church are facing. Yet there are subtle differences between the two letters. Paul himself had expected the parousia in a very short time, whereas the Paulinist knows that it has now been a very considerable time and the parousia is still delayed. So in presenting the scenario for the parousia, the Paulinist attempts to make sense of this delay.[53]

This perspective fell out of favor by the last quarter of the twentieth century because it was based on a certain assumption about the development of thought of the early Christians, an assumption that is difficult to defend.[54] In 1980 Richard Bauckham argued that "the problem of the

---

53. N. Perrin, *New Testament Introduction* (New York: Harcourt Brace Jovanovich, 1974), 134.
54. For examples of those who favored such approaches, see H. Conzelmann, *The Theology of St. Luke* (London: Faber and Faber, 1961); J. A. T. Robinson, *Redating the New Testament* (London: SCM, 1976). For a forceful critique of this perspective, see S. Smalley, "The Delay of the Parousia,"

delay of the *parousia* was the same problem of eschatological delay which had long confronted Jewish apocalyptic eschatology."[55] Indeed, apocalyptic discourse in Jewish tradition has always held in tension "imminence and delay," the point being that building an evolutionary chronology based on transitions from imminence to delay is dubious.[56] More recently Dunn has argued that too much has been put on texts like 2 Thessalonians, situational letters where the context must be more carefully considered: "Neither the early nor the later letters can be treated as universal statements of Paul's eschatological expectation."[57] On the matter of 2 Thessalonians outlining intervening events before the end, Dunn argues that even in 2:5 it is pointed out that this was part and parcel of basic (and early) Christian teaching.[58]

On the subject of the delay of the parousia, the most insightful essay that has been written on the history of interpretation of this subject is by David Aune in 1975.[59] Aune notes how Q and the Synoptics carry a strong interest in the themes of viligance and eschatological watchfulness.[60] Aune finds no evidence of the presumption of an imminent parousia, though he admits "the lack of specificity with regard to the exact date of the parousia made it impossible for its nonoccurrence to become a critical problem at any point in the subsequent history of early Christianity."[61] Overall, Aune finds that any attempt to trace a development in Christian thought on the matter of the parousia in the first or early second centuries is bound to fail, because the relevant evidence is limited. He lists only five pertinent texts from the New Testament (as well as 1 Clem. 23:3, 11–12).[62] He concludes: "It must be observed that even if all of these texts are viewed as direct expressions of the anxiety caused by the delay of the parousia,

JBL 83.1 (1964): 41–54: "I want to suggest that instead of a radical departure from Paul's earlier view of the parousia, the delay of which gave rise to hasty revisions, we are confronted in the Pauline epistles with a homogenous eschatological outlook, in which Paul's own background and intellect, as well as the differing milieux and problems of his readers, cause more or less the same thing to be said in different ways. . . . The differences of eschatological *genre*, in fact, are apparent rather than real" (50, emphasis original). See also the analysis and incisive comments of I. H. Marshall, "Palestinian and Hellenistic Christianity: Some Critical Comments," *NTS* 19 (1973): 271–87.

55. R. J. Bauckham, "The Delay of the Parousia," *TynBul* 31 (1980): 3–36.
56. Bauckham, "Delay of the Parousia, 36.
57. Dunn, *Theology of Paul the Apostle*, 311.
58. Dunn, *Theology of Paul the Apostle*, 312.
59. D. E. Aune, "The Significance of the Delay of the Parousia," in *Current Issues in Biblical and Patristic Interpretation*, ed. G. F. Hawthorne (Grand Rapids: Eerdmans, 1975), 87–109.
60. Aune, "Significance of the Delay of the Parousia," 97–98.
61. Aune, "Significance of the Delay of the Parousia," 98.
62. Aune, "Significance of the Delay of the Parousia," 98.

the infrequency with which the problem comes to the surface may be taken to indicate how generally unimportant the matter actually was.[63]

WHAT'S GOING ON IN 2 THESSALONIANS SCHOLARSHIP?

As we did with 1 Thessalonians (see pp. 170–78), here too we will survey key works related to 2 Thessalonians in the twentieth and twenty-first centuries. Much of this will focus on the late twentieth century and onward, mostly because prior to that, aside from discussions of the authorship of 2 Thessalonians, the letter was neglected and was often treated as an appendage to the study of 1 Thessalonians. Topically, we will consider four trends: rhetoric, authorship, apocalyptic, and the Thessalonian situation.

2 Thessalonians and Rhetoric

In the 1980s and 1990s, scholars took special interest in examining New Testament texts via rhetorical criticism.[64] In 1984 Frank W. Hughes wrote his doctoral dissertation on this,[65] later published as *Early Christian Rhetoric and 2 Thessalonians*.[66] Hughes argues that 2 Thessalonians is an example of deliberative rhetoric, penned by a later pseudepigrapher, in order to correct the misguided "realized eschatology" of certain followers of Paul.[67] Using classical rhetorical divisions, Hughes outlines 2 Thessalonians as follows: *exordium* (1:1–12); *partitio* (2:1–2); *probatio I* (2:3–12); *probatio II* (2:13–15); *peroratio* (2:16–17); *exhortatio* (3:1–15); and postscript (3:16–18).

Robert Jewett also argued in favor of the value of analyzing 2 Thessalonians through rhetorical categories, and he too labeled 2 Thessalonians as "deliberative," though Jewett made a case for 2 Thessalonians being genuine.[68] Charles Wanamaker's 1990 commentary on 1–2 Thessalonians can also be considered an advocate for rhetorical criticism, Wanamaker agreeing with Hughes that 2 Thessalonians "seeks to persuade its readers to adopt a different understanding of the day of the Lord than the one that

---

63. Aune, "Significance of the Delay of the Parousia," 100; cf. 109.

64. See Kennedy, *New Testament Interpretation through Rhetorical Criticism.*

65. F. W. Hughes, "Second Thessalonians as a Document of Early Christian Rhetoric" (PhD diss., Northwestern University, 1984).

66. Hughes, *Early Christian Rhetoric and 2 Thessalonians.*

67. Hughes also wrote an essay on 1 Thess called "The Rhetoric of 1 Thessalonians," in Collins, *Thessalonian Correspondence,* 94–116; see too A. Smith, *Comfort One Another: Reconstructing the Rhetoric and Audience of 1 Thessalonians* (Louisville: Westminster John Knox, 1995).

68. Jewett, *Thessalonian Correspondence.*

they seem to hold and to act against the disruptive influence of the idle."[69] So quickly did this field of study grow that in 1993 Karl Donfried could refer to "an emerging consensus" on the treatment of 2 Thessalonians as "deliberative" and posit that rhetorical criticism helps to open up the intentions of the author more clearly.[70]

Authorship

We have already provided a technical discussion of the scholarship on the authorship question and 2 Thessalonians (see pp. 197–220); here we will briefly point out key studies that have shaped the discussion. Before getting to contemporary scholarship, we must mention the importance of the work of W. Wrede,[71] and we offer its significance (via the aid of Trilling's analysis). Trilling comments that "Wrede's work provided a powerful impulse in scholarship which continues to exercise influence even today."[72] While previously there were no legitimate theories about how one could make sense of 2 Thessalonians as a pseudepigraphal letter separated from 1 Thessalonians by several decades, Wrede supplied such a hypothesis.[73] What Trilling found most convincing from Wrede's argument is the notion that 2 Thessalonians is completely dependent on 1 Thessalonians's structure. Wrede wondered, *Why would the same author, writing to the same community, repeat so much of the same structure and content from a former letter written so recently?*[74] Trilling argues that Pauline scholarship has not put this Wredian line of questioning out of its mind since it was raised.

Trevor Thompson offers an insightful look into an important conversation on 2 Thessalonians that took place at the Thessalonian Seminar of the Society of Biblical Literature in 1983. At that time, Thompson explains, Anglophone scholarship largely supported the authenticity of 2 Thessalonians, though there were exceptions, such as G. Krodel.[75] At this SBL meeting, Edgar Krentz and John C. Hurd were invited to revisit the authorship question, Krentz favoring pseudonymity and Hurd maintaining Pauline authorship. Interestingly, Krentz's paper was not immediately

---

69. Wanamaker, *Thessalonians*, 48. In terms of whether to study Paul's letters through rhetorical interpretation or epistolary analysis, Wanamaker rejects this binary approach; he argues that one may both label 2 Thess as a "letter of advice" and read it as deliberative rhetoric (48).

70. See Donfried, "2 Thessalonians and the Church of Thessalonica," 50.

71. Wrede, *Die Echtheit des zweiten Thessalonicherbriefes*.

72. Trilling, "Die beiden Briefe des Apostels Paulus an die Thessalonicher," 3375 (trans. mine).

73. Trilling, "Die beiden Briefe des Apostels Paulus an die Thessalonicher," 3375.

74. Trilling, "Die beiden Briefe des Apostels Paulus an die Thessalonicher," 3375.

75. Krodel, "2 Thessalonians," 73–96.

published, though his thoughts on the matter did appear in his *Anchor Bible Dictionary* entry.[76] Hurd's arguments appeared over a decade later in a volume entitled *The Earlier Letters of Paul—and Other Studies.*[77] While there are many good, lengthy defenses of Pauline authorship, Thompson is probably correct that Krentz's paper (now published) is still "the most comprehensive and detailed argument against the authenticity of Second Thessalonians in English."[78]

Within a few years of this SBL meeting, Glenn Holland completed his dissertation at the University of Chicago on issues pertaining to the authorship of 2 Thessalonians, later published as *The Tradition That You Received from Us: 2 Thessalonians in the Pauline Tradition.*[79] In this book Holland argues that 2 Thessalonians was written in the late first century when questions were raised by the delay of the parousia.

Finally, mention should be made here of M. J. J. Menken's 1994 commentary on 2 Thessalonians. Menken treats 2 Thessalonians as pseudonymous, and like Holland and Hughes, Menken argues that 2 Thessalonians was written to challenge a problematic realized eschatology.[80]

Apocalyptic

In the middle and late twentieth century we see a surge in interest in biblical scholarship on apocalyptic literature,[81] which created the oppor-

---

76. "Thessalonians, First and Second Epistles to the," *ABD* 6:515–23.

77. See J. C. Hurd, "Concerning the Authenticity of 2 Thessalonians," 135–61. I cannot help but mention, even if only for the "time capsule," as it were, a record of Hurd's participation in an online list-serve in 1999, just as scholars became more comfortable using the internet for academic discussion. In one interesting exchange, Hurd mentions the importance of Wrede, but he concludes that his line of thought is "fatally flawed." He also talks about fallacies in the argument that basically finds the work of a forger whether 2 Thess shows similarities to or differences from 1 Thess. Hurd calls this a "heads-I-win," "tails-you-lose" argument. He writes, "Anything about 2 Thess. which is similar to 1 Thess. is counted as evidence of 'slavish copying'; anything which seems dissimilar is taken as evidence of non authenticity." The crux, Hurd argues, should not involve only a comparison of 1 and 2 Thess but of a general style for Paul and how 2 Thess stacks up against all the Pauline letters in terms of differences. At the end of his post, Hurd requests any information on "papyrus letters with a coda in the handwriting of the one who dictated the body of the letter." Hurd finds this approach potentially illuminating for the study of 2 Thess (esp 3:17). See J. C. Hurd, "Pseudonymity and 2 Thessalonians," https://lists.ibiblio.org/pipermail/corpus-paul/19990502/000478.html.

78. T. Thompson, "A Stone that *Still* Won't Fit," 434.

79. Holland, *Tradition That You Received from Us.*

80. Menken's work is also noteworthy for being the only stand-alone academic commentary on 2 Thess written in the modern period (to my knowledge).

81. See, e.g., D. Russell, *The Method & Message of Jewish Apocalyptic, 200 BC–AD 100* (Philadelphia; Westminster, 1964); J. Schmidt, *Die jüdische Apokalyptik: Die Geschichte ihrer Erforschung von die Anfängen bis zu die Textfunden von Qumran* (Neukirchen-Vluyn: Neukirchener Verlag, 1969); K. Koch, *The Rediscovery of Apocalyptic* (London: SCM, 1972); M. G. Reddish, *Apocalyptic Literature: A Reader* (Peabody, MA: Hendrickson, 1990); J. Collins, *The Apocalyptic Imagination:*

tunity for 2 Thessalonians to be treated as a form (or modified form) of apocalyptic literature. This allowed 2 Thessalonians to break free from being bogged down in conversations only about authorship and to enter fresh discussions about the nature and authority of Jewish (and by extension Christian) apocalyptic texts.[82]

At the 2012 meeting of the Colloquium Oecumenicum Paulinum, a group of scholars gathered together to discuss 2 Thessalonians with an interest in its eschatology.[83] Here 2 Thessalonians and its apocalyptic imagination proved to be a topic of deep interest.

The Thessalonian Situation

Finally, we address conversations in Thessalonian scholarship related to the Thessalonian situation. In this case, the discussion has been almost exclusively among those who consider 2 Thessalonians genuine and attempt to relate 1 and 2 Thessalonians in their shared sociohistorical context. We have already discussed Jewett's approach and his "millenarian" model on pp. 63–64. Jewett posits that 2 Thessalonians was written to correct the false assumption that the millennium had come. His work has been engaged extensively by scholars, but few (if any) have adopted his approach. Nevertheless, Jewett modeled a primary concern for deep methological reflection.

Karl Donfried has also contributed extensively to questions surrounding the situation behind 2 Thessalonians, most of the pertinent essays now collected in his *Paul, Thessalonica, and Early Christianity*.[84] Donfried's essay, "2 Thessalonians and the Church of Thessalonica," is his most direct discussion of the Thessalonian situation and the place where he articulates his hypothesis that perhaps Timothy was responsible for writing 2 Thessalonians.[85] Donfried leans in favor of the view that Paul was attempting, in his second letter, to refute the misguided notion that the Thessalonians were living in a fully realized eschaton.

An Introduction to Apocalyptic Literature (Grand Rapids: Eerdmans, 1998); F. J. Murphy, *Apocalypticism in the Bible and Its World* (Grand Rapids: Baker, 2012).

82. See Gupta, "Apocalyptic Reading of Psalm 78," 179–94; see too P. G. R. de Villiers, "The Glorious Presence of the Lord: The Eschatology of 2 Thessalonians," in *Eschatology of the New Testament and Some Related Documents*, ed. J. G. van der Watt (Tübingen: Mohr Siebeck, 2011), 333–61.

83. Cf. also H. Koester, "From Paul's Eschatology to the Apocalyptic Schemata of 2 Thessalonians," in Collins, *Thessalonian Correspondence*, 441–58.

84. Donfried, *Paul, Thessalonica, and Early Christianity*.

85. Found in *Paul, Thessalonica, and Early Christianity*, 49–68.

Colin Nicholl's important monograph offers what is the most comprehensive study of the Thessalonian situation, explicitly attempting to establish a scenario that makes sense of 2 Thessalonians as a genuine Pauline letter written after 1 Thessalonians (see pp. 81–83). He argues that their false belief that the day of the Lord had *already* come was a cause for terror at the thought of impending or experienced divine wrath; hence they moved from *hope* to *despair*.[86]

Todd Still and James Harrison wrote monographs with focused interest in sociopolitical dynamics that related to the Thessalonian situation. Still concentrated on the conflict and persecution from community members in Thessalonica. He looked mostly at 1 Thessalonians but included 2 Thessalonians.[87] Harrison investigated political and imperial dimensions of the situation behind 1–2 Thessalonians and examined 2 Thessalonians 2 in detail.[88]

CONCLUSION

As is obvious from the above discussion, in most ways the interpretation of 2 Thessalonians has been tethered closely to 1 Thessalonians. Second Thessalonians has experienced a problematic neglect due to its brevity and similarity to 1 Thessalonians. It has also been a lively topic of conversation as a possible forgery or pseudepigraph and more recently as a text that bears features of or influence from Jewish apocalyptic thought. Trends obviously change over time, but what is clear in a wider frame is that 2 Thessalonians is receiving increasing attention as a document for study in its own right.

RECOMMENDED READING

Bray, G., ed. *Ambrosiaster: Commentaries on Galatians–Philemon.* ACT. Downers Grove, IL: InterVarsity Press, 2009.

Gorday, P., ed. *Colossians, 1–2 Thessalonians, 1–2 Timothy, Titus, Philemon.* ACCS. Downers Grove, IL: InterVarsity Press, 2000.

Murphy, F. A. "Thomas' Commentaries on Philemon, 1 and 2 Thessalonians and Philippians." Pages 167–96 in *Aquinas on Scripture: An Introduction to His*

---

86. Nicholl, *From Hope to Despair*, 115–82.
87. Still, *Conflict at Thessalonica*, 191–206.
88. Harrison, *Paul and the Imperial Authorities*, 71–96.

Biblical Commentaries. Edited by T. G. Weinandy, D.A. Keating, and J. P. Yocum. London: T&T Clark, 2005.

Thiselton, A. *1 and 2 Thessalonians through the Centuries*. Oxford: Wiley-Blackwell, 2011.

Thompson, T. "As If Genuine: Interpreting the Pseudepigraphic Second Thessalonians." Pages 471–88 in *Pseudepigraphie und Verfasserfiktion in frühchristlichen Briefen*. Edited by J. Frey et al. WUNT 246. Tübingen: Mohr Siebeck, 2009.

———. "A Stone that *Still* Won't Fit: An Introductory and Editorial Note for Edgar Krentz's 'A Stone That Will Not Fit.'" Pages 433–38 in *Pseudepigraphie und Verfasserfiktion in frühchristlichen Briefen*. Edited by J. Frey et al. WUNT 246. Tübingen: Mohr Siebeck, 2009.

Trilling, W. "Die beiden Briefe des Apostels Paulus an die Thessalonicher: Eine Forschungsübersicht." *ANRW* 25.4:3365–403. Part 2, *Principat*, 25.4. Edited by H. Temporini and W. Haase. New York: de Gruyter, 1989.

Primary Sources

Calvin, J. *Commentaries on the Epistles of Paul the Apostle to the Philippians, Colossians, and Thessalonians*. Translated by J. Pringle. Edinburgh: Calvin Translation Society, 1851.

Luther, Martin. *Word and Sacrament I*. Edited by E. T. Bachmann. Luther's Works 35. Philadelphia: Muhlenberg, 1960.

Nestle, E., and K. Aland, eds. *Novum Testamentum Graece*. 28th ed. Stuttgart: Deutsche Bibelgesellschaft, 2012.

BIBLIOGRAPHY

Aasgaard, R. *My Beloved Brothers and Sisters: Christian Siblingship in Paul.* JSNTSup 265. London: T&T Clark, 2004.

Achtemeier, P. J., J. B. Green, and M. M. Thompson. *The New Testament: Its Literature and Theology.* Grand Rapids: Eerdmans, 2001.

Adam-Veleni, P. "Thessalonike." Pages 545–62 in *Brill's Companion to Ancient Macedon: Studies in the Archaeology and History of Macedon, 650 BC–300AD.* Edited by R. J. L. Fox. Leiden: Brill, 2011.

Adams, E. "The 'Coming of God' Tradition and Its Influence on New Testament Parousia Texts." Pages 1–19 in *Biblical Traditions in Transmission: Essays in Honour of Michael A. Knibb.* Edited by C. Hempel and J. Lieu. JSJSup 111. Leiden: Brill, 2006.

———. *The Stars Will Fall from Heaven: Cosmic Catastrophe in the New Testament and Its World.* LNTS 347. London: T&T Clark, 2007.

Adams, S. A. *The Genre of Acts and Collected Biography.* SNTSMS 156. Cambridge: Cambridge University Press, 2013.

Aernie, M. *Forensic Language and the Day of the Lord Motif in Second Thessalonians 1 and the Effects on the Meaning of the Text.* Eugene, OR: Wipf & Stock, 2010.

Allamani-Souri, V. "Brief History of Imperial Thessaloniki as Derived from Epigraphic and Archaeological Evidence." Pages 80–91 in *Roman Thessaloniki.* Edited by D. Grammenos. Thessaloniki: Archaeological Museum of Thessaloniki, 2003.

———. "The Imperial Cult." Pages 98–120 in *Roman Thessaloniki.* Edited by D. Grammenos. Thessaloniki: Archaeological Museum of Thesssaloniki, 2003.

———. "The Province of Macedonia in the Roman Imperium." Pages 67–79 in *Roman Thessaloniki.* Edited by D. Grammenos. Thessaloniki: Archaeological Museum of Thessaloniki, 2003.

———. "The Social Composition of the City." Pages 92–97 in *Roman Thessaloniki.* Edited by D. Grammenos. Thessaloniki: Archaeological Museum of Thessaloniki, 2003.

Allison, D. C. *A Critical and Exegetical Commentary on James.* ICC. London: Bloomsbury, 2013.

———. "Day of the Lord." *NIDB* 2:46–47.

———. "Jesus and the Victory of Apocalyptic." Pages 126–46 in *Jesus and the Restoration of Israel: A Critical Assessment of N. T. Wright's* Jesus and the Victory of God. Edited by C. C. Newman. Downers Grove, IL: InterVarsity Press, 1999.

Arnal, W. E. "Bridging Paul and the Corinthians Together? A Rejoinder and Some Proposals on Redescription and Theory." Pages 75–104 in *Redescribing Paul and the Corinthians*. Edited by R. Cameron and M. P. Miller. Atlanta: SBL Press, 2011.

Arzt-Grabner, P. "Paul's Letter Thanksgiving." Pages 129–58 in *Paul and the Ancient Letter Form*. Edited by S. E. Porter and S. A. Adams. PAST 6. Leiden: Brill, 2010.

Ascough, R. S. *1 and 2 Thessalonians: Encountering the Christ Group at Thessalonike*. Sheffield: Sheffield Phoenix Press, 2014.

———. "Of Memories and Meals: Greco-Roman Associations and the Early Jesus-Group at Thessalonikē." Pages 49–72 in *From Roman to Early Christian Thessalonikē*. Edited by L. Nasrallah, C. Bakirtzis, and S. Friesen. Cambridge: Harvard University Press, 2010.

———. *Paul's Macedonian Associations: The Social Context of Philippians and 1 Thessalonians*. WUNT 2/161. Tübingen: Mohr Siebeck, 2003.

———. Review of *Paul between Synagogue and State*, by M. Tellbe. *JBL* 122.4 (2003): 772–74.

———. "The Thessalonian Christian Community as a Professional Voluntary Association." *JBL* 119.2 (2000): 311–28.

———. "Translocal Relationships among Voluntary Associations and Early Christianity." *JECS* 5.2 (1997): 223–41.

———. *What Are They Saying about the Formation of Pauline Churches?* New York: Paulist, 1999.

Ascough, R. S., and P. A. Harland. *Associations in the Greco-Roman World: A Sourcebook*. Minneapolis: Fortress, 2012.

Aune, D. E. *The New Testament in Its Literary Environment*. Louisville: Westminster John Knox, 1987.

———. "The Significance of the Delay of the Parousia." Pages 87–109 in *Current Issues in Biblical and Patristic Interpretation*. Edited by G. F. Hawthorne. Grand Rapids: Eerdmans, 1975.

Aus, R. "Comfort in Judgment: The Use of Day of the Lord and Theophany Traditions in Second Thessalonians 1." PhD diss., Yale University, 1971.

———. "God's Plan and God's Power: Isaiah 66 and the Restraining Factors of 2 Thess 2:6–7." *JBL* 96 (1977): 537–53.

———. "Liturgical Background of the Necessity and Propriety of Giving Thanks according to 2 Thess 1:3." *JBL* 92.3 (1973): 432–38.

———. "The Relevance of Isaiah 66.7 to Revelation 12 and 2 Thessalonians 1." *ZNW* 67 (1976): 252–68.

Aymer, M. "'Mother Knows Best': The Story of Mother Paul Revisited." Pages 187–98 in *Mother Goose, Mother Jones, Mommie Dearest: Biblical Mothers and*

Their Children. Edited by C. A. Kirk-Duggan and T. Pippin. SemeiaSt 61. Atlanta: SBL Press, 2009.

Baarda, T. "1 Thess. 2:14–16. Rodrigues in 'Nestle-Aland.'" *Nederlands theologische tijdschrift* 39 (1985): 186–93.

Bailey, J. A. "Who Wrote II Thessalonians?" *NTS* 25 (1978–79): 131–45.

Bammel, E. "Ein Beitrag zur paulinischen Staatsanschauung." *TLZ* (1960): 837–40.

———. "Judenverfolgung und Naherwartung: Zur Eschatologie des Ersten Thessalonicherbriefs." *ZTK* 56.3 (1959): 294–315.

Barclay, J. M. G. "Conflict in Thessalonica." *CBQ* 55 (1993): 512–30.

———. "Mirror-Reading a Polemical Letter: Galatians as a Test Case." *JSNT* 31 (1987): 73–97.

———. "Thessalonica and Corinth: Social Contrasts in Pauline Christianity." *JSNT* 15.47 (1992): 49–74.

Barr, G. K. *Scalometry and the Pauline Epistles.* JSNTSup 261. London: T&T Clark, 2004.

Barth, M. *The Letter to Philemon.* ECC. Grand Rapids: Eerdmans, 2000.

Bartlett, D. L. *Ministry in the New Testament.* Philadelphia: Fortress, 1993.

Barton, S. C. "Spirituality and the Emotions." Pages 171–93 in *The Bible and Spirituality.* Edited by A. T. Lincoln et al. Eugene, OR: Wipf & Stock, 2013.

Bassler, J. M. "The Enigmatic Sign: 2 Thessalonians 1:5." *CBQ* 46 (1984): 496–510.

———. "Peace in All Ways: Theology in the Thessalonian Letters: A Response to R. Jewett, E. Krentz, and E. Richard." Pages 71–85 in *Pauline Theology, Volume 1: 1 Thessalonians, Philippians, Galatians, Philemon.* Edited by J. M. Bassler. Minneapolis: Fortress, 1991.

———. "SKEUOS: A Modest Proposal for Illuminating Paul's Use of Metaphor in 1 Thessalonians 4:4." Pages 53–66 in *The Social World of the First Christians.* Edited by L. M. White and O. L. Yarbrough. Minneapolis: Fortress, 1995.

Bates, M. W. *Salvation by Allegiance Alone: Rethinking Faith, Works, and the Gospel of Jesus the King.* Grand Rapids: Baker, 2017.

Bauckham, R. J. "The Delay of the Parousia." *TynBul* 31 (1980): 3–36.

Baum, A. "Authorship and Pseudepigraphy in Early Christian Literature: A Translation of the Most Important Source Texts and An Annotated Bibliography." Pages 11–64 in *Paul and Pseudepigraphy.* Edited by S. E. Porter and G. P. Fewster. PAST. Boston: Brill, 2013.

———. *Pseudepigraphie und literarische Fälschung im frühen Christentum: mit ausgewählten Quellentexten samt deutscher Übersetzung.* WUNT 2/138. Tübingen: Mohr Siebeck, 2001.

Baumert, N. "Brautwerbung—das einheitliche Thema von 1 Thess 4,3–8." Pages 316–39 in *The Thessalonian Correspondence.* Edited by R. F. Collins. Leuven: Leuven University Press, 1990.

Bauspiess, M., C. Landmesser, and D. Lincicum. *Ferdinand Christian Baur and the History of Early Christianity.* Oxford: Oxford University Press, 2017.

Beale, G. K. *1–2 Thessalonians.* IVPNTC. Downers Grove, IL: InterVarsity Press, 2003.

Becker, E.-M. "Ὡς δι' ἡμῶν in 2 Thess 2.2 als Hinweis auf einem verlorenen Brief." *NTS* 55.1 (2009): 55–72.

Beker, J. C. *Paul the Apostle: The Triumph of God in Life and Thought.* Philadelphia: Fortress, 1984.

Berding, K. *Polycarp and Paul: An Analysis of Their Literary and Theological Relationship in Light of Polycarp's Use of Biblical and Extra-Biblical Literature.* Leiden: Brill, 2002.

Bernett, M. "Roman Imperial Cult in Galilee." Pages 337–56 in *Religion, Ethnicity, and Identity in Ancient Galilee: A Region in Transition.* Edited by J. Zangenberg, H. W. Attridge, and D. B. Martin. WUNT 210. Tübingen: Mohr Siebeck, 2012.

Bernhardt, R. *Polis und römische Herrschaft in der späten Republik.* Berlin: de Gruyter, 1985.

Best, E. *A Commentary on the First and Second Epistles to the Thessalonians.* BNTC. Peabody, MA: Hendrickson, 1972.

Bienert, W. *Die Arbeit nach der Lehre der Bibel. Eine Grundlegung evangelischer Socialethik.* Stuttgart: Evangelisches Verlagswerk, 1954.

Binder, D. *Into the Temple Courts: The Place of the Synagogues in the Second Temple Period.* SBLDS 169. Atlanta: SBL Press, 1999.

Binder, H. "Paulus und die Thessalonicherbrief." Pages 87–93 in *The Thessalonian Correspondence.* Edited by Raymond F. Collins. BETL 87. Leuven: Leuven University Press, 1990.

Bird, M. F. "Reassessing a Rhetorical Approach to Paul's Letters." *ExpTim* 119.8 (2008): 374–79.

Black, C. C., and D. F. Watson, eds. *Words Well Spoken: George Kennedy's Rhetoric of the New Testament.* Studies in Rhetoric and Religion 8. Waco, TX: Baylor University Press, 2008.

Blumell, L. H. *Lettered Christians: Christians, Letters, and Late Antique Oxyrhynchus.* NTTSD 39. Leiden: Brill, 2012.

Bockmuehl, M. N. A. "1 Thess 2:14–16 and the Church in Jerusalem." *TynBul* 52 (2001): 1–31.

Boers, H. "The Form Critical Study of Paul's Letters: 1 Thessalonians as a Case Study." *NTS* 22.2 (1975–76): 140–58.

Boring, M. E. *1 and 2 Thessalonians.* NTL. Louisville: Westminster John Knox, 2015.

Bornemann, W. *Die Thessalonicherbriefe.* Göttingen: Vandenhoeck & Ruprecht, 1894.

Bornkamm, G. *Paul.* Translated by D. M. G. Stalker. New York: Harper & Row, 1971.

Bray, G., ed. *Ambrosiaster: Commentaries on Galatians–Philemon.* ACT. Downers Grove, IL: InterVarsity Press, 2009.

Breytenbach, C. *Grace, Reconciliation, Concord.* Boston: Brill, 2010.

Bridges, L. M. *1 & 2 Thessalonians.* SHBC. Macon, GA: Smyth & Helwys, 2008.

———. Review of *Conflict at Thessalonica,* by T. D. Still. *RevExp* 97 (2000): 110–11.

Brocke, C. vom. *Thessaloniki—Stadt des Kassander und Gemeinde des Paulus: eine frühe christliche Gemeinde in ihrer heidnischen Umwelt.* WUNT 2/125. Tübingen: Mohr Siebeck, 2001.

———. "Work in the New Testament and in Greco-Roman Antiquity." Pages 23–34 in *Dignity of Work*. Edited by K. Mtata. Minneapolis: Lutheran University Press, 2011.

Broer, I. "Antijudaismus im Neuen Testament? Versuch einer Annäherung anhand von zwei Texten (1 Thess 2,14–16 und Mt 27,24f.)." Pages 321–55 in *Salz der Erde*. Edited by A. Vögtle, L. Overlinner, and P. Fiedler. Stuttgart: Katholisches Bibelwerk, 1991.

———. "'Antisemitismus' und Judenpolemik im Neuen Testament: Ein Beitrag zum besseren Verständnis von 1 Thess 2:14–16." *Biblische Notizen* 20 (1983): 59–91.

———. "'Der ganze Zorn ist schon über sie gekommen': Bemerkungen zur Interpolationshypothese und zur Interpretation von 1 Thes 2,14–16." Pages 137–59 in *The Thessalonian Correspondence*. Edited by R. F. Collins. BETL 87. Leuven: Leuven University Press, 1990.

Brown, A. "Paul and the Parousia." Pages 47–76 in *The Return of Jesus in Early Christianity*. Edited by J. T. Carroll. Peabody, MA: Hendrickson, 2000.

Brown, R. *Introduction to the New Testament*. Garden City, NY: Doubleday, 1997.

Brown, S. G. "The Intertextuality of Isaiah 66.17 and 2 Thessalonians 2.7: A Solution to the 'Restrainer' Problem." Pages 254–77 in *Studies in Scripture in Early Judaism and Christianity*. Edited by C. A. Evans and J. A. Sanders. Sheffield: JSOT Press, 1993.

Bruce, F. F. *1 and 2 Thessalonians*. WBC. Waco, TX: Word, 1982.

Buckmann, J. "1 Thessalonians: Opposing Death by Building Community." Pages 810–20 in *Feminist Biblical Interpretation: A Compendium of Critical Commentary on the Books of the Bible and Related Literature*. Ed. L. Schottroff and M.-T. Wacker. Grand Rapids: Eerdmans, 2012.

Burke, T. *Family Matters: A Socio-Historical Study of Kinship Metaphors in 1 Thessalonians*. JSNTSup 247. London: T&T Clark, 2003.

Bystrom, R. O. "God as Worker: How It Affects Life and Ministry." *Direction* 32.2 (2003): 166–72.

Campbell, D. A. *Framing Paul: An Epistolary Biography*. Grand Rapids: Eerdmans, 2014.

Carney, E. "Macedonian Women." Pages 409–27 in *A Companion to Ancient Macedonia*. Edited by J. Roisman and I. Worthington. West Sussex: Wiley-Blackwell, 2010.

Carter, W. *The Roman Empire and the New Testament: An Essential Guide*. Nashville: Abingdon, 2006.

Chapa, J. "Consolatory Patterns? 1 Thes 4,13–18; 5,11." Pages 220–28 in *The Thessalonian Correspondence*. Edited by R. F. Collins. BETL 87. Leuven: Leuven University Press, 1990.

———. "Is First Thessalonians a Letter of Consolation?" *NTS* 40 (1994): 150–60.

Clarke, A. D. *A Pauline Theology of Church Leadership*. London: T&T Clark, 2008.

Colish, M. L. *Studies in Scholasticism*. Burlington, VT: Ashgate, 2006.

Collins, A. Y. "The Transformation of Paul's Apocalyptic Ideas in the First Two Centuries." Pages 138–54 in *Revealed Wisdom: Studies in Apocalyptic in Honour of Christopher Rowland*. Edited by J. Ashton. Boston: Brill, 2014.

Collins, J. *The Apocalyptic Imagination: An Introduction to Apocalyptic Literature.* Grand Rapids: Eerdmans, 1998.

Collins, R. F. "Apropos the Integrity of 1 Thess." *ETL* 65 (1979): 67–106.

———. *Letters That Paul Did Not Write: The Epistle to the Hebrews and Pauline Pseudepigrapha.* Wilmington, DE: Glazier, 1988.

———. *The Power of Images in Paul.* Collegeville, MN: Liturgical Press, 2008.

———. "A Significant Decade: The Trajectory of the Hellenistic Epistolary Thanksgiving." Pages 159–84 in *Paul and the Ancient Letter Form.* Edited by S. E. Porter and S. A. Adams. PAST 6. Leiden: Brill, 2010.

———. *Studies on the First Letter to the Thessalonians.* BETL 66. Leuven: Leuven University Press, 1984.

Comfort, P. W. *A Commentary on Textual Additions to the New Testament.* Grand Rapids: Kregel, 2017.

———. *A Commentary on the Manuscripts and Text of the New Testament.* Grand Rapids: Kregel, 2015.

Controzzi, S. "1 Thes 2:7—A Review." *Filologia Neotestamentaria* 12.23–24 (1999): 155–60.

Conzelmann, H. *The Theology of St. Luke.* London: Faber and Faber, 1961.

Cosden, D. *The Heavenly Good of Earthly Work.* Peabody, MA: Hendrickson, 2006.

Coulet, C. "Paul à Thessalonique (1Th 2.1–12)." *NTS* 52 (2006): 377–93.

Cousar, C. *Reading Galatians, Philippians, and 1 Thessalonians.* Macon, GA: Smyth & Helwys, 2013.

Crook, Z. *Reconceptualising Conversion: Patronage, Loyalty, and Conversion in the Religions of the Ancient Mediterranean.* BZNW 130. Berlin: de Gruyter, 2004.

Crüsemann, M. "'Wer nicht arbeiten will, soll auch nicht essen': Sozialgeschichtliche Beobachtungen zu 2 Thess 3,6–13." Pages 212–23 in *Essen und Trinken in der Bibel.* Edited by M. Geiger et al. Gütersloh: Gütersloher, 2009.

Cullmann, O. "Le caractère eschatologique du devoir missionnaire et de la conscience apostolique de S. Paul." *RHPR* 16 (1936): 210–45.

Cuvillier, E. "Vérité et historicité de la fiction littéraire. La seconde épître aux thessaloniciens comme pseudépigraphe." *Études théologiques et religieuses* 88.4 (2013): 515–28.

Dahmen, K. "The Numismatic Evidence." Pages 41–62 in *A Companion to Ancient Macedonia.* Edited by J. Roisman and I. Worthington. West Sussex: Wiley-Blackwell, 2010.

Deissmann, A. *Light from the Ancient East: The New Testament Illustrated by Recently Discovered Texts of the Graeco-Roman World.* 4th ed. Translated by L. R. M. Strachan. London: Hodder and Stoughton, 1927.

deSilva, D. *Honor, Patronage, Kinship, and Purity: Unlocking New Testament Culture.* Downers Grove, IL: InterVarsity Press, 2000.

———. *An Introduction to the New Testament.* Downers Grove, IL: InterVarsity Press, 2004.

———. *Transformation: The Heart of Paul's Gospel.* Bellingham, WA: Lexham, 2014.

Dobschütz, E. von. *Die Thessalonicher-Briefe*. KEK 10. Göttingen: Vandenhoeck & Ruprecht, 1909.

Doering, L. *Ancient Jewish Letters and the Beginnings of Christian Epistolography*. WUNT 298. Tübingen: Mohr Siebeck, 2012.

Donaldson, T. L. *Jews and Anti-Judaism in the New Testament*. Waco, TX: Baylor University Press, 2010.

———. *Paul and the Gentiles: Remapping the Apostle's Convictional World*. Minneapolis: Fortress, 1997.

Donfried, K. P. "2 Thessalonians and the Church of Thessalonica." Pages 128–44 in *Origins and Method: Toward a New Understanding of Judaism and Christianity: Essays in Honour of John C. Hurd*. Edited by B. H. McLean. JSNTSup 86. Sheffield: JSOT Press, 1993. Reprinted on pages 49–68 in *Paul, Thessalonica, and Early Christianity*. London: T&T Clark, 2002.

———. "The Cults of Thessalonica and the Thessalonian Correspondence." *NTS* 31.3 (1995): 336–56.

———. "The Imperial Cults of Thessalonica and Political Conflict in 1 Thessalonians." Pages 215–23 in *Paul and Empire*. Edited by R. A. Horsley. Harrisburg, PA: Trinity Press International, 1997.

———. "Issues of Authorship in the Pauline Corpus: Rethinking the Relationship Between 1 and 2 Thessalonians." Pages 81–114 in *2 Thessalonians and Pauline Eschatology*. Edited by C. Tuckett and C. Breytenbach. Leuven: Peeters, 2013.

———. "Paul and Judaism: 1 Thessalonians 2:13–16 as a Test Case." *Interpretation* 38.3 (1984): 242–53.

———. *Paul, Thessalonica, and Early Christianity*. London: T&T Clark, 2002.

———. "The Theology of 1 Thessalonians as a Reflection of Its Purpose." Pages 243–60 in *To Touch the Text*. Edited by M. P. Horgan and P. J. Kobelski. New York: Crossroad, 1989.

Donfried, K. P., and I. H. Marshall. *Theology of the Shorter Pauline Letters*. NTT. Cambridge: Cambridge University Press, 1993.

Donfried, K. P., and J. Beutler, eds. *The Thessalonians Debate: Methodological Discord or Methodological Synthesis?* Grand Rapids: Eerdmans, 2000.

Duff, J. "A Reconsideration of Pseudepigraphy in Early Christianity." PhD diss., Oxford University, 1998.

Dunn, J. D. G. *Beginning from Jerusalem*. Christianity in the Making 2. Grand Rapids: Eerdmans, 2009.

———. "Deutero-Pauline Letters." Pages 130–44 in *Early Christian Thought in Its Jewish Context*. Edited by J. M. G. Barclay. Cambridge: Cambridge University Press, 1996.

———. "Jesus Tradition in Paul." Pages 155–78 in *Studying the Historical Jesus*. Edited by B. Chilton and C. A. Evans. NTTS 19. Leiden: Brill, 1998.

———. *The Theology of Paul the Apostle*. Grand Rapids: Eerdmans, 1998.

Eadie, J. A. *Commentary on the Greek Text of the Epistles of Paul to the Thessalonians*. London: Macmillan, 1877.

Edson, C. F. *Inscriptiones Thessalonicae et Viciniae*. Berlin: de Gruyter, 1972.

Edwards, Jonathan. *The Works of Jonathan Edwards.* 2 volumes. Peabody, MA: Hendrickson, 1998.

Ehrman, B. D. *Forgery and Counter-Forgery: The Use of Literary Deceit in Early Christian Polemics.* Oxford: Oxford University Press, 2014.

Ehrman, B. D., and M. W. Holmes, eds. *The Text of the New Testament in Contemporary Research: Essays on the Status Quaestionis.* 2nd ed. NTTSD 42. Leiden: Brill, 2013.

Elgvin, T. "'To Master His Own Vessel': 1 Thess 4.4 in Light of New Qumran Evidence." *NTS* 43 (1997): 604–19.

Ellicot, C. J. *A Critical and Grammatical Commentary on St Paul's Epistle to the Thessalonians.* Andover: W. F. Draper, 1864.

Elliger, W. *Paulus in Griechenland: Philippi, Thessaloniki, Athen, Korinth.* Stuttgart: Katholisches Bibelwerk, 1978.

Elliott, N., and M. Reasoner. *Documents and Images for the Study of Paul.* Minneapolis: Fortress, 2010.

Ellul, J. "From the Bible to a History of Non-Work." *Cross Currents* 35 (1985): 43–48. Translated by D. Lovekin.

Erdman, C. R. *The Return of Christ.* New York: George H. Doran, 1922.

Ernst, M. *Distanzierte Unpersönlichkeit: Analyse von Sprache und Stil des zweiten Thessalonicherbriefes im Vergleich mit paulinischen Texten.* Salzburg: Institut für Neutestamentliche Bibelwissenschaft, 1998.

Esler, P. E. "1 Thessalonians." Pages 1200–12 in *The Oxford Bible Commentary.* Edited by J. Barton and J. Muddiman. Oxford: Oxford University Press, 2001.

———. "2 Thessalonians." Pages 1213–19 in *The Oxford Bible Commentary.* Edited by J. Barton and J. Muddiman. Oxford: Oxford University Press, 2001.

Fearghail, F. Ó. "The Jews in the Hellenistic Cities of Acts." Pages 39–54 in *Jews in the Hellenistic and Roman Cities.* Edited by J. R. Bartlett. London: Routledge, 2002.

Fee, G. D. *The First and Second Letters to the Thessalonians.* NICNT. Grand Rapids: Eerdmans, 2009.

Findlay, G. *The Epistles to the Thessalonians.* Cambridge: Cambridge University Press, 1894.

Fishwick, D. "A Critical Assessment: On the Imperial Cult in Religions of Rome." *Religious Studies and Theology* 28.2 (2009): 129–74.

Fitzmyer, J. *The Acts of the Apostles.* AB. New Haven: Yale University Press, 1998.

Foster, P. "The Eschatology of the Thessalonian Correspondence: An Exercise in Pastoral Pedagogy and Constructive Theology." *JSPL* 1.1 (2011): 57–82.

———. "Who Wrote 2 Thessalonians? A Fresh Look at an Old Problem." *JSNT* 35.2 (2012): 150–75.

Fowl, S. *Ephesians.* NTL. Louisville: Westminster John Knox, 2012.

———. "A Metaphor in Distress: A Reading of νήπιοι in 1 Thessalonians 2.7." *NTS* 36.3 (1990): 469–73.

Frame, J. E. *A Critical and Exegetical Commentary on the Epistles of St. Paul to the Thessalonians.* New York: Scribner's, 1912.

Frayer-Griggs, D. *Saved through Fire: The Fiery Ordeal in New Testament Eschatology.* Eugene, OR: Pickwick, 2016.

Fredriksen, P. "Judaizing the Nations: The Ritual Demands of Paul's Gospel." *NTS* 56 (2010): 232–52.

———. "Paul's Letter to the Romans, the Ten Commandments, and Pagan 'Justification by Faith.'" *JBL* 133.4 (2014): 801–8.

Friedrich, G. "I. Thessalonicher 5, 1–11, der apologetische Einschub eines Späteren." *ZTK* 70.3 (1973): 288–315.

———. *Die erste Brief an die Thessalonicher.* NTD 8. Göttingen: Vandenhoeck & Ruprecht, 1976.

Friesen, S. J. *Twice Neokoros: Ephesus, Asia and the Cult of the Flavian Imperial Family.* Leiden: Brill, 1993.

Fuchs, E. "Meditation über 1 Thess 1,2–10." *Göttinger Predigtmediationen* 18 (1963–64): 299–303.

Furnish, V. P. *1–2 Thessalonians.* ANTC. Nashville: Abingdon, 2007.

———. "The Jesus-Paul Debate: From Baur to Bultmann." Pages 18–50 in *Paul and Jesus: Collected Essays.* Edited by A. J. M. Wedderburn. Sheffield: Sheffield Academic Press, 1989.

Garland, D. E. Review of *The Thessalonian Correspondence*, by R. Jewett. *RevExp* 85 (1988): 132–33.

Gaventa, B. R. *First and Second Thessalonians.* IBC. Louisville: Westminster John Knox, 1998.

———. *Our Mother Saint Paul.* Louisville: Westminster John Knox, 2007.

Gilliard, F. D. "The Problem of the Antisemitic Comma between 1 Thessalonians 2.14 and 15." *NTS* 35 (1989): 498–501.

Gillihan, Y. M. "Rapture." Pages 347–54 in *Encyclopedia of Millennialism and Millennial Movements.* Edited by R. Landes. New York: Routledge, 2000.

Gillman, J. L. Review of *The Thessalonian Correspondence*, by R. Jewett. *CBQ* 50 (1988): 325–26.

Ginsberg, L. D. *Staging Memory, Staging Strife: Empire and Civil War in the Octavia.* Oxford: Oxford University Press, 2016.

Glancy, J. A. *Slavery in Early Christianity.* Oxford: Oxford University Press, 2002.

Goff, M. J. *4QInstruction.* Atlanta: SBL Press, 2013.

Goold, W. H., ed. *The Works of John Owen.* 16 volumes. Edinburgh: Banner of Truth, 1965.

Gorday, P., ed. *Colossians, 1–2 Thessalonians, 1–2 Timothy, Titus, Philemon.* ACCS. Downers Grove, IL: InterVarsity Press, 2000.

Gorman, M. J. *Apostle of the Crucified Lord.* 2nd ed. Grand Rapids: Eerdmans, 2017.

———. *Becoming the Gospel.* Grand Rapids: Eerdmans, 2015.

———. *Cruciformity: Paul's Narrative Spirituality of the Cross.* Grand Rapids: Eerdmans, 2001.

———. *Inhabiting the Cruciform God: Kenosis, Justification, and Theosis in Paul's Narrative.* Grand Rapids: Eerdmans, 2009.

Gradel, I. *Emperor Worship and Roman Religion.* Oxford: Clarendon, 2002.

Grant, R. M. *Early Christianity and Society: Seven Studies*. San Francisco: Harper & Row, 1977.

Grayston, K., and G. Herdan. "The Authorship of the Pastorals in the Light of Statistical Linguistics." *NTS* 6 (1959): 1–15.

Greef, W. *The Writings of John Calvin*. Translated by L. D. Bierma. Louisville: Westminster John Knox, 2008.

Green, G. L. *The Letters to the Thessalonians*. PNTC. Grand Rapids: Eerdmans, 2002.

Greenspoon, L. "By the Letter? Word for Word? Scriptural Citation in Paul." Pages 9–24 in *Paul and Scripture: Extending the Conversation*. Edited by C. D. Stanley. Atlanta: SBL Press, 2012.

Greer, R. A. *Theodore of Mopsuestia: Commentary on the Minor Pauline Epistles*. Atlanta: SBL Press, 2010.

Gregson, R. "A Solution to the Problems of the Thessalonian Epistles." *EvQ* 38 (1966): 76–80.

Griffith-Jones, R. Review of *The First and Second Letters to the Thessalonians*, by G. D. Fee. *JTS* 62.1 (2011): 323–27.

———. Review of *The Thessalonians Debate*, by K. P. Donfried and J. Beutler. *JTS* 52.2 (2001): 816–20.

Gundry, R. H. *The Old Is Better: New Testament Essays in Support of Traditional Interpretations*. WUNT 178. Tübingen: Mohr Siebeck, 2005.

Gupta, N. K. *1–2 Thessalonians*. NCCS. Eugene, OR: Wipf & Stock, 2016.

———. "An Apocalyptic Reading of Psalm 78 in 2 Thessalonians 3." *JSNT* 31.2 (2008): 179–94.

———. "Mirror-Reading Moral Issues in Paul's Letters." *JSNT* 34 (2012): 361–81.

———. "The 'Not . . . But' (*ou . . . alla*) New Testament Rhetorical Pattern." *Ashland Theological Journal* 42 (2010): 13–24.

———. "Paul and the *Militia Spiritualis* Topos in 1 Thessalonians." Pages 13–32 in *Paul and the Greco-Roman Philosophical Tradition*. Edited by J. R. Dodson and A. W. Pitts. LNTS. London: Bloomsbury, 2017.

———. "What Is in a Name? The Hermeneutics of Authorship Analysis concerning Colossians." *CBR* 11 (2013): 196–217.

———. *Worship That Makes Sense to Paul*. BZNW 175. Berlin: de Gruyter, 2010.

Hadorn, W. "Die Abfassung der Thessalonicherbriefe auf der dritten Missionsreise und der Kanon des Marcion." *ZNW* 19 (1919–20): 67–72.

Hagner, D. *The New Testament: A Historical and Theological Introduction*. Grand Rapids: Baker, 2012.

———. "Paul's Quarrel with Judaism." Pages 128–50 in *Anti-Semitism and Early Christianity: Issues of Polemic and Faith*. Edited by C. A. Evans and D. A. Hagner. Minneapolis: Fortress, 1993.

Hamerton-Kelly, R. *Politics and Apocalypse*. East Lansing, MI: Michigan State University Press, 2007.

Hannah, D. D. "Isaiah within Judaism of the Second Temple Period." Pages 7–33 in *Isaiah in the New Testament*. Edited by S. Moyise and M. J. J. Menken. London: T&T Clark, 2005.

Harris, M. J. "The Thessalonian Correspondence." Pages 269–301 in *All Things to All Cultures*. Edited by M. Harding and A. Nobbs. Grand Rapids: Eerdmans, 2013.

Harrison, J. R. *Paul and the Imperial Authorities at Thessalonica and Rome: A Study in the Conflict of Ideology*. WUNT 273. Tübingen: Mohr Siebeck, 2011.

Haufe, G. *Der erste Brief des Paulus an die Thessalonicher*. THKNT 12.1. Leipzig: Evangelische Verlagsanstalt, 1999.

Hays, R. B. *Echoes of Scripture in the Letters of Paul*. New Haven: Yale University Press, 1989.

———. "Lost in Translation: A Reflection on Romans in the Common English Bible." Pages 83–101 in *The Unrelenting God: Essays on God's Action in Scripture in Honor of Beverly Roberts Gaventa*. Edited by D. J. Downs and M. L. Skinner. Grand Rapids: Eerdmans, 2013.

Hellerman, J. "Brothers and Friends in Philippi: Family Honor in the Roman World and in Paul's Letter to the Philippians." *BTB* 39.1 (2009): 15–25.

———. *Embracing Shared Ministry: Power and Status in the Early Church and Why It Matters Today*. Grand Rapids: Kregel, 2013.

Hendrix, H. L. "Archaeology and Eschatology at Thessalonica." Pages 107–18 in *The Future of Early Christianity: Essays in Honor of Helmut Koester*. Edited by B. A. Pearson. Minneapolis: Fortress, 1991.

———. "Beyond 'Imperial Cult' and 'Cults of Magistrates.'" *SBL Seminar Papers* 25 (1986): 301–8.

———. Review of *The Thessalonian Correspondence*, by R. Jewett. *JBL* 107.4 (1988): 763–66.

———. "Thessalonicans Honor Romans." ThD diss., Harvard Divinity School, 1984.

Hengel, M. *Acts and the History of Earliest Christianity*. London: SCM, 1979.

Hill, R. C. *Theodoret: Commentary on the Letters of St. Paul*. Vol. 2. Brookline, MA: Holy Cross Orthodox Press, 2001.

Hock, R. F. "The Problem of Paul's Social Class: Further Reflections." Pages 7–18 in *Paul's World*. PAST 4. Edited by S. E. Porter. Leiden: Brill, 2008.

———. "Simon the Shoemaker as an Ideal Cynic." *GRBS* 17 (1976): 41–53.

———. *The Social Context of Paul's Ministry: Tentmaking and Apostleship*. Philadelphia: Fortress, 1980.

Hoehner, H. "Did Paul Write Galatians?" Pages 150–69 in *History and Exegesis: New Testament Essays in Honor of Dr. E. Earle Ellis for His 80th Birthday*. Edited by S.-W. Son. New York: T&T Clark, 2006.

Hoffmann, Y. "The Day of the Lord as a Concept and a Term in the Prophetic Literature." *ZAW* 83 (1987): 37–50.

Holladay, C. R., J. T. Fitzgerald, J. W. Thompson, and G. E. Sterling, eds. *Light from the Gentiles: Hellenistic Philosophy and Early Christianity: Collected Essays, 1959–2012, by Abraham J. Malherbe*. NovTSup 150. 2 vols. Boston: Brill, 2013.

Holland, G. S. "'A Letter Supposed from Us': A Contribution to the Discussion about the Authorship of 2 Thessalonians." Pages 394–402 in *The Thessalonian*

Correspondence. Edited by R. F. Collins. Leuven: Leuven University Press, 1990.

———. *The Tradition That You Received from Us: 2 Thessalonians in the Pauline Tradition.* Hermeneutische Untersuchungen zur Theologie 24. Tübingen: Mohr Siebeck, 1986.

Hollmann, G. "Die Unechtheit des zweiten Thessalonicherbriefs." *ZNW* 5 (1904): 28–38.

Holmes, J. "Lectures on 2 Thessalonians: A New Translation." *Letter & Spirit* 5 (2009): 211–38.

Holmes, M. W. *1 & 2 Thessalonians.* NIVAC. Grand Rapids: Zondervan, 1998.

Holtz, T. "The Judgment on the Jews and the Salvation of All Israel: 1 Thes 2,15–16 and Rom 11,25–26." Pages 284–94 in *The Thessalonian Correspondence.* Edited by R. F. Collins. Leuven: Peeters, 1990.

———. "Paul and the Oral Gospel Tradition." Pages 380–93 in *Jesus and the Oral Gospel Tradition.* Edited by H. Wansbrough. London: Bloomsbury, 2004.

Hooker, M. *From Adam to Christ.* Eugene, OR: Wipf & Stock, 1990.

Hoppe, R. "Der Topos Prophetenverfolgung bei Paulus." *NTS* 50.4 (2004): 535–49.

Horrell, D. *1 Peter.* NTG. London: T&T Clark, 2008.

———. "The Imperial Cult and the New Testament." *JSNT* 27.3 (2005): 251–373.

———. *Solidarity and Difference: A Contemporary Reading of Paul's Ethics.* 2nd ed. London: T&T Clark, 2015.

Hughes, F. W. *Early Christian Rhetoric and 2 Thessalonians.* JSNTSup 30. Sheffield: JSOT, 1989.

———. "The Rhetoric of Letters." Pages 194–240 in *The Thessalonians Debate.* Edited by K. P. Donfried and J. Beutler. Grand Rapids: Eerdmans, 2000.

———. "Second Thessalonians as a Document of Early Christian Rhetoric." PhD diss., Northwestern University, 1984.

———. "Thessalonians, First and Second Letters to the." Pages 111–16 in *New Testament: History of Interpretation.* Edited by J. H. Hayes. Nashville: Abingdon, 2004.

Hughes, K. L. *Constructing Antichrist: Paul, Biblical Commentary, and the Development of Doctrine in the Early Middle Ages.* Washington, DC: Catholic University of America Press, 2005.

Hultberg, A., ed. *Three Views on the Rapture: Pretribulation, Prewrath, and Posttribulation.* Grand Rapids: Zondervan, 1996.

Humphrey, E. *Scripture and Tradition: What the Bible Really Says.* Grand Rapids: Baker, 2013.

Hurd, J. C. "Concerning the Authenticity of 2 Thessalonians." Pages 135–61 in *The Earlier Letters of Paul—And Other Letters.* New York: Peter Lang, 1998.

———. "Paul Ahead of His Time: 1 Thess. 2.13–16." Pages 21–36 in *Antijudaism in Early Christianity: Paul and the Gospels.* Edited by P. Richardson and D. Granskou. Waterloo: Wilfrid Laurier University Press, 1986.

Hurtado, L. W. *Destroyer of the Gods: Early Christian Distinctiveness in the Roman World.* Waco, TX: Baylor University Press, 2016.

Hyldahl, N. *Die paulinische Chronologie*. Acta Theologica Danica 19. Leiden: Brill, 1986.

Jeremias, J. *Unknown Sayings of Jesus*. 2nd ed. London: SPCK, 1964.

Jervis, L. A. *At the Heart of the Gospel*. Grand Rapids: Eerdmans, 2007.

———. *The Purpose of Romans: A Comparative Letter Structure Investigation*. JSNTSup 55. Sheffield: JSOT Press, 1991.

Jewett, R. *The Thessalonian Correspondence: Pauline Rhetoric and Millenarian Piety*. Philadelphia: Fortress, 1986.

Johanson, Bruce. *To All the Brethren: A Text-Linguistic and Rhetorical Approach to 1 Thessalonians*. ConBNT 16. Stockholm: Almqvist & Wiksell, 1987.

Johnson, A. *1 and 2 Thessalonians*. THNT. Grand Rapids: Eerdmans, 2016.

———. *Holiness and the Missio Dei*. Eugene: Wipf & Stock, 2016.

———. "Paul's 'Anti-Christology' in 2 Thess 2:3–12 in Canonical Context." *JTI* 8.1 (2014): 125–43.

Johnson, E. E. "Paul's Reliance on Scripture in 1 Thessalonians." Pages 143–62 in *Paul and Scripture: Extending the Conversation*. Edited by C. D. Stanley. Atlanta: SBL Press, 2012.

Johnson, L. T. *Acts of the Apostles*. SP. Collegeville, MN: Liturgical Press, 1992.

———. "The New Testament's Slander and the Conventions of Ancient Polemic." *JBL* 108.3 (1989): 419–41.

———. *Writings of the New Testament: An Interpretation*. Rev. ed. Minneapolis: Fortress, 1999.

Johnson, S. "Notes and Comments." *ATR* 23 (1941): 173–76.

Johnson-DeBaufre, M. "'Gazing upon the Invisible': Archaeology, Historiography, and the Elusive Women of 1 Thessalonians." Pages 73–108 in *From Roman to Early Christian Thessalonikē*. Edited by L. Nasrallah, C. Bakirtzis, and S. Friesen. Cambridge: Harvard University Press, 2010.

Kampling, R. "Freude bei Paulus." *Trierer theologische Zeitschrift* 101 (1992): 69–79.

Karrer, M. "Der zweite Thessalonicherbrief und Gottes Widersacher." *HBT* 29.2 (2007): 101–31.

Keener, C. S. *Acts: An Exegetical Commentary, Volume 1: Introduction and 1:1–2:47*. Grand Rapids: Baker, 2012.

Keesmaat, S. C. "In the Face of the Empire: Paul's Use of Scripture in the Shorter Epistles." Pages 182–212 in *Hearing the Old Testament in the New Testament*. Edited by S. E. Porter. Grand Rapids: Eerdmans, 2006.

Kennedy, G. A. *Classical Rhetoric and Its Christian and Secular Tradition from Ancient to Modern Times*. 2nd edition. Chapel Hill, NC: University of North Carolina Press, 1999.

———. *New Testament Interpretation through Rhetorical Criticism*. Chapel Hill: University of North Carolina Press, 1984.

Kenny, A. *A Stylometric Study of the New Testament*. Oxford: Clarendon, 1986.

Kister, M. "A Qumranic Parallel to 1 Thess 4:4? Reading and Interpretation of 4Q416 2 II 21." *DSD* 10.3 (2003): 365–70.

Klauck, H.-J. *Ancient Letters and the New Testament*. Louisville: Westminster John Knox, 1986.

Klijn, A. F. "1 Thess 4,13–18 and Its Background in Apocalyptic Literature." Pages 67–73 in *Paul and Paulinism: Essays in Honour of C. K. Barrett.* Edited by M. D. Hooker and S. G. Wilson. London: SPCK, 1982.

Kloppenborg, J., and R. S. Ascough. *Greco-Roman Associations: Texts, Translations, and Commentary: I. Attica, Central Greece, Macedonia, Thrace.* Berlin: de Gruyter, 2011.

Knopf, R. *Das nachapostolische Zeitalter.* Tübingen: Mohr Siebeck, 1905.

Koch, A. *Commentar über den ersten Brief des Apostels Paulus an die Thessalonicher.* Berlin: L. Oehmigke, 1855.

Koch, K. *The Rediscovery of Apocalyptic.* London: SCM, 1972.

Koester, H. "Archäologie und Paulus in Thessalonike." Pages 1–9 in *Frühchristliches Thessaloniki.* Edited by C. Breytenbach. Studien und Texte zu Antike und Christentum 44. Tübingen: Mohr Siebeck, 2012.

———. "Egyptian Religion in Thessalonica: Regulation for the Cult." Pages 133–50 in *From Roman to Early Christian Thessalonikē.* Edited by L. Nasrallah, C. Bakirtzis, and S. J. Friesen. Cambridge: Harvard University Press, 2010.

———. "From Paul's Eschatology to the Apocalyptic Schemata of 2 Thessalonians." Pages 441–58 in *The Thessalonian Correspondence.* Edited by R. F. Collins. Leuven: Leuven University Press, 1990.

———. "Imperial Ideology and Paul's Eschatology in 1 Thessalonians." Pages 158–66 in *Paul and Empire.* Edited by R. A. Horsley. Harrisburg, PA: Trinity Press International, 1997.

———. *Introduction to the New Testament: History and Literature of Early Christianity II.* Philadelphia: Fortress, 1982.

Konradt, M. "Εἰδέναι ἕκαστον ὑμῶν τὸ ἑαυτοῦ σκεῦος κτᾶσθαι . . . : zu Paulus' sexualethischer Weisung in 1 Thess 4,4f." *ZNW* 92.1–2 (2001): 128–35.

Kooten, G. H. van. "Broadening the New Perspective." Pages 319–44 in *Abraham, the Nations, and the Hagarites.* Edited by M. Goodman, G. H van Kooten, and J. T. A. G. M. van Ruiten. Leiden: Brill, 2010.

———. "'Wrath Will Drip in the Plains of Macedonia': Expectations of Nero's Return in the Egyptian Sibylline Oracles (Book 5), 2 Thessalonians, and Ancient Historical Writings." Pages 177–215 in *The Wisdom of Egypt: Jewish, Early Christian, and Gnostic Essays in Honour of Gerard P. Luttikhuizen.* Edited by A. Hilhorst and G. H. van Kooten. Boston: Brill, 2005.

Kraftchick, S. Review of *The Thessalonian Correspondence*, by R. Jewett. *Interpretation* 42.4 (1988): 410–12.

Kreinecker, C. M. "The Imitation Hypothesis: Pseudepigraphic Remarks on 2 Thessalonians with Help from Documentary Papyri." Pages 197–219 in *Paul and Pseudepigraphy.* Edited by S. E. Porter and G. P. Fewster. Boston: Brill, 2013.

Kremendahl, D. *Die Botschaft der Form: Zum Verständnis von antiker Epistolographie und Rhetorik im Galaterbrief.* Göttingen: Vandenhoeck & Ruprecht, 2000.

Krentz, E. "2 Thessalonians." Pages 515–25 in *The Blackwell Companion to the New Testament.* Edited by D. E. Aune. Oxford: Wiley-Blackwell, 2010.

————. "A Stone That Will Not Fit: The Non-Pauline Authorship of 2 Thessalonians." Pages 456–63 in *Pseudepigraphie und Verfasserfiktion in frühchristlichen Briefen.* Edited by J. Frey et al. WUNT 256. Tübingen: Mohr Siebeck, 2009.

Krodel, G. "2 Thessalonians." Pages 73–96 in *Ephesians, Colossians, 2 Thessalonians, and the Pastoral Epistles.* Proclamation. Philadelphia: Fortress, 1978.

————. *Acts.* Minneapolis: Augsburg, 1986.

————. "The 'Religious Power of Lawlessness' (*Katechon*) as Precursor of the 'Lawless One' (*Anomos*) 2 Thess 2:6–7." *Currents in Theology and Missions* 17.6 (1990): 440–46.

Kümmel, W. "Das literarische und geschichtliche Problem des ersten Thessalonicherbriefes." Pages 213–27 in *Neotestamentica et Patristica.* Edited by W. C. van Unnik. NovTSup 6. Leiden: Brill, 1962.

Kyrtatas, D. J. "Early Christianity in Macedonia." Pages 585–99 in *Brill's Companion to Ancient Macedon.* Edited by R. J. L. Fox. Leiden: Brill, 2011.

Ladd, G. E. *The Blessed Hope: A Biblical Study of the Second Advent and the Rapture.* Grand Rapids: Eerdmans, 1956.

Lakoff, G., and M. Johnson. *Metaphors We Live By.* Chicago: University of Chicago Press, 1980.

Laub, F. *1 und 2 Thessalonicher.* Würzburg: Echter, 1985.

Légasse, S. *Les épitres de Paul aux Thessaloniciens.* Paris: Cerf, 1999.

Lenker, J. N. *The Precious and Sacred Writings of Martin Luther.* Minneapolis: Lutheran in All Lands, 1903.

Levine, L. I. *The Ancient Synagogue: The First Thousand Years.* New Haven: Yale University Press, 2005.

Lieu, J. "Letters." Page 449 in *The Oxford Handbook of Biblical Studies.* Edited by J. M. Lieu and J. W. Rogerson. Oxford: Oxford University Press, 2006.

Lincoln, A., J. G. McConville, and L. K. Peterson, eds. *The Bible and Spirituality.* Eugene, OR: Wipf & Stock, 2013.

Lintott, J. *Imperium Romanum: Politics and Administration.* London: Routledge, 1993.

Llewelyn, S. R., J. R. Harrison, with E. J. Bridge. *New Documents Illustrating Early Christianity.* Volume 10: A Review of the Greek and Other Inscriptions and Papyri Published between 1988 and 1992. Grand Rapids: Eerdmans, 2012.

Lo, J. "Pastoral Theology in the Letters of Paul: The Basis for Paul's Pastoral Responsibility." *Hill Road* 17.2 (2014): 25–50.

Longenecker, R. N. *Paul, Apostle of Liberty.* 2nd ed. Grand Rapids: Eerdmans, 2015.

Luckensmeyer, D. *The Eschatology of First Thessalonians.* NTOA 71. Göttingen: Vandenhoeck & Ruprecht, 2009.

Lull, T. F. "Luther's Writings." Pages 39–61 in *The Cambridge Companion to Luther.* Edited by D. M. McKim. Cambridge: Cambridge University Press, 2003.

Lünemann, G. *Kritisch exegetisches Handbuch über die Briefe an die Thessalonicher.* KEK 10. Göttingen: Vandenhoeck & Ruprecht, 1878.

Lütgert, D. W. *Die Vollkommenen in Philippi und die Enthusiasten in Thessalonich.* BFCT 13. Gütersloh: Bertelsmann, 1909.

Lyons, G. *Pauline Autobiography: Toward a New Understanding.* SBLDS 73. Atlanta: Scholars, 1985.

MacDougall, D. W. *The Authenticity of 2 Thessalonians.* Paternoster Biblical Monograph Series. Milton Keynes: Paternoster, 2016.

Malherbe, A. "Exhortation in First Thessalonians." Pages 167–86 in *Light from the Gentiles: Hellenistic Philosophy and Early Christianity: Collected Essays, 1959–2012, by Abraham J. Malherbe.* Edited by C. R. Holladay et al. Boston: Brill, 2013.

———. "Gentle as a Nurse: The Cynic Background to 1 Thess 2." *NovT* 12.2 (1970): 203–17.

———. *The Letters to the Thessalonians.* AB. New York: Doubleday, 2000.

———. *Paul and the Popular Philosophers.* Minneapolis: Fortress, 1989.

———. *Paul and the Thessalonians: The Philosophic Tradition of Pastoral Care.* Philadelphia: Fortress, 1987.

———. "Paul: Hellenistic Philosopher or Christian Pastor." Pages 197–208 in *Light from the Gentiles: Hellenistic Philosophy and Early Christianity: Collected Essays, 1959–2012, by Abraham J. Malherbe.* Edited by C. R. Holladay et al. Boston: Brill, 2013.

Manson, T. W. "St. Paul in Greece: The Letters to the Thessalonians." *BJRL* 35 (1953): 428–47.

Marguerat, D. "Imiter l'apôtre, père et mère de la communauté (1 Th 2,1–12)." Pages 25–54 in *Not in the Word Alone: The First Epistle to the Thessalonians.* Edited by M. D. Hooker. Rome: Benedictina, 2003.

Marshall, I. H. *1 and 2 Thessalonians.* Grand Rapids: Eerdmans, 1983.

———. *New Testament Theology.* Downers Grove, IL: InterVarsity Press, 2010.

———. "Palestinian and Hellenistic Christianity: Some Critical Comments." *NTS* 19 (1973): 271–87.

Martin, R. P. *New Testament Foundations.* Vol. 2. Grand Rapids: Eerdmans, 1994.

Marxsen, W. *Der erste Brief an die Thessalonicher.* Zürich: Theologischer, 1979.

———. *Der zweite Thessalonicherbrief.* Zurich: TVZ, 1982.

März, C.-P. "Das Gleichnis vom Dieb. Überlegungen zur Verbindung von Lk 12,39 par Mt 24,43 und 1 Thess 5,2.4." Pages 635–48 in *The Four Gospels: Festschrift for Franz Neirynck.* Edited by F. van Segbroeck et al. BETL 100. Leuven: Leuven University Press, 1992.

McGehee, M. "A Rejoinder to Two Recent Studies Dealing with 1 Thessalonians 4:4." *CBQ* 51 (1989): 82–89.

McKim, D. *Historical Handbook of the Major Biblical Interpreters.* Downers Grove, IL: InterVarsity Press, 1998.

McKinion, S., ed. *Isaiah 1–39.* ACCS. Downers Grove, IL: InterVarsity Press, 2014.

McNeel, J. H. *Paul as Infant and Nursing Mother: Metaphor, Rhetoric, and Identity in 1 Thessalonians 2:5–8.* Atlanta: SBL Press, 2014.

Menken, M. J. J. *2 Thessalonians.* NTR. New York: Routledge, 1994.

Metzger, B. M. "Literary Forgeries and Canonical Pseudepigrapha." *JBL* 91.1 (1972): 3–24.

———. *A Textual Commentary on the Greek New Testament*. 2nd ed. Stuttgart: Deutsche Bibelgesellscaft/German Bible Society, 1994.

Metzger, P. *Katechon: II Thess 2,1–12 im Horizont apokalyptischen Denkens*. Berlin: de Gruyter, 2005.

Miguez, N. O. *Practice of Hope*. Minneapolis: Fortress, 2012.

Miller, C. "The Imperial Cult in the Pauline Cities of Asia Minor and Greece." *CBQ* 72.2. (2010): 314–32.

Milligan, G. *St. Paul's Epistles to the Thessalonians*. London: Macmillan, 1908.

Mitchell, A. C. Review of *From Hope to Despair*, by C. Nicholl. *Journal of Religion* 85.4 (2005): 654–56.

Mitchell, M. M. "1–2 Thessalonians." Pages 51–63 in *The Cambridge Companion to St Paul*. Edited by J. D. G Dunn. Cambridge: Cambridge University Press, 2003.

———. *Paul and the Rhetoric of Reconciliation: An Exegetical Investigation*. Louisville: Westminster John Knox, 1991.

Morgan, Teresa. *Roman Faith and Christian Faith: Pistis and Fides in the Early Roman Empire and Early Churches*. Oxford: Oxford University Press, 2015.

Morris, L. *1, 2 Thessalonians*. Word Biblical Themes. Dallas: Word, 1989.

———. *1 and 2 Thessalonians*. TNTC. Grand Rapids: Eerdmans, 1984.

Morton, A. Q., and J. McLeman. *Christianity in the Computer Age*. New York: Harper & Row, 1964.

Mount, C. *Pauline Christianity: Luke-Acts and the Legacy of Paul*. NovTSup 104. Boston: Brill, 2002.

Müller, P.-G. *Der Erste und Zweite Brief an die Thessalonicher*. Regensburger Neues Testament. Regensburg: Pustet, 2001.

Müller, U. B. "Apocalyptic Currents." Pages 281–329 in *Christian Beginnings*. Edited by J. Becker. Translated by A. S. Kidder and R. Krauss. London: Westminster John Knox, 1993.

Munck, J. *Paul and the Salvation of Mankind*. Translated by F. Clarke. London: SCM, 1959.

Murphy, F. A. "Thomas' Commentaries on Philemon, 1 and 2 Thessalonians and Philippians." Pages 167–96 in *Aquinas on Scripture: An Introduction to His Biblical Commentaries*. Edited by T. G. Weinandy, D. A. Keating, and J. P. Yocum. London: T&T Clark, 2005.

Murphy, F. J. *Apocalypticism in the Bible and Its World*. Grand Rapids: Baker, 2012.

Murphy-O'Connor, J. *Paul: A Critical Life*. Oxford: Clarendon, 1996.

———. *Paul the Letter-Writer*. Collegeville, MN: Liturgical Press, 1995.

Murrell, N. S. "The Human Paul of the New Testament: Anti-Judaism in 1 Thess 2:14–16." *Eastern Great Lakes Biblical Society* 14 (1994): 169–86.

Nasrallah, L. S. "Empire and Apocalypse in Thessaloniki: Interpreting the Early Christian Rotunda." *JECS* 13.4 (2005): 465–508.

Nasrallah, L., C. Bakirtzis, and S. J. Friesen, eds. *From Roman to Early Christian Thessalonikē: Studies in Religion and Archaeology*. Cambridge: Harvard University Press, 2010.

Neufeld, T. R. *Put on the Armour of God: The Divine Warrior from Isaiah to Ephesians.* Sheffield: Sheffield Academic, 1997.

Neutel, K. B. "Slaves Included? Sexual Regulations and Slave Participation in Two Ancient Religious Groups." Pages 133–48 in *Slaves and Religions in Graeco-Roman Antiquity and Modern Brazil.* Edited by S. Hodkinson and D. Geary. Newcastle upon Tyne: Cambridge Scholars, 2012.

Nicholl, C. R. *From Hope to Despair in Thessalonica: Situating 1 and 2 Thessalonians.* SNTSMS 126. Cambridge: Cambridge University Press, 2004.

———. "Michael, the Restrainer Removed (2 Thess 2:6–7)." *JTS* 51.1 (2000): 27–53.

Nicklas, T. "'Der Tag des Herrn ist schon da' (2 Thess 2:2b): ein Schlüsselproblem zum Verständnis des 2. Thessalonicherbriefs." *HTS* 71.1 (2015): 1–10.

Nigdelis, P. Επιγραφικά Θεσσαλονίκεια. Συμβολή στην πολιτική και κοινωνική ιστορία της Αρχαίας Θεσσαλονίκης (*Epigraphica Thessalonicensia. A Contribution to the Political and Social History of Ancient Thessaloniki*). Thessaloniki: University Studio Press, 2006.

———. "Roman Thessalonica." Pages 51–87 in *The History of Macedonia.* Edited by I. Koliopoulos. Thessaloniki: Museum of the Macedonian Struggle Foundation, 2007.

———. "Synagoge(n) und Gemeinde der Juden in Thessaloniki: Fragen Aufgrund einer neuen jüdischen Grabinschrift der Kaiserzeit." *ZPE* 120 (1994): 298–306.

———. "Thessaloniki: The Age of the Macedonian Kingdom and the Period of Roman Rule." http://site.lpth.gr/en/texts/Nigdelis_en.pdf. Online only.

Norton, J. D. H. *Contours in the Text: Textual Variation in the Writings of Paul, Josephus, and the Yahad.* LNTS 430. London: T&T Clark, 2011.

Oakes, P. *Reading Romans in Pompeii: Paul's Letter at Ground Level.* Minneapolis: Fortress, 2009.

———. Review of *From Hope to Despair*, by C. Nicholl. *JSNT* 27.5 (2005): 113–14.

———. Review of *Paul between Synagogue and State*, by M. Tellbe. *BibInt* 12.3 (2004): 341–44.

———, ed. *Rome in the Bible and the Early Church.* Grand Rapids: Baker, 2002.

Okeke, G. E. "I Thessalonians 2.13–16: The Fate of Unbelieving Jews." *NTS* 27 (1980): 127–36.

Omanson, R. L. *A Textual Guide to the Greek New Testament.* Stuttgart: Deutsche Bibelsgesellschaft, 2006.

Oropeza, B. J. *Jews, Gentiles, and the Opponents of Paul.* Eugene, OR: Wipf & Stock, 2012.

Ovadiah, A. "Ancient Jewish Communities in Macedonia and Thrace." Pages 185–98 in *Hellenic and Jewish Arts: Interaction, Tradition and Renewal.* Edited by A. Ovadiah. Tel Aviv: Ramot, 1998.

Paddison, A. *Theological Hermeneutics and 1 Thessalonians.* SNTSMS 133. Cambridge: Cambridge University Press, 2005.

Pahl, M. W. *Discerning the "Word of the Lord": The "Word of the Lord" in 1 Thessalonians 4:15.* LNTS 389. London: T&T Clark, 2009.

Pao, D. "Gospel within the Constraints of an Epistolary Form: Pauline Introductory Thanksgivings and Paul's Theology of Thanksgiving." Pages 101–28 in *Paul and the Ancient Letter Form*. PAST 6. Edited by S. E. Porter and S. A. Adams. Leiden: Brill, 2010.

———. *Thanksgiving: An Investigation of a Pauline Theme*. Downers Grove, IL: InterVarsity Press, 2002.

Pearson, B. "1 Thessalonians 2:13–16: A Deutero-Pauline Interpolation." *HTR* 64 (1971): 79–94.

Peerbolte, L. J. L. *The Antecedents of Antichrist: A Traditio-Historical Study of the Earliest Christian Views on Eschatological Opponents*. JSJSup 49. Leiden: Brill, 1996.

———. "The κατέχον/κατέχων of 2 Thess. 2:6–7." *NovT* 49.2 (1997): 138–50.

Perrin, N. *New Testament Introduction*. New York: Harcourt Brace Jovanovich, 1974.

Peterson, E. "Pastor Paul." Pages 283–94 in *Romans and the People of God*. Edited by S. Soderlund and N. T. Wright. Grand Rapids: Eerdmans, 1999.

Pillar, E. *Resurrection as Anti-Imperial Gospel: 1 Thessalonians 1:9b–10 in Context*. Minneapolis: Fortress, 2013.

Pitts, A. W. "Style and Pseudonymity in Pauline Scholarship: A Register Based Configuration." Pages 113–52 in *Paul and Pseudepigraphy*. Edited by S. E. Porter and G. P. Fewster. Boston: Brill, 2013.

Plevnik, J. "The Parousia as Implication of Christ's Resurrection: An Exegesis of 1 Thess 4:13–18." Pages 199–277 in *Word and Spirit: Essays in Honor of David Michael Stanley*. Edited by J. Plevnik. Willowdale: Regis College, 1975.

———. *Paul and the Parousia. An Exegetical and Theological Investigation*. Peabody, MA: Hendrickson, 1997.

Plummer, A. *A Commentary on St. Paul's First Epistle to the Thessalonians*. London: R. Scott, 1918.

Pobee, J. S. *Persecution and Martyrdom in the Theology of Paul*. JSNTSup 6. Sheffield: JSOT Press, 1985.

Porter, J. S. *Principles of Textual Criticism*. London: Simms and M'Intyre, 1848.

Porter, S. E. "On Pauline Pseudepigraphy: An Introduction." Pages 1–10 in *Paul and Pseudepigraphy*. Edited by S. E. Porter and G. P. Fewster. PAST. Boston: Brill, 2013.

———. "Paul and His Bible: His Education and Access to the Scriptures of Israel." Pages 97–124 in *As It Is Written: Studying Paul's Use of the Old Testament*. Edited by S. E. Porter and C. D. Stanley. Atlanta: SBL Press, 2008.

———, ed. *Paul: Jew, Greek, and Roman*. PAST. Boston: Brill, 2008.

———. "Pauline Authorship and the Pastoral Epistles: Implications for Canon." *BBR* 5 (1995): 105–23.

———. "Translation, Exegesis, and 1 Thessalonians 2:14–15: Could a Comma Have Changed the Course of History?" *Bible Translator* 64.1 (2013): 82–98.

Porter, S. E., and A. Pitts. *Fundamentals of New Testament Textual Criticism*. Grand Rapids: Eerdmans, 2015.

Porter, S. E., and S. A. Adams. "Pauline Epistolography: An Introduction." Pages 1–7 in *Paul and the Ancient Letter Form*. Edited by S. E. Porter and S. A. Adams. PAST. Leiden: Brill, 2010.

Poster, C. "A Conversation Halved: Epistolary Theory in Greco-Roman Antiquity." Pages 21–51 in *Letter-Writing Manuals and Instructions from Antiquity to the Present*. Edited by C. Poster and L. C. Mitchell. Studies in Rhetoric/Communication Columbia: University of South Carolina Press, 2007.

Powell, A. *The Greek World*. London: Routledge, 2002.

Powell, C. E. "The Identity of the 'Restrainer' in 2 Thessalonians 2:6–7." *BibSac* 154 (1997): 320–32.

Powell, M. A. *Introducing the New Testament*. Grand Rapids: Baker, 2009.

———. *What Are They Saying about Acts?* Mahwah, NJ: Paulist, 1991.

Price, S. R. F. *Rituals and Power: The Roman Imperial Cult in Asia Minor*. Cambridge: Cambridge University Press, 1984.

Ranke, L. von. "Preface to the First Edition of the Histories of the Latin and Germanic Nations." Pages 85–88 in *The Theory and Practice of History*. Edited by G. G. Iggers. London: Routledge, 2011.

Reasoner, M. *Roman Imperial Texts: A Sourcebook*. Minneapolis: Fortress, 2013.

Redalie, Y. "Work with One's Hands." Pages 282–89 in *Paul and the Heritage of Israel*. Edited by D. P. Moessner et al. London: Bloomsbury, 2012.

Reddish, M. G. *Apocalyptic Literature: A Reader*. Peabody, MA: Hendrickson, 1990.

Reinmuth, E. "Die erste Brief an die Thessalonicher." Pages 105–58 in *Die Briefe an die Philipper, Thessalonicher und an Philemon*. Edited by N. Walter, E. Reinmuth, and P. Lampe. NTD 8/2. Göttingen: Vandenhoeck & Ruprecht, 1998.

———. "Der zweite Brief an die Thessalonicher." Pages 159–204 in *Die Briefe an die Philipper, Thessalonicher und an Philemon*. Edited by N. Walter, E. Reinmuth, and P. Lampe. NTD 8/2. Göttingen: Vandenhoeck & Ruprecht, 1998.

Richard, E. J. "Early Pauline Thought: An Analysis of 1 Thessalonians." Pages 71–85 in *Pauline Theology*. Edited by J. M. Bassler. Minneapolis: Fortress, 1991.

———. *First and Second Thessalonians*. SP. Collegeville, MN: Liturgical Press, 1995.

Richards, E. R. *Paul and First-Century Letter Writing: Secretaries, Composition and Collection* (Downers Grove, IL: InterVarsity Press, 2004).

———. *The Secretary in the Letters of Paul*. WUNT 2/42. Tübingen: Mohr Siebeck, 1991.

Richardson, N. *Paul's Language about God*. JSNTSup 99. Sheffield: Sheffield Academic, 1994.

Riesner, R. "Pauline Chronology." Pages 9–29 in *Blackwell Companion to Paul*. Edited by S. Westerholm. Oxford: Wiley-Blackwell, 2011.

———. *Paul's Early Period: Chronology, Mission Strategy, Theology*. Grand Rapids: Eerdmans, 1998.

Rigaux, B. *Les Épitres aux Thessaloniciens*. Paris: Gabalda, 1956.

Rist, M. "Pseudepigraphy and the Early Christians." Pages 75–91 in *Studies in New Testament and Early Christian Literature*. Edited by D. E. Aune. Leiden: Brill, 1972.

Ritter, B. *Judeans in the Greek Cities of the Roman Empire*. Boston: Brill, 2015.

Robinson, J. A. T. *Redating the New Testament*. London: SCM, 1976.

Roetzel, C. *Paul, a Jew on the Margins*. Louisville: Westminster John Knox, 2003.

———. "Theodidaktoi and Handiwork in Philo and 1 Thessalonians." Pages 324–31 in *L'Apôtre Paul: Personnalité, style et conception du ministère*. Edited by A. Vanhoye. BETL 73. Leuven: Leuven University Press, 1986.

Rollens, S. E. "Inventing Traditions in Thessalonica: The Appropriation of the Past in 1 Thess 2:14–16." *BTB* 46.3 (2016): 123–32.

Roose, H. "'A Letter as by Us': Intentional Ambiguity in 2 Thessalonians 2.2." *JSNT* 29 (2006): 107–24.

Roosen, A. *De Brieven van Paulus aan de Tessalonicenzen*. Rome: Roermond, 1971.

Rossano, P. "Note archeologiche sulla antica Tessalonica." *Revista Bíblica* 6 (1958): 242–47.

Rossing, B. *The Rapture Exposed*. Boulder, CO: Westview, 2004.

Rothschild, C. K. *Hebrews as Pseudepigraphon: The History and Significance of the Pauline Attribution of Hebrews*. Tübingen: Mohr Siebeck, 2012.

Royse, J. R. "The Early Text of Paul (and Hebrews). Pages 175–203 in *The Early Text of the New Testament*. Edited by C. E. Hill and M. J. Kruger. Oxford: Oxford University Press, 2012.

Rulmu, C. "Between Ambition and Quietism: The Sociopolitical Background of 1 Thessalonians 4,9–12." *Biblica* 91.3 (2010): 393–417.

Russell, D. *The Method & Message of Jewish Apocalyptic, 200 BC–AD 100*. Philadelphia; Westminster, 1964.

Russell, R. "The Idle in 2 Thess 3:6–12: An Eschatological or a Social Problem?" *NTS* 34 (1988): 105–19.

Sailors, T. B. "Wedding Textual Criticism and Rhetorical Criticism." *JSNT* 80 (2000): 81–92.

Sampley, J. P., ed. *Paul in the Greco-Roman World*. 2nd ed. 2 vols. London: Bloomsbury, 2016.

———. *Walking in Love: Moral Progress and Spiritual Growth with the Apostle Paul*. Minneapolis: Fortress, 2016.

Schlatter, A. *Die Briefe an die Thessalonicher und Philipper*. Stuttgart: Vereinsbuchhandlung, 1910.

Schmidt, D. "1 Thess 2:13–16: Linguistic Evidence for an Interpolation." *JBL* 102.2 (1983): 269–79.

Schmidt, J. *Die jüdische Apokalyptik: die Geschichte ihrer Erforschung von den Anfängen bis zu den Textfunden von Qumran*. Neukirchen-Vluyn: Neukirchener, 1969.

Schmidt, U. "1 Thess 2.7b, c: 'Kleinkinder, die wie eine Amme Kinder versorgen." *NTS* 55.1 (2009): 116–20.

Schmiedel, P. *Die Briefe an die Thessalonicher und an die Korinther*. Frieburg: J. C. B. Mohr, 1892.

Schmithals, W. *Paulus und die Gnostiker: Untersuchungen zu den kleinen Paulusbriefen*. Hamburg: Herbert Reich, Evangelischer Verlag, 1965. ET: *Paul and the Gnostics*. Nashville: Abingdon, 1972.

————. "Die Thessalonicherbriefe als Briefkompositionen." Pages 295–315 in *Zeit und Geschichte: Dankesgabe an Rudolf Bultmann zum 80 Geburtstag.* Edited by E. Dinkler and H. Thyen. Tübingen: Mohr Siebeck, 1964.

Schnabel, E. Review of *Paul's Macedonian Associations*, by R. S. Ascough. *Trinity Journal* 26.2 (2005): 335–36.

Schnelle, U. *Einleitung in das Neue Testament.* 5th ed. Göttingen: Vandenhoeck & Ruprecht, 2005.

Schreiber, S. *Der erste Brief an die Thessalonicher.* Gütersloh: Gütersloher Verlaghaus, 2014.

Schröter, J. "Lukas als Historiograph. Das lukanische Doppelwerk und die Entdeckung der christlichen Heilsgeschichte." Pages 237–62 in *Die antike Historiographie und die Anfänge der christlichen Geschichtsschreibung.* Edited by E.-M. Becker. Berlin: de Gruyter, 2005.

Schweitzer, A. "The Solution of Thoroughgoing Eschatology." Pages 6–49 in *The Historical Jesus in Recent Research.* Edited by J. D. G. Dunn and S. McKnight. Winona Lake, IN: Eisenbrauns, 2005.

Shillington, V. G. "A New Testament Perspective on Work." *Conrad Grabel Review* 10 (1992): 139–55.

Shogren, G. *1 and 2 Thessalonians.* ZECNT. Grand Rapids: Zondervan, 2012.

Simpson, J. W. "The Problems Posed by 1 Thessalonians 2:15–16 and a Solution." *HBT* 12.1 (1990): 42–72.

Smalley, S. "The Delay of the Parousia." *JBL* 83.1 (1964): 41–54.

Smiga, G. M. Review of *Paul between Synagogue and State*, by M. Tellbe. *CBQ* 64.2 (2002): 395–96.

Smith, A. *Comfort One Another: Reconstructing the Rhetoric and Audience of 1 Thessalonians.* Louisville: Westminster John Knox, 1995.

————. "The First Letter to the Thessalonians: Introduction, Commentary, and Reflections." Pages 671–737 in vol. 9 of *The New Interpreter's Bible Commentary.* Edited by L. E. Keck. 10 vols. Nashville: Abingdon, 2015.

————. *The Social and Ethical Implications of the Pauline Rhetoric in 1 Thessalonians.* Ph.D. diss., Vanderbilt University, 1989.

————. "'Unmasking the Powers': Toward a Postcolonial Analysis of 1 Thessalonians." Pages 47–66 in *Paul and the Roman Imperial Order.* Edited by R. A. Horsley. London: Bloomsbury, 2004.

Smith, J. E. "1 Thessalonians 4:4: Breaking the Impasse." *BBR* 11 (2001): 65–105.

————. "Another Look at 4Q416 2ii.21, a Critical Parallel to First Thessalonians 4:4." *CBQ* 63 (2001): 499–504.

Smith, L. *The Glossa Ordinaria: The Making of a Medieval Bible Commentary.* Boston: Brill, 2009.

Söding, T. *Das Liebesgebot bei Paulus: Die Mahnung zur Agape im Rahmen der paulinischen Ethik.* NTAbh 26. Münster: Aschendorff, 1995.

Spicq, C. *Theological Lexicon of the New Testament.* 3 vols. Translated by J. Ernest. Peabody, MA: Hendrickson, 1994.

Spinks, C. *The Bible and the Crisis of Meaning: Debates on the Theological Interpretation of Scripture.* London: T&T Clark, 2007.

Stacy, R. W. "Introduction to the Thessalonian Correspondence." *RevExp* 96 (1999): 175–94.

Stanley, C. D. *Arguing with Scripture: The Rhetoric of Quotations in the Letters of Paul.* London: T&T Clark, 2004.

———. "Who's Afraid of a Thief in the Night?" *NTS* 48.4 (2002): 468–86.

Strecker, G. *Theology of the New Testament.* Berlin: de Gruyter, 2014.

Stefanidou-Tiveriou, T. "Thessaloniki from Cassander to Galerius." http://site.lpth .gr/en/texts/Tiveriou_en.pdf. Online only.

Stegemann, E. *Paulus und die Welt: Aufsätze.* Edited by C. Tuor-Kurth and P. Wick. Zürich: Theologischer Verlag, 2005.

———. "Remarques sur la polemique antijudaïque dans 1 Thessaloniciens 2,14–16." Pages 99–112 in *Le déchirement: juifs et chrétiens au premier siècle.* Edited by D. Marguerat. Geneva: Labor et Fides, 1996.

Steimle, C. *Religion im römischen Thessaloniki: Sakraltopographie, Kult und Gesellschaft.* Tübingen: Mohr Siebeck, 2008.

Stenschke, C. "Hinweise zu einem wiederentdeckten Gebiet der Actaforschung . . ." *Communio Viatorum* 41 (1999): 65–91.

———. Review of *Paul's Macedonian Associations*, by R. S. Ascough. *Religion & Theology* 12.1 (2005): 74–79.

Stevens, R. P. *The Other Six Days: Vocation, Work, and Ministry in Biblical Perspective.* Grand Rapids: Eerdmans, 2000.

Still, T. D. *Conflict at Thessalonica: A Pauline Church and Its Neighbours.* JSNTSup 183. Sheffield: Sheffield Academic, 1999.

———. "Did Paul Loathe Manual Labor?: Revisiting the Work of Ronald F. Hock on the Apostle's Tentmaking and Social Class." *JBL* 125.4 (2006): 781–95.

———. "Eschatology in the Thessalonian Letters." *RevExp* 96.2 (1999): 195–210.

Stowers, S. K. *Letter Writing in Greco-Roman Antiquity.* Philadelphia: Westminster, 1986.

Strugnell, J., and D. J. Harrington, eds. *Qumran Cave 4.XXIV: Sapiential Texts, Part 2. 4QInstruction: 415ff. With a Re-edition of 1Q26.* Oxford: Clarendon, 1999.

Suhl, A. *Paulus und seine Briefe: Ein Beitrag zur paulinischen Chronologie.* SNT 11. Gütersloh: Gütersloher Verlagshaus Mohn, 1975.

Talbert, C. *Ephesians and Colossians.* Paideia. Grand Rapids: Baker, 2007.

———. *Learning through Suffering: The Educational Value of Suffering in the New Testament and Its Milieu.* Collegeville, MN: Liturgical Press, 1991.

Taylor, N. H. "Caligula, the Church of Antioch and the Gentile Mission." *Religion & Theology* 7.1 (2000): 1–23.

Tellbe, M. *Paul between Synagogue and State: Christians, Jews, and Civic Authorities in 1 Thessalonians, Romans, and Philippians.* ConBNT 34. Stockholm: Almqvist & Wiksell, 2001.

Thiselton, A. *1 and 2 Thessalonians through the Centuries.* Oxford: Wiley-Blackwell, 2011.

———. *The First Epistle to the Corinthians.* NIGTC. Grand Rapids: Eerdmans, 2000.

———. *The Living Paul.* Downers Grove, IL: InterVarsity Press, 2009.

Thomas, C. G. "The Physical Kingdom." Pages 65–80 in *A Companion to Ancient Macedonia*. Edited by J. Roisman and I. Worthington. West Sussex: Wiley-Blackwell, 2010.

Thompson, J. W. *Moral Formation according to Paul: The Context and Coherence of Pauline Ethics*. Grand Rapids: Baker, 2011.

———. *Pastoral Ministry according to Paul*. Grand Rapids: Baker, 2006.

———. "Paul as Missionary Pastor." Pages 25–36 in *Paul as Missionary*. Edited by T. Burke and B. Rosner. London: T&T Clark, 2011.

Thompson, T. "A Stone That Still Won't Fit: An Introductory and Editorial Note for Edgar Krentz's 'A Stone That Will Not Fit.'" Pages 433–38 in *Pseudepigraphie und Verfasserfiktion in frühchristlichen Briefen*. Edited by J. Frey et al. WUNT 256. Tübingen: Mohr Siebeck, 2009.

Thurston, R. "The Relationship between the Thessalonian Epistles." *ExpTim* 85 (1973–74): 52–56.

Tonstad, S. K. "The Restrainer Removed: A Truly Alarming Thought (2 Thess 2:1–12)." *HBT* 29.2 (2007): 133–51.

Trebilco, P. R. *Self-Designation and Group Identity in the New Testament*. Cambridge: Cambridge University Press, 2014.

Trilling, W. "Die beiden Briefe des Apostels Paulus an die Thessalonicher: Eine Forschungsübersicht." *ANRW* 25.4:3365–403. Part 2, *Principat*, 25.4. Edited by H. Temporini and W. Haase. New York: de Gruyter, 1989.

———. *Untersuchungen zum zweiten Thessalonischerbrief*. Leipzig: St. Benno, 1972.

———. *Der zweite Brief an die Thessalonicher*. EKKNT 14. Zürich: Benzinger/ Neukirchener, 1980.

Trozzo, L. M. "Thessalonian Women: The Key to the 4:4 Conundrum." *PRSt* 39.1 (2012): 39–52.

Tuckett, C. "Synoptic Tradition in 1 Thessalonians." Pages 316–39 in *From the Sayings to the Gospels*. WUNT 328. Tübingen: Mohr Siebeck, 2014.

Tzanavari, K. "The Worship of Gods and Heroes in Thessaloniki." Pages 177–262 in *Roman Thessaloniki*. Edited by D. Grammenos. Thessaloniki: Archaeological Museum of Thessaloniki, 2003.

Unger, M. "Historical Research and the Church at Thessalonica." *BibSac* 119 (1962): 38–44.

Van Aarde, A. G. "The Second Letter to the Thessalonians Re-Read as Pseudepigraph." *HTS* 56.1 (2000): 105–36.

Villiers, P. G. R. de. "The Glorious Presence of the Lord: The Eschatology of 2 Thessalonians." Pages 333–61 in *Eschatology of the New Testament and Some Related Documents*. WUNT 2/315. Edited by J. G. van der Watt. Tübingen: Mohr Siebeck, 2011.

Volf, M. *Work in the Spirit: Toward a Theology of Work*. Oxford: Oxford University Press, 1991.

Wachtel, K., and M. W. Holmes. *The Textual History of the Greek New Testament: Changing Views in Contemporary Research*. Atlanta: SBL Press, 2011.

Walker Jr., W. O. *Interpolations in the Pauline Letters*. JSNTSup 213. Sheffield: Sheffield Academic, 2001.

Walton, S. "What Has Aristotle to Do with Paul? Rhetorical Criticism and 1 Thessalonians." *TynBul* 46.2 (1995): 229–50.

Wanamaker, C. A. *The Epistles to the Thessalonians.* NIGTC. Grand Rapids: Eerdmans, 1990.

Watson, D. "The Three Species of Rhetoric and the Study of the Pauline Epistles." Pages 25–47 in *Paul and Rhetoric.* Edited by Sampley et al. London: Bloomsbury, 2013.

Weima, J. A. D. *1–2 Thessalonians.* BECNT. Grand Rapids: Baker, 2014.

———. "1–2 Thessalonians." Pages 871–90 in *Commentary on the New Testament Use of the Old Testament.* Edited by G. K. Beale and D. A. Carson. Grand Rapids: Baker, 2007.

———. "An Apology for the Apologetic Function of 1 Thessalonians 2:1–12," *JSNT* 68 (1997): 73–99.

———. "'But We Became Infants among You': The Case for NHΠIOI in 1 Thess 2.7." *NTS* 46.4 (2000): 547–64.

———. "The Function of 1 Thessalonians 2:1–12 and the Use of Rhetorical Criticism: A Response to Otto Merk." Pages 114–31 in *The Thessalonian Debate.* Edited by K. P. Donfried and J. Beutler. Grand Rapids: Eerdmans, 2000.

———. "Infants, Nursing Mother, and Father: Paul's Portrayal of a Pastor." *CTJ* 37.2 (2002): 209–29.

———. *Neglected Endings.* Sheffield: JSOT Press, 1994.

———. *Paul the Ancient Letter Writer.* Grand Rapids: Baker, 2016.

———. "'Peace and Security' (1 Thess 5.3): Prophetic Warning or Political Propoganda?" *NTS* 58.3 (2012): 331–59.

———. "The Slaying Satan's Superman and the Sure Salvation of the Saints." *CTJ* 41 (2006): 67–88.

Weima, J. A. D., and S. E. Porter. *An Annotated Bibliography of 1 and 2 Thessalonians.* NTTS 26. Leiden: Brill, 1998.

Weima, J. A. D., and S. M. Baugh. *1 & 2 Thessalonians, 1 & 2 Timothy, Titus.* ZIBBC. Grand Rapids: Zondervan, 2002.

Wengst, K. *Pax Romana and the Peace of Jesus Christ.* London: SCM, 1987.

Wenham, D. *Paul: Follower of Jesus or Founder of Christianity?* Grand Rapids: Eerdmans, 1995.

Werner, M. *The Formation of Christian Dogma.* London: Black, 1957.

White, J. R. "'Peace and Security' (1 Thessalonians 5.3): Is It Really a Roman Slogan?" *NTS* 59 (2013): 382–95.

Wick, P. "Ist 1 Thess 2,13–16 antijüdisch?: Der rhetorische Gesamtzusammenhang des Briefes als Interpretationshilfe für eine einzelne Perikope." *TZ* 50.1 (1994): 9–23.

Williams, D. J. *1 and 2 Thessalonians.* NIBC 12. Peabody, MA: Hendrickson, 1992.

Winter, B. *Divine Honours for the Caesars: The First Christians' Responses.* Grand Rapids: Eerdmans, 2015.

———. "'If a Man Does Not Wish to Work . . .': A Cultural and Historical Setting for 2 Thessalonians 3:6–16." *TynBul* 40 (1989): 303–15.

Wischmeyer, O. *Paul: Life, Setting, Work, Letters*. London: Bloomsbury, 2012.

Witherington III, B. *1 and 2 Thessalonians: A Socio-Rhetorical Commentary*. Grand Rapids: Eerdmans, 2006.

———. *New Testament Rhetoric: An Introductory Guide to the Art of Persuasion in and of the New Testament*. Eugene, OR: Wipf & Stock, 2009.

———. *Work*. Grand Rapids: Eerdmans, 2011.

Wold, B. "Reading and Reconstructing 4Q416 2 II 21: Comments on Menahem Kister's Proposal." *DSD* 12 (2005): 205–11.

Woodward, M. S. *The Glossa Ordinaria on Romans*. Kalamazoo: Western Michigan University, 2011.

Wortham, R. "The Problem of Anti-Judaism in 1 Thessalonians 2:14–16 and Related Pauline Texts." *BTB* 25 (1995): 37–44.

Wrede, W. *The Authenticity of the Second Letter to the Thessalonians*. Translated by R. Rhea. Eugene, OR: Wipf & Stock, 2017. Original German volume: *Die Echtheit des zweiten Thessalonicherbriefes*. TU 9/2. Leipzig: C. J. Henrich, 1903.

Wright, N. T. *The New Testament and the People of God*. Minneapolis: Fortress, 1992.

———. *Paul and the Faithfulness of God*. Minneapolis: Fortress, 2013.

———. "Putting Paul Together Again: Toward a Synthesis of Pauline Theology." Pages 193–211 in *Pauline Theology*. Edited by J. Bassler. Minneapolis: Fortress, 1991.

———. *Surprised by Hope: Rethinking Heaven, the Resurrection, and the Mission of the Church*. New York: HarperOne, 2008.

Wrzól, J. *Die Echtheit des zweiten Thessalonicherbriefes*. Biblische Studien 19.4. Freiburg: Herder, 1916.

Yarbrough, O. L. *Not Like the Gentiles: Marriage Rules in the Letters of Paul*. SBLDS 80. Atlanta: Scholars Press, 1985.

Young, S. "Paul's Ethnic Discourse on 'Faith': Christ's Faith and Gentile Access to the Judean God in Rom 3:21–5:1." *HTR* 108 (2015): 30–51.

Zanker, P. *The Power of Images in the Age of Augustus*. Ann Arbor: University of Michigan Press, 1988.

SCRIPTURE INDEX

OTHER ANCIENT LITERATURE INDEX

SUBJECT INDEX

GREEK WORD INDEX

AUTHOR INDEX